T0226247

Lecture Notes in Computer Science　　　10753

Commenced Publication in 1973
Founding and Former Series Editors:
Gerhard Goos, Juris Hartmanis, and Jan van Leeuwen

Editorial Board

More information about this series at http://www.springer.com/series/7408

Erik Kamsties · Jennifer Horkoff
Fabiano Dalpiaz (Eds.)

Requirements Engineering: Foundation for Software Quality

24th International Working Conference, REFSQ 2018
Utrecht, The Netherlands, March 19–22, 2018
Proceedings

 Springer

Editors
Erik Kamsties 🆔
Dortmund University
  of Applied Sciences and Arts
Dortmund
Germany

Fabiano Dalpiaz 🆔
Utrecht University
Utrecht
The Netherlands

Jennifer Horkoff 🆔
Chalmers and University of Gothenburg
Gothenburg
Sweden

ISSN 0302-9743   ISSN 1611-3349 (electronic)
Lecture Notes in Computer Science
ISBN 978-3-319-77242-4   ISBN 978-3-319-77243-1 (eBook)
https://doi.org/10.1007/978-3-319-77243-1

Library of Congress Control Number: 2018934362

LNCS Sublibrary: SL2 – Programming and Software Engineering

Printed on acid-free paper

This Springer imprint is published by the registered company Springer International Publishing AG
part of Springer Nature
The registered company address is: Gewerbestrasse 11, 6330 Cham, Switzerland

Preface

It is our great pleasure to welcome you to the proceedings of the 24th International Working Conference on Requirements Engineering Foundation for Software Quality. The REFSQ working conference series is a leading international forum for discussing requirements engineering (RE) and its many relations to quality. REFSQ aims at establishing an inclusive forum in which experienced researchers, PhD candidates, practitioners, and students can inform each other, learn about, discuss, and advance the state-of-the-art research and practice in the discipline of RE. The first REFSQ meeting took place in 1994. The conference has been organized as a stand-alone conference since 2010 and is now well established as a premier conference series on RE, located in Europe. REFSQ 2018 was held in Utrecht, The Netherlands, during March 19–22, 2018. We were excited to return to the location of the first REFSQ meeting in 1994.

RE is a critical factor in developing high-quality and successful software, systems, and services. Today, RE is expected to support engineering diverse types of systems of different scale and complexity such as information systems, embedded systems, mobile systems, or cyber-physical systems and is applied in diverse domains. Since the term "requirements engineering" was popularized 40 years ago by a special issue of the *IEEE Transactions on Software Engineering* in 1977, the community of practitioners and researchers have been working tirelessly on the identification, characterization, and evaluation of the multifaceted relationships between aspects of requirements processes, artifacts, and methods and aspects of software quality. We chose "RE and Digital Transformation" as the REFSQ 2018 special theme, to emphasize an important issue: the role RE can play in the dramatic changes that take place in our society today to innovate and design new heterogeneous systems and services to fit the needs of users and to take into account the values of society.

We are pleased to present this volume comprising the REFSQ 2018 proceedings. It features 23 papers included in the technical program of REFSQ 2018, presented during the conference. These papers were selected by an international Program Committee of leading experts in RE from both academia and industry. The committee evaluated the papers via a thorough peer-review process. This year, 73 abstracts were initially submitted. Eleven abstracts were not followed up by papers, one paper was withdrawn, and four papers were desk rejected. The review process included 57 papers. Each paper was reviewed by three members of the REFSQ 2018 Program Committee. An extensive online discussion among the Program Committee members enriched the reviews during the evaluation of the possible decision-making outcomes for each paper. During a face-to-face Program Committee meeting that took place on December 1, 2017, in Utrecht, The Netherlands, the papers were discussed and selected for inclusion in the conference proceedings. Authors of rejected papers were encouraged to submit their papers to the REFSQ 2018 satellite events.

The REFSQ 2018 conference was organized as a three-day symposium. Two conference days were devoted to presentation and discussion of scientific papers. The keynote speaker was Tanja Vos from the Open Universiteit and Universitat Politècnica de València. One conference day was devoted to presentation and discussion of industry experiences. This Industry Track offered an industrial keynote by Michiel van Genuchten from VitalHealth Software, followed by a full day program of talks. In a world cafe session at the end, industry practitioners discussed with the participating researchers various issues of industrial requirements engineering. In addition, the REFSQ conference program also included two live experiments as well as posters and tool presentations. Furthermore, satellite events, including several workshops and a doctoral symposium, were co-located with the conference. All papers from the main conference track can be found in the present proceedings. The papers included in the satellite events can be found in the REFSQ 2018 workshop proceedings published with CEUR.

REFSQ 2018 would not have been possible without the engagement and support of many individuals who contributed in many different ways. As editors of this volume, we would like to thank the REFSQ Steering Committee members, in particular Barbara Paech and Kurt Schneider, for their availability and for the excellent guidance they provided. Special thanks go to Klaus Pohl for his long-term engagement for REFSQ. We are indebted to Anna Perini and Paul Grünbacher, the REFSQ 2017 co-chairs, for their extremely helpful advice. We are grateful to all the members of the Program Committee for their timely and thorough reviews of the submissions and for their time dedicated to the online discussion and the face-to-face meeting. In particular, we thank those Program Committee members who volunteered to serve in the role of mentor, shepherd, or gatekeeper to authors of conditionally accepted papers. We would like to thank the members of the local organization at the Utrecht University for their ongoing support and determination to make sure all operational processes ran smoothly at all times. We are grateful to the chairs, who organized the various events included in REFSQ 2018.

Finally, we would like to thank Vanessa Stricker and Eric Schmieders for their excellent work in coordinating the background organization processes, and Anna Kramer for her support in preparing this volume.

We believe this volume provides an informative perspective on the conversations that shape the REFSQ 2018 conference. We hope you will find research results and truly new ideas to innovate and design new heterogeneous systems and services to fit the needs of users and to take into account the values of society.

January 2018

Erik Kamsties
Jennifer Horkoff
Fabiano Dalpiaz

Organization

Organizing Committee

Local Organization

Fabiano Dalpiaz   Utrecht University, The Netherlands

Background Organization

Vanessa Stricker   University of Duisburg-Essen, Germany
Eric Schmieders   University of Duisburg-Essen, Germany

Research Track

Erik Kamsties   Dortmund University of Applied Sciences and Arts, Germany
Jennifer Horkoff   Chalmers and the University of Gothenburg, Sweden

Research Methodology

Nazim Madhavji   University of Western Ontario, Canada

Workshops

Klaus Schmid   Stiftung Universität Hildesheim, Germany
Paola Spoletini   Kennesaw State University, USA

Posters and Tools

Mehrdad Sabetzadeh   University of Luxembourg, Luxembourg
Eya Ben Charrada   University of Zurich, Switzerland

Doctoral Symposium

Jolita Ralyté   University of Geneva, Switzerland
Pete Sawyer   Aston University, UK

Industry Track

Kim Lauenroth   adesso AG, Dortmund, Germany
Garm Lucassen   Utrecht University, The Netherlands

Social Media and Publicity

Itzel Morales-Ramírez   Infotec, Mexico
Henning Femmer   Technische Universität München, Germany

Website

Fatma Başak Aydemir   Utrecht University, The Netherlands

Proceedings

Fabian Kneer   Dortmund University of Applied Sciences and Arts,
                      Germany

Program Committee

Raian Ali	Bournemouth University, UK
Joao Araujo	Universidade Nova de Lisboa, Portugal
Fatma Başak Aydemir	Utrecht University, The Netherlands
Richard Berntsson Svensson	Blekinge Institute of Technology, Sweden
Daniel Berry	University of Waterloo, Canada
Sjaak Brinkkemper	Utrecht University, The Netherlands
Simone Bürsner	Hochschule Bonn-Rhein-Sieg, Germany
Nelly Condori-Fernández	VU University of Amsterdam, The Netherlands
Maya Daneva	University of Twente, The Netherlands
Oscar Dieste	Universidad Politécnica de Madrid, Spain
Jörg Dörr	Fraunhofer IESE, Germany
Alessio Ferrari	ISTI-CNR, Pisa, Italy
Xavier Franch	Universitat Politècnica de Catalunya, Spain
Samuel Fricker	FHNW, Switzerland
Vincenzo Gervasi	University of Pisa, Italy
Martin Glinz	University of Zurich, Switzerland
Michael Goedicke	University of Duisburg-Essen, Germany
Paul Grünbacher	Johannes Kepler University Linz, Austria
Renata Guizzardi	Universidade Federal do Espirito Santo, Brazil
Irit Hadar	University of Haifa, Israel
Hermann Kaindl	Vienna University of Technology, Austria
Marjo Kauppinen	Aalto University, Finland
Alessia Knauss	Autoliv, Sweden
Eric Knauss	Chalmers — University of Gothenburg, Sweden
Anne Koziolek	Karlsruhe Institute of Technology, Germany
Kim Lauenroth	adesso AG, Germany
Soren Lauesen	IT University of Copenhagen, Denmark
Emmanuel Letier	University College London, UK
Nazim Madhavji	University of Western Ontario, Canada
Patrick Mäder	Technische Universität Ilmenau, Germany
Fabio Massacci	University of Trento, Italy
Raimundas Matulevicius	University of Tartu, Estonia
John Mylopoulos	University of Ottawa, Canada
Andreas L. Opdahl	University of Bergen, Norway
Barbara Paech	Universität Heidelberg, Germany
Elda Paja	University of Trento, Italy

Liliana Pasquale — Lero, Ireland
Oscar Pastor Lopez — Universitat Politècnica de València, Spain
Anna Perini — Fondazione Bruno Kessler Trento, Italy
Klaus Pohl — Paluno, University of Duisburg-Essen, Germany
Jolita Ralyté — University of Geneva, Switzerland
Björn Regnell — Lund University, Sweden
Mehrdad Sabetzadeh — University of Luxembourg, Luxembourg
Camille Salinesi — CRI, Université de Paris 1 Panthéon-Sorbonne, France
Nicolas Sannier — SNT - University of Luxembourg, Luxembourg
Pete Sawyer — Aston University, UK
Klaus Schmid — Stiftung Universität Hildesheim, Germany
Kurt Schneider — Leibniz Universität Hannover, Germany
Norbert Seyff — FHNW and University of Zurich, Switzerland
Alberto Siena — University of Trento, Italy
Paola Spoletini — Kennesaw State University, USA
Angelo Susi — Fondazione Bruno Kessler - Irst, Italy
Michael Vierhauser — Johannes Kepler University Linz, Austria
Yves Wautelet — Katholieke Universiteit Leuven, Belgium
Roel Wieringa — University of Twente, The Netherlands
Krzysztof Wnuk — Lund University, Sweden
Tao Yue — Simula Research Laboratory and University of Oslo, Norway
Yuanyuan Zhang — University College London, UK
Didar Zowghi — University of Technology, Sydney, Australia

Steering Committee

Kurt Schneider (Chair)
Barbara Paech (Vice Chair)
Richard Berntsson Svensson
Fabiano Dalpiaz
Maya Daneva
Samuel Fricker
Rainer Grau

Paul Grünbacher
Jennifer Horkoff
Erik Kamsties
Eric Knauss
Oscar Pastor
Anna Perini
Klaus Pohl

Additional Reviewers

Muneera Bano
Axel Busch
Catarina Gralha
Eduard Groen
Anne Hess
Paul Hübner
Rashidah Kasauli

Matthias Koch
Christian Kücherer
Garm Lucassen
Ibtehal Noorwali
Thomas Olsson
Marcela Ruiz
Marcus Seiler

Melanie Stade
Christian Stier
Naomi Unkelos-Shpigel
Karina Villela

Fernando Wanderley
Dominik Werle
Rebekka Wohlrab
Dustin Wüest

Sponsors

Supporters

Organizers

**Fachhochschule
Dortmund**
University of Applied Sciences and Arts

UNIVERSITY OF
GOTHENBURG

CHALMERS

Invited Talks

Testing Without Requirements?

Tanja Vos[1,2]

[1]Open Universiteit, The Netherlands
[2]Universitat Politècnica de València, Spain
mailto:Tanja.Vos@ou.nl

Abstract. Good requirements are the basis for high quality software. However, in industrial practice, the availability of decent requirements are still more an exception than common practice. One of the activities, the quality of which depends highly on requirements, is testing. Testing software systems without requirements can lead to unstructured testing that cannot give good insights into the quality of the System Under Test (SUT). We propose a completely different way of testing, that starts from having no requirements documented and will build up a test-suite and requirements while we test. For this we will present TESTAR, a tool for automated testing at the user interface level. TESTAR is different from existing approaches for testing at the user interface in that it does not need scripts nor does it generate scripts. TESTAR just tests on the fly looking for faults. TESTAR has predefined oracles that can automatically test general-purpose system requirements. To make TESTAR test specific requirements we need to refine these oracles and direct the tests. This can be done incrementally while we are already testing! In the keynote we will describe this approach and explain the future need of a test tool that learns itself what the best strategy is for testing.

No Free Lunch for Software After All

Michiel van Genuchten

VitalHealth Software
mvgenuchten@vitalhealthsoftware.com

Abstract. The impact of software on products, industries and society is significant. Software put the computer industry upside down in the 1990's. Mobile phones followed in the first decade of this century. Medtech, the car industry and the financial industry are changing rapidly as we speak. The talk will be based on the personal experience of the presenter in various industries and the 40 columns that have been published in 'Impact' in IEEE Software. Insiders from companies such as Microsoft, Oracle, NASA, Hitachi, Tomtom and ASML have discussed the impact of software on their products and industries in the columns. Lessons learned include that software keeps growing at a surprisingly steady rate and volume (number of users of the software) is the key to success. A more sobering lesson is that software can easily be turned into a weapon of mass deceit, as has been proven by spammers, phishers, and an automobile company.

The lessons learned will be applied to better understand the requirements engineering and quality we need to create the software of the future. A couple of questions to be discussed: will we ever be able to engineer requirements and build proper roadmaps for future products? Is the quality we can achieve good enough for the applications we build? What foundations are needed for the next generation of software systems and where can science contribute?

Contents

RE Previews and Visions

Big Data

Mindmapping and Requirements Modeling

RE in Industrial Practice

Problem-Oriented Requirements in Practice – A Case Study

Soren Lauesen[(✉)]

IT University of Copenhagen, Copenhagen, Denmark
slauesen@itu.dk

Abstract. **[Context and motivation]** Traditional requirements describe what the system shall do. This gives suppliers little freedom to use what they have already. In contrast, problem-oriented requirements describe the customer's *demands*: what he wants to use the system for and which problems he wants to remove. The supplier specifies how his system will deal with these issues. The author developed the problem-oriented approach in 2007 on request from the Danish Government, and named it SL-07. **[Question/problem]** SL-07 has been used in many projects – usually with success. However, we had no detailed reports of the effects. **[Principal ideas/results]** This paper is a case study of SL-07 in acquisition of a complex case-management system. The author wrote the requirements and managed the supplier selection. Next, he was asked to run the entire acquisition project, although he was a novice project manager. Some of the results were: The problem-oriented requirements were a factor 5 shorter than traditional requirements in the same domain. Stakeholders understood them and identified missing demands. Suppliers could write excellent proposals with a modest effort. The requirements were a good basis for writing test cases and resolving conflicts during development. The delivery was 9 months late, but this was not related to the requirements. **[Contribution]** This is a publication of a full, real-life, complex requirements specification, the selection document, error lists, etc. The full texts are available on the author's web-site. The paper discusses the results and illustrates them with samples from the full texts.

Keywords: Problem-oriented requirements · SL-07 · COTS-based
Case study · Supplier selection · Issue resolution · Fixed-price contract
Usability requirements

1 Background

Requirements can be written in many ways: traditional system-shall requirements, various kinds of use cases, user stories, UML-diagrams, etc. Does it matter which kind of requirements we use, e.g. which of the many kinds of use cases or user stories we use? It does. It influences whether stakeholders can check that requirements cover their needs (validate them), suppliers can provide meaningful proposals, the parties can agree whether issues are bugs or requests for change, etc. The author has seen many real-life requirements specifications and published five very different ones in his textbook (Lauesen [5]), where he also explains the consequences of each kind of

© Springer International Publishing AG, part of Springer Nature 2018
E. Kamsties et al. (Eds.): REFSQ 2018, LNCS 10753, pp. 3–19, 2018.
https://doi.org/10.1007/978-3-319-77243-1_1

requirements. Some of the consequences have been disastrous, such as losing a business opportunity of 100 M$ because of traditional system-shall-requirements.

What does research say about the way we write requirements? Amazingly very little. Publications rarely provide examples of real-life requirements, and how they worked in practice. Many papers have statistics and general discussions of requirements (e.g. Nurmuliani et al. [13] about requirements volatility), but the reader wonders what the real requirements looked like. As another example Bruijn and Dekkers [1] investigated how many requirements in a specific project were ambiguous and how many of them actually caused problems. However, we don't see any of the requirements, not even the one that caused serious problems. Maiden and Ncube [11] wrote about acquisition of a COTS system and gave advice on how to do it better. Here too, we don't see any requirements. Even in textbooks about requirements, we rarely see real requirements. The focus is on the requirements processes. Exceptions are Robertson and Robertson [15], who illustrate all kinds of requirements with tiny pieces, primarily from a road de-icing system, Kotonya and Sommerville [4], who show tiny pieces from a university library system, and Cockburn [2], who shows examples of many kinds of use cases. None of them show a full, real requirements specification or substantial parts of one, nor the supplier's proposal or reports of how the requirements worked in practice.

In 2007, the author published Requirements SL-07, an exemplary requirements specification for an electronic health record system with a guide booklet. It covered all kinds of requirements in a problem-oriented way: we don't specify what the system shall do, but what the user will use it for. The Danish government had requested it as part of their standard contract for software acquisitions, K02. Analysts can download it, replace irrelevant requirements with their own and reuse large parts.

SL-07 was intended for software acquisitions where large parts existed already (COTS). However, SL-07 proved equally useful for other kinds of projects, such as product development or agile in-house development.

In this paper, we show how SL-07 was used in a real-life project: acquisition of a COTS-based system for complex case management. We show how the spec developed, how the suppliers reacted, how we selected the winner, how issues were resolved during development, and why the project was 9 months late. You can download the full specification with the supplier's proposal, the selection document, the list of errors/issues, the test script, etc. from the author's web-site:

http://www.itu.dk/people/slauesen/Y-foundation.html.

Method

This is a report of a real project. The project was not action research, nor planned to be part of any research. As a consultant, the author had helped many customers with requirements, but left project management and acquisition to the customer. The Y-Foundation project started in the same way, but developed into the author being also the project manager. Later he got permission to anonymize and publish papers from the project. This paper is based on 795 emails, other existing documents, discussions and meetings that the author participated in. In addition, the author later contacted the new foundation secretary and the supplier to get their view on the system after more than two years of use. The documents have been translated from Danish and anonymized.

There is an obvious validity threat since the author reports about a project where he had a significant influence. The threat is reduced by giving the reader access to the original documents, which were shared with stakeholders and suppliers. However, it has not been possible to anonymize the emails.

2   The Y-Foundation Case

Twice a year the Danish Y-Foundation (synonym) receives around 300 applications and gives grants to some of them. There are two grant areas: Engineering and Medical. The Foundation has two full-time employees (a secretary and the CEO) and two part-time (an accountant and a web-editor). The board of the Foundation has four members - two business members and two domain experts, one in engineering and one in medicine. All board members look at all the applications. At a board meeting, the board decides which applications to grant. Next, it is a clerical task to send accepts or rejects to the applicants, pay grants and receive final reports.

The entire process was manual. The applications were paper documents. They circulated between the board members prior to the board meeting. The secretary maintained a spreadsheet that gave an overview of the applications.

In January 2013, the foundation decided to acquire a grant management system and a new CMS on a fixed-price contract. Applicants would upload grant applications on the foundation's web site. The board members would in parallel look at the applications and see the other board member's ratings. At the board meeting, they might modify their rating, and the other board members would see it live. After the meeting, the secretary would send bulk emails to applicants; handle payment of grants; remind applicants to send a final report, etc.

The foundation contracted with the author to write the requirements, later to handle also supplier selection, and finally to be the project manager (PM) of the entire project. He wrote and maintained the requirements based on the problem-oriented requirements in the SL-07 template [7]. Most of the system existed already. The new parts were developed in an agile way. The system was deployed March 2014 with several open issues and completed October 2014, nine months late.

3   Problem-Oriented Requirements and SL-07

Jackson [3] distinguished between the problem space (outside the computer system) and the solution space (inside the system). He pointed out that requirements should describe the problem domain, leaving the solution domain to the developers. However, it wasn't clear where the boundary - the user interface - belonged.

When we use the term *problem-oriented requirements*, we don't specify the user interface. It is part of the solution space. The developer/supplier has to provide it. We describe not only functional requirements in a problem-oriented way, but also usability, security, documentation, phasing out, etc.

Here is an example of problem-oriented requirements from the Y-Foundation. It is the requirements for how to support the board members during the board meeting.

From the board member's point of view, discussion of applications during the meeting is one task, carried out without essential interruptions. At first sight, a task description looks like a typical use case, but it is profoundly different:

Task C21. During the board meeting
This task describes what a board member does with the grant applications during the meeting.

Start:	When discussion of the applications starts.
End:	When all applications have been discussed for now.
Frequency:	Twice a year.
Users:	Board members. The four board members and the secretary look at the applications at the same time and note their own comments directly in the system. See also access rights in H1

Subtasks:	*Proposed* solution:	Code:
1. Look at each application. See what the other board members mean, preferably live as soon as they have indicated something. Look at the full application and attached documents.	*As task C20.* [C20 shows the proposed screen with a list of applications, each with a traffic light for each board member] *The system updates the list of applications without the board members having to click a "refresh".*	
2. Record your conclusion and your private comments.	*As task C20.*	
3. Maybe record the joint conclusion.	*As task C20.*	

The text before the table is not requirements, but assumptions the supplier can make and the context in which the task is carried out. The requirements are in the table. In this case there are three requirements, each of them being a subtask of the full task. Column one shows the user's demand, what he wants to do. Column 2 may initially show the customer's idea of a possible solution, later the supplier's proposed solution. In the real document, the proposed solution is in red, here shown also in italics. Column three (the code column) is for assessment, reference to test cases, etc.

The subtasks can be repeated and carried out in almost any sequence. The user decides. A subtask could also be a problem the user has today. We might have written this "problem subtask":

Notice that the task doesn't describe an interaction between user and system. It describes what the user wants to achieve. The requirement is that the system supports it.

1p. Problem. Today you cannot see what the other board members mean. You have to wait and hear.	*The system updates the list of applications without the board members having to click a "refresh".*	

We have shown experimentally that tasks perform much better than use cases in many ways, for instance in their ability to deal with the business-critical needs of the customer (Lauesen and Kuhail [6]).

User stories have become widely used. We might translate each task step to a user story. Using Lucassen [9] as a guide, step 2 would become this user story:

As a board member, I want to see the application's traffic lights, so that I can record my conclusion and my private comments.

The traffic lights have now become requirements. In the task version, the traffic lights are potential solutions. This makes user stories less suited for COTS-based systems where most of the system exists already. An existing system might not use traffic lights at all, yet provide a good solution. If we replace all the task steps with user stories, we have defined a solution: a rather detailed description of the functions on the user interface. However, we cannot go the other way from user stories to task descriptions, because we have lost information about the larger context in which these user stories take place. It will for instance be hard to see which user stories should be supported by a single user screen. An Epic might help here, but there are no traditions or guidelines that ensure that it will group user stories in a useful way. With SL-07, grouping and context description are compulsory.

Stakeholders like user stories [10], probably because they have a simpler and more rigid structure than use cases, and have more user focus than system-shall requirements. However, there are no experience reports about how successful user stories are in fixed-price projects, how stable they are, and how many customer-supplier conflicts they resolve.

Table 1 shows the table of contents for the final SL-07 spec, including the supplier's proposal. Around 30% of the pages are tasks (Chapter C). Another 20% are descriptions of data the system must store (Chapter D). It includes a slim E/R data model and a detailed data description. Business aspects, system integration and non-functional requirements take up the rest. All requirements are written in a problem-oriented way. Around 90% of Chapters G to L can usually be reused word-by-word.

The spec contains a total of 275 requirements. Of these, 100 are task steps, 80 are descriptions of the fields in the data model (each field is a requirement). The remaining 95 requirements are system integration and non-functional requirements.

User stories and use cases cover only what corresponds to the 100 task steps.

SL-07 is not just a problem-oriented way to express requirements. It provides a convenient format that makes it easy to match requirements with the supplier's proposal, track requirements to test cases, and track business goals to requirements. It also serves as a checklist for what to remember, with realistic examples of everything. Based on experience with many projects, it has grown over the years to deal with new topics, e.g. supplier selection criteria and recently (version 5) EU's General Data Protection Regulation (GDPR).

Usability requirements

Usability is important in most projects, but it is hard to specify in a verifiable way. In the Y-Foundation, usability requirements played a major role in determining whether an issue was an error or a request for change.

Table 1. The Y-Foundation requirements

The SL-07 template, Chapter I, covers usability requirements. It requires what usability specialists agree on: Make early, unguided usability tests of the user interface (or a mockup) with potential real users; redesign and test with new users until the test results are acceptable (Nielsen [12], Redish et al. [14]).

This cannot be used directly in our case where the complex part of the user interface has only one user (the secretary) and the medium complex part has only four users (the board members). We came up with these problem-oriented requirements:

Usability I1. Ease-of-learning and task efficiency

Requirements:	*Proposed* solution	Code
1. The secretary must be able to carry out the tasks in Work Area 1 without serious usability problems ["Serious" defined below the table]	With a functional version of the system, a secretary carries out examples of tasks without guidance. On the way, the secretary may ask the supplier's expert. The secretary assesses whether the system is sufficiently efficient and easy to use. *Offered.*	
2. Board members ... (similar)	(similar) *Offered.*	
3. Potential applicants must be able to carry out the tasks in Work Area 4 without serious usability problems.	A think-aloud test with three potential applicants is made. The user cannot ask when in doubt. *This is the customer's own responsibility.*	

A **serious** usability problem is a situation where the user:

a. is unable to complete the task on his own,
b. or believes it is completed when it is not,
c. or complains that *it is really cumbersome,*
d. or the test facilitator observes that the user doesn't use the system efficiently.

The first requirement (I1-1) worked well in practice. It says that the users may not encounter serious usability problems during their tasks, and it defines what a serious usability problem is.

The requirements were used in this way: During acceptance testing, the secretary carried out various test tasks. When she was stuck, we recorded it as an issue ("defect"), according to requirement I1-1. Later, the secretary sat next to a supplier specialist, carried out the tasks and asked when needed. Some of the issues were true defects; others were things we learned how to do.

The user interface for the board members was tailor-made, based on the secretary's vision and agile (iterative) development with the supplier. The user interface became intuitive to the board members, but there were many errors in the detail (bugs). They were gradually removed.

For the potential applicant's user interface, we accepted the responsibility (I1-3) and paid the supplier for changes, as we in an agile way developed the web part.

4 Elicitation and Specification of the Requirements

The PM (the author) used 11 weeks to elicit and write the requirements that we sent to the potential suppliers. He spent 40 work hours on it. A month-by-month timeline of the project with hours spent and number of emails handled, is available at the author's web site [8]. Here is a summary:

18-01-2013: The consultant (the author) started his work.
02-04-2013: Requirements version 2.4 was ready (34 pages + 3 page data examples). The requirements had been through versions 1.0, 1.1, 2.0, 2.1, 2.2 and 2.3. Each version was the result of interviews, study of existing documents, comments from stakeholders, and a focus group with

potential applicants. The contents grew almost chapter by chapter according to the TOC in Table 1. Chapters C (tasks to support) and D (data to record) required most of the work. The last parts from Chapter H (security) to Chapter L (maintenance) were around 90% reuse of the template example.

10-04-2013:   We sent this version to the three suppliers we had selected and asked for a meeting with each of them. They should show how their system supported the requirements. They could also suggest changes to the requirements. They did not have to write anything.

06-06-2013:   Requirements version 2.5 was ready (still 34 + 3 pages). After the meetings with the suppliers, we had 6 comments that we included in version 2.5. An important one was to allow other accounting systems than the present one. No major changes were needed. We sent this version to the three suppliers asking for a written proposal. The supplier should write his proposed solution in column 2 of the requirement tables or as *solution notes* above or below the table. He should also quote the price.

28-06-2013:   Contract version 1.0 was ready (44 pages). We got proposals from all three suppliers and selected one of them. His version of the requirements with his proposed solution became version 1.0 of the contractual requirements.

13-09-2013:   Contract version 2.1 was ready (44 pages). During the contract work, we made a few minor changes in the contractual requirements. This is the version available at the author's web site [8]. It includes a detailed change log.

During development, we did not make further changes to the requirements. We managed errors and changes through a list of issues, as explained in the development section below. In two cases, we made an amendment to the contract.

During elicitation, we received many stakeholder comments, but we usually had to restructure them to fit them into the template. Many analysts simply make each comment a new requirement. In fact, some analysts consider requirements a list of the user's wishes. However, this leads to unstructured requirements that are hard to implement and keep track of. In addition, user wishes may be solutions that conflict with the supplier's way of doing things. In our case, we took care to translate the comments into the SL-07 style and insert them in the proper template part. Here are two of the wishes we got, the resulting requirements, and the selected supplier's proposed solution (red in the real document, italics here). In several cases, we had to add more than one requirement to meet the wish:

Wish from a domain expert

I want a "private space" for my own comments on the grant application. We translated it into a task step (functional requirement) and a data requirement. It looked like this, including the supplier's proposed solution in italics:

Task C20. Assess applications before the board meeting

Subtasks and variants:	*Proposed* solution	Code
1. Look at the applications you have to assess …	*The system shows a list of …*	
…	…	
6 [new]. Note your private comments that are not intended for others.	*Noted directly in the list.*	

Data D5. Application role [Name of a data class]

Fields and relationships:	*Proposed* solution	Code
1. roleType: …	*The customer can maintain a list …*	
…	…	
9 [new]. private_comment: The board member's private comments. Not visible to others.	*Yes*	

Wish from the auditor

It shall not be possible to pay money to an applicant's bank account until the account number has been approved by someone else than the one who created the account number in the system. We needed an elaboration. He explained that he had seen fraud where a secretary handled a large grant by changing the applicant's bank account number to his own, paying the amount to it and informing the applicant that the application had been rejected. It became these two new requirements:

Task C14. Pay grants

Subtasks and variants:	*Proposed* solution	Code
1. Make a list of payments …	*The system creates the list …*	
…	…	
4 [new]. Check that account numbers are what the applicant specified.	*If the account number has been changed, this is clearly flagged.*	

Security H5. Protection against threats

Threats to protect against:	*Proposed* solution	Code
…	…	
5 [new]. The system must prevent that someone forges the bank account number prior to the payment.	*The system can in the payment list show what originates directly from the applicant …*	

5   Supplier Selection

In general, suppliers spend a lot of time and money on proposal writing and customer meetings, often more than 500 h for a proposal. Making it easy for them is important for getting good proposals. In our case, the three suppliers found it easy to reply. According to their comments, a supplier spent only 20–30 work hours. There are several reasons for this.

First, the requirements were short, just 34 pages. According to the suppliers, traditional requirements in this domain are hundreds of pages.

Second, the suppliers did not have to write anything before the first meeting. They just had to present their solution and explain how it met our requirements.

Third, when they sent their written proposal, they could easily write how their system met each of the requirements, because the demand (e.g. the task step) was clearly visible. However, only two of the three suppliers did this.

Fourth, when we had received and discussed the proposal with the supplier, we took the burden of editing the proposal and sending it to the supplier before he quoted a price.

Supplier A offered a solution based on Microsoft's CRM-system (for managing communication with customers), Microsoft's SharePoint, etc. SharePoint was used also to develop the Foundation's web-site. Everything was standard components that were configured and combined. No programming was necessary.

Supplier A didn't reply to each of the requirements. He described the solution as a list of modules to be delivered, e.g. "customer management, segmentation, internal case management". We couldn't see how all of this related to the Foundation's work.

However, we had the promised meeting where we discussed their proposal. During the meeting, we managed to walk through all the SL-07 requirements, listen to the way they planned to support them, and take notes. Next, the PM edited the notes into the SL-07 requirements and returned them as the agreed solution.

Supplier B offered a solution based on their own extensions to SharePoint, Outlook (e-mail) and either Navision or eConomic (accounting). SharePoint was also used to develop the Foundation's web site. Possibly, a bit of programming would be needed for the Foundation.

B had carefully written their solution proposal for each of the Foundation's requirements, but in several essential places they just wrote "needs more analysis". For instance, it was obscure how the accounting system would be integrated. Some solution proposals showed a misunderstanding of the needs.

Supplier C offered a solution based on their existing case management system (an extension of Microsoft's SharePoint), Outlook (e-mail), Navision (accounting) and Wordpress (Open source system for development of the Foundation's web-site). Possibly, a bit of programming would be needed for the Foundation.

C had carefully written their solution proposal for each requirement. As an example, the most important central overview screen (the list of grant applications) was shown in graphical detail. The SL-07 requirements including solutions were 44 pages. The most uncertain parts would be tested early in the project and both parties could terminate the contract if the test failed (proof-of-concept, requirements B3).

Choice: We chose supplier C based on three factors: Financial benefit, risk, and cost of product including 4-years of operation. See details on the author's web-site.

6 Development

The plan was that the system should be acceptance-tested early December 2013 and the 4-week operational test completed before New Year. Actually, full delivery didn't take place until end of September 2014 (a delay of 9 months). Here is a summary of the development steps:

18-09-2013: We sign the contract with supplier C and start development. The supplier had identified integration with the accounting system, tax reporting and automatic bank transfer as the most risky parts. He had not tried this before. The plan was to make a POC (Proof of Concept, B3) to reduce the risk. However, it turned out that the bank needed many weeks to give electronic access.

11-10-2013: We accept the POC although we have not completed an electronic bank transfer. However, the system can do all the preparatory work. The system is able to make the basic communication with the accounting system, which is supposed to handle also the tax reporting. Implementation of the applicant's parts, the board's parts, and the secretary's parts continues.

11-11-2013: According to the contract, the supplier should have completed the system test by now, but he needs just a few more days. Everything looks promising.

14-11-2013: To speed up things, we run our first acceptance test. We don't get very far. We encounter and report 23 issues (defects, mistakes, etc.).

20-11-2013: The supplier reports *system test passed*. We try acceptance testing again, but don't get much further. The list of issues grows, some issues are resolved, many remain open or are reopened. The ambition was to deploy the entire system before Christmas, where applicants become busy sending grant applications. We decide to focus on the on-line application part and delay other parts.

23-12-2013: We deploy the on-line application part. It works fine, although some applicants need assistance to circumvent system issues. At the application deadline 15-01-2014, we have 225 applications. There are now 69 issues on the list, including the closed ones.

31-01-2014: We have now been in operational test for the four weeks specified in the contract. There are only 12 open issues on the list. They seem tiny and we agree that they can be handled during the warranty period. We accept delivery and pay the supplier the full amount (around 100,000 $) plus 40 h for changes.

25-02-2014: The system parts for the board and the secretary work miserably. Often the users have to login for each document they want to see. This is extremely cumbersome because a grant application contains several documents. Errors come and go. We focus on repairing the issues. The PM strives to postpone discussions about issues being defects or changes, to meetings in the steering committee.

27-03-2014:   The great grant meeting in the board. The supplier has an expert in the room to offer support. Fortunately, the meeting is a success. Although a bit slow, everybody can see each other's vote. Earlier the board spent the whole day discussing the applications. Now they have already agreed on most of them (those with four red lights or four green lights in the list of applications). In around an hour, they deal with the applications that need discussion. They spend the rest of the meeting discussing strategic issues, which they did not have time for earlier.

15-04-2014:   The secretary cannot handle the grants. There are things she doesn't know how to do and outright errors in the system. The supplier is silent. There is no financial incentive anymore. We escalate the problems to the CEO level and things move on slowly.

01-09-2014:   There are still 9 open issues on the list.

01-10-2014:   The last issues have been resolved or renounced. The business goals are met and the users are happy with the system.

Test cases and user manual

For the acceptance test, we developed a test script that would cover test of most of the requirements. It had one or more sections for each of the requirements sections. Here is part of the script for tasks C12 and C21:

Test script: Section 6.   C12 and C21. During the board meeting
NN [Secretary] and a [simulated] board member work concurrently with the system.
1.   Board member writes own public and private comments for application L and M. Votes yellow for both.
2.   Check that NN and other board members can see the vote and the public comments.
3.   NN records for application L: green, M: red, C: green.
4.   NN records that C is worth publishing.
5.   Ask the board to confirm that everything is correct. Start time monitoring, 12 hours.

In a copy of the requirements, we made the code columns refer to the line or lines in the test script that would test this requirement. Now it was easy to spot the requirements that were not tested.

User manual. As explained above, the secretary's part of the system was not intuitive. New secretaries would come aboard and would need help. Since the task part of the requirements corresponded to observable periods of working with the system, it was obvious to make a guide section for each task.

So we did. Basically, each guide section consisted of a screenshot of the situation, and for each button a callout with a short explanation of the subtask which would use it. We tested the first part of the user manual with a potential secretary. The result was that it would not suffice as a stand-alone manual, but with a bit of initial personal expla-nation, it allowed a new secretary to experiment on his own.

7   Error Handling and Issue Resolution

During the project, the list of issues grew to 130 (including 23 from the first test). At the end, they were all closed, i.e. resolved or renounced.

We can classify issues in this way:

1. Defect: The system violates the requirements. The supplier must cover the cost of repair. Includes serious usability problems where the system could do what the user wanted, but the user couldn't figure out how (requirements I1-1 and I1-2).
2. Failed expectation: Although not specified as a requirement, the developer should have known and must cover the cost. Includes obvious errors. Danish contract law uses this principle.
3. Change: A new or changed requirement. The developer couldn't know. The customer must pay for the repair.
4. Ignore: A mistake, a duplicate, cannot be reproduced, or the customer decides to accept it as it is.

Using these definitions, we get the number of issues shown in Table 2.

There are 45 defects (violated requirements). From the customer's point of view, it is an advantage that issues are classified as defects, rather than changes (for which he has to pay). More than 60% of the defects were violation of usability requirements and security requirements (H4-2 and H4-3, protecting against human mistakes). See examples below.

The 49 failed expectations can be obvious bugs or issues the supplier should know. See examples below. There are 22 change issues. The customer had to pay. Here, better elicitation might have helped (see the *discussion* section below).

Table 2. Issues according to type

45 defects related to these requirements:
18 related to usability (Chapter I)
10 to security (H)
7 to deployment (J)
5 to tasks (C)
2 to data (D)
1 to system integration (F)
1 to response time (L1)
49 failed expectations
22 changes
14 ignore
130 Total

Examples of defects (violated requirements)

#F8   When the user scrolls far down the application list, the list headings disappear. [Violates I1-2. It was a serious usability problem for the board. See discussion of #F8 below.]

#F13   The test person applied for 81.000 DKK, but it ended up as 81 DKK. [Denmark uses decimal comma. Violates H4-2: All data entered must be checked for format, consistency and validity.]

#25   When sending bulk emails to all rejected applicants, we need to make a few individual changes. Not possible, said the supplier. [Violates C13-11, where the supplier had proposed this solution: *The secretary can change them individually before sending them.* So he had to find a solution – and he did.]

#28 Wanted to pay an applicant. By mistake, the secretary clicked one with red lights, meaning *reject*. The system couldn't undo it. [Violates H4-3: The user must be able to correct mistakes easily.]

Examples of failed expectations

#F23 File names in the application form: Only the top half of the letters are visible. [This is an obvious error. You would not write a requirement about such details.]

#71 Port 80 must be used in the upload part of the web-site. For security reasons, many companies block other ports. [The supplier used another port, and as a result many professional applicants couldn't upload their application. We argued that port 80 was the usual default, and that the supplier had announced the solution as accessible from everywhere.]

Examples of changes

#44 It must not be allowed to upload travel applications without an Excel budget.

#70 The grant receiver's bank account should show the payment with the receiver's project ID. We showed the foundation ID only. Important for universities that receive grants for many projects. They couldn't trace the payment to a department. [We had missed this rule because we forgot to treat the receiver's accountants as stakeholders. Fortunately, the error was easy to repair.]

Example of issue resolution

#F8 Scrolling a list with headings. The board member's list of applications has a line for each of the 200-300 applications. It has 16 columns, including 5 "traffic lights", one for each member and one for the secretary. When the user scrolled down the list, the headers moved away too and the user couldn't see what was what. It was a serious usability problem. We had this dialog with the supplier:

- Supplier: It is web-based, so it is impossible to do it better.
- The PM found a solution on the web and gave the supplier the link. It *is* possible.
- Supplier: It will be costly.
- We: It is a usability defect (I1-2), so do it, please.

8   Discussion

Why was delivery late?
The selected supplier suggested developing and deploying the system in 3 months, based on his COTS system. Actually, it took 11 months. The reasons were:

1. The supplier had been too optimistic with system integration. The POC (Proof of Concept) had not revealed the complexities, partly because we had not anticipated that the bank needed many weeks to provide electronic access.

2. For a complex web application that handled also Office documents, browsers turned out to behave differently and it was hard to figure out what to do.
3. For programming, the supplier used a subcontractor without domain knowledge. This caused many misunderstandings, also because the communication path became long.
4. We had accepted the delivery and paid the supplier, assuming that the few open issues could be handled as maintenance. This removed the financial incentive for the supplier, and things went very slowly.

It is hard to see that additional requirements would have reduced the delay. Better project management would.

Would traditional requirements help?

Traditional requirements in this domain are hundreds of pages, told the suppliers. The author has experienced it himself. The university where he works wanted a case-management system for the entire university. It was a bit more complex than the Y-foundation system, e.g. because it had to handle many types of cases. The project manager and the author wrote SL-07 requirements similar to the ones for the Y-foundation. We spent around 60 h to do this. The spec was 45 pages. However, in order to speed up the process and avoid a full EU acquisition, the university wanted to build on an existing requirements framework for case management systems, where several suppliers had been prequalified. So the university hired two consultants. They spent around 100 h to move various SL-07 requirements into the system-shall framework. They refused to include usability requirements because *it was impossible to define usability, so forget about it.* (As explained above, usability requirements saved many troubles in the Y-Foundation case.)

The result was a requirements specification of 240 pages with lots of mandatory requirements. The contract part was an additional 120 pages. Just having suppliers send a proposal was a problem. We got two proposals, only one of which met the mandatory requirements. The conclusion is that this kind of requirements would not have helped. SL-07 doesn't use mandatory requirements because requirements can rarely be assessed in isolation. They interact. Instead you may insist on adequate support of requirements *areas*, e.g. board meetings or usability. In the Y-Foundation, the mandatory "requirement" was that the business value of the entire acquisition shall be positive (requirements section B4).

Avoiding the issues

Issue handling takes time, also for the issues where the supplier has to cover the cost. To what extent could we have prevented the issues? Let us look at the issue classes one by one:

Defects: Defects are violated requirements, so defects are a sign that requirements work well. Otherwise, the issues would have been changes at the customer's expense. But it still makes sense to prevent them. More than 60% of the defects were usability issues and handling human mistakes. You would expect that they might be prevented by early prototyping, but most of them are of a very technical nature and would not have been caught in this way. As an example, it seems unlikely that any of the four defects above would have been caught by prototyping. Would agile development help? No, all the new parts of the system were developed in an agile way.

Failed expectations: Again, most of them are very technical, and better requirements would not help.

Changes: Thirteen out of the 22 change requests were about data not being shown when needed, doubts about mandatory data fields, or confusing labeling of data fields on the user interface. If the supplier had accepted responsibility for usability of the applicant's web interface, these issues would have been defects. A more profound change was that a new application state was needed in addition to the nine specified. Fortunately, none of the changes were costly to implement (40 h total).

Better requirements elicitation would have helped, e.g. the customer exploring the data presentation with prototypes or wireframes. The wire frames would fit into SL-07 as *solution notes*, in that way not being requirements.

COTS or tailor-made: As expected, the problem-oriented requirements were equally suited for the COTS parts and the tailor-made parts. Traditional *system-shall* requirements or user stories are less suited for COTS, because the COTS system may support the need, but not in the system-shall/user story way.

9 Conclusion

The case study has shown the following benefits of problem-oriented requirements in this project. Since there is no similar study of other ways to specify requirements, we have little to compare with. The hypothesis is that the benefits below can be expected in other projects too, if they are based on SL-07 and have an analyst with solid SL-07 experience.

1. The problem-oriented requirements were 5 times shorter than traditional requirements in the same area.
2. The requirements were well suited for COTS-based solutions, since they didn't specify what the system should do, but only what it was to be used for.
3. Elicitation and requirements writing took just 40 h. This was due to reuse of the SL-07 template example and the way it expresses requirements, but also to the author having extensive experience with SL-07.
4. Stakeholders could understand the requirements and explain what they missed.
5. Suppliers could write excellent proposals with a modest effort (20–30 h).
6. It was easy to select the winner because we could se what each proposal supported well and poorly.
7. The requirements were a good basis for resolving conflicts about who pays when issues came up during development.
8. They were also a good basis for writing test cases and user manual.
9. The SL-07 usability requirements and the security requirements about guarding against human errors, eliminated a lot of change requests.

References

1. de Bruijn, F., Dekkers, H.L.: Ambiguity in natural language software requirements: a case study. In: Wieringa, R., Persson, A. (eds.) REFSQ 2010. LNCS, vol. 6182, pp. 233–247. Springer, Heidelberg (2010). https://doi.org/10.1007/978-3-642-14192-8_21
2. Cockburn, A.: Writing Effective Use Cases. Addison Wesley, Reading (2001)
3. Jackson, M.: Problem Frames: Analysing and Structuring Software Development Problems. Addison-Wesley, New York (2001)
4. Kotonya, G., Sommerville, I.: Requirements Engineering, Processes and Techniques. Wiley, Chichester (1998)
5. Lauesen, S.: Software Requirements – Styles and Techniques. Addison-Wesley, Boston (2002)
6. Lauesen, S., Kuhail, M.: Task descriptions versus use cases. Requir. Eng. 17, 3–18 (2012). https://doi.org/10.1007/s00766-011-0140-1
7. Lauesen, S.: Guide to Requirements SL-07 - Template with Examples (2016). ISBN: 9781523320240. http://www.itu.dk/people/slauesen/index.html
8. Lauesen, S.: Requirements for the Y-Foundation. Full requirements specification including the supplier's reply, the selection document, and the list of errors/issues (2017). http://www.itu.dk/people/slauesen/Y-foundation.html
9. Lucassen, G., et al.: Improving agile requirements. Requir. Eng. 21, 383–403 (2016)
10. Lucassen, G., Dalpiaz, F., Werf, J., Brinkkemper, S.: The use and effectiveness of user stories in practice. In: Daneva, M., Pastor, O. (eds.) REFSQ 2016. LNCS, vol. 9619, pp. 205–222. Springer, Cham (2016). https://doi.org/10.1007/978-3-319-30282-9_14
11. Maiden, N.A., Ncube, C.: Acquiring COTS software selection requirements. IEEE Softw. 15, 46–56 (1998)
12. Nielsen, J.: The usability engineering life cycle. IEEE Comput. 25, 12–22 (1992)
13. Nurmuliani, N., Zowghi, D., Fowell, S.: Analysis of requirements volatility during software development life cycle. IEEE (2004). https://opus.lib.uts.edu.au/bitstream/10453/2603/3/2004001816.pdf
14. Redish, J., Molich, R., Bias, R.G., Dumas, J., Bailey, R., Spool, J.M.: Usability in practice: formative usability evaluations — evolution and revolution. In: CHI 2002, Minneapolis, USA, 20–25 April 2002
15. Robertson, S., Robertson, J.: Mastering the Requirements Process. Addison-Wesley, Harlow (2012)

An Exploratory Study on How Internet of Things Developing Companies Handle User Experience Requirements

Johanna Bergman[1], Thomas Olsson[2]([envelope]) [ORCID], Isabelle Johansson[1],
and Kirsten Rassmus-Gröhn[1]

[1] Department of Design Sciences, Lund University, Lund, Sweden
johanna.e.bergman@gmail.com, isabelle.a.e.johansson@gmail.com,
kirsten.rassmus-grohn@certec.lth.se
[2] RISE SICS AB, Lund, Sweden
thomas.olsson@ri.se

Abstract. [**Context and motivation**] Internet of Things (IoT) is becoming common throughout everyday lives. However, the interaction is often different from when using e.g. computers and other smart devices. Furthermore, an IoT device is often dependent on several other systems, heavily impacting the user experience (UX). Finally, the domain is changing rapidly and is driven by technological innovation.

[**Question/problem**] In this qualitative study, we explore how companies elicit UX requirements in the context of IoT. A key part of contemporary IoT development is also data-driven approaches. Thus, these are also considered in the study.

[**Principal idea/results**] There is a knowledge gap around data-driven methodologies, there are examples of companies that collect large amount of data but do not always know how to utilize it. Furthermore, many of the companies struggle to handle the larger system context, where their products and the UX they control are only one part of the complete IoT ecosystem.

[**Contribution**] We provide qualitative empirical data from IoT developing companies. Based on our findings, we identify challenges for the companies and areas for future work.

1 Introduction

Internet of Things (IoT) is rapidly growing and will have a fundamental impact on our lives. IoT is advancing into many domains, facing new contexts and usages, such as hospitals, smart buildings, wearables and smart vehicles. The interaction with IoT is often different than for e.g. a computer or smart phone [1].

The nature of IoT extends the interaction possibilities through mobile and wireless networks, social and collaborative applications, connected data, and the use of intelligent agents [1]. The diverse nature of interaction possibilities with IoT results in that the product being developed will be part of a whole

© Springer International Publishing AG, part of Springer Nature 2018
E. Kamsties et al. (Eds.): REFSQ 2018, LNCS 10753, pp. 20–36, 2018.
https://doi.org/10.1007/978-3-319-77243-1_2

ecosystem of devices [2]. Furthermore, the combination of hardware and software design is a distinguishing part of the design methodology for IoT [3]. IoT affects the design methodology and processes through increased importance of the user-centeredness of design where the user actively can determine the design outcome, increased use of higher level tools and applying new, agile, and exploratory design methods [1]. At the same time, innovation and deciding what to implement is more customer-driven and based on data from actual usage [4].

The term User Experience (UX) can be defined as *"a person's perceptions and responses resulting from the use and/or anticipated use of a product, system or service"* [5]. As such, UX attempts at capturing all aspects of the experience of using a product, system or service, such as emotions and perceptions in all stages of use, the perception of brand image, performance, and the context of use. Similar to usability *"the extent to which a system, product or service can be used by specified users to achieve specified goals with effectiveness, efficiency and satisfaction in a specified context of use"* [5], UX is typically considered to be a quality requirement (QR) or non-functional requirement (NFR) [6,7]. However, UX is inherently difficult to measure, while usability can be measured objectively, e.g. time to complete tasks, and subjectively, e.g. the system usability scale (SUS) [8]. Usability can furthermore be seen as a subpart of UX, which underlines the attempt of UX at capturing universal and overall qualities of an individual using a product, system or service. Fraifer et al. proposes a quantifiable way of communicating and describing UX based on 84 different (mainly subjective) evaluation methods such as hedonic qualities, diary studies, interview and questionnaire guides, experience sampling, etc. [9]. They create a radar diagram based on the overarching qualities *Look* (Visual Design, Information structure, Branding), *Feel* (Mastery of interaction, Satisfaction, Emotional Attachment) and *Usability*. The concept of UX also touches on the meaning it creates in a user's life, and what needs it fulfills [10,11]. Hassenzahl comments that even though the concept of UX (in his words: *proposition to consider the experience before the thing*), has been adopted by academics and HCI practitioners, not much has changed in the general design approach [10].

In this paper, we study how IoT development companies address IoT UX. This is part of our ongoing efforts to understand the overall decision process around IoT system development. Specifically, this paper aims at understanding the activities performed in the context of data-driven development to decide how to address UX requirements. We define the following research questions:

RQ1 How are UX requirements elicited in the context of IoT development in general?

RQ2 How are data-driven methodologies specifically utilized for IoT development to elicit UX requirements?

RQ3 Which are the challenges for UX and IoT?

This paper is organized as follows: In Sect. 2, the related work is outlined. The research method used is described in Sect. 3. Section 4 presents the main results and Sect. 5 summarizes the discussion. The paper is concluded in Sect. 6.

2   Related Work

IoT interfaces pose certain challenges, in that a large part of the interaction going on is invisible to the user (ubiquitous cf. [12]). Furthermore, the technology is, in itself, distributed and asynchronous and each IoT device typically consists of a combination of a physical product, underlying software and network services [3]. This affect the way the user is able to interact with it. IoT therefore impacts the design process, putting a larger focus on UX evaluation and design methods that can enhance UX [1,2,13]. This is accomplished by, for example, using agile [14] development, iterative design and prototyping, and applying user-centered design principles (e.g. [5]), rather than traditional requirements engineering.

One way of accomplishing an iterative design, that meets the users' needs and expectations, is to improve the system continuously after it has been released to the market, for example by collecting usage data (analytics) [3]. However, the physical design of the device is less flexible, and changing the physical product after launch is typically never performed and entails large costs. Therefore, iteration and parallel design, and conceptualizing the product in the design process become more important for the hardware part. Lin et al. attempt at creating a framework for how to combine the data-driven approach with product form design [15]. The main part of the framework consists of conducting a UX scenario experiment with the product. However, they conclude that the limitation of working iteratively with the physical object results in that the presented framework can mainly be used by newly launched products with short life cycles.

According to Pallot et al. [16], there is in general more research conducted on UX evaluation (subjective) rather than UX measurement (objective). Furthermore, they consider that, due to the complexity of UX, most papers in the field describe a narrow UX evaluation, focusing on ergonomic and hedonic qualities. In the context of an experiential living lab for IoT, they have elaborated on the UX life-cycle described by Roto et al. [17], and proposed a UX framework and model with a combination of 42 different properties in three categories: Knowledge, Social and Business.

In addition to hedonic and ergonomic qualities, they single out three of the Business UX elements specifically concerning IoT; automation level, connectivity, and reliability. However, their ideas of how to conduct measurements per se are not elaborated.

One large part of consumer IoT is wearables. The increasing use of wearables is referred to by Barricelli et al. [18], as the *quantified-self* movement. In [19], Oh and Lee discuss UX issues for quantified-self. It is stated that the wearables are often regarded as fashion items and therefore aesthetics is important. The size and shape are also said to play a role in order not to disturb the user. Shin investigates the term quality of experience (QoE), that he describes as encompassing both UX and the quality of service (QoS), and shows how they are interrelated [20]. However, Shin does not define what they mean by UX, but describes it to be related to usefulness and enjoyment.

Ovad and Larsen conducted a study on UX and usability in eight different Danish companies [21]. Their mainly focused on how to combine agile development methods with UX. Three were software companies and five were companies working with embedded software in physical products. They argue that there is a gap between industry and academy when it comes to UX and usability methods. Holmström-Olsson et al. studied five different Swedish companies' view on interaction and ecosystems for IoT [22]. Their study also presents a model (User Dimensions in IoT, UDIT), that is focused on user interaction rather than a broader view of UX.

Customer-driven innovation and a close communication with the users is an important trend in software engineering. Customer-driven understanding means understanding the specific and detailed needs of the customers as a vehicle for innovation rather than being technology driven [4]. There is also a movement to work with concrete data rather than informed opinions [23]. This is closely related to working with continuous deployment and creating an atmosphere where the users are used to "being experimented on" [24]. With the study presented in this article, the existing work is complemented with how IoT development companies actually use data and analytics to understand the UX requirements, both for hardware and software.

3   Research Method

Considering the exploratory nature of this study and the aim to describe the diversities among companies within the defined area, the qualitative approach was found to be the most suitable [25]. The overall design of the study is found in Fig. 1.

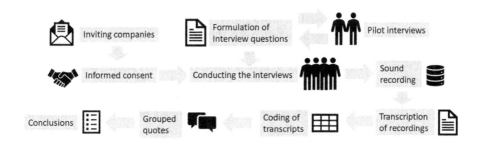

Fig. 1. Overview of the method for the exploratory case study.

3.1   Data Collection

Data was collected through semi-structured interviews [26]. The interview instrument was structured according to the funnel model meaning that the character of the questions moved from general to specific [26]. The instrument was evaluated in two pilot interviews, resulting in some adjustments. The interview instrument used can be found in [27].

3.2   Execution

The analysis was qualitative with the aim to explore and gain understanding; not to explain and statistically analyze. The selection of companies was based on a combination of convince sampling and maximum variation [28] (cf. [27] for details). The participating companies all develop IoT products or systems. All companies have an office in the south part of Sweden, and all interviews except from one took place at their respective office. The companies and interviewees' roles are summarized in Table 1. Companies A-C and E-G are consultancy companies, where Company G is a design studio and the others cover the complete process. Companies D and H-K are product development companies. Software is central to all of the companies and they develop complete software systems. That is, they do not merely develop the software embedded in their hardware products. The older companies (A, E, F and H) come from other domains and have over time started working with IoT.

The interviews were performed by the first and third author. All the interviews were recorded and lasted for approximately one hour. Both interviewers asked questions and interacted in with the interviewees. In two cases (E and C), there were two interviewees. The interviewees were selected based on their insights into the requirements and UX processes.

3.3   Data Analysis

The analysis consisted of coding the transcripts, which involves dividing the qualitative data into parts with coherent content and assigning codes to these different parts [26]. The coding was conducted by applying the two main types of data analysis methods: generation of theory and confirmation of theory. The aim of theory generation methods is to find hypotheses from the data, whereas theory confirmation methods are used to find support for previously generated hypotheses [29]. Our initial codes originated from the goals of the study, the research questions, and other related variables of interest. As the analysis progressed, a number of codes were added. These post-formed codes were found iteratively by identifying recurring themes in the data and finding text parts which could not be coded with any of the preformed codes [29]. In total, 28 codes where used, 16 of them was preformed. The coding was performed by the first and third author. The first interview was coded separately by both authors and combined into a resulting coded transcript. Because of the similarities between the selected codes of each author, the consequent interviews were equally divided between the authors instead. After a transcript had been coded by one author, it was validated by the other. If there were any disagreements regarding the assignment of codes, the particular text part was immediately discussed to agree on a final selection of codes.

Table 1. Participating companies. Category (Cat.): P = Product company, C = Consulting company. The sizes of the companies are displayed as number of employees, and the age in years.

Id	Size	Age	Cat.	Description	Interviewee(s)
A	600	30	C	Specialized in embedded systems. Operating in industrial automation and product development.	Senior software developer
B	270	4	C	Design and product development of IoT technology within e.g. interior, automotive, health care.	Head of design
C	8	2	C	Specialized in IoT with focus on industrial IoT, e-health, energy.	C1: CEO C2: Ind. designer
D	10	4	P	Start-up company with a sensor used within retail and facility management.	Sales director
E	45	30	C	Product development within IoT and other areas.	E1: SW developer E2: R&D manager
F	4000	40	C	Global IT management company. Provides IT solutions and services.	Lead of IoT
G	10	2	C	Design studio. Develops concepts, pitches, stories, and visions.	Lead interaction designer
H	1000	15	P	International mobile communication company. Develops and sells products.	Senior UX designer
I	30	2	P	Start-up automotive company. Develops and sells products.	Software developer
J	70	2	P	Development of smart B2C products. The main domain is wearables.	UX director
K	9	3	P	Start-up company with a home security system.	CEO

3.4 Threats to Validity

The threats to validity are outlined in this section. The threats to validity are discussed from an empirical validity point of view, which involves construct validity, internal validity, external validity, and reliability [25,26].

A threat to the **construct validity** is that the interview questions are not interpreted by the interviewees as the interviewers intended. This is addressed by commencing each interview with asking the interviewee to define the concepts of UX and IoT, respectively. When summarizing the answers, we use these definitions, together with the role of the interviewee, to judge from what point of view the development process is described. An additional threat to the construct validity is the semi-structure of the interviews. In some cases, an open question was used where it may have been preferable to use a closed question. For example, the question about UX activities was an open question and we did not ask the interviewee to list any activities in particular.

In our case, the **internal validity** foremost regards the interview situation. One such threat is that the interviewee's personal opinions may not represent that of the company. In that way, the answers could possibly be more related to the person rather than the company. Moreover, the interviewee's role can be assumed to highly influence the answers and how much the interviewee knows about the subject in question. This threat is smaller for the small companies but for the larger companies, the threat cannot be ignored. For example, Intervie-wee F was not informed about details of the company's UX work. During the interviews, we may have been more inclined to ask follow-up questions when the interviewees gave an answer which confirmed our theories, possibly resulting in confirmation bias. However, none of the persons who performed the interviews had any previous dealings with any of the companies or other relationships with them. In combination with a literature study, we consider the confirmation bias threat to be small.

The external validity regards the aspect of the extent to which the results are generalizable to companies not part of the study. We interviewed both con-sultancy companies as well as product companies. In addition, we interviewed both young and old companies. However, only one larger product company was interviewed. The results are thus based mostly on consulting companies and start-ups. Hence, we cannot ignore the threats to validity. However, as argued by Flyvbjerg, the threats to generalizability should not be exaggerated [28].

One threat to the **reliability** concerns the coding. When the results were to be compiled from the tabulated and coded transcripts, we discovered that the way that the codes had been defined were too general. Furthermore, all interviews, except from the two at Company C and G were held in Swedish. We consider it as a threat to the reliability that information and meaning can be lost or changed due to the translation of quotes from Swedish to English. The translation has, to limited extent, also involved rephrasing and shorting some of the quotes, which may also contribute to this threat.

4   Results

This section summarizes the results from the 12 interviews performed with inter-viewees from 11 different companies. The following sub sections elaborate the results for each of the research questions presented in Sect. 1.

4.1   RQ1 How Are UX Requirements Elicited in the Context of IoT Development in General?

All participating companies state that they apply agile or iterative development methods. The consulting companies (Company A, B, C, E, F and G) are similar in the way that they are dependent on their customers' desires and it is generally the customer who directs how rigorous the requirements are specified. However, there are differences among the consultancy companies. In the initial part of the process, Company A and E focus on specifying mostly functional requirements, while Company B, C and G instead concentrate on exploring the underlying problem and origin of the customer's idea. Since company F is a large company with a separate UX department, Interviewee F could not describe their UX pro-cess in detail. The characterization of the development processes at the product companies varies from applying short iterations (Company D and J) or being directed by UX (Company J and K), to being unstructured and self-organizing (Company I and K). Apart from company A and E all companies describe their UX work as exploratory using for example prototypes and user stories instead of defining requirements. The development process at the innovation department at Company H is different to the process at Company H by being more iterative. Except from that Interviewee H explained that the innovative character of the development demands a more rapid process, the reason for applying a different development model *"[It] is also that it's about Internet of Things. That is to say, it's unknown ground. The values are entirely untried"*.

When describing the UX development process, the interviewees were asked if they apply any UX techniques. The techniques are presented in Table 2, categorized as either qualitative or quantitative. Extensive user research is foremost described by Interviewee G, H, J and K. Identifying the user groups and the underlying problem are seen as important. When asked how their UX decisions are made, Interviewee G answers *"Research! [. . .] Both market research and then concept testing, basically"*. Interviewee J, describes that they have focused on the underlying needs rather than the product itself. Interviewee B, G, H, J, and K emphasize the importance of involving the end-users during the development process. For example, Company J have had beta testers, that provided both qualitative feedback and analytics data. Interviewee H sees it as one of their main activities during the process to go out in the field and talk to the end-users. Interviewee I bring up that they have had people testing their product using virtual reality. Even though it primarily was a marketing event, Interviewee I mention that they received valuable suggestions during that activity. Both interviewees from Company E believe that involving the end-user would be beneficial for their development process. However, it is rarely done. Interviewee E1 mentions that *"In some cases, it may be that you may have to run some user test to test a hypothesis. But usually, it's enough to use our knowledge, i.e. previous experiences or [. . .] e.g. design guidelines."*.

Prototyping is also something that is emphasized. Interviewee D stresses the use of 3D printing in order to be able to test different use cases early on. Interviewee B argues the use of easy and quick prototyping. However, the interviewee sees a problem with proceeding to generating solutions too quickly, since this involves a risk of losing the underlying meaning. Interviewee D experiences that it is easier to discuss a prototype than requirements, because *"if you take [the prototype] to the developers, they exactly know what it's supposed to look like"*.

To address RQ1, the handling of UX requirements are dependent on the customer's demands in the case of the consulting companies. However, company B, C and G tend to focus more on defining the problem together with the customer compared to company A and E that are more focused on requirements. When it comes to the product companies, UX requirements are generally not defined. Instead it is an ongoing process where for example user stories and prototypes are used to direct development.

Table 2. UX techniques during the development process, Category (Cat.): P = Product company, C = Consulting company

Id	Cat.	Qualitative techniques	Quantitative techniques
A	C	-	-
B	C	Prototyping, User test	User data
C	C	Prototyping	-
D	P	Prototyping	*Unknown*
E	C	Occasional user tests, Depends on customer	-
F	C	Mock-ups, User feedback	-
G	C	User research, User tests, Scenarios, Story boards, personas	User data, A/B testing
H	P	Personas, Surveys, Interviews with end users	Google Analytics, A/B testing
I	P	Indirect user feedback, Conceptual sketches	-
J	P	User research, Feedback from beta testers, Personas, Focus groups, Sketches	Google Analytics, In-house A/B testing
K	P	User research, User feedback, Prototyping	*Unknown*

4.2   RQ2 How Are Data-Driven Methodologies Specifically Utilized for IoT Development to Elicit UX Requirements?

Companies that work in a more data-driven way do not generally see the product as finished when it has been released to market. For example, Interviewee K said *"For us, it's not binary. It's not the traditional business mindset that you develop a product for a long time and then you release it and everyone will have access to it at the same time."*.

Among the product companies, Company D, J, and K have all released their products to the market. None of them considers their product as finished and they explicitly describe that they use quantitative data from the product to develop the product also after-market release. Company D updates their products with new features and also collects data and statistics from the devices. Interviewee D emphasizes that update and data collection are important to their development and strategy; *"In fact, all data that comes there can be used to create a better product"*. Company J uses Google Analytics data for various purposes, such as finding bugs, determining which functions that are used the most, and evaluating the set-up time. Information that comes from Google Analytics is seen as either a warning of that something is wrong or a sign of approval that it works as expected. However, Interviewee J claims that they are, to some extent, immature when it comes to using the data. The interviewee sees future possibilities with collecting other data than just which features that are used. One such possibility could be to extend the studying of behavioral data. In addition, the company is interested in behavioral data that concerns the physical product and not only the software.

When it comes to A/B testing, Company J does it during the development process but not after-market release. Interviewee J means that the reason for not applying A/B testing in the field is that they *"don't have that many customers yet. So we dare not risk that one particular solution may be bad"*. Company K develops new features that are released to a limited number of users. Interviewee K described that when *"The product is out, it's already in thousands of homes. And we can do such a thing as doing a new feature, deploy it to a hundred users, and see if they are using it or if we want to do something more."*.

Most interviewees that say that their company uses metrics related to UX, also argue that the quantitative data can be problematic and need to be complemented with data from, for instance, user tests or feedback from users. For example, as Interviewee G mean that numbers can be used to tell that something is important, but not why. Interviewee H stresses that *"You have to use it with other data. You have to make interviews, and have contact with focus groups also to put it in context"*. Interviewee J sees Google Analytics data as an indication of that something is wrong; *"It's usually just a catalyst, an indication that here's something strange."* Interviewee B mentions that they collect data in terms of different kind of feedback from users. In addition to working with Google Analytics, Company J also collects data from social media, support mail, and opinions from beta testers. Also, Interviewee D and K describe that they use customer feedback to improve the product.

The consequences are that companies that apply data-driven methodologies (D, J, and K) are using the data as either confirmatory or as a warning that something is wrong. None of the companies let their UX design process be directed entirely by the quantitative data.

4.3   RQ3 Which Are the Challenges for UX and IoT?

The interviewees identified some UX related challenges that are specific or more prominent when developing IoT compared to other systems.

Interviewee D, E2, and J identify a challenge related to the IoT development process, which involves combining an agile software development process with hardware development. Interviewee J described this challenge as: *"It's an obvious problem that, in a certain phase of the project, it's somewhat contradictory that [the software developers] want to wait as long as possible with deciding while the [hardware developers] must decide earlier"*.

Furthermore, Interviewee G argues that privacy and security is a UX challenge; *"It's not necessarily a technical challenge, [it] is a UX challenge"*. Interviewee F stresses the connection between UX and security and means that an insecure device results in poor UX.

Interviewee H means that UX for IoT can be seen as *"an ecosystem of experiences"* and emphasizes that there is a number of factors that affects the experience that cannot be controlled but are affecting the UX. Something that is also mentioned by for example Interviewee D, is the problem of being dependent on other systems, such as the user's router or poor WiFi connection. Interviewee K argues that *"The big challenges are when you have to build on systems that are not that good"*. Interviewee I and G sees it as an issue that it cannot be ensured that there is Internet connection available everywhere.

Interviewee H describes an interoperability issue as *"One very basic thing is something that has been around for a long time, but is still difficult. And that is to connect things to each other."*. Interviewee G highlights the user perspective, which involves that the digitized products communicate with each other invisibly and consider it as a trap for IoT that the user does not have an intuitive perception towards that communication. Interviewee F regards it as problematic when different industries or even companies develop their own platforms and standards; *"It will never work that each industry owns whole ecosystems. What is needed is openness and finding standards."*. In accordance, Interviewee G also describes the challenge of compatibility; *"There's so many different solutions, applications out there [...]. There's just no standard"*.

Interviewee D believes that it is easy to make too advanced services and that the installation needs to be simple. This was also stressed by for example Interviewee C1 who said that they *"call it plug-and-play"*, and Interviewee A that argued: *"Anyone should be able to [install it] by picking it out of the box and starting it"*.

Summarizing the challenges, there are challenges that are related to the development process at each company, but there are also challenges related to requirements that is not always controllable by the company itself since it involves also other systems.

5   Discussion and Future Work

Based on the analysis of the transcriptions and codes of the interviews, we identify three topics of special interest that affect UX in IoT design in companies: *Adapting to the situation*, *Proactive vs. reactive*, and the *The system context*. They are elaborated in the three following sub-sections. We conclude the discussion with a perspective on future work.

5.1   Adapting to the Situation

Company A and E tend to define requirements early in the process to a larger extent than the other companies. One explanation can be that both companies are relatively old and have a tradition in hardware development respective industrial automation. The focus is also mainly on functional requirements, which also may be due to their respective background. The consulting companies, on the other hand, with a strong innovation and design profile (B and G) tend to define the problem together with their customer and focus on the underlying problem rather than defining requirements. However, as Interviewee E2, D and J mentioned, hardware in agile processes can be difficult since it is both expensive and time consuming to make hardware changes late in the process.

A majority of the interviewees seems to consider prototyping as a natural part of their process. The use of different software prototyping tools described by Interviewee D, H, J and K is in line with contemporary UX research [1,13]. The use of rapid prototyping [13] is favored by Interviewee B, who at the same time considers it a risk that prototyping can undermine user research activities; there is a risk of being too confident if focusing on prototyping which leads to neglecting user research.

There are examples among the companies that indicate that their design processes are both iterative, prototype-based, user-centered, and exploratory which is in accordance with how de Haan consider the development process to change due to IoT [1]. Drawn from our results, we cannot confirm that the companies design process and their way of handling of UX requirements are due to the fact that they are developing for IoT. We consider that it is more likely that factors such as type of product, degree of innovation, company organization, and age of the company plays a greater role than the fact that it is IoT.

The interviewees in our study brought up that the quantitative usage data itself does not tell anything about the underlying reason. Therefore, the interviewees propose that the quantitative data should be used together with qualitative data in order to understand, for instance, why a feature is used or not. Which is similar to what is proposed by Holmström-Olsson et al. [30].

The companies are more or less immature in the use of quantitative data, something that they are also well aware of. Among the companies that collects data, they do not always know how to use the data. There is also a common skepticism regarding how useful the quantitative data is. However, there is a hype around data-driven methodologies that possibly lead to companies are afraid of lag behind if not adopting the new techniques. Data-driven methodologies are likely not always suitable. For example, Company J is using A/B testing during the development process, but not as the product are released to the market. They do not want to employ A/B testing as their customer base is too small and products too new.

With the advent of data-driven techniques, there is a knowledge gap and at the same time a hype which result in that companies collect large amount of data but are not mature in their way to make use of it. We hypothesize that there is a need for a better understanding of when and how a particular method or technique is appropriate to use to elicit, analyze and validate UX requirements.

5.2 Proactive or Reactive?

Almost all of the companies apply some kind of prototyping whereas only a couple use data-driven approaches systematically. Company D, J, and K apply data-driven activities both during the development process and after the product is released to market. They have in common several of the preconditions for applying data-driven development suggested by Holmtröm-Olsson et al. [31].

Firstly, none of the three companies consider their product as finished. Secondly, they have a product released to the market that they automatically collect data from. Thirdly, they have an organization where UX, software development, and product management are closely integrated.

The interviewees agree that the data is difficult to use without interpretation. When it comes to UX, the data is mostly used as either confirmatory or as a warning that something is wrong. We believe that IoT is relatively unexplored which requires more creativity and innovation since there is a fewer number of applications to copy or take inspiration from. There seems to be a connection to the maturity of the products and markets and whether there is an emphasis on creative and proactive techniques (such as story boards and user and market research) or confirmatory and reactive techniques (such as usage data and user tests). The former is utilized more in more immature products and markets. Similar to De Haan [1], who states reactive and data-driven approaches *"may simply lead to the most average HCI design ever created"*, there is also a connection to how radical innovation is being deployed and how long the iterations are. Hence, we hypothesize that longer iterations with more radical innovation is less suited for data-driven approaches whereas incremental innovation in short iterations are more suited for data-driven approaches. Obviously, hardware development has by nature longer iterations and hence more reliant on proactive approaches.

5.3   The System Context

An IoT device is always part of a larger system, dependent on a network, sometimes referred to as an ecosystem. This network may be of varied quality and will therefore in turn affect the quality of the Internet connection of the device. Furthermore, the other parts of the system are often developed by other companies with different goals. As expressed by Interviewee D, this is something that is out of the company's control, but it will still affect the UX of their IoT device. If the device also depends on additional systems, such as other IoT devices, interoperability issues may arise. The lack of standardization is an example of such an issue. This is brought up by Interviewee F and G during their respective interviews. These factors that are outside each company's control are also discussed by [20], who argues that these affect the QoS and thus the QoE (but are not part of UX according to them).

When the development of an ecosystem requires different industries to collaborate, it is an obstacle that, as Interviewee F described, separate industries wants to own the ecosystem. A collaboration requires standardization, but presumably, the reverse relationship - that standardization requires collaboration - is also a premise. Even though the concept of developing different systems part of a larger ecosystem is not new, we believe it is still largely not appropriately addressed. An IoT ecosystem will likely be even more diverse and coming from more vendors which emphasizes this problem from an UX perspective.

5.4   Future Work

One of the major challenges to IoT specifically but all software development in general is how to handle UX requirements when the products are part of a larger system, with less standards and control. In essence, there need to be a flexibility and adaptability to an unknown usage context. Especially when addressing immature markets and perhaps with immature products, the compromise between radical incremental innovation in relation to the UX will be key to product success. To study this, we suggest combining studies of comparative domains as well as applied research together with IoT companies to in depth understand their challenges and potential solutions. Furthermore, this study was conducted in a relatively limited geographical area. It would therefore be beneficial to extend the study into including companies in different geographical areas.

The relationship between UX and the challenge of privacy and in the context of IoT is something that, to our knowledge, there is little research on. A study could focus on the question if a high security and privacy level can have a positive impact on UX when it comes to IoT, especially with an ecosystem perspective.

One interesting question that arises in the context of data-driven development, is how this approach to the development process affect the creativity when it comes to UX. As the quantitative measures becomes increasingly popular, it would be interesting to investigate the benefits and drawbacks from a creativity and innovation perspective and when different types of techniques and methods are the most suited.

The interest in UX among the companies could be described by the increased user-centeredness described by de Haan [1] and the general shift towards UX found by Ovad et al. [21] and is not necessarily due to the fact that the companies develop IoT. A narrower categorization could be done, e.g. by comparing companies that all develop consumer IoT products. As an example, Company A and D do not involve their end-users to the same extent as Company J, H and K, for which a reason might be that they are B2B and not B2C. It is likely that the type of product influences the design process, which would be preferable to also compare with non-IoT companies.

Designing IoT can be particularly challenging since it, in many cases, does not have a traditional UI [12] and is highly interconnected with other products, systems and services which affects the users' perceptions of the experience of use. From a user experience perspective, the actual size of the IoT system is irrelevant, and thus, many of the UX requirements may therefore be independent of size, but this would need to be investigated further.

6   Conclusion

In this study, we interviewed 11 companies working with IoT. The main characterizing factors are the hardware-software dilemma, agile and iterative development, fast-changing markets and technology as well as new usage contexts and interaction modes. Even though many aspects of IoT are not new, when combined they pose unique challenges for the companies when handling UX requirements. We believe that there is a need to better understand when a specific method is suited to help companies adapt to the specific situation at hand. Furthermore, there is a compromise to be made between an upfront, proactive analysis principle and an analysis of usage in running software, in a reactive manner. Even though there are proponents of data-driven, reactive methods, it is not clear that it leads to the best innovation in all situations. Lastly, UX requirements in a larger system of loosely connected companies are not well understood. Hence, there is a need to improve UX requirements elicitation and analysis methods in this context.

Based on our study, indications are that there is no single solution which works for all companies and situations. Hence, we firmly believe in empirical understanding of the context and supporting companies with their unique problems and tailoring solutions that work in practice.

References

1. de Haan, G.: HCI design methods: where next? From user-centred to creative design and beyond. In: Proceedings of the European Conference on Cognitive Ergonomics, pp. 1–8 (2015)
2. Fauquex, M., Goyal, S., Evequoz, F., Bocchi, Y.: Creating people-aware IoT applications by combining design thinking and user-centered design methods. In: IEEE World Forum on Internet of Things, pp. 57–62 (2015)
3. Rowland, C., Goodman, E., Charlier, M., Light, A., Lui, A.: Designing Connected Products - UX for the Consumer Internet of Things, vol. 1. O'Reilly Media, Sebastopol (2015)
4. Bosch, J.: Speed, data, and ecosystems: the future of software engineering. IEEE Softw. **33**(1), 82–88 (2016)
5. ISO: 9241–210:2010 Ergonomics of human-system interaction - part 210: Human-centered design for interactive systems. Technical report (2010)
6. Glinz, M.: On non-functional requirements. In: 2007 15th IEEE International Conference on Requirements Engineering, RE 2007, pp. 21–26. IEEE (2007)
7. ISO: 25010 Systems and software engineering-systems and software quality requirements and evaluation (SQuaRE). Technical report (2011)
8. Brooke, J., et al.: SUS: a quick and dirty usability scale. Usabil. Eval. Ind. **189**(194), 4–7 (1996)
9. Fraifer, M., Kharel, S., Hasenfuss, H., Elmangoush, A., Ryan, A., Elgenaidi, W., Fernström, M.: Look before you leap: exploring the challenges of technology and user experience in the internet of things. In: Forum on Research and Technologies for Society and Industry, pp. 1–6, September 2017
10. Hassenzahl, M.: Experiences before things: a primer for the (yet) unconvinced. In: Extended Abstracts on Human Factors in Computing Systems, pp. 2059–2068 (2013)
11. Hassenzahl, M., Wiklund-Engblom, A., Bengs, A., Hägglund, S., Diefenbach, S.: Experience-oriented and product-oriented evaluation: psychological need fulfillment, positive affect, and product perception. Int. J. Hum. Comput. Interact. **31**(8), 530–544 (2015)

12. Resnick, M.L.: Ubiquitous computing: UX when there is no UI. In: Proceedings of the Human Factors and Ergonomics Society Annual Meeting, vol. 57, pp. 1007–1011. Sage Publications, Los Angeles (2013)
13. Kranz, M., Holleis, P., Schmidt, A.: Embedded interaction: interacting with the internet of things. IEEE Internet Comput. 14(2), 46–53 (2010)
14. Warden, S., Shore, J.: The Art of Agile Development: With Extreme Programming. O'Reilly Media, Sebastopol (2007)
15. Lin, K.Y., Chien, C.F., Kerh, R.: UNISON framework of data-driven innovation for extracting user experience of product design of wearable devices. Comput. Ind. Eng. 99, 487–502 (2016)
16. Pallot, M., Pawar, K., Santoro, R.: A user experience framework and model within experiential living labs for Internet of Things. In: 2013 International Conference on Engineering, Technology and Innovation, ICE 2013 and IEEE International Technology Management Conference, ITMC 2013 (2015)
17. Roto, V., Law, E., Vermeeren, A., Hoonhout, J.: User experience white paper. Outcome of the Dagstuhl Seminar on Demarcating User Experience, Germany (2011)
18. Barricelli, B.R., Valtolina, S.: A visual language and interactive system for end-user development of internet of things ecosystems. J. Vis. Lang. Comput. 40, 1–19 (2017)
19. Oh, J., Lee, U.: Exploring UX issues in quantified self technologies. In: 2015 8th International Conference on Mobile Computing and Ubiquitous Networking, ICMU 2015, pp. 53–59 (2015)
20. Shin, D.-H.: Conceptualizing and measuring quality of experience of the internet of things: exploring how quality is perceived by users. Inf. Manage. 54(8), 998–1011 (2017). https://doi.org/10.1016/j.im.2017.02.006. ISSN 0378-7206
21. Ovad, T., Larsen, L.B.: The prevalence of UX design in agile development processes in industry. In: Proceedings of the 2015 Agile Conference, Agile 2015, pp. 40–49 (2015)
22. Olsson, H.H., Bosch, J., Katumba, B.: Exploring IoT user dimensions. In: Abrahamsson, P., Jedlitschka, A., Nguyen Duc, A., Felderer, M., Amasaki, S., Mikkonen, T. (eds.) PROFES 2016. LNCS, vol. 10027, pp. 477–484. Springer, Cham (2016). https://doi.org/10.1007/978-3-319-49094-6_33
23. Olsson, H.H., Bosch, J.: From opinions to data-driven software r&d: a multi-case study on how to close the 'open loop' problem. In: Software Engineering and Advanced Applications (SEAA), pp. 9–16. IEEE (2014)
24. Parnin, C., Helms, E., Atlee, C., Boughton, H., Ghattas, M., Glover, A., Holman, J., Micco, J., Murphy, B., Savor, T., et al.: The top 10 adages in continuous deployment. IEEE Softw. 34(3), 86–95 (2017)
25. Easterbrook, S., Singer, J., Storey, M.A., Damian, D.: Selecting empirical methods for software engineering research. In: Shull, F., Singer, J., Sjøberg, D.I.K. (eds.) Guide to Advanced Empirical Software Engineering, pp. 285–311. Springer, London (2008). https://doi.org/10.1007/978-1-84800-044-5_11
26. Runeson, P., Host, M., Rainer, A., Regnell, B.: Case Study Research in Software Engineering: Guidelines and Examples. Wiley, Hoboken (2012)
27. Bergman, J., Johansson, I.: The user experience perspective of Internet of Things development. Master's thesis, Department of Design Sciences, Lund University, Sweden (2017)
28. Flyvbjerg, B.: Five misunderstandings about case-study research. Qual. Inq. 12(2), 219–245 (2006)

29. Seaman, C.B.: Qualitative methods in empirical studies of software engineering. IEEE Trans. Softw. Eng. **25**(4), 557–572 (1999)
30. Olsson, H.H., Bosch, J.: Towards continuous validation of customer value. In: Scientific Workshop Proceedings of the XP2015, June 2016, pp. 1–4 (2015)
31. Olsson, H.H., Alahyari, H., Bosch, J.: Climbing the "Stairway to heaven" - a mulitiple-case study exploring barriers in the transition from agile development towards continuous deployment of software. In: Software Engineering and Advanced Applications, pp. 392–399 (2012)

NLP in Theory and Practice

Inferring Ontology Fragments from Semantic Role Typing of Lexical Variants

Mitra Bokaei Hosseini[1]([✉]) [iD], Travis D. Breaux[2]([✉]), and Jianwei Niu[1]([✉])

[1] Computer Science Department, University of Texas, San Antonio, TX, USA
{mitra.bokaeihosseini,jianwei.niu}@utsa.edu
[2] Institute of Software Research, Carnegie Mellon University, Pittsburgh, USA
breaux@cs.cmu.edu

Abstract. **[Context and Motivation]** Information systems depend on personal data to individualize services. To manage privacy expectations, companies use privacy policies to regulate what data is collected, used and shared. However, different terminological interpretations can lead to privacy violations, or misunderstandings about what behavior is to be expected. **[Question/Problem]** A formal ontology can help requirements authors to consistently check how their data practice descriptions relate to one another and to identify unintended interpretations. Constructing an empirically valid ontology is a challenging task since it should be both scalable and consistent with multi-stakeholder interpretations. **[Principle Ideas/Results]** In this paper, we introduce a semi-automated semantic analysis method to identify ontology fragments by inferring hypernym, meronym and synonym relationships from morphological variations. The method employs a shallow typology to categorize individual words, which are then matched automatically to 26 reusable semantic rules. The rules were discovered by classifying 335 unique information type phrases extracted from 50 mobile privacy policies. The method was evaluated on 109 unique information types extracted from six privacy policies by comparing the generated ontology fragments against human interpretations of phrase pairs obtained by surveying human subjects. The results reveal that the method scales by reducing the number of otherwise manual paired comparisons by 74% and produces correct fragments with a 1.00 precision and 0.59 recall when compared to human interpretation. **[Contributions]** The proposed rules identify semantic relations between a given lexeme and its morphological variants to create a shared meaning between phrases among end users.

Keywords: Requirements engineering · Natural language processing · Ontology

1 Introduction

Mobile and web applications (apps) are increasingly popular due to the convenient services they provide in different domains of interest. According to a 2015 PEW Research Center study, 64% of Americans own a smart phone [1]. They found that smart phone users typically check health-related information online (62% of Americans), conduct online banking (54%), and look for job-related information (63%). To fulfill user needs and business requirements, these apps collect different categories of personal information, such as

© Springer International Publishing AG, part of Springer Nature 2018
E. Kamsties et al. (Eds.): REFSQ 2018, LNCS 10753, pp. 39–56, 2018.
https://doi.org/10.1007/978-3-319-77243-1_3

friends' phone numbers, photos and real-time location. Regulators require apps to provide users with a legal privacy notice, also called a privacy policy, which can be accessed by users before installing the app. For example, the California Attorney General's office recommends that privacy policies list what kind of personally identifiable data is collected, how it is used, and with whom it is shared [2]. Privacy policies contain critical requirements that inform stakeholders about data practices [3]. Due to different stakeholder needs, there can be disparate viewpoints regarding what is essentially the same subject matter [4]. Stakeholders use different words for the same domain, which reduces shared understanding of the subject and leads to a misalignment among the designers' intention, and expectations of policy writers and regulators [5].

Data practices are commonly described in privacy polices using hypernymy [6], which occurs when a more abstract information type is used instead of a more specific information type. Hypernymy permits multiple interpretations, which can lead to ambiguity in the perception of what exact personal information is used. To address this problem, companies can complement their policies with a formal ontology that explicitly states what kinds of information are included in the interpretations of data-related concepts. Initial attempts to build any ontology can require comparing each information type phrase with every other phrase in the policy, and assigning a semantic relationship to each pair. However, considering a lexicon built from 50 policies that contains 351 phrases, an analyst must make $(351 \times 350)/2 = 61{,}425$ comparisons, which is over 200 h of continuous comparison by one analyst.

In this paper, we describe a semi-automated semantic analysis method that uses lexical variation of information type phrases to infer ontological relations, such as hypernyms. Instead of performing paired comparisons, the analyst spends less than one hour typing the phrases, and then a set of semantic rules are automatically applied to yield a subset of all possible relations. The rules were first discovered in a grounded analysis of information types extracted from 50 privacy policies for a manual ontology construction approach [7]. To improve the semantic relations inferred using these initial set of rules, we established a ground truth by asking human subjects to perform the more time-consuming task of comparing phrases in the lexicon. We then compared the results of the semantic rules against these human interpretations, which led to identifying additional semantic rules. Finally, we evaluated the improved semantic rules using 109 unique information types extracted from six privacy policies, and human subject surveys to measure the correctness of the results produced by the semantic rules.

This paper is organized as follows: in Sect. 2, we discuss terminology and the theoretical background; Sect. 3 presents a motivating example; in Sect. 4, background and related work are discussed; in Sect. 5, we introduce our semi-automated method for discovering ontology fragments consisting of hypernyms, meronyms and synonyms; In Sect. 6, we explain the experimental setup; in Sect. 7, we present results of evaluating this technique against human subject-surveyed information type pairs, before presenting our discussion and conclusion in Sects. 8 and 9.

2   Important Terminology and Theoretical Background

In this section, we define the terminology and present the theoretical background.

2.1   Terminology

- *Hypernym* – a noun phrase, also called a superordinate term, that is more generic than another noun phrase, called the hyponym or subordinate term.
- *Meronym* – a noun phrase that represents a part of a whole, which is also a noun phrase and called a holonym.
- *Synonym* – a noun phrase that has a similar meaning to another noun phrase.
- *Lexicon* – a collection of phrases or concept names that may be used in an ontology.
- *Ontology* – a collection of concept names and logical relations between these concepts, including hypernymy, meronymy and synonymy, among others [8].

2.2   Theoretical Background on Description Logic

Description Logic (DL) ontologies enable automated reasoning, including the ability to infer which concepts subsume or are equivalent to other concepts in the ontology. We chose the DL family $\mathcal{AL}$, which is PSPACE-complete for concept satisfiability and concept subsumption. In this paper, reasoning in DL begins with a TBox T that contains a collection of concepts and axioms based on an interpretation $\mathcal{I}$ that consists of a nonempty set $\Delta^{\mathcal{I}}$, called the domain of interpretation. The interpretation function $.^{\mathcal{I}}$ maps concepts to subsets of $\Delta^{\mathcal{I}}$: every atomic concept C is assigned a subset $C^{\mathcal{I}} \subseteq \Delta^{\mathcal{I}}$, the top concept $\top^{\mathcal{I}} = \Delta^{\mathcal{I}}$ has the interpretation $\top$.

The $\mathcal{AL}$ family includes operators for concept union and intersection, and axioms for subsumption, and equivalence with respect to the TBox. Subsumption is used to describe individuals using generalities, and we say a concept C is subsumed by a concept D, written $T \vDash C \sqsubseteq D$, if $C^{\mathcal{I}} \subseteq D^{\mathcal{I}}$ for all interpretations $\mathcal{I}$ that satisfy the TBox T. The concept C is equivalent to a concept D, written $T \vDash C \equiv D$, if $C^{\mathcal{I}} = D^{\mathcal{I}}$ for all interpretations $\mathcal{I}$ that satisfy the TBox T.

The DL enables identifying which lexicon phrases directly or indirectly share meanings, called an interpretation in DL. Each lexicon phrase is mapped to a concept in the TBox T. We express a hyponym concept C in relation to a hypernym concept D using subsumption $T \vDash C \sqsubseteq D$, and for two concepts C and D that correspond to synonyms, we express these as equivalent concepts $T \vDash C \equiv D$. For meronymy, we define a part-whole relation *partOf* that maps parts to wholes as follows: a part concept C that has a whole concept D, such that $T \vDash C \sqsubseteq (partOf\ D)$. We express the DL ontology using the Web Ontology Language[1] (OWL) version 2 DL and the HermiT[2] OWL reasoner.

---

[1] https://www.w3.org/TR/owl-guide.
[2] http://www.hermit-reasoner.com/.

3   Motivating Example

We now provide an example statement from the WhatsApp privacy policy with example interpretations inferred from the statement to demonstrate the problem.

Statement: You must provide certain devices, software, and data connections to use our Services, which we otherwise do not supply.

In this statement, "device" is an abstract information type that can be interpreted in many ways. Here are three example strategies for obtaining an interpretation:

1. If device is a super-ordinate concept, then we infer that mobile device is a kind device, therefore, the collection of information also applies to mobile devices.
2. If device is a kind of system with components, settings, etc., and we know that a device can have an IP address, then WhatsApp may collect device IP address. This interpretation is reached using a meronymy relationship between device and device IP address.
3. By use both strategies (1) and (2), together, we can infer that the collection statement applies to mobile device IP address, using both hypernymy and meronymy.

These interpretations are based on human knowledge and experience, and there is a need to bridge the gap between linguistic information types in privacy policies and knowledge of the world. In the above examples, mobile device, device IP address, and mobile device IP address are variants of a common lexeme: "device." We use the syntactic structure of lexical variants to infer semantics and construct lexical ontologies that are used to bridge this knowledge gap.

4   Related Work

In requirements engineering, two approaches are defined for codifying knowledge: naïve positivism, and naturalistic inquiry [9]. Positivism refers to the world with a set of stable and knowable phenomena, often with formal models. Naturalistic inquiry (NI) refers to constructivist views of knowledge that differ across multiple human observations. The research in this paper attempts to balance among these two viewpoints by recognizing that information types are potentially unstable and intuitive concepts. Our approach permits different interpretations, before reducing terminological confusion to reach a shared understanding through formal ontologies. We now review prior research on ontology in privacy.

4.1   Ontology in Security and Privacy Policy

Heker et al. developed a privacy ontology for e-commerce transactions which includes concepts about privacy mechanisms and principles from legislative documents [10]. Bradshaw et al. utilize an ontology that distinguishes between authorization and obligations for a policy service framework that forces agents to check their behavior with specifications [11]. Kagal et al. constructed an ontology to enforce access control policies in a web service model [12]. Syed et al. developed an ontology that provides a common understanding of cybersecurity and unifies commonly used cybersecurity standards [13]. Breaux et al. utilize an ontology that includes simple hierarchies for actors and information types to infer data flow traces across separate policies in multi-tier applications [14]. To our knowledge, our work is the first privacy-related lexical ontology that formally conceptualizes information types extracted from policies with their implied semantic relations. The initial version of this ontology has been used to find conflicts between mobile app code-level method calls and privacy policies [15].

4.2 Constructing an Ontology

There is no standard method to build an ontology [4], yet, a general approach includes identifying the ontology purpose and scope; identifying key concepts leading to a lexicon; identifying relations between lexicon concepts; and formalizing those relations. A lexicon consists of terminology in a domain, whereas ontologies organize terminology by semantic relations [16]. Lexicons can be constructed using content analysis of source text, which yields an annotated corpus. Breaux and Schaub empirically evaluated crowdsourcing to create corpora from annotated privacy policies [17]. Wilson et al. employed crowd-sourcing to create a privacy policy corpus from 115 privacy policies [18].

WordNet is a lexical database which contains English words and their forms captured from a newswire corpus, and their semantic relations, including hypernymy and synonymy [19]. Our analysis shows that only 14% of our lexicon was found in WordNet, mainly because our lexicon is populated with multi-word phrases. Moreover, meronymy relations are missing from WordNet.

Snow et al. presented a machine learning approach using hypernym-hyponym pairs in WordNet to identify additional pairs in parsed sentences of newswire corpus [20]. This approach relies on explicit expression of hypernymy pairs in text. Bhatia et al. [21] identified and applied a set of 72 Hearst-related patterns [22] to 30 privacy policies to extract hypernymy pairs. This approach yields hypernyms for only 24% of the lexicon. This means the remaining 76% of the lexicon must be manually analyzed to construct an ontology. These approaches fail to consider the semantic relations between the morphological variants of a nominal, which may not be present in the same sentence as the nominal. Our proposed model identifies these variants with semantic relations.

5   Ontology Construction Method Overview

The ontology construction method (see Fig. 1) consists of 7 steps: (1) collecting privacy policies; (2) itemizing paragraphs in the collected privacy policies; (3) annotating the itemized paragraphs by crowd workers based on a specific coding frame; (4) employing an entity extractor developed by Bhatia and Breaux [6] to analyze the annotations and extract information types which results in an information type lexicon (artifact A in Fig. 1); (5) pre-processing the phrases in the lexicon; (6) assigning role types to each pre-processed phrase that yields information type phrases with associated role sequences; (7) automatically matching the type sequence of each phrase to a set of semantic rules to yield a set of ontology fragments consisting of hypernym, meronym, and synonym relationships. Steps

1–3 are part of a crowdsourced content analysis task based on Breaux and Schaub [17]. Our contribution in this paper includes steps 5–7 which utilizes an information type lexicon to construct an ontology.

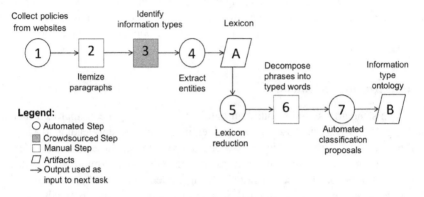

Fig. 1. Overview of ontology construction method

5.1 Acquiring the Mobile Privacy Policy Lexicon

The mobile privacy policy lexicon (artifact A in Fig. 1) was constructed using a combination of crowdsourcing, content analysis and natural language processing (NLP). In step 1 (see Fig. 1), we selected the top 20 mobile apps across each of 69 sub-categories in Google Play[3]. From this set, we selected apps with privacy policies, removing duplicate policies when different apps shared the same policy. Next, we selected only policies that match the following criteria: format (plain text), language (English), and explicit statements for privacy policy; yielding 501 policies, from which we randomly selected 50 policies. In step 2, the 50 policies were segmented into ~120 word paragraphs using the method described by Breaux and Schaub [17]; yielding 5,932 crowd worker annotator tasks with an average 98 words per task for input to step 3.

In step 3, the annotators select phrases corresponding to one of two category codes in a segmented paragraph as described below for each annotator task, called a Human Intelligence Task (HIT). An example HIT is shown in Fig. 2.

- *Platform Information:* any information that the app or another party accesses through the mobile platform which is not unique to the app.
- *Other Information:* any other information the app or another party collects, uses, shares or retains.

These two category codes were chosen, because our initial focus is on information types that are automatically collected by mobile apps and mobile platforms, such as "IP address," and "location information." The other information code is used to ensure that annotators remain vigilant by classifying and annotating all information types.

---

3 https://play.google.com.

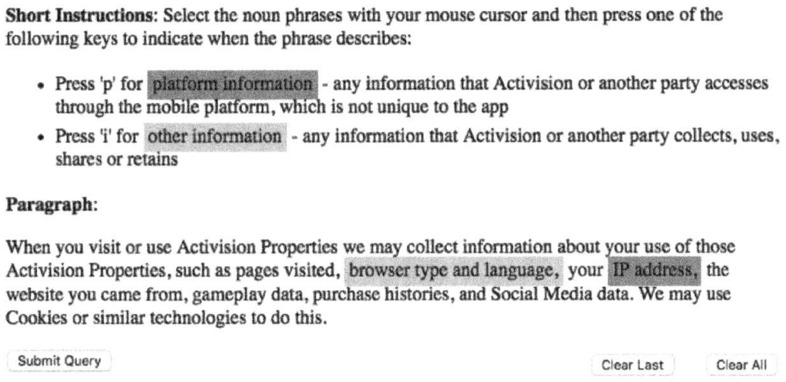

Short Instructions: Select the noun phrases with your mouse cursor and then press one of the following keys to indicate when the phrase describes:

- Press 'p' for platform information - any information that Activision or another party accesses through the mobile platform, which is not unique to the app
- Press 'i' for other information - any information that Activision or another party collects, uses, shares or retains

Paragraph:

When you visit or use Activision Properties we may collect information about your use of those Activision Properties, such as pages visited, browser type and language, your IP address, the website you came from, gameplay data, purchase histories, and Social Media data. We may use Cookies or similar technologies to do this.

Submit Query   Clear Last   Clear All

Fig. 2. Example HIT shown to a crowd worker

In step 4, we selected only platform information types when two or more annotators agreed on the annotation to construct the lexicon. This number follows the empirical analysis of Breaux and Schaub [17], which shows high precision and recall for two or more annotators on the same HIT. Next, we applied an entity extractor [6] to the selected annotations to itemize the platform information types into unique entities included in the privacy policy lexicon.

Six privacy experts, including the authors, performed the annotations. The cumulative time to annotate all HITs was 59.8 h across all six annotators, yielding a total 720 annotations in which two or more annotators agreed on the annotation. The entity extractor reduced these annotations down to 351 unique information type names, which comprise the initial lexicon.

In step 5, the initial lexicon was reduced as follows:

a. Plural nouns were changed to singular nouns, e.g., "peripherals" is reduced to "peripheral."
b. Possessives were removed, e.g., "device's information" is reduced to "device information."
c. Suffixes "-related," "-based," and "-specific" are removed, e.g., "device-related information" is reduced to "device information."

This reduced the initial lexicon by 16 types to yield a final lexicon with 335 types.

5.2 Semantic Role Typing of Lexicon Phrases

Figure 3 shows an example phrase, "mobile device IP address" that is decomposed into the atomic phrases: "mobile," "device," "IP," "address," based on a 1-level, shallow typology. The typology links atomic words from a phrase to one of six roles: (M) modifiers, which describe the quality of a thing, such as "mobile" and "personal;" (T) things, which is a concept that has logical boundaries and which can be composed of other things; (E) events, which describe action performances, such as "usage," "viewing," and "clicks;" (G) agents, which describe actors who perform actions or possess things; (P) property, which describes the functional feature of an agent, place or thing, such as "date," "name," "height;" and (α) which is an abstract type that indicates "information," "data," "details," and any other synonym of "information." In an information type ontology, the concept that corresponds to the α type is the most general, inclusive concept.

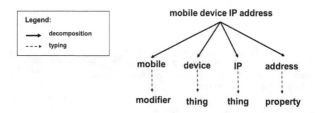

Fig. 3. Example lexicon phrase, grouped and typed

In step 6, the analyst reviews each information type phrase in the lexicon and assigns role types to each word. The phrase typing is expressed as a continuous series of letters that correspond to the role typology. Unlike the quadratic number of paired comparisons required to identify relationships among lexicon phrases, this typing step is linear in the size of the lexicon. Furthermore, word role types can be reused across phrases that reuse words to further reduce the time needed to perform this step. Next, we introduce the semantic rules that are applied to the typed phrases in the lexicon.

5.3   Automated Lexeme Variant Inference

We now describe step 7, which takes as input the typed, atomic phrases produced in step 6 to apply a set of semantic rules to infer variants and their ontological relationships, which we call *variant relationships*. Rules consist of a type pattern and an inferred ontological relationship. The type pattern is expressed using the typology codes described in Sect. 5.2. The rules below were discovered by the first and second author who classified the 335 pre-processed lexicon phrases using the typology as a second-cycle coding, which is a qualitative research method [23]. Subscripts indicate the order of same-typed phrases in asymmetric ontological relations:

Hypernymy Rules

H1. M_α implies that $M\_\alpha \sqsubseteq \alpha$, e.g., "unique information" is a kind of "information."

H2. $M_1\_M_2\_\alpha$ implies that $M_1\_M_2\_\alpha \sqsubseteq (M_1\_\alpha \sqcup M_2\_\alpha)$, e.g., "anonymous demographic information" is a kind of "anonymous information" and "demographic information."

H3. $M\_T_1\_T_2$ implies $M\_T_1\_T_2 \sqsubseteq (M\_\alpha \sqcup T_1\_T_2)$ and $T_1\_T_2 \sqsubseteq partOf\ M\_T_1$, e.g., "mobile device hardware" is a kind of "mobile information," "device hardware," and "device hardware" is a part of "mobile device."

H4. M_T_α implies $M\_T\_\alpha \sqsubseteq (M\_\alpha \sqcup T\_\alpha)$, e.g., "mobile device information" is a kind of "mobile information" and "device information."

H5. M_T_P implies $M\_T\_P \sqsubseteq M\_\alpha$ and $M\_T\_P \sqsubseteq partOf\ M\_T$ and $T\_P \sqsubseteq partOf\ M\_T$, e.g., "mobile device name" is a kind of "mobile information" and a part of "mobile device" and "device name" is a part of "mobile device."

H6. M_G_α implies that $M\_G\_\alpha \sqsubseteq (M\_\alpha \sqcup G\_\alpha)$, e.g. "aggregated user data" is a kind of "aggregated data" and "user data."

H7. T_α implies $T\_\alpha \sqsubseteq \alpha$, e.g., "device information" is a kind of "information."

H8. $T_1\_T_2\_\alpha$ implies $T_1\_T_2\_\alpha \sqsubseteq (T_1\_\alpha \sqcup T_2\_\alpha)$, e.g., "device log information" is a kind of "device information" and "log information."

H9. G_α implies that $G\_\alpha \sqsubseteq \alpha$, e.g. "user information" is a kind of "information."

H10. G_T implies that $G\_T \sqsubseteq (G\_\alpha \sqcup T)$, e.g., "user content" is a kind of "user information" and "content."

H11. G_P implies that $G\_P \sqsubseteq (G\_\alpha \sqcup P)$ and $G\_P \sqsubseteq partOf\ G$, e.g., "user name" is a kind of "user information" and "user name" is a part of "user."

H12. E_α implies that $E\_\alpha \sqsubseteq \alpha$, e.g. "usage data" is a kind of "data."

H13. T_E implies that $T\_E \sqsubseteq (T \sqcup E \sqcup E\_lemma)$, e.g., "page viewed" is a kind of "page," "viewed," and "view."

Meronymy Rules

M1. $T_1\_T_2$ implies $T_1\_T_2 \sqsubseteq partOf\ T_1$ and $T_1\_T_2 \sqsubseteq T_2$, e.g., "device hardware" is a part of "device" and is a kind of "hardware."

M2. $T_1\_M\_T_2$ implies $T_1\_M\_T_2 \sqsubseteq partOf\ T_1$ and $M\_T_2\ partOf\ T_1$, e.g., "device unique id" is a part of "device," and "unique id" is a part of "device."

M3. T_P implies $T\_P \sqsubseteq partOf\ T$ and $T\_P \sqsubseteq P$, e.g., "device name" is a part of "device" and a kind of "name."

M4. E_T implies that $E\_T \sqsubseteq partOf\ E$ and $E\_T \sqsubseteq T$, e.g., "advertising identifier" is part of "advertising" and a kind of "identifier."

M5. E_P implies $E\_P \sqsubseteq partOf\ E$ and $E\_P \sqsubseteq P$, e.g., "click count" is part of "click" and a kind of "count."

M6. T_E_α implies that $T\_E\_\alpha \sqsubseteq partOf\ T$ and $T\_E\_\alpha \sqsubseteq (T\_\alpha \sqcup E\_\alpha)$, e.g., "language modeling data" is a part of "language" and a kind of "language data" and "modeling data."

M7. $M_1\_T_1\_M_2\_T_2$ implies $M_1\_T_1\_M_2\_T_2 \sqsubseteq partOf\ M_1\_T_1$ and $M_1\_T_1\_M_2\_T_2 \sqsubseteq M_2\_T_2$, e.g., "mobile device unique identifier" is a part of "mobile device" and a kind of "unique identifier."

M8. $T_1\_E\_T_2$ implies that $T_1\_E\_T_2 \sqsubseteq partOf\ T_1\_E$ and $T_1\_E\_T_2 \sqsubseteq (E\_T_2 \sqcup T_1\_information \sqcup T_2\_information)$, e.g., "Internet browsing behavior" is a part of "Internet browsing" and a kind of "browsing behavior" and "Internet information" and "behavior information."

M9. T_E_P implies that $T\_E\_P \sqsubseteq partOf\ T\_E$ and $T\_E\_P \sqsubseteq (E\_P \sqcup T\_\alpha \sqcup P)$, e.g., "website activity date" is a part of "website activity" and a kind of "activity date," "website information," and "date."

Synonymy Rules

S1. T implies $T \equiv T\_\alpha$, e.g., "device" is a synonym of "device information."

S2. P implies $P \equiv P\_\alpha$, e.g., "name" is a synonym of "name information."

S3. E implies $\equiv (E\_\alpha \sqcup E\_lemma)$, e.g., "views" is a synonym of "views information" and "view."

S4. G implies $G \equiv G\_\alpha$, e.g., "user" is a synonym of "user information."

The automated step 7 applies the rules to phrases and yields variant relationships for evaluation in two steps: (a) the semantic rules are matched to the typed phrases to infer new candidate phrases and relations; and (b) for each inferred phrase, we repeat step (a) with the inferred phrase. The technique terminates when no rules match a given input phrase. An inferred phrase can be either *explicit concept name,* which refers to an inferred phrase that exists in the lexicon, or *tacit concept name* referring to an inferred phrase that does not exist in the lexicon.

For example, in Fig. 3, we perform step (a) by applying the rule H5 to infer that "mobile device IP address" is a kind of "mobile information" and a part of "mobile device IP" and "device IP address" is a part of "mobile device IP." Rule H5 has the implication that $M\_T\_P \sqsubseteq M\_\alpha$, which yields an information class for M_α that includes information about things distinguished by a modifier M. In practice, these classes describe all things personal, financial, and health-related and, in this example, all things mobile. Continuing with the example, the phrases "device IP address" and "mobile device IP" are not in the lexicon, i.e., they are potentially implied or *tacit concept names*. Thus, we re-apply the rules to "device IP address" and "mobile device IP." Rule M3 matches the "device IP address" typing to infer that "device IP address" is part of "device IP" and is a kind of "address." Since "device IP" is not in the lexicon, we re-apply the rules to this phrase. Rule M1 matches the type sequence of this phrase to yield "device IP" is a part of "device" and "device IP" is a kind of "IP." Both "device" and "IP" are *explicit concept names*. Therefore, we accept both inferences for further evaluation. We continue performing step (a) on "mobile device IP" by applying rule H3 that infers additional concept names and relations. The axioms from re-applying the rules to the explicit and tacit concepts names yield ontology fragments. We evaluate these axioms using the individual preference relationships described in the next section.

6   Experiment Setup

In psychology, preferences reflect an individual's attitude toward one or more objects, including a comparison among objects [24]. We designed a survey to evaluate and improve the ontological relationship prospects produced by step 7. We used 50 privacy policies and 335 pre-processed unique information types in a training set to improve the semantic rules. Because the prospects produced by the semantic rules all share at least one common word, we asked 30 human subjects to compare each 2,365 phrase-pair from the lexicon that shares at least one word. The survey asks subjects to classify each pair by choosing a relationship from among one of the following six options:

S: Phrase A is subsumed by phrase B in pair (A, B)

S: Phrase B is subsumed by phrase A in pair (A, B)
P: Phrase A is part of Phrase B in pair (A, B)
W: Phrase B is part of Phrase A in pair (A, B)
E: Phrase A is equivalent to phrase B in pair (A, B)
U: Phrase A is unrelated to phrase B in pair (A, B)

Figure 4 presents a survey excerpt: the participant checks one option to indicate the relationship, and they can check a box to swap the word order, e.g., in the first pair, the subject can check the box to indicate that "web browser type" is a part of "browser." We recruited 30 participants to compare each pair using Amazon Mechanical Turk, in which three pairs were shown in one Human Intelligence Task (HIT). Qualified participants completed over 5,000 HITs, had an approval rate of at least 97%, and were located in the United States. The average time for participants to compare a pair is 11.72 s.

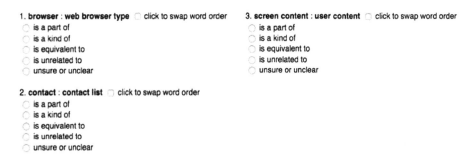

Fig. 4. Example survey questions to collect relation preferences

The participant results are analyzed to construct a ground truth (GT) in Description Logic. In the results, participants can classify the same phrase pair using different ontological relations. There are several reasons that explain multiple ontological relations for each pair: participants may misunderstand the phrases, or they may have different experiences that allow them to perceive different interpretations (e.g., "mac" can refer to both a MAC address for Ethernet-based routing, and a kind of computer sold by Apple, a manufacturer). To avoid excluding valid interpretations, we built a multi-viewpoint GT that accepts multiple, competing interpretations. For the entire survey results, we define *valid interpretations* for a phrase pair to be those interpretations where the observed number of responses per category exceeds the expected number of responses in a Chi-square test, where $p < 0.05$, which means there is at least a 95% chance that the elicited response counts are different than the expected counts. The expected response counts for an ontological relationship are based on how frequently participants chose that relationship across all comparisons. We constructed a multi-viewpoint GT as follows: for each surveyed pair, we add an axiom to GT for the relation category, if the number of participant responses is greater than or equal to the expected Chi-square frequency; except, if the number of unrelated responses exceeds the expected Chi-square frequency, then we do not add any axioms. We published the ground truth dataset[4] that

---
[4] http://gaius.isri.cmu.edu/dataset/plat17/preferences.csv.

includes phrase pairs, the ontological relation frequencies assigned by participants to each pair, and the Chi-square expected values for each relation per pair.

We measure the number of true positives (TPs), true negatives (TNs), false positives (FPs), and false negatives (FNs) by comparing the variant relationships with the ground truth ontology to compute precision = TP/(TP + FP) and recall = TP/(TP + FN). A variant relation is a TP, if it is logically entailed by GT, otherwise, that relationship is a FP. An unrelated phrase pair in the preferences results is considered as TN, if we cannot match any inferred variant relationship with it. For all phrase pairs with valid interpretations (hypernymy, meronymy, synonymy) that do not match an inferred variant relationship, we count these as FN. We use logical entailment to identify true positives, because subsumption is transitive and whether a concept is a hypernym to another concept may rely on the transitive closure of that concept's class relationships. Next, we present results from improving the semantic rules using the training dataset and describe our approach for building the test set to evaluate the final rule set.

7 Evaluation and Results

This section presents the results for the training and testing of the approach. The training has been done in two incremental phases: (1) we first evaluated a set of 17 initial rules applied to the 335 pre-processed unique information types; (2) based on the results of phase 1 and analysis of false negatives, we extended the initial rules to 26 rules and evaluated the application of the extended rule set using the 335 pre-processed unique information types. In the testing stage, we utilized a separate 109 pre-processed unique information types to evaluate the extended rule set.

7.1 Preference Relations with Initial Rule Set

We began with a set of 17 rules that summarized our intuition on 335 pre-processed unique information types for variant relationship inference. After typing and decomposition, the technique yields 126 *explicit concept names* from the original lexicon, 182 potential *tacit concept names*, and 1,355 total axioms. Comparing the inferred relations with the individuals' preferences in the training ground truth (GT) results in 0.984 precision and 0.221 recall. Overall, the method correctly identifies 256/1,134 of related phrase pairs in the training GT. The total number of true positives (TPs), true negatives (TNs), false positives (FPs), and false negatives (FNs) are 256, 1092, 4, and 901, respectively. To improve the results, we analyzed the FNs and extended the initial 17 rules to 26 total rules that are discussed in Sect. 5.3. Next, we report the results from applying the extended rules to the original 335 pre-processed unique information types.

7.2 Preference Relations with Extended Rule Set

The extended rule set consists of the initial and nine additional rules to improve the semi-automated technique. We also extended rules H3 and H5 with a new meronymy-inferred relationship as defined in Sect. 5.3. Using the extended rule set, the technique yields 186 *explicit concept names*, 286 potential *tacit concept names*, and 2,698 total axioms. The ontology fragments computed by applying the extended rule set can be found online in the OWL format.[5] Table 1 shows results for the semi-automated method with the initial and extended rule sets. This table also includes the number of hypernymy, meronymy, and synonymy relations that are inferred using the two rule sets. The extended rule set correctly identifies 782 preference relations out of 1,134 related pairs in the training GT. Also, the recall is improved to 0.569 with the extended rule set.

Table 1. Evaluations of relations using initial and extended rule set on training GT

	Initial rules	Extended rules
Explicit/tacit concept names	126/182	194/289
Number of inferred hypernyms	580	1,122
Number of inferred meronyms	192	535
Number of inferred synonyms	583	1041
Precision	0.984	0.996
Recall	0.221	0.569

The total number of TPs, TN, FPs, and FNs are 782, 878, 3, and 590, respectively. We observed that 477/590 of false negatives (FNs) depend on semantics beyond the scope of the 6-role typology. For example, the training GT shows the participants agreed that "mobile phone" is a kind of "mobile device," possibly because they understood that "phone" is a kind of "device." We observed that 22/477 of semantically related FNs exclusively concern synonyms that require additional domain knowledge, e.g., "postal code" is equivalent to "zip code," or in the case of acronyms, "Internet protocol address" is equivalent to "IP address." Moreover, 10/477 of semantically related FNs exclusively concern meronymy, e.g., "game activity time" is a part of "game system." Only 1/477 of semantically related FNs is exclusively mentioned for hypernymy: "forwarding number" is a kind of "valid mobile number." Finally, 444/477 of semantically related FNs can have multiple valid interpretations (meronymy, hypernymy, and synonymy) in the training GT.

In addition, we discovered that 53/590 of FNs were due to individual preference-errors that were inconsistent with the automated method, e.g., individual preferences identified "mobile device identifier" equivalent to "mobile device unique identifier," which ignores the fact that an identifier is not necessarily unique. Finally, we identified 60/590 relations that can be identified by introducing new semantic rules.

The training GT also contains a special relationship identified by individuals between 40 pairs that we call *part-of-hypernymy*. For example, individuals identified "device id" as a part of "mobile device," because they may have assumed that mobile device (as a hyponym of device) has an id. Therefore, we extended rules H3 and H5 to infer *part-of-hypernymy* in the extended rule set.

---

[5] http://gaius.isri.cmu.edu/dataset/plat17/variants.owl.

7.3   Method Evaluation

To evaluate our extended rule set, we randomly selected six additional privacy policies from the pool of 501 policies discussed in Sect. 5.1. We used the same approach and annotators from Sect. 5.1 to extract the unique information types and construct the test lexicon. The resulting 110 information types were reduced to 109 information types which were then typed and analyzed by the extended rule set, resulting in 76 *explicit concept names*, 139 potential *tacit concept names*, and 831 total axioms. We acquired the preference relations[6] for the test lexicon by surveying 213 phrase pairs resulting in 121 related phrase pairs included in the testing ground truth (GT) using the method discussed in Sect. 6. In further analysis, the relations in the testing GT were compared with the relations provided by the extended rule set. Overall, the extended rule set correctly identifies 79 preference relations out of 121 related pairs in the training GT. Table 2 presents the results including the precision and recall for this analysis. The ontology fragments computed using the extended rule set are online in OWL.[7]

Table 2. Evaluations of relations using extended rule set on testing GT

	Extended rules
Explicit/tacit concept names	194/289
Number of inferred hypernyms	385
Number of inferred meronyms	80
Number of inferred synonyms	366
Precision	1.000
Recall	0.593

In summary, the results show total number of 79 TPs, 80 TNs, zero FPs, and 54 FNs. We observed that 44/54 of FNs in the test set depend on semantics beyond the scope of the role typology and syntactic analysis of information types. We published a list of these concept pairs, including the human preferences.[8] Some examples include: "device open udid" as a kind of "device identifier," "in-app page view" as a kind of "web page visited," and "page viewed" as equivalent to "page visited." We also observed 7/54 of FNs that require introducing six new rules. Finally, by comparing the total number of TPs and TNs with 213 phrase pairs, we can conclude that the semi-automated semantic analysis method can infer $\left(\dfrac{79 + 80}{213} \times 100 \right) = 74\%$ of paired comparisons.

8   Discussion

We now discuss and interpret our results and threats to validity.

---

[6] http://gaius.isri.cmu.edu/dataset/plat17/study-utsa-prefs-test-set.csv.
[7] http://gaius.isri.cmu.edu/dataset/plat17/variants-test-set.owl.
[8] http://gaius.isri.cmu.edu/dataset/plat17/supplements-test-set.csv.

8.1   Interpretation of Extended Rule Set Results

Comparing the ontology fragments to preferences, we observe that preferences imply new axioms that explain a portion of the FNs in training and testing. These preferences are influenced by individual interpretations of relations between two phrases. Analyzing these FNs, we identified four cases where individuals report incorrect interpretations:

(1) The meaning of modifiers in a phrase are ignored and an equivalent relationship is identified for a pair of phrases, e.g., "unique id" and "id."
(2) Different modifiers are interpreted as equivalent, e.g., "approximate location information" and "general location information."
(3) The superordinate and subordinate phrase's relationship is diminished and an equivalent relation is assumed, e.g., "hardware" and "device", "iPhone" and "device."
(4) Information as a whole that contains information is confused with information as a sub-ordinate concept in a super-ordinate category, e.g., "mobile application version" is both a part of, and a kind of, "mobile device information."

One explanation for the inconsistencies is that individuals conflate interpretations when comparing two phrases as a function of convenience. Without prompting individuals to search their memory for distinctions among category members (e.g., iPhone is different from Android, and both are kinds of device), they are inclined to ignore these distinctions when making sense of the comparison. In requirements engineering, this behavior corresponds to relaxing the interpretation of constraints or seeking a narrower interpretation than what the natural language statement implies. When relaxing constraints, stakeholders may overlook requirements: e.g., if "actual location" and "physical location" are perceived as equivalent, then stakeholders may overlook requirements that serve to more closely approximate the "actual" from noisy location data, or requirements to acquire location from environmental cues to more closely approximate a "physical" location. Furthermore, this behavior could yield incomplete requirements, if analysts overlook other, unstated category members.

8.2   Threats to Validity

In this section, we discuss the internal and external validity for our approach.

Internal Validity. Internal validity is the extent to which observed causal relations actually exist within the data, and whether the investigator's inferences about the data are valid [25]. In this method, the inferred semantic relations are highly dependent on the role typing system and any inconsistencies in the types affect the final results. For this reason, two analysts assigned roles to the phrases in the training lexicon. We used Fliess' Kappa to measure the degree of agreement for this task [26]. Two analysts reached Kappa of 0.72, which shows a high, above-chance agreement. However, there is still a need for automating the role typing system to reduce potential inconsistencies.

External Validity. External validity is the extent to which our approach generalizes to the population outside the sample used in the study [25]. Based on our study, 7/54 of false negatives in test set evaluation require six new semantic rules. Moreover, we cannot claim that the extended rule set will cover all the information types extracted from privacy policies, since we only analyzed specific information types called platform information. To assure that the rules have saturated for information type analysis, further studies on different information types are required.

9   Conclusion and Future Work

Privacy policies contain legal requirements with which company information systems need to comply. In addition, they serve to communicate those requirements to other stakeholders, such as consumers and regulators. Because stakeholders use different words to describe the same domain concept, how these policies use abstraction and variability in concept representation can affect ambiguity and reduce the shared under-standing among policy authors, app developers, regulators and consumers. To address this problem, we present results of a semi-automated, semantic analysis method to construct privacy policy ontologies that formalize different interpretations of related concepts.

The method was evaluated on 213 pairs of phrases that share at least one word from a set of 109 unique phrases in the lexicon acquired from six mobile app privacy policies. The individual preference data set contains 80/213 pairs that are identified as unrelated (37%) and 121/213 relations identified as related through hypernymy, meronymy, and synonymy in the testing GT. The technique yields 79/121 of axioms in testing GT with an average precision $= 1.00$ and recall $= 0.59$.

In future work, we envision a number of extensions. To increase coverage, we propose to formalize the rules as a context free grammar with semantic attachments using the rule-to-rule hypothesis [27]. We also envision expanding the knowledge base to include relations that cannot be identified using syntactic analysis, such as hypernymy between "phone" and "device." To improve typing, we considered identifying role types associated with part-of-speech (POS) tagging and English suffixes. However, prelimi-nary results on 335 pre-processed phrases from the training lexicon shows only 22% of role type sequences can be identified using POS and English suffixes. Therefore, instead of relying on POS and suffix features, we envision using deep learning methods [28] to learn the features for identifying the semantic relations between phrases. Finally, we envision incorporating these results in requirements analysis tools to help detect and remediate variants that can increase ambiguity and misunderstanding.

Acknowledgement. We thank Jaspreet Bhatia, Rocky Slavin, and Xiaoyin Wang for their annotations of the 50 mobile app policies, and the CMU RE Lab for their helpful feedback. A short version of this paper, which compared a manually-constructed ontology to the initial rule set, was presented at the AAAI Fall Symposium on Privacy and Language Technologies and appears online as a non-archival technical report. This research was supported by NSF CAREER #1453139, NSA #141333, NSF #1330596, and NSF #0964710.

References

1. Smith, A.: US smartphone use in 2015. Pew Research Center, 1 (2015)
2. Harris, K.D.: Privacy on the go: recommendations for the mobile ecosystem (2013)
3. Anton, A.I., Earp, J.B.: A requirements taxonomy for reducing web site privacy vulnerabilities. Requir. Eng. **9**(3), 169–185 (2004)
4. Uschold, M., Gruninger, M.: Ontologies: principles, methods and applications. Knowl. Eng. Rev. **11**(02), 93–136 (1996)
5. Breaux, T.D., Baumer, D.L.: Legally "reasonable" security requirements: a 10-year FTC retrospective. Comput. Secur. **30**(4), 178–193 (2011)
6. Bhatia, J., Breaux, T.D.: Towards an information type lexicon for privacy policies. In: 2015 IEEE Eighth International Workshop on Requirements Engineering and Law (RELAW), pp. 19–24. IEEE (2015)
7. Hosseini, M.B., Wadkar, S., Breaux, T.D., Niu, J.: Lexical similarity of information type hypernyms, meronyms and synonyms in privacy policies. In: 2016 AAAI Fall Symposium Series (2016)
8. Martin, J.H., Jurafsky, D.: Speech and language processing. Int. Ed. **710**, 117–119 (2000)
9. Potts, C., Newstetter, W.C.: Naturalistic inquiry and requirements engineering: reconciling their theoretical foundations. In: 1997 Proceedings of the Third IEEE International Symposium on Requirements Engineering, pp. 118–127. IEEE (1997)
10. Hecker, M., Dillon, T.S., Chang, E.: Privacy ontology support for e-commerce. IEEE Internet Comput. **12**(2), 54–61 (2008)
11. Bradshaw, J., Uszok, A., Jeffers, R., Suri, N., Hayes, P., Burstein, M., Acquisti, A., Benyo, B., Breedy, M., Carvalho, M., Diller, D.: Representation and reasoning for DAML-based policy and domain services in KAoS and Nomads. In: Proceedings of the Second International Joint Conference on Autonomous Agents and Multiagent Systems, pp. 835–842. ACM (2003)
12. Kagal, L., et al.: Authorization and privacy for semantic web services. IEEE Intell. Syst. **19**(4), 50–56 (2004)
13. Syed, Z., Padia, A., Finin, T., Mathews, M.L., Joshi, A.: UCO: a unified cybersecurity ontology. In: AAAI Workshop: Artificial Intelligence for Cyber Security (2016)
14. Breaux, T.D., Smullen, D., Hibshi, H.: Detecting repurposing and over-collection in multi-party privacy requirements specifications. In: 2015 IEEE 23rd International Requirements Engineering Conference (RE), pp. 166–175. IEEE (2015)
15. Slavin, R., Wang, X., Hosseini, M.B., Hester, J., Krishnan, R., Bhatia, J., Breaux, T.D., Niu, J.: Toward a framework for detecting privacy policy violations in android application code. In: Proceedings of the 38th International Conference on Software Engineering, pp. 25–36. ACM (2016)
16. Huang, C.R. (ed.): Ontology and the Lexicon: A Natural Language Processing Perspective. Cambridge University Press, Cambridge (2010)
17. Breaux, T.D., Schaub, F.: Scaling requirements extraction to the crowd: experiments with privacy policies. In: 2014 IEEE 22nd International Requirements Engineering Conference (RE), pp. 163–172. IEEE (2014)
18. Wilson, S., Schaub, F., Dara, A.A., Liu, F., Cherivirala, S., Leon, P.G., Andersen, M.S., Zimmeck, S., Sathyendra, K.M., Russell, N.C., Norton, T.B.: The creation and analysis of a website privacy policy corpus. In: ACL, vol. 1 (2016)
19. Miller, G.A.: WordNet: a lexical database for English. Commun. ACM **38**(11), 39–41 (1995)
20. Snow, R., Jurafsky, D., Ng, A.Y.: Learning syntactic patterns for automatic hypernym discovery. In: Advances in Neural Information Processing Systems, vol. 17 (2004)

21. Bhatia, J., Evans, M.C., Wadkar, S., Breaux, T.D.: Automated extraction of regulated information types using hyponymy relations. In: IEEE International Requirements Engineering Conference Workshops (REW), pp. 19–25. IEEE (2016)
22. Hearst, M.A.: Automatic acquisition of hyponyms from large text corpora. In: Proceedings of the 14th Conference on Computational Linguistics, vol. 2, pp. 539–545. Association for Computational Linguistics (1992)
23. Saldaña, J.: The Coding Manual for Qualitative Researchers. Sage, London (2015)
24. Lichtenstein, S., Slovic, P. (eds.): The Construction of Preference. Cambridge University Press, Cambridge (2006)
25. Yin, R.K.: Case Study Research: Design and Methods. Sage publications, Thousand oaks (2009)
26. Fleiss, J.L.: Measuring nominal scale agreement among many raters. Psychol. Bull. **76**(5), 378 (1971)
27. Bach, E.: An extension of classical transformational grammar (1976)
28. Zeng, D., Liu, K., Lai, S., Zhou, G., Zhao, J.: Relation classification via convolutional deep neural network. In: COLING, pp. 2335–2344 (2014)

Using Tools to Assist Identification of Non-requirements in Requirements Specifications – A Controlled Experiment

Jonas Paul Winkler$^{(\boxtimes)}$ and Andreas Vogelsang

Technische Universität Berlin, Berlin, Germany
{jonas.winkler,andreas.vogelsang}@tu-berlin.de

Abstract. [**Context and motivation**] In many companies, textual fragments in specification documents are categorized into requirements and non-requirements. This categorization is important for determining liability, deriving test cases, and many more decisions. In practice, this categorization is usually performed manually, which makes it labor-intensive and error-prone. [**Question/problem**] We have developed a tool to assist users in this task by providing warnings based on classification using neural networks. However, we currently do not know whether using the tool actually helps increasing the classification quality compared to not using the tool. [**Principal idea/results**] Therefore, we performed a controlled experiment with two groups of students. One group used the tool for a given task, whereas the other did not. By comparing the performance of both groups, we can assess in which scenarios the application of our tool is beneficial. [**Contribution**] The results show that the application of an automated classification approach may provide benefits, given that the accuracy is high enough.

Keywords: Requirements engineering · Machine learning
Convolutional neural networks · Natural language processing

1 Introduction

Requirements specifications are used in many requirements engineering (RE) processes to document results. The purpose of these documents is to define the properties that a system must meet to be accepted. Moreover, in contexts, where one company or department acts as a customer and another company acts as a supplier, the requirements specification also defines liability between the partners (i.e., what must be achieved to fulfill the contract). For this reason, requirements specifications should undergo a rigorous quality assessment process especially in industries where systems are created by a collaboration of many suppliers (e.g., automotive).

Besides actual and legally binding requirements, requirements specifications usually contain auxiliary content (e.g., explanations, summaries, examples,

© Springer International Publishing AG, part of Springer Nature 2018
E. Kamsties et al. (Eds.): REFSQ 2018, LNCS 10753, pp. 57–71, 2018.
https://doi.org/10.1007/978-3-319-77243-1_4

and references to other documents). These content elements are not requirements, which must be fulfilled by the supplier but they may facilitate the process of understanding requirements and their context. To distinguish this auxiliary information from legally binding requirements, one of our industry partners annotates all content elements in their requirements specifications with specific labels for *requirements* and *information*. However, this manual labeling task is time-consuming and error-prone. By analyzing a set of requirements specifications from our partner, we observed that labels (i.e., requirement and information) are often not added when the content is created. This impedes the usage of these documents for following activities, such as creating a test specification based on a requirements specification. Adding the labels at a later stage is expensive since every content element has to be read and understood again.

To assist requirements engineers in performing this task, we have created a tool that automatically classifies the content elements of requirement specifications and issues warnings if the actual label deviates from the automatically predicted one. This tool is used by requirements authors and reviewers for creating new requirements or inspecting already existing requirements.

The tool uses neural networks to classify content elements as either information or requirement. This neural network is trained on a large corpus of reviewed requirements taken from requirements specifications of our industry partner. As with all neural networks, performance is not perfect and thus the tool will sometimes issue warnings on correctly labeled items and will sometimes ignore actual defects. In earlier evaluations, the classifier achieved an accuracy of 81% [1]. This might impede the usefulness of our tool. Thus, we currently do not know whether using the tool actually helps increasing the classification quality compared to not using the tool.

Therefore, we have conducted a controlled experiment with computer science students trained on requirements engineering to evaluate the usefulness of our tool for the given task. The students were split into two equally sized groups. Both groups performed a given task independently. One group used our tool, whereas the other did not. In this paper, we present the goals, setup, and results of this experiment.

The results indicate that given high accuracy of the provided warnings, users of our tool are able to perform slightly better than the users performing manual review. They managed to find more defects, introduce less new defects, and did so in shorter time. However, when many false warnings are issued, the situation may be reversed. Thus, the actual benefit is largely dependent on the performance of the underlying classifier. False negatives (i.e., defects with no warnings) are an issue as well, since users tend to focus less on elements with no warnings.

2   Background

At our industry partner, documentation and review of requirements are independent processes. After creation, requirements documents are reviewed during quality audits. Each requirement is assessed as to whether it is necessary, conflict free, well written, etc. Some assessments are automatically checked by a requirements specification analysis tool using predefined rule sets (e.g., is the requirement phrased using certain modal verbs, weak work analysis, are the required attributes set). However, most of the assessments require context knowledge of the requirements engineer and thus cannot be performed by such simple analysis methods. The task of separating information and requirements is one example of such an assessment.

In our previous works [1,2], we have presented a method to perform this task automatically. At its core, our approach uses a convolutional neural network as presented in [3]. The network is trained on requirement content elements and information content elements taken from requirements specifications of our industry partner. The approach has been integrated in the aforementioned requirements specification analysis tool.

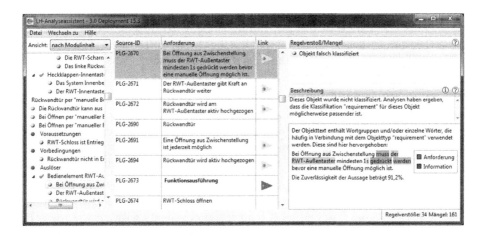

Fig. 1. Screenshot of the tool (Color figure online)

Figure 1 shows a screenshot of the tool. It closely resembles the requirements engineering tool used at our industry partner (IBM Rational DOORS), featuring a tree view on the left and a tabular view of the requirements in its center. The tool issues warnings (yellow markers) and errors (red markers) on content elements where the predicted classification differs from the actual one. On the right hand side, an explanation of the error is provided: Words and groups of words leading to the classification decision are identified and highlighted using a back tracing technology [4]. Additionally, content elements for which no class could be reliably detected are also marked. These might need to be rephrased.

By explicitly pointing out content elements with questionable phrasing and/or classification, we expect that requirements engineers will identify more issues within their documents and may do so in shorter time. This will shorten the time spent during quality audits and hopefully reveal more issues compared to fully manual reviews. However, using such a tool also bears the risk of hiding actual errors. If requirements engineers start to trust the tool and rely on it, it is less likely that they identify defects not found by our tool.

3 Research Methodology

In order to assess the impact of our tool on the task of reviewing requirements/information classification, we conducted a controlled experiment with students. We followed the guidelines provided in Ko et al. [5] and Jedlitschka et al. [6].

3.1 Research Questions

The overall goal of our experiment is to examine whether and how the use of a tool improves the process of finding *defects* in requirements documents compared to completely manual review. In this paper, a defect is a misclassified content element (i.e., requirement marked as information or information marked as requirement). As there are various ways of improving this process, we aim to analyze different aspects. Therefore, we followed five research questions.

RQ1: Does the usage of our tool enable users to detect more defects? This is the primary goal of our tool. By focusing the attention of users on possibly misclassified content elements, we assume they will be able to detect more defects within their documents.

RQ2: Does the usage of our tool reduce the number of defects introduced by users? Requirements engineers tend to make errors during quality audits (e.g., dismissing a requirement as an information). By decreasing the focus on possibly correctly classified content elements, we assume they will less likely edit those elements and introduce less defects into their documents.

RQ3: Are users of our tool prone to ignoring actual defects because no warning was issued? As our tool issues warnings to focus the attention of users, it is possible that they will tend to skip elements with no warnings. If these content elements contain defects, users are likely to miss them. Thus, we need to analyze whether users miss more unwarned defects when using our tool.

RQ4: Are users of our tool faster in processing the documents? One of our primary goals is to allow requirements engineers to work more efficiently. Therefore, we analyze whether users of our tool are able to work faster.

RQ5: Does our tool motivate users to rephrase requirements and information content elements? Our tool also shows explanations for each issued warning, i.e., which words caused the internal neural network to decide on either requirement or information. If an actual requirement was classified as information by our tool due to bad phrasing, these explanations could lead users into rethinking the phrasing and reformulating it, thus improving the quality of the requirement.

3.2 Experiment Design

We utilized a two-by-two crossover design [7], using two sessions and two groups of subjects (see Table 1). The treatment group worked within our tool environment that we described in Sect. 2, later referred to as the tool-assisted group

Table 1. Experimental design

	Group 1	Group 2
Session 1 (wiper control)	M	TA
Session 2 (window lift)	TA	M

(TA), while the control group was working without the help of our tool. We refer to the control group as the manual group (M). The difference between sessions is the requirements specification that was used. In the first session, we used a requirements specification of a wiper control system and in the second session, we used a requirements specification of a window lift system.

3.3 Participants

The experiment was conducted as part of a university masters course on automotive software engineering at TU Berlin. The participants of this course were undergraduate students in their last year. The majority was enrolled for the study programs computer science, computer engineering, or automotive systems. The course included lectures on basic principles of requirements and test engineering. As a result, the students understood what requirements engineering is used for and how requirements should be documented. They were especially aware of the consequences of bad requirements engineering on subsequent development steps.

The experiment was announced beforehand. We especially emphasized that a large number of participants would be crucial for acquiring useful results. We motivated the students to take part in the experiment by telling them that they would gain insight into real world requirements engineering. At the time of the experiment, 20 students were present, which reflects about two-thirds of all students enrolled in the course.

3.4 Experimental Materials

The experiment was conducted using real-world requirements documents available at our industry partner. We selected two documents describing common systems in any modern car: the wiper control system and the window lift system. The documents contain requirements in a tabular format. Each row contains one content element, consisting of its identifier, the content text, and its object type. Three object types were present in these documents: heading, requirement, and information.

The documents are very long, containing about 3000 content elements each. Since the students cannot possibly read, understand, and find defects in the entire document within the time limit (see Sect. 3.7), the documents were truncated to a reasonable size. Also, as per request of our industry partner, certain confidential information such as the names of persons, signals, and other systems were replaced by generic strings (e.g., "SIGNAL-1", "SYSTEM-3").

To assess whether the students with or without tool perform better, we created a gold standard by identifying all defects the students had to find in the two documents by ourselves. This gold standard serves as reference for comparing the performance of the groups.

Each document was then prepared in two different formats: a csv like format readable by our tool for assisted review and an MS Excel version for unassisted review. Both formats contain exactly the same data. Colors and font sizes in the Excel spreadsheet were selected to mimic the tool as close as possible.

Table 2 lists the relevant characteristics of the documents, such as number of elements, number of defects, numbers about warnings issued by our tool, and overall accuracy of the tool on this document. The Wiper Control document has many obviously misclassified elements and many of the false warnings are easily dismissible as such. On the Window Lift document, our tool issued many false warnings due to an inconsistent writing style within the document.

Table 2. Characteristics of the used requirements specifications

	Wiper control	Window lift
Total elements	115	261
Total requirements	85	186
Total information	30	75
Total defects	20	17
Total warnings	24	70
Correct warnings	12	12
Unwarned defects	8	5
Accuracy	82.6%	75.8%

3.5   Tasks

The task given to the students was designed to resemble the procedure taken during actual quality audits. Each student had to read and understand the requirements specifications and correct defects within these documents. The students were instructed to search for the following defects:

- Requirement content elements incorrectly classified as information
- Information content elements incorrectly classified as requirements
- Badly phrased requirements (i.e., ambiguous, missing modal verb, . . .)

The students were asked to fix the defects by either changing the object type, the phrasing, or both.

3.6   Data Analysis Procedure

We perform the analysis of our research questions using metrics defined in this section and formulate working hypotheses about what outcome we expect. The independent variable in our experiment is the review method used by the student, which is either *Manual*, or *Tool-Assisted*.

RQ1: Does the usage of our tool enable users to detect more defects? We evaluate this question by calculating the *Defect Correction Rate (DCR)*:

$$DCR = \frac{DefectsCorrected}{DefectsInspected}$$

DefectsCorrected is the number of defects identified and corrected by a student, *DefectsInspected* is the number of defects examined by the student. We do not base this metric on the total number of defects in the document because a student might not have had the time to review the whole document. For the DCR, we are only interested in the likelihood that a defect is identified and corrected if the respective object has at least been examined by a student. We expect that the warnings issued by our tool help students to identify and correct defects. Thus, we expect a higher DCR:

$$H_1 : DCR(\text{Tool-Assisted}) > DCR(\text{Manual})$$

RQ2: Does the usage of our tool reduce the number of defects introduced by users? Similar to RQ1, we evaluate this question by calculating the *Defect Introduction Rate (DIR)*:

$$DIR = \frac{DefectsIntroduced}{ElementsInspected}$$

where *DefectsIntroduced* is the number of modified elements that were originally correct and *ElementsInspected* the total number of elements examined by the student. We expect that

$$H_2 : DIR(\text{Tool-Assisted}) < DIR(\text{Manual})$$

RQ3: Are users of our tool prone to ignoring actual defects because no warning was issued? For evaluating this question, we only consider elements on which our tool issued no warnings. The *Unwarned Defect Miss Rate (UDMR)* is defined as

$$UDMR = \frac{UnwarnedDefectsMissed}{UnwarnedDefectsInspected}$$

where *UnwarnedDefectsInspected* is the number of examined defects for which the tool did not give any warnings and *UnwarnedDefectsMissed* is the subset of these that were not corrected. Since we suspect that the users of our tool will be more focused on the elements with warnings, we expect the following (which would be a negative property of using the tool):

$$H_3 : UDMR(\text{Tool-Assisted}) > UDMR(\text{Manual})$$

RQ4: Are users of our tool faster in processing the documents? This question is answered by examining how much time the users spent on each element. The *Time Per Element (TPE)* is calculated as follows:

$$TPE = \frac{TotalTimeSpent}{ElementsInspected}$$

TotalTimeSpent is the time the students needed to complete the document or the total time of the experiment if they did not finish. We suspect that users of our tool will be faster in processing the documents:

$$H_4 : TPE(\text{Tool-Assisted}) > TPE(\text{Manual})$$

RQ5: Does our tool motivate users to rephrase requirements and information content elements?

$$ERR = \frac{ElementsRephrased}{ElementsInspected}$$

This metric captures how many content elements are rephrased by users. We did not inspect whether the change improved the requirement or not. We expect that users of the tool may be more eager to rephrase content elements since the tool points to linguistic weaknesses by providing visual explanations of its decisions.

$$H_5 : ERR(\text{Tool-Assisted}) > ERR(\text{Manual})$$

3.7   Procedure

The experiment was scheduled to take 90 min. The time available was divided into four segments:

- **Introduction, setup, data distribution, and group assignment (20 min):** The session was started with a presentation on requirements quality, how our industry partner performs quality audits, the importance of differentiation between requirements and information, details on the structure of the experiment itself, and details on the documents necessary to understand them.

  After that, we randomly divided the students into two groups and distributed the requirements documents to them. The tool was distributed to the students a week before the experiment without any data to reduce the time needed for setup.
- **Session 1: Wiper Control (20 min):** During the experiment, students worked through the document from top to bottom and made modifications where they thought it is necessary. We allowed them to form teams of two or three students of the same group. This way, they were able to discuss their opinions, much like requirements engineers will do during real quality audits. We prohibited them from sharing information between teams or groups. After time was up, the students were asked to mark the position they were at.

– **Session 2: Window Lift (30 min):** The second run was executed exactly like the first but with switched groups and with a different document.
– **Conclusions (10 min):** After the second run, we collected the modified documents and presented how we are going to evaluate the data and what kind of results we expect.

3.8 Piloting

Prior to performing the actual experiment, we simulated the experiment. Some of our co-workers were briefed and performed the same tasks as the students in the experiment. We used the results of the experiment to adjust certain parameters of the experiment, such as the size of the documents and allocated time for each session. The test run also allowed us to verify that our planned evaluation methodology yields usable results.

4 Study Results

For the first document, we received a total of 14 reviews, 7 reviews with tool usage and 7 reviews without tool usage. We received less reviews for the second document (3 with tool usage and 4 without tool usage) because some students had to leave. We also had to discard 2 reviews because one did not contain any changes and the other was done by a student who had major difficulties in understanding the documents due to language barriers.

An overview of all collected data is available online[1]. Figure 2 shows boxplots of the calculated metrics over all reviews and for each review document separately. In the following, we discuss our research questions based on these results.

4.1 Discussion

In Fig. 2a, the Defect Correction Rate (DCR) is displayed for each document and review method. Regarding the Wiper Control document, the students with the tool performed better than the students without tool support. The average correction rate is 11% higher. However, on the Window Lift document, results were opposite: The students doing manual review corrected 61% of all examined defects, whereas the students doing assisted review only corrected 45%. One explanation for this could be the lower quality of the warnings issued by our tool (see the difference in accuracy in Table 2) due to the low linguistic quality of the Window Lift document. Therefore, it is possible that the students were misled by the false warnings of the tool.

Figure 2b shows the Defect Introduction Rate (DIR), i.e., how many new defects were introduced per examined element by changing content elements with no defect. The students doing the assisted review performed better on both documents, introducing only half as many new defects on average as the students without tool. We assume that students refrained from changing content elements if no warning was issued by the tool.

---

[1] https://doi.org/10.6084/m9.figshare.5469343.v1.

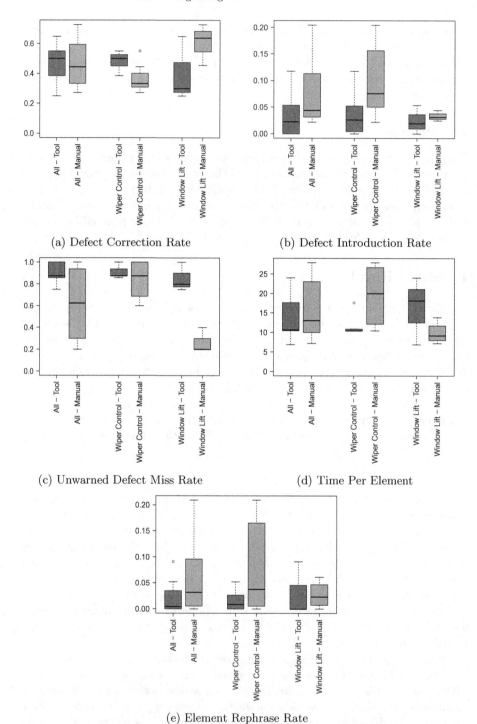

(a) Defect Correction Rate

(b) Defect Introduction Rate

(c) Unwarned Defect Miss Rate

(d) Time Per Element

(e) Element Rephrase Rate

Fig. 2. Study results

An unwarned defect is a defect for which our tool did not issue a warning. We analyzed how likely it is that these defects are missed by tool users. We compare this with the performance of the manual review group on the same set of defects (those without warnings). Of course, students in the manual group did not know which defects had warnings in the tool. Figure 2b shows that if the tool is used, 90% of defects without a warning are not corrected. As expected, the group doing manual review performed better, missing only 62% of all unwarned defects. This is in line with our expectation that students with tool support will focus less on elements without warnings.

The time spent by the students on each element is shown in Fig. 2d. Students spent less time on each element in the Window Lift document (mean: 10.8 s) than on the Wiper Control document (mean: 13.9 s). This may be the result of a learning effect: Students became used to the task and learned for which information they need to look. On the first document, the students performing assisted review were considerably faster (11.2 s per element on average compared to 16.6 s for the manual review). In addition, 4 out of 7 teams using the tool completed their review, whereas only 1 out of 7 teams finished using manual review. On the second document, the students using the tool were slower, most likely because they analyzed the false warnings and tried to decide whether to change or not to change a content element.

Figure 2e shows how many content elements were rephrased. Overall, only 3.8% of the examined content elements were changed. In 8 out of 21 reviews, no element was changed at all. We expected more changes, considering that the overall text quality of the documents was rather low. The students not working with the tool changed more content elements, especially on the Wiper Control document. We assume that the students working with the tool were more focused on the warnings than changing the text of content elements.

To summarize the discussion, we provide answers to our research questions:

RQ1: Users of our tool may be able to detect and fix more defects than users without the tool. However, this depends on the accuracy of our tool. Bad accuracy may even have a negative effect on defect identification.

RQ2: If our tool is used, less new defects are introduced during a review.

RQ3: Our students missed more unwarned defects (i.e., false negatives) if warnings were present.

RQ4: Given that the accuracy of the tool is high enough, users of our tool may be able to complete the task much faster.

RQ5: In our experiment, usage of the tool did not motivate users to rephrase more content elements.

5 Threats to Validity

In this section, we discuss the various threats to construct, internal and external validity of our experiment.

Number of participants [construct]. A major threat to our results is the low number of participants. Since we allowed students to work in teams, the number of results is even smaller. This allowed them to engage in discussions within the team, which, in our opinion, is more important for the experiment setup than having a larger sample size. On the other hand, the small sample size forbids making any statistical tests on the hypothesis described in this paper. Therefore, we do not claim that we can reject or support any of the hypothesis with our results. Our goal was to check and refine the working hypothesis that we came up with to see which (additional) parameters might influence the results.

Definition of gold standard [construct]. We compared the results of the two review methods with a gold standard that we created ourselves, i.e., we defined what a defect is in the documents. This definition has an impact on the performance assessment of the review methods. The authors of this article are working on this classification problem for more than 3 years in close collaboration with an industry partner. Therefore, we claim that the created gold standard is close to what the industry partner would consider as truth.

Differences in knowledge between students [internal]. We assumed that the students have no prior knowledge in requirements engineering apart from what was taught during the lecture. Some students may have more knowledge in requirements engineering than others and thus may perform better at the task. We diminished the effects of this by having each students perform the task with both review methods.

Maturation [internal]. Maturation is an effect that occurs over time and may change a subject's behavior due to learning, fatigue, or changes in motivation. The students in our experiment may have learned from the first session of the experiment and applied that knowledge in the second session. It is also possible that students have lost motivation or performed worse due to fatigue after completing the first session.

Communication between groups [internal]. We have especially stated during the experiment that it is important not to share information about defects between groups. However, since the experiment was conducted in a classroom setting and students were able to discuss within the group, information may have been shared between groups nonetheless. As such, not all reviews may be independent.

Time limit [internal]. The time limit was set for two reasons: First, the time in actual quality audits is limited as well, and second, we only had a total of 90 min available. We told the students that it is not necessary to complete a document within the time limit. However, the students could have aimed for completing the review nonetheless and thus may have performed worse than without a time limit.

Students are no RE experts [external]. Compared with people who actually perform quality audits, students are no requirements engineering experts. They lack both general knowledge about the processes in which requirements specifications are involved in as well as special knowledge about the documents themselves. However, students may inspect the documents more carefully whereas RE experts may tend to dismiss possible defects either due to them being the authors or due to process constraints (changes may induce additional costs). Falessi et al. state that controlled experiments with students are as valid as experiments with experts [8].

The most relevant threat to validity is the number of participants. Our sample size is not sufficiently large to be used for statistical significance tests and therefore, experiments on larger groups of participants may show different results. An experiment on a larger user base should be performed next.

6 Related Work

Machine learning techniques are applied for many requirements engineering tasks, especially for classification. A few of these works are outlined here.

Hayes et al. [9] present a tool that integrates with Weka and provides a convenient way for users to perform classification tasks. For example, their tool is able to differentiate between temporal and non-temporal requirements.

Huang et al. [10] present and approach to classify different types of non-functional requirements, achieving 81% recall and 12% precision on their dataset, averaged above all classes.

Ott [11] presents an approach to increase the efficiency of requirements specification reviews by assigning requirements to topics (e.g., temperature, voltage). He argues that a block of requirements belonging to the same topic may be reviewed faster than requirements of mixed topics. However, no validation of that claim is provided.

Perini et al. [12] use a prioritization algorithm based on machine learning techniques to sort software requirements by their importance. This allows stakeholders to discern important and less important requirements more easily. Its effectiveness is demonstrated using empirical evaluation methods.

There is currently a discussion in the community around the empirical investigation of the effectiveness of automated tools for RE tasks. In an earlier paper, Berry et al. [13] claim that in some scenarios, for some tasks, any tool with less than 100% recall is not helpful and the user may be better off doing the task entirely manually. In fact, our experiment supports this claim by indicating that the accuracy of the tool may have an effect on the observed performance. In a follow-up paper [14], Berry relaxes his first claim by saying that a human working with the tool on the task should at least achieve better recall than a human working on the task entirely manually. Our experimental setup follows this idea by comparing tool-assisted and manual reviews.

7 Conclusions

At our industry partner, each content element of a requirements specification document needs to be classified as either requirement or non-requirement ("information"). A requirement is legally binding and needs to be tested. This does not apply to non-requirements. This classification is currently performed manually.

We have built a tool that classifies content elements of specification documents as either information or requirement and issues warnings when the classification seems to be wrong. We assume that by using our tool, RE experts will be able to perform this classification more effectively and efficiently.

In this paper, we have presented the results of a controlled experiment, showing the benefits and limitations of our tool. Two groups of students analyzed requirements specification documents and were asked to fix any defects in them. One group used the tool, whereas the other did not.

The results show that, given high accuracy of the provided warnings, users of our tool are able to perform slightly better than the users performing manual review. They managed to correct more defects, introduce less new defects, and did so in shorter time. However, when many false warnings are issued, the situation may be reversed. Thus, the actual benefit is largely dependent on the performance of the underlying classifier. False negatives (i.e., defects with no warnings) are an issue as well, since users tend to focus less on elements with no warnings.

The sample size used in our experiment is not high enough to underpin our conclusions with measures on statistical significance, as we were limited to the students visiting the lecture. We plan to perform the experiment again with more students. However, the results presented in this paper already show that improvements can be achieved by using our tool.

Since the tool is based on machine learning algorithms, achieving perfect accuracy, or at least perfect recall, is impossible. Therefore, our tool may not be needed when a requirements engineer is doing a complete review of a specification document and is able to detect all defects. However, in the real world, humans do errors due to various reasons such as fatigue and inattention. Our approach may help them to do fewer errors and achieve higher quality specification documents (with regard to requirement vs. information classification) compared with manual review.

To assess which accuracy or recall the tool must provide to outperform a completely manual review is an interesting question that we want to follow in future experimental setups.

References

1. Winkler, J.P., Vogelsang, A.: Automatic classification of requirements based on convolutional neural networks. In: 3rd IEEE International Workshop on Artificial Intelligence for Requirements Engineering (AIRE), pp. 39–45 (2016)
2. Winkler, J.P.: Automatische Klassifikation von Anforderungen zur Unterstützung von Qualitätssicherungsprozessen. In: Mayr, H.C., Pinzger, M. (eds.) INFORMATIK 2016, Bonn. Lecture Notes in Informatics (LNI), pp. 1537–1549 (2016)
3. Kim, Y.: Convolutional neural networks for sentence classification. In: Proceedings of the 2014 Conference on Empirical Methods in Natural Language Processing (EMNLP), pp. 1746–1751 (2014)

4. Winkler, J.P., Vogelsang, A.: "What Does My Classifier Learn?" a visual approach to understanding natural language text classifiers. In: Proceedings of the 22nd International Conference on Natural Language and Information Systems, pp. 468–179. NLDB (2017)

5. Ko, A.J., LaToza, T.D., Burnett, M.M.: A practical guide to controlled experiments of software engineering tools with human participants. Empir. Softw. Eng. **20**(1), 110–141 (2015)

6. Jedlitschka, A., Ciolkowski, M., Pfahl, D.: Reporting experiments in software engineering. In: Shull, F., Singer, J., Sjøberg, D.I.K. (eds.) Guide to Advanced Empirical Software Engineering, pp. 201–228. Springer, London (2008). https://doi.org/10.1007/978-1-84800-044-5_8

7. Wohlin, C., Runeson, P., Höst, M., Ohlsson, M.C., Regnell, B., Wesslén, A.: Experimentation in Software Engineering. Springer, Heidelberg (2012). https://doi.org/10.1007/978-3-642-29044-2

8. Falessi, D., Juristo, N., Wohlin, C., Turhan, B., Münch, J., Jedlitschka, A., Oivo, M.: Empirical software engineering experts on the use of students and professionals in experiments. Empir. Softw. Eng. **23**, 452–489 (2017)

9. Hayes, J.H., Li, W., Rahimi, M.: Weka meets TraceLab: toward convenient classification: machine learning for requirements engineering problems: a position paper. In: 1st IEEE International Workshop on Artificial Intelligence for Requirements Engineering (AIRE), pp. 9–12. AIRE (2014)

10. Cleland-Huang, J., Settimi, R., Zou, X., Solc, P.: Automated classification of non-functional requirements. Requir. Eng. **12**(2), 103–120 (2007)

11. Ott, D.: Automatic requirement categorization of large natural language specifications at Mercedes-Benz for review improvements. In: Doerr, J., Opdahl, A.L. (eds.) REFSQ 2013. LNCS, vol. 7830, pp. 50–64. Springer, Heidelberg (2013). https://doi.org/10.1007/978-3-642-37422-7_4

12. Perini, A., Susi, A., Avesani, P.: A machine learning approach to software requirements prioritization. IEEE Trans. Softw. Eng. **39**(4), 445–461 (2013)

13. Berry, D., Gacitua, R., Sawyer, P., Tjong, S.F.: The case for dumb requirements engineering tools. In: Regnell, B., Damian, D. (eds.) REFSQ 2012. LNCS, vol. 7195, pp. 211–217. Springer, Heidelberg (2012). https://doi.org/10.1007/978-3-642-28714-5_18

14. Berry, D.M.: Evaluation of tools for hairy requirements and software engineering tasks. In: 2017 IEEE 25th International Requirements Engineering Conference Workshops (REW), pp. 284–291 (2017)

Empirical Insights into Traceability

Evaluation of Techniques to Detect Wrong Interaction Based Trace Links

Paul Hübner$^{(\boxtimes)}$ and Barbara Paech

Institute for Computer Science, Heidelberg University,
Im Neuenheimer Feld 205, 69120 Heidelberg, Germany
{huebner,paech}@informatik.uni-heidelberg.de

Abstract. [**Context and Motivation**] In projects where trace links are created and used continuously during the development, it is important to support developers with an automatic trace link creation approach with high precision. In our previous study we showed that our interaction based trace link creation approach achieves 100% precision and 80% relative recall and thus performs better than traditional IR based approaches. [**Question/problem**] In this study we wanted to confirm our previous results with a data set including a gold standard created by developers. Moreover we planned further optimization and fine tuning of our trace link creation approach. [**Principal ideas/results**] We performed the study within a student project. It turned out that in this study our approach achieved only 50% precision. This means that developers also worked on code not relevant for the requirement while interactions were recorded. In order to improve precision we evaluated different techniques to identify relevant trace link candidates such as focus on edit interactions or thresholds for frequency and duration of trace link candidates. We also evaluated different techniques to identify irrelevant code such as the developer who created the code or code which is not related to other code in an interaction log. [**Contribution**] Our results show that only some of the techniques led to a considerably improvement of precision. We could improve precision almost up to 70 % while keeping recall above 45% which is much better than IR-based link creation. The evaluations show that the full benefits of an interaction based approach highly depend on the discipline of the developers when recording interactions for a specific requirement. Further research is necessary how to support the application of our approach in a less disciplined context.

Keywords: Traceability · Interaction · Requirement · Source code
Precision

1 Introduction

Existing trace link creation approaches are typically based on information retrieval (IR) and on structured requirements like use cases or user stories. Also, they often

© Springer International Publishing AG, part of Springer Nature 2018
E. Kamsties et al. (Eds.): REFSQ 2018, LNCS 10753, pp. 75–91, 2018.
https://doi.org/10.1007/978-3-319-77243-1_5

focus on links between requirements [2]. It is known that precision of IR created links is often not satisfying [8] for their direct usage even in the case of structured requirements. Thus, handling of false positive IR created trace links requires extra effort in practice which is even a research subject on its own [7,9,19].

Still, the research focus in RE is to improve recall, since security critical domains like the aeronautics and automotive industry require complete link sets and thus accept the effort to remove many false positives [3]. These links are created periodically, when needed for certification to justify the safe operation of a system.

However, in many companies requirements are managed in issue tracking systems (ITS) [15]. For open source projects ITS are even the de facto standard for all requirements management activities [17]. In ITS the requirements text is unstructured, since ITS are used for many purposes, e.g. development task and bug tracking in addition to requirement specification. This impairs the results of IR-based trace link creation approaches [18]. Furthermore, for many development activities it is helpful to consider links between requirements and source code during development, e.g. in maintenance tasks and for program comparison [16]. If these links are created continuously, that means after each completion of an issue, they can be used continuously during the development. In these cases, large effort for handling false positives and thus, bad precision is not practicable. Therefore, a trace link creation approach for links between unstructured requirements and code is needed with perfect precision and good recall. Recall values are reported as good above 70% [9].

In a previous paper [10] we provided such a trace link creation approach (called IL in the following) based on interaction logs and code relations. Interaction logs capture the source code artifacts touched while a developer works on an issue. Interaction logs provide more fine-grained interaction data than VCS change logs [6]. Code relations such as references between classes provide additional information. In a previous study using data from an open source project we showed that our approach can achieve 100% precision and 80% relative recall and thus performs much better than traditional IR based approaches [11]. As there are no open source project data available with interaction logs and a gold standard for trace links, we only could evaluate recall relative to all correct links found by our approach and IR.

In contrast to the previous paper we now present a study based on interaction log data, requirements and source code from a student project. We used a student project in order to be able to create a gold standard with the help of the students. This enabled the calculation of the recall against the gold standard.

The presented study consists of two parts. In the first part we calculated precision and real recall values for our IL approach. The first results of the study showed that IL has only around 50% precision. We therefore evaluated the wrong links identified by IL. We found out that these links were caused by developers not triggering the interaction recording for requirements correctly. They worked on different requirements without changing the requirement in the IDE. Thus, all trace links were created for one requirement.

In consequence, in the second part of our study, we evaluated different techniques to improve precision by identifying relevant trace link candidates such as focus on edit interactions or thresholds for frequency and duration of interactions. We also evaluated different techniques to identify irrelevant code such as the developer who created the code, or code which does not refer to other code in an interaction log. In the best cases we could improve the precision up to almost 70% with still reasonable recall above 45%.

The remainder of this paper is structured as follows. Section 2 gives a short introduction into the evaluation of trace link creation approaches and the project used for the evaluation. Section 3 presents our interaction based trace link creation approach. Section 4 introduces the experimental design along with the creation of data sets for our study, states the research questions and introduces the improvement techniques to detect wrong trace links for our approach developed in this study. In Sect. 5 we present the results of the study and answer the research questions including a discussion. Section 6 discusses the threats to validity of the study. In Sect. 7 we discuss related work. Section 8 concludes the paper and discusses future work.

2   Background

In this section we introduce the basics of trace link evaluation and the study context.

2.1   Trace Link Evaluation

To evaluate approaches for trace link creation [2,8] a gold standard which consists of the set of all correct trace links for a given set of artifacts is important. To create such a gold standard it is necessary to manually check whether trace links exist for each pair of artifacts. Based on this gold standard precision and recall can be computed.

Precision (P) is the amount of correct links (true positives, TP) within all links found by an approach. The latter is the sum of TP and not correct links (false positive, FP). Recall (R) is the amount of TP links found by an approach within all existing correct links (from the gold standard). The latter is the sum of TP and false negative (FN) links:

$$P = \frac{TP}{TP + FP} \qquad R = \frac{TP}{TP + FN} \qquad F_\beta = (1 + \beta^2) \cdot \frac{P \cdot R}{(\beta^2 \cdot P) + R}$$

F_β-scores combine the results for P and R in a single measurement to judge the accuracy of a trace link creation approach. As shown in the equation for F_β above, β can be used to weight P in favor of R and vice versa. In contrast to other studies our focus is to emphasize P, but still consider R. Therefore we choose $F_{0.5}$ which weights P twice as much as R. In addition we also calculate F_1-scores to compare our results with others. In our previous paper [11] information about typical values of P and R in settings using structured [9] and unstructured [18] data for trace link creation approaches can be found. Based on these sources for unstructured data good R values are between 70 and 79% and good P values are between 30 and 49%.

2.2   Evaluation Project

Due to the labor intensity of creating a trace link gold standard often student projects are used [5]. In the following we describe the student project in which we recorded the interactions, the application of the used tools and how we recorded the interactions. The project lasted from Oct. 2016 to March 2017 and was performed Scrum oriented. Thus it was separated into seven sprints with the goal to get a working product increment in each sprint. The projects aim was to develop a so called *master patient index* for an open ID oriented organization of health care patient data. A typical use case for the resulting product would be to store and manage all health care reports for a patient in a single data base. The project involved the IT department of the university hospital as real world customer. Further roles involved were the student developers and a member of our research group with the role of a product owner. Seven developers participated in the project. In each of the sprints one of developer acted as scrum master.

All requirements related activities were documented in a Scrum Project of the ITS JIRA[1]. This included the specification of requirements in the form of user stories and the functional grouping of the requirements as epics. For instance the epic *Patient Data Management* comprised user stories like *View Patients* or *Search Patient Data*. Complex user stories in turn comprised sub-tasks documenting more and often technical details. For instance the *Search Patient Data* user story comprised the sub-tasks *Provide Search Interface* or *Create Rest Endpoint*. The project started with an initial vision of the final product from the customer and was broken down by the developers using the scrum backlog functionality of JIRA to a set of initial user stories which evolved during the sprints.

For implementation the project used JavaScript which was requested by the customer. Furthermore the MongoDB[2] NOSQL database and the React[3] UI framework were used. The developers used the Webstorm[4] version of IntelIJ IDE along with Git as version control system. Within the JIRA project and the JavaScript source code we also applied our feature management approach [21]. A feature in this project corresponded to an epic. This approach ensures that all artifacts are tagged with the name of the feature they belong to. So that a user story is tagged with the epic it corresponds to, but also the sub-tasks of the user stories and the code implementing the user story are tagged.

The developers installed and configured IntelliJ plug-ins we used for interaction recording (cf. Sect. 3) and were supported whenever needed. They got a short introduction about interaction recording and associating requirements

---

[1] https://www.atlassian.com/software/jira.
[2] https://www.mongodb.com/.
[3] https://reactjs.org/.
[4] https://www.jetbrains.com/webstorm/.

and source code files. The plug-ins recorded all interactions in the IDE in locally stored csv and xml files. The developers were asked to send us their interaction log files by email after each sprint on voluntary basis so that we had the possibility to check the plausibility of the recorded interactions. In the first sprints some of the developers had problems with activating interaction recording and using the desired IntelliJ plug-in to interact with requirements. After detecting such problems we explained it to them and asked them to solve these problems for the processing of the next sprint. However some of the developers only sent their interaction logs once or twice in the final project phase. Therefore four of the seven log files received were not usable for our evaluation. One was almost empty due to technical problems, in the other three only a very low number of requirements were logged. The corresponding developers stopped to record changes to requirements at a certain point in time and thus all following interactions were associated with the last activated requirement. We used the three correctly recorded interaction logs to apply our IL approach. Overall the interaction logs of the three developers contained more than two million log entries. The developers recorded these interactions while working on 42 distinct user stories and sub-tasks and touching 312 distinct source code files.

3   Interaction Based Trace Link Approach

Figure 1 shows our interaction based trace link creation approach (IL) and the improvement step IL_i. First we use an IDE Plug-in to capture the interactions of the developer while working on requirements and code. In a second step trace links are created between requirements and code based on the interactions. The last step is an improvement step that uses source code structure and interaction log data. In the following we explain the steps in more detail.

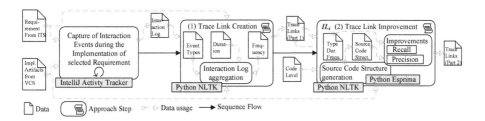

Fig. 1. IL trace link creation overview: interaction capturing, trace link creation and improvement IL_i

3.1 Interaction Logs

In contrast to our last study we used the IntelliJ IDE[5] and implemented the first interaction capturing step of our IL approach with two IntellJ Plug-ins:

1. To log interactions we used the *IntellJ Activity Tracker* Plug-in which we modified to our needs. We extended the Plug-ins ability to track the interactions with requirements. The only action to be performed by the developers for this plug-in was to activate it once. After this all interactions within the IDE of the developer were recorded, comprising a time stamp, the part of the IDE and the type of interactions performed. The most important part of the IDE for us are the editor for the source code, the navigator which displays a structural tree of all resources managed by the IDE, and dialogs which are often involved in high level actions like committing to Git and performing JIRA Issue related actions. The interaction types can be low level interactions like editor keystrokes, but also high level interactions (selected from the context menu) like performing a refactoring or when committing changes to Git.
2. To associate interactions with requirements the *Task & Context* IntellJ functionality was used. The developers connected this Plug-in with the JIRA project. When working on a requirement the developers selected the specific JIRA issue with the *Task & Context* functionality. When committing their code changes to the Git repository the *Task & Context* plug-in supported the finishing of the respective JIRA issue.

The following listing shows two abridged log entries as created by the modified version of the activity tracker tool.

```
1   2016−10−04T10:14:50.910;dev2;Action;EditorSplitLine;ise;Editor;
      /git/Controller.js;
2   2016−10−13T13:28:26.414;dev2;Task Activation;ISE2016−46:Enter Arrays;
      ise;
```

The first log entry is a typical edit interaction starting with a time stamp, the developers user name, the kind of performed action, the performed activity (which is entering a new line), the used Git project, the involved component of the IDE (*editor*) and the used source code file (*/git/Controller.js*). The second log entry shows an interaction with a user story from JIRA including its issue ID and name (*ISE2016-46:Enter Arrays*).

3.2 Trace Link Creation and Improvement

The actual IL trace link creation has been implemented in our Python NLTK[6] based tool. As shown in Fig. 1 in step *IL-Trace Link Creation (1)* interactions of the same requirements are aggregated and trace link candidates are created using the data of interaction logs, the source code touched by the interactions extracted from the version control system and the requirements from the ITS. The candidates relate the requirement associated to the interaction and the source code touched in the interaction.

---

[5] https://www.jetbrains.com/idea/.
[6] http://www.nltk.org/.

In the IL_i-*Trace Link Improvement (2)* step source code structure and inter-action log data such as duration and frequency are used to improve recall (cf. Fig. 1). The source code structure based improvement of this step has been implemented with the Esprima[7] JavaScript source code parser. With source code structure we denote the call and data dependencies between code files and classes [14]. Using the code structure to improve trace link creation is part of traceability research [13]. In our previous study we added additional links to a requirement by utilizing the code structure of source code files already linked to the requirement [11]. As we aim at trace links with perfect precision this recall improvement only makes scene, if the trace links have excellent precision. Otherwise utilization of code structure might increase recall but very likely also decrease precision.

In this paper we also use the code structure to support precision by utilizing the relations between source code files involved in the interaction logs of one requirement (cf. Sect. 4.4).

4 Experiment Design

In this section we describe the details of our study (cf. Fig. 2), in particular wrt. the data sets and the techniques to detect wrong interaction links.

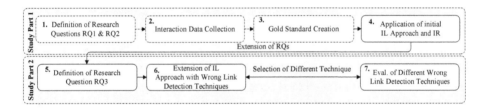

Fig. 2. Experimental design: overview of performed activities

4.1 Research Questions

The initial purpose of this study was to calculate precision and real recall values instead of relative recall as in our last study, for our approach (RQ_1) and for comparison also for IR (RQ_2) [11]. After we realized that the precision of our IL approach was not sufficient for direct usage of the trace links with the data of the student project we investigated the improvement of precision and thus detection techniques for wrong trace links (RQ_3). Thus the research questions we answer in the two parts of our study are:

RQ_1: *What is the precision and recall of IL created trace links?* Our hypothesis was that IL has very good precision and good recall.

---

[7] http://esprima.org/.

RQ$_2$: *What is the precision and recall of IR created trace links?* Our hypothesis was that IR has bad precision and good recall.

RQ$_3$: *What is the precision and recall of IL with detection techniques for wrong trace links?* Our hypothesis was that detection techniques utilizing details of the interaction log like the time stamp, and detection techniques considering the source code like using the source code structure should enhance precision considerably and keep reasonable recall.

4.2   Gold Standard Creation

The left side of Table 1 shows the overview of all recorded interactions for user stories or sub-tasks and the number of involved source code files of the three developers which we used for further processing and evaluation in our study.

Table 1. Interaction data and gold standard

	Interaction logs			Gold standard creation					
	#Req.	#Interactions	#Code. Files	#Req.	#Code. Files	#Link Cand.	#Rated Correct	#Rated Wrong	#Rated Unknown
Dev_1	12	628.502	155	3	99	139	37	90	2
Dev_2	20	506.726	273	11	141	374	128	241	5
Dev_3	16	893.390	256	5	83	189	52	123	14
Sum	42[a]	2.028.618	312[a]	19	151[a]	692	217	454	21

[a]Same issues and source files used by different developers have been accumulated

The right side of Table 1 shows the overview of the gold standard. For the gold standard creation we first selected 21 user stories of the 42 requirements, since these 21 user stories were assigned directly to the three developers. The others had been assigned to other developers or had a different issue type. Through this we made sure that the developers knew the requirements very well. We further excluded two of the 21 user stories. For one user story one developer had not stopped the interaction recording and thus links to almost all source code files in the Git repository had been created. The other user story was the first in the interaction logs of a developer and no activation event was recorded for that user story.

To limit the link candidates to a reasonable amount we considered all possible link candidates between user stories and code files tagged with the same feature. For the remaining 19 user stories we selected all code files from the Git repository with the same feature tag (cf. Sect. 2.2). This excluded in particular files with a format different than *javascript and json and xml*. Examples for such files are html files and build scripts. After this 151 code files, as shown in the sixth column of the last row of Table 1, remained. Then we created all possible link candidates between user stories and code files with the same tag. This resulted in 692 link candidates.

We provided a personalized questionnaire with link candidates for the three developers. The developers labeled the links as correct (217), wrong (454)

or unknown (21). The latter means they did not have the competence to judge. The developers also confirmed that all feature labels were correct. The three developers worked on their personalized questionnaire in individual sessions lasting between two to three hours in a separate office room in our department and had the possibility to ask questions if something was unclear. Thus initially all links of the gold standard were only rated by one developer. After the first part of our study we checked the link ratings of the developers for plausibility. By inspecting the source code files and requirements involved in each link we manually checked 113 wrong links created by our approach.

4.3   Part 1: Trace Link Creation with IL and IR

We initially created trace links with our IL approach (cf. Sect. 3) and with the common IR methods vector space model (VSM) and latent semantic indexing (LSI) [2,4]. We applied both approaches to the user stories together with their sub-tasks (see Sect. 2.2) and to the 151 code files used for the gold standard creation. We only used these code files, as we only had the gold standard links for them.

For IL we combined the interactions of a user story with the interactions of the corresponding sub-task for further evaluations, as the sub-tasks describe details for implementing the user story. From the resulting link candidates we removed all links to code files not included in the gold standard. We applied IR to the texts of user stories and corresponding sub-tasks and to the 151 code files used for the gold standard. In addition we performed all common IR pre-processing steps [1,2], i.e. stop word removal, punctuation character removal and stemming. We also performed camel case identifier splitting (e.g. *PatientForm* becomes *Patient Form*), since this notation has been used in the source code [4]. Since the user stories contained only very short texts, the used threshold values for the IR methods had to be set very low.

4.4   Part 2: Detection Techniques for Wrong Trace Links

Since our IL approach had worse precision values as we expected, we decided to investigate how IL can be extended by the detection of wrong trace links. Thus we extended our initial study with a second part in which we wanted to answer RQ_3 (cf. Sect. 4.1) for the evaluation of wrong link detection techniques. We looked at two different kind of wrong trace link detection techniques. The first set of techniques was based on the data available in the interaction logs. The second set of techniques used the source code files touched by interactions and data around these files. The main idea was to directly detect link candidates not relevant for a user story or code files not relevant for a user story.

For the interactions logs we used (a) the type of interaction, i.e. whether an interaction is a select or a edit, (b) the duration of interactions based on the logged time stamp and (c) the frequency how often an interaction with a source code file occurred for a user story. The rationale was that (a) edit events are more likely than select events to identify code necessary for a user story and that (b, c) a longer duration of the interaction or higher frequency signify that the developer made a more comprehensive change and not only a short edit e.g. correcting a typo noticed when looking at a file.

For source code we used (a) the ownership that is the developer who created the interaction, as one developer might have worked less disciplined than others (b) the number how often source code files were interacted with for different user stories, as files used for different user stories might be base files which had not been considered relevant for the gold standard by the developers (c) filtering on only JavaScript source code files as other formats might not be so relevant for a user story and (d) the code structure for the source code files involved in one user story to detect files which had no relation in the code structure to other files, as the unrelated code files might signify a different purpose than the user story. We then combined the most promising techniques. Altogether we implemented wrong link detection so that link candidates were removed when their logged values were below a certain threshold, different of a certain type or when the source code file did not match the aforementioned criteria. We choose the threshold, the type and the combination of thresholds and source code filter criteria to optimize the precision of the links created by IL and minimize the effect on the recall.

5 Results

This section reports the results of evaluations along with answering the RQs.

5.1 Part 1: Precision and Recall for the Initial Evaluation

Table 2 gives an overview of the evaluations performed as described in Sect. 4.3. Our approach created 372 link candidates, 212 of them were wrong. 57 correct links were not found. We can answer RQ_1 as follows: The precision for our IL approach is 43.0% and recall is 73.7%

Table 2. Precision and recall for IL and IR

Approach	GS links	Link Cand.	Correct links	Wrong links	Not found	Precision	Recall	$F_{0.5}$	F_1
IL	217	372	160	212	57	0.430	0.737	0.469	0.543
$IR_{VSM(0.3)}$	217	191	38	153	179	0.199	0.175	0.194	0.186
$IR_{VSM(0.2)}$	217	642	104	538	113	0.162	0.480	0.187	0.242
$IR_{LSI(0.1)}$	217	102	35	67	182	0.343	0.161	0.280	0.219
$IR_{LSI(0.05)}$	217	363	77	286	140	0.212	0.355	0.231	0.266

We can answer RQ_2 looking at the different IR variants with different thresholds: with very low thresholds the best achievable precision is 34.3% (LSI(0.1))

Table 3. Duration based IL improvement

Dur. (sec)	GS links	Link Cand. All	Link Cand. Edit	Correct All	Correct Edit	Wrong All	Wrong Edit	Not found	Precision All	Precision Edit	Recall All	Recall Edit	$F_{0.5}$	F_1
1	217	372	220	160	107	212	113	57	0.430	0.486	0.737	0.493	0.488	0.490
10	217	317	199	144	104	173	95	73	0.454	0.523	0.664	0.479	0.513	0.500
60	217	231	167	113	90	118	77	104	0.489	0.539	0.521	0.415	0.508	0.469
180	217	183	142	93	78	90	64	124	0.508	0.549	0.429	0.359	0.497	0.435
300	217	154	122	81	70	73	52	136	0.526	0.574	0.373	0.323	0.496	0.413

and the best achievable recall 48.0% (VSM(0.2)). These results are bad compared to IL and bad compared to typical IR-results on structured data [9] (cf. Sect. 2.1).

As the IL precision was much lower than expected, we investigated whether there was a problem with the gold standard. We therefore checked manually 113 wrong links which resulted from edit interactions (see next section) and confirmed that these links are really wrong. We concluded that the developers had not used the interaction logging properly and worked on code not relevant for the activated user story. This happened typically for smaller code changes on the fly beside the implementation of the activated user story. So for example developers updated a file from which they had copied some code, but they did not activate the requirement the change should have been associated with.

5.2 Part 2: Precision and Recall Using Wrong Link Detection

In this section we report on the answers to RQ_3. Table 3 shows the results for focusing on edit interactions and different minimal duration. The first row corresponds to our IL approach without any restrictions. It shows that by focusing on edit interactions the precision slightly improves from 43.0% to 48.6%. As focus on edit always improved the precision a little, we only report the F-measure for IL focused on edits and we only describe these numbers in the following text. When increasing the minimum duration for an interaction precision can be

Table 4. Frequency based IL improvement

Frequency	GS links	Link Cand. All	Link Cand. Edit	Correct All	Correct Edit	Wrong All	Wrong Edit	Not found	Precision All	Precision Edit	Recall All	Recall Edit	$F_{0.5}$	F_1
1	217	372	220	160	107	212	113	57	0.430	0.486	0.737	0.493	0.488	0.490
2	217	314	220	142	107	172	113	75	0.452	0.486	0.654	0.493	0.488	0.490
5	217	220	191	113	98	107	93	104	0.514	0.513	0.521	0.452	0.499	0.480
10	217	181	169	99	93	82	76	118	0.547	0.550	0.456	0.429	0.521	0.482
20	217	158	151	90	87	68	64	127	0.570	0.576	0.415	0.401	0.530	0.473
100	217	86	86	59	59	27	27	158	0.686	0.686	0.272	0.272	0.526	0.389

improved up to 57.4%. This impairs of course recall. We show at the end of this section how recall can be improved by using the code structure.

Table 4 shows the results for different minimal frequencies within one interaction log. Again row one gives the numbers for the original approach. Here the improvement is stronger leading to a precision of 68.6% for a frequency of 100. In particular, by this restriction all select interactions are removed. However, recall is even more impaired.

Table 5. Developer specific differences

Developer	GS links	Link Cand.		Correct		Wrong		Not found	Precision		Recall		$F_{0.5}$	F_1
		All	Edit	All	Edit	All	Edit		All	Edit	All	Edit		
Dev_1	37	41	17	19	6	22	11	18	0.463	0.353	0.514	0.162	0.286	0.222
Dev_2	128	252	155	110	79	142	76	18	0.437	0.510	0.859	0.617	0.528	0.558
Dev_3	52	77	46	30	21	47	25	22	0.390	0.457	0.577	0.404	0.445	0.429

Table 5 shows the distribution for the three developers. One can see that developer Dev_2 was the most active and Dev_3 contributed more than Dev_1. However, for all three the interactions led to more wrong than correct links. So precision does not differ much.

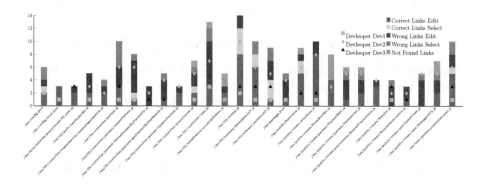

Fig. 3. Code files which had interactions in 3 or more user stories

Figure 3 shows the 28 code files which have been touched in interactions for three or more user stories. Furthermore it shows how often each developer touched these files. The developer distribution shows that some of the files have been touched by different user stories from one developer and some from several developers. One can see that only three out of 28 files have only wrong link candidates. Also files which have many link candidates sometimes have many correct link candidates and sometimes not. So there is no clear pattern that these files are the reason for more wrong link candidates.

Table 6. Source code based improvements

Code Res.	GS links	Link Cand. All	Edit	Correct All	Edit	Wrong All	Edit	Not found	Precision All	Edit	Recall All	Edit	$F_{0.5}$	F_1
none	217	372	220	160	107	212	113	57	0.430	0.486	0.737	0.493	0.488	0.490
>3 US	217	208	92	83	43	125	49	134	0.399	0.467	0.382	0.198	0.368	0.278
Only .js	186	327	203	129	99	198	104	57	0.394	0.488	0.694	0.532	0.496	0.509
Con.	217	274	169	147	99	127	70	70	0.536	0.586	0.677	0.456	0.554	0.513

This is confirmed in Table 6 which shows the results for the different source code restrictions with the first row showing the numbers without restrictions. The second row shows the precision for code which was touched by interactions in three or more user stories. Here the precision increased slightly to 46.7%. The third row shows a precision 48.8% when only looking at Javascript files. The best precision of 58.6% could be achieved when removing code files which were not connected by source code relations to other code files of the same user story.

When looking at the individual techniques for detecting wrong links we thus can answer RQ3 as follows: The best precision 68.6% can be achieved with a minimum frequency of 100. This leads to a recall of 27.2%. The second best precision 58.2% can be achieved with removing files which are not connected. This leads to a recall of 45.6%.

Table 7. Combination of improvements

Code Con.	Freq.	Code Struct	GS links	Link Cand. All	Edit	Correct All	Edit	Wrong All	Edit	Not found	Precision All	Edit	Recall All	Edit	$F_{0.5}$	F_1
True	20	0	217	124	123	82	82	42	41	135	0.661	0.667	0.378	0.378	0.578	0.482
True	20	4	217	151	148	101	101	50	47	116	0.669	0.682	0.465	0.465	0.624	0.553
True	100	0	217	71	71	47	47	24	24	170	0.662	0.662	0.217	0.217	0.469	0.326
True	100	4	217	87	87	58	58	29	29	159	0.667	0.667	0.267	0.267	0.513	0.382

We therefore also investigated in the combination of these two techniques. We first removed the not connected code files and then restricted the remaining interaction links wrt. frequency. Table 7 shows the resulting precision of 66.7% for frequency 20 ($F_{0.5}$ is 0.578) and 66.2% for frequency 100 ($F_{0.5}$ is 0.469).

So for frequency 100 precision decreased when looking at connected files. For frequency 20 we get the best $F_{0.5}$-measure of all evaluations. We applied the recall improvement (IL_i) to both settings. Again frequency 20 yielded the best results.

Altogether RQ3 can be answered as follows: with the wrong link detection techniques we could improve precision from 43.0% up to 68.2% (increase of 25.2%). The recall decreased from 73.7% without wrong link detection to 46.5%. This yields the best $F_{0.5}$-measure of 0.624.

5.3   Discussion

In the following we discuss all of our hypotheses wrt. IL and the rationale for the detection techniques. The bad precision compared to our previous study for IL clearly indicates that the developers did not use the recording in a disciplined way. The detailed evaluations for the developers did not show big differences, so this was true for all three developers. We tried several detection techniques for wrong links: Focus on edit interactions, duration, source code owner, source code type and removing of files with many links did not yield considerable precision improvement. Only frequency and removal of non-connected files improved the precision considerably up to almost 70% with recall above 45%. (cf. Sect. 2.1). For our purpose they are not sufficient, as this still means that our approach would create thirty percent links not directly usable for the developers.

We thus see three further directions of research. (a) We can try to come up with further techniques to detect wrong links which yield a precision close to 100%. (b) We can try to support the developers in applying interaction recording in a more disciplined way. The results of our previous paper [11] on the Mylyn project showed that it is possible for developers to use interaction recording in a disciplined way. It could be that students are particularly bad with this discipline. (c) Instead of automatic link creation support we can generate links through IL as recommendations to the developers.

In previous research [6] we had used more coarse-grained VCS change logs to create links and had given the developers different means to create links based on the logs during a sprint or at the end of a project. We could use our IL approach to give recommendations to the developers at different points in the sprint or project which links to create based on their interactions. Then developers have to detect the wrong links themselves. However, we would like to avoid such overhead for the developers as much as possible.

6   Threats to Validity

In this section we discuss the threats to validity of our study. The internal validity is threatened as manual validation of trace links in the gold standard was performed by the students working as developers in a project context of our research group. However, this ensured that the experts created the gold standard. Also the evaluation of the links was performed after the project had already been finished so that there was no conflict of interest for the students to influence their grading.

When comparing the results achieved with our approach to IR the setup of the IR algorithms is a crucial factor. Wrt. preprocessing we performed all common steps including the identifier splitting which is specific to our used data set. However, the low threshold values impair the results for the precision of IR. Thus, further comparison of IL and IR in which higher threshold values are possible (e.g. with more structured issue descriptions) is necessary.

The external validity depends on the availability of interaction logs and respective tooling and usage of the tooling by developers. The generalizability based on one student project is clearly limited. In the Mylyn open source project, used in our last study, the developers used their own implemented interaction logging approach and thus worked very disciplined. It is very likely that the student developers did not apply the interaction logging as disciplined as the Mylyn developers, since they had no awareness for it. Interaction recording is not yet applied often in industry. So it is an open question how disciplined interaction logging can be achieved.

7   Related Work

In our previous paper [11] we discuss other work on IR and interaction logging such as the systematic literature review of Borg on IR trace link creation [2] or Konopkas approach [12] to derive links between code through interaction logs. Most similar to our work is the approach of Omoronyia et al. [20] who capture interactions between source code and structured requirements specified as use cases. We adopt their approach using select and edit events for trace link creation. In contrast to our goal their tool support focuses on visualizing the trace links after a task has been performed and not on direct availability and usage of trace links.

For this paper most relevant is research on the quality of recorded interaction. We only found a very recent study of Soh et al. [22] studying interactions recorded in Mylyn. They show that the assumptions that the time recorded for an interaction is the time spent on a task and that an edit event recorded by Mylyn corresponds to modification in the code are not true. They could detect these differences by comparing the interactions and videos capturing developer behavior in a quasi-experiment. These differences are not due to any misbehavior of the developers, but only due to Mylyns recording algorithm. For example searching and scrolling is not counted in the time spent and idle time is not treated correctly. In this study these problems do not apply as we used a different logging environment. We are not aware of any noise problems with this environment. Similar to their work, we also use duration as an indicator for a relevant event.

8   Conclusion and Outlook

In this paper we investigated the precision and recall of our IL-approach for trace link creation in a student project. Contrary to our previous work the original approach only achieved a precision of about 50%. We therefore implemented several techniques for the detection of wrong links: Focus on edit interactions, duration, source code owner, source code type and removing of files with many links did not yield considerable precision improvement. Only frequency and removal of non-connected files improved the precision considerably up to almost 70% with above 45% recall. As discussed in Sect. 5.3 this is not sufficient for our purpose.

We are starting to apply the IL-approach in another student project. In this project we will make sure through regular inspections that the students apply the approach in a disciplined way. We will use the two best improvement techniques as quick indicators for undisciplined usage and interview the students for reasons of such usage. Given sufficient precision we plan to also create the links immediately after each interaction and observe the use of the links in the project.

Acknowledgment. We thank the students of the project for the effort.

References

1. Baeza-Yates, R., Ribeiro-Neto, B.: Modern Information Retrieval, 2nd edn. Pearson/Addison-Wesley, Harlow, Munich (2011)
2. Borg, M., Runeson, P., Ardö, A.: Recovering from a decade: a systematic mapping of information retrieval approaches to software traceability. Empir. Softw. Eng. **19**(6), 1–52 (2013)
3. Briand, L., Falessi, D., Nejati, S., Sabetzadeh, M., Yue, T.: Traceability and SysML design slices to support safety inspections. ACM ToSEM **23**(1), 1–43 (2014)
4. De Lucia, A., Di Penta, M., Oliveto, R.: Improving source code lexicon via traceability and information retrieval. IEEE TSE **37**(2), 205–227 (2011)
5. De Lucia, A., Fasano, F., Oliveto, R., Tortora, G.: Recovering traceability links in software artifact management systems using information retrieval methods. ACM ToSEM **16**(4), 1–50 (2007)
6. Delater, A., Paech, B.: Tracing requirements and source code during software development: an empirical study. In: International Symposium on Empirical Software Engineering and Measurement, Baltimore, MD, USA, pp. 25–34. IEEE/ACM, October 2013
7. Falessi, D., Di Penta, M., Canfora, G., Cantone, G.: Estimating the number of remaining links in traceability recovery. Empir. Softw. Eng. **22**(3), 996–1027 (2016)
8. Gotel, O., Cleland-Huang, J., Hayes, J.H., Zisman, A., Egyed, A., Grunbacher, P., Antoniol, G.: The quest for ubiquity: a roadmap for software and systems traceability research. In: RE Conference, pp. 71–80. IEEE, September 2012
9. Hayes, J., Dekhtyar, A., Sundaram, S.: Advancing candidate link generation for requirements tracing: the study of methods. IEEE TSE **32**(1), 4–19 (2006)
10. Hübner, P.: Quality improvements for trace links between source code and requirements. In: REFSQ Workshops, Doctoral Symposium, Research Method Track, and Poster Track, Gothenburg, Sweden, vol. 1564. CEUR-WS (2016)
11. Hübner, P., Paech, B.: Using interaction data for continuous creation of trace links between source code and requirements in issue tracking systems. In: Grünbacher, P., Perini, A. (eds.) REFSQ 2017. LNCS, vol. 10153, pp. 291–307. Springer, Cham (2017). https://doi.org/10.1007/978-3-319-54045-0_21
12. Konopka, M., Navrat, P., Bielikova, M.: Poster: discovering code dependencies by harnessing developer's activity. In: ICSE, pp. 801–802. IEEE/ACM, May 2015
13. Kuang, H., Nie, J., Hu, H., Rempel, P., Lü, J., Egyed, A., Mäder, P.: Analyzing closeness of code dependencies for improving IR-based traceability recovery. In: SANER, pp. 68–78. IEEE, February 2017

14. Kuang, H., Mäder, P., Hu, H., Ghabi, A., Huang, L., Lü, J., Egyed, A.: Can method data dependencies support the assessment of traceability between requirements and source code? J. Softw. Evol. Process **27**(11), 838–866 (2015)

15. Maalej, W., Kurtanovic, Z., Felfernig, A.: What stakeholders need to know about requirements. In: EmpiRE, pp. 64–71. IEEE, August 2014

16. Mäder, P., Egyed, A.: Do developers benefit from requirements traceability when evolving and maintaining a software system? Empir. Softw. Eng. **20**(2), 413–441 (2015)

17. Merten, T., Falisy, M., Hübner, P., Quirchmayr, T., Bürsner, S., Paech, B.: Software feature request detection in issue tracking systems. In: RE Conference. IEEE, September 2016

18. Merten, T., Krämer, D., Mager, B., Schell, P., Bürsner, S., Paech, B.: Do information retrieval algorithms for automated traceability perform effectively on issue tracking system data? In: Daneva, M., Pastor, O. (eds.) REFSQ 2016. LNCS, vol. 9619, pp. 45–62. Springer, Cham (2016). https://doi.org/10.1007/978-3-319-30282-9_4

19. Niu, N., Mahmoud, A.: Enhancing candidate link generation for requirements tracing: the cluster hypothesis revisited. In: RE Conference, pp. 81–90. IEEE, September 2012

20. Omoronyia, I., Sindre, G., Roper, M., Ferguson, J., Wood, M.: Use case to source code traceability: the developer navigation view point. In: RE Conference, Los Alamitos, CA, USA, pp. 237–242. IEEE, August 2009

21. Seiler, M., Paech, B.: Using tags to support feature management across issue tracking systems and version control systems. In: Grünbacher, P., Perini, A. (eds.) REFSQ 2017. LNCS, vol. 10153, pp. 174–180. Springer, Cham (2017). https://doi.org/10.1007/978-3-319-54045-0_13

22. Soh, Z., Khomh, F., Guéhéneuc, Y.G., Antoniol, G.: Noise in Mylyn interaction traces and its impact on developers and recommendation systems. Empir. Softw. Eng. 1–48 (2017). https://doi.org/10.1007/s10664-017-9529-x

Second-Guessing in Tracing Tasks Considered Harmful?

Bhushan Chitre[1], Jane Huffman Hayes[1(✉)], and Alexander Dekhtyar[2]

[1] Computer Science, University of Kentucky, Lexington, KY, USA
{bhushan.chitre,jane.hayes}@uky.edu
[2] CSSE, California Polytechnic State University, San Luis Obispo, CA, USA
dekhtyar@calpoly.edu

Abstract. **[Context and motivation]** Trace matrices are lynch pins for the development of mission- and safety-critical software systems and are useful for all software systems, yet automated methods for recovering trace links are far from perfect. This limitation makes the job of human analysts who must vet recovered trace links more difficult. **[Question/Problem]** Earlier studies suggested that certain analyst behaviors when performing trace recovery tasks lead to decreased accuracy of recovered trace relationships. We propose a three-step experimental study to: (a) determine if there really are behaviors that lead to errors of judgment for analysts, (b) enhance the requirements tracing software to curtail such behaviors, and (c) determine if curtailing such behaviors results in increased accuracy. **[Principal ideas/results]** We report on a preliminary study we undertook in which we modified the user interface of RETRO.NET to curtail two behaviors indicated by the earlier work. We report on observed results. **[Contributions]** We describe and discuss a major study of potentially unwanted analyst behaviors and present results of a preliminary study toward determining if curbing these behaviors with enhancements to tracing software leads to fewer human errors.

Keywords: Requirements tracing · Study of the analyst · Trace vetting
RETRO.NET · User interface · Empirical study

1 Introduction and Motivation

Automated tracing, generating or recovering the relationship between artifacts of the software development process, has been well researched over the past 15 years [4], but this automation doesn't come without inherent costs. One such cost is the need for human analysts to interact with the results of the automated methods. What we currently know about such interactions is that they tend to end disappointingly [1, 2, 6]. As long as we are using automated tracing methods for safety- and mission-critical systems, we must have humans vet the links. Therefore, we need to figure out how to make humans more accurate as they work with the results of automated methods. In prior studies we noticed some unwanted behaviors [1, 2, 6]. Can we curb them? Will curbing them yield fewer human errors?

© Springer International Publishing AG, part of Springer Nature 2018
E. Kamsties et al. (Eds.): REFSQ 2018, LNCS 10753, pp. 92–98, 2018.
https://doi.org/10.1007/978-3-319-77243-1_6

A trace matrix is a collection of trace links, defined as "a specified association between a pair of artifacts, one comprising the source artifact and one comprising the target artifact." by the Center of Excellence for Software and System Traceability (COEST) [3]. A plethora of researchers have designed techniques for automatically or semi-automatically generating trace matrices, many discussed in a comprehensive survey by Borg [4]. Most of the focus in that work was on improving the quality of the candidate trace matrix, the matrix generated by a software method. While that work continues, recent work has segued into study of the analyst who works with the candidate matrix to generate the final trace matrix — the one that is used in application.

A typical trace tool, such as RETRO.NET used in this work [5], displays the candidate trace matrix and shows the list of source (high level) elements, and the list of candidate target (low level) elements that were automatically mapped to the source element. The texts of all elements can also be viewed. The key function of a tracing tool is to allow the analyst to vet individual candidate links.

Cuddeback et al. [1] and Dekhtyar et al. [2] studied the work of analysts with candidate trace matrices produced by automated software. The analysts were presented a candidate trace matrix and were asked to evaluate the individual links and correct any errors of omission or commission. The accuracy of candidate trace matrices varied from analyst to analyst — from high-accuracy matrices that contained few omitted links and few false positives to low-accuracy ones which contained many errors of both types. The studies found that analysts working with high accuracy candidate traces tended to decrease the accuracy — i.e., introduce false links into the matrix and remove true links, whereas the analysts who had low accuracy matrices tended to improve the accuracy significantly[1]. A follow-up study collected logs of analyst activity during the tracing process, and looked at behaviors that correlated with improved or decreased accuracy [6]. While that study did not have enough data points to allow for statistical significance of the results, the authors observed a number of analyst behaviors that tended to lead to errors of judgement. Specifically, two behaviors briefly described below were observed.

Long time to decide. When analysts took unusually long (for their pace) time to decide whether a candidate link needed to be kept in the trace, *they tended to make an incorrect decision* [6].

Revisiting a link (backtracking). When analysts revisited a link on which they already entered a decision and reversed that decision, *they tended to err* [6].

Our motivation for the continuing study of analyst behavior in tracing tasks comes from the key observations from the prior work [1, 2, 4, 6]. On one hand, the lack of traceability as a byproduct of development in large software projects demonstrates a clear need for accurate automatic tracing methods [4]. At the same time, human analysts, when asked to curate automatically obtained traceability relations, make mistakes and decrease the overall accuracy of the trace [1, 2]. We observe that one possible way to resolve this, and to improve the accuracy of curated trace relations is, potentially, to curb analyst behaviors that result in errors. In fact, psychologists studying human decision-making have observed that humans tend to operate in one of two decision-making

---

[1] As reported earlier [2], the accuracy of the starting RTM affected the changes in precision, recall, and f2-measure, and the final precision in statistically significant ways, but did not affect final recall or final f2-measure in statistically significant ways.

systems — System 1 (S1) (or fast, instinctive thinking) or System 2 (S2) (slow, deliberate, logical thinking) [8]. The observed behaviors leading to decrease in accuracy belong to System 2. This motivates an additional research question expressed below.

2   Curbing Unwanted Analyst Behavior

The latter observation serves as the inspiration for our next step in the study of the behavior of human analysts. In this section we discuss the overall plan for the study, as well as the preliminary work we conducted.

2.1   Research Preview

The study we are planning to undertake consists of three key research questions.

1. **RQ1:** *Are there analyst behaviors that tend to reliably lead to analysts making errors, and where do these behaviors fall on the Kahneman's thinking system dichotomy* [8]*?* We hypothesize that such behaviors can be observed as statistically significant. We additionally conjecture that such behaviors would correspond to the decision-making System 2 [8].
2. **RQ2:** *What software enhancements for automated tracing tools can be designed and developed to curb the discovered unwanted behaviors?* We hypothesize that each unwanted behavior can be curbed via UI and workflow changes to the requirements tracing software.
3. **RQ3:** *Is there an improvement in the accuracy of final trace matrices constructed by the analysts using software with the implemented enhancements?* We hypothesize that the software enhancements will improve the accuracy (i.e., decrease the number of errors that analysts make in vetting candidate links and in discovery of omitted links).

The basic outline of the study is as follows.

Discovery of analyst behaviors. In the first stage we plan to replicate the tracing experiment of Kong et al. [6] in which we collected activity logs from a group of analysts performing a tracing task with a version of RETRO.NET enhanced with event logging. The original study included only a few data points, and did not allow the authors to observe any specific harmful behaviors with any degree of statistical rigor. Our intent is to collect significantly more data points (i.e., logs documenting analyst's work with a tracing tool on a tracing task), so that log analysis may reveal clear analyst behaviors that either tend to lead to errors, or tend to reliably improve accuracy, and provide more than just anecdotal evidence in support of such observations.

RETRO.NET logs information about individual analyst interactions with the software — keys pressed, elements selected, linking decisions made and confirmed, searches performed, etc. Each log record is keyed by a timestamp, making it easy to map analyst behavior, and in particular to map their correct and erroneous decisions along the time axis.

Initial replicated experiments were conducted in Spring 2017 and Fall 2017 quarters. We have been able to collect over 80 data points, and are currently in the process of analyzing the results to see if the prior observations [1, 2] are confirmed. In the immediate future, we plan to replicate the analysis of Kong et al. [6] on the 80+ tracing logs we now have.

The first observed behaviors leading to errors belonged to Kahneman's System 2 (slow and deliberate) way of thinking. This leads us to ask the following question during the discovery process: *is RTM analysis a process that can be performed best within the System 1 (fast, intuitive)* [8] *of decision-making?* To answer this question, we can classify the observed harmful behaviors within the S1 — S2 dichotomy.

Development of software enhancements. Once we identify analyst behaviors that tend to lead to errors in link vetting, we plan to develop software-supported strategies for curbing such unwanted behaviors. For each behavior discovered, we will design one or more features to enhance RETRO.NET in a way that would reduce behavior incidence. We will explore the following approaches:

1. *Warnings.* This is a very basic approach: detect an unwanted behavior, and as soon as it is observed produce a warning within the tracing software suggesting that the analyst reconsider.
2. *Prohibitions.* This approach starts the same way as a warning with the detection of the unwanted behavior, but instead of simply producing a warning, the software will simply refuse to grant the analyst the ability to complete the unwanted behavior.
3. *Restructuring.* Certain unwanted behaviors may be eliminated or reduced if the way the analyst interacts with the tracing software is changed, and the use cases where such unwanted behaviors were observed are altered in significant ways. An example of a restructuring solution may be a change from allowing the analyst to review candidate links in arbitrary order to an interaction model where the analyst is shown each link once in a predefined order and is not allowed to revisit a link.

Study of the impact. We want to know the answers to two key questions:

1. *Do software enhancements designed to curb unwanted behaviors **actually curb** these behaviors?*
2. *Is the decrease in unwanted behaviors accompanied by a decrease in the number of errors analyst make?* (and thus by an increase in the accuracy of the trace relation).

To answer these questions we plan to conduct a second replication of the prior study [6], only this time we will use control and experimental groups of analysts. The control group will work with the standard version of the RETRO.NET tool, without any enhancements implemented in Stage 2 of the study. The experimental group will work with a version of RETRO.NET enhanced with specific solutions for curbing unwanted behavior. To test different ways of curbing the same behavior, we may need to conduct multiple rounds of such study.

2.2 Preliminary Study

To test the feasibility of our approach we conducted a preliminary study. We briefly describe the structure of the study and its results below.

Unwanted analyst behaviors. The study concentrated on the two analyst behaviors described in Sect. 1 (a) taking an *unusually* long amount of time to make a decision on a candidate link, and (b) revising an explicitly conveyed decision on a link. These were the two clearest behaviors observed previously [6] that tended to result in errors.

Software enhancements. We elected to start with very simple modifications to RETRO.NET. For each behavior, RETRO.NET was enhanced with code working in the background designed to detect it, and with UI elements that would produce a warning message to the analyst when the behavior was discovered. Specifically, the enhanced RETRO.NET, upon detecting either of the two behaviors, displayed a pop-up window informing the user that their behavior could lead to an error. In the case of the user trying to revisit a decision, the user is given an option to backtrack. In both cases, the user can also dismiss the prompt and simply continue with their action. In making decisions about the enhancements of RETRO.NET we tried to make the changes simple and non-prohibitive. We understand that UI design principles suggest that pop-up messages that disrupt the flow of user interaction with the software may reduce productivity and decrease user satisfaction with the software and its UI. At the same time, we wanted the warnings in our first experiment to be "blatant," easy to see, and hard to miss. We took the risk of implementing the warnings via the pop-up message UI elements fully realizing that we may be sacrificing some user satisfaction with the software.

The study. A total of 14 subjects participated in a preliminary study conducted in Spring of 2017 at the University of Kentucky. Five (5) subjects were in the control group and worked with non-enhanced RETRO.NET. Nine (9) subjects were in the experimental group and worked with the RETRO.NET version enhanced with backtracking and taking-too-long warnings[2]. Each subject received a brief training session on their version of RETRO.NET using the same toy dataset. Later, they were presented with the ChangeStyle dataset [1, 2] to trace. All subjects started with the same initial candidate trace matrix. We measured the *precision, recall, f2-measure,* and *lag* [7] of the resulting trace matrix the subjects submitted and the *time* it took them to complete the work. The results of the preliminary study are shown below.

2.3 Preliminary Study Results

In our preliminary study, the experimental group showed higher mean precision (15.6% vs. 8.3%), higher mean recall (96% vs. 77.6%), and higher mean f2-measure (0.329 vs. 0.262), as well as better (lower) lag (1.85 vs. 2.55) for the submitted traces. Only two mean values were better for the control group: the mean time (75 min versus 82) and the change in true

---

[2] Originally, the control and the experimental groups were of the same size, but we had a significantly larger number of non-completions in the control group.

positives was higher (1.6 versus 1.222). This could be explained by the extra prompts that were shown to the user: (a) that had to at least be dismissed, and (b) that had to be at most obeyed.

3   Discussion and Conclusions

The preliminary study tentatively indicates that basic prompts (discussed in Sect. 2.1 as warnings) may suffice to move analysts away from undesired behaviors without having to resort to more restrictive measures, but at the expense of time taken to perform tracing. The main, and very useful, outcome of the preliminary study is a list of items that we must add to our future study: collect the number of times that prompts appear, collect the amount of time that an analyst takes when dismissing and reacting to the prompt, track the action taken by the analyst after a prompt, track the number of false positives (true negatives, false positives, and false negatives) added and removed, and potentially track each individual true positive link displayed by RETRO.NET to learn its final disposition.

As mentioned in Sect. 2.1, we envision a three stage approach to investigating our main research question: can we help analysts vet trace matrices? For the first phase of the study, discovery of the analyst behaviors leading to errors, we plan to undertake studies (and have already undertaken some of them) using a software tracing tool in order to discover what behaviors analysts exhibit when tracing. We posit that we will discover good behaviors (those that lead to improved trace matrices) as well as unwanted behaviors - those that lead to errors. Our early work discussed above is a first step toward addressing the second of the three phases: enhance tracing software to curtail unwanted behaviors and learn whether or not the software enhancements do indeed curtail them. For phase three, we plan to undertake a study similar to that of our preliminary study, but with a wider scope. We plan to collect richer data from significantly larger control and experimental groups. We also envision undertaking a statistical study of our data, as we will have sufficient data points to permit such analysis. It is our hope that these three stages of our study will contribute to our field and more importantly to software tracing tools put in the hands of practitioners so that analyst tracing work won't end in disappointment, but rather in effective and efficient use of the analysts' time.

Acknowledgment. We thank Dr. Dan Berry for insightful comments and suggestions on prior versions that resulted in a greatly improved paper. We thank all participants from upper division software engineering classes who took their time to participate in our study. We thank NASA and NSF as prior grants funded the development of RETRO.NET. We thank Jody Larsen, the developer of RETRO.NET. We thank NSF for partially funding this work under grants CCF-1511117 and CNS- 1642134.

References

1. Cuddeback, D., Dekhtyar, A., Hayes, J.H.: Automated requirements traceability: the study of human analysts. In: Proceedings of IEEE International Conference on requirements Engineering (RE), Sydney, Australia, pp. 231–240, September 2010

2. Dekhtyar, A., Dekhtyar, O., Holden, J., Hayes, J.H., Cuddeback, D., Kong, W.-K.: On human analyst performance in assisted requirements tracing: statistical analysis. In: The Proceedings of IEEE International Conference on Requirements Engineering (RE) 2011, Trento, Italy (2011)
3. Huang, J., Gotel, O., Zisman, A.: Software and Systems Traceability. Springer, London (2014). https://doi.org/10.1007/978-1-4471-2239-5
4. Borg, M., Runeson, P., Ardö, A.: Recovering from a decade: a systematic mapping of information retrieval approaches to software traceability. Empirical Softw. Eng. **19**(6), 1565–1616 (2014)
5. Hayes, J.H., Dekhtyar, A., Sundaram, S., Holbrook, A., Vadlamudi, S., April, A.: REquirements TRacing On target (RETRO): improving software maintenance through traceability recovery. Innov. Syst. Softw. Eng. NASA J. (ISSE) **3**(3), 193–202 (2007)
6. Kong, W.-K., Hayes, J., Dekhtyar, A., Holden, J.: How do we trace requirements? An initial study of analyst behavior in trace validation tasks. In: Proceedings of the 4th International Workshop on Cooperative and Human Aspects of Software Engineering, (CHASE 2011) (2011)
7. Hayes, J., Dekhtyar, A., Sundaram, S.: Advancing candidate link generation for requirements tracing: the study of methods. IEEE Trans. Softw. Eng. **32**(1), 4–19 (2006)
8. Kahneman, D.: Thinking, Fast and Slow. Farrar, Straus, New York (2011)

Taming Ambiguity

Interview Review: An Empirical Study on Detecting Ambiguities in Requirements Elicitation Interviews

Paola Spoletini[1](✉), Alessio Ferrari[2](✉) (iD), Muneera Bano[3,4], Didar Zowghi[4], and Stefania Gnesi[2]

[1] Kennesaw State University, Kennesaw, GA, USA
pspoleti@kennesaw.edu
[2] CNR-ISTI, Pisa, Italy
{alessio.ferrari,stefania.gnesi}@isti.cnr.it
[3] Swinburne University of Technology, Melbourne, Australia
mbano@swin.edu.au
[4] University of Technology Sydney, Ultimo, Australia
{muneera.bano,didar.zowghi}@uts.edu.au

Abstract. [**Context and Motivation**] Ambiguities identified during requirements elicitation interviews can be used by the requirements analyst as triggers for additional questions and, consequently, for disclosing further – possibly *tacit* – knowledge. Therefore, every unidentified ambiguity may be a missed opportunity to collect additional information. [**Question/problem**] Ambiguities are not always easy to recognize, especially during highly interactive activities such as requirements elicitation interviews. Moreover, since different persons can perceive ambiguous situations differently, the unique perspective of the analyst in the interview might not be enough to identify all ambiguities. [**Principal idea/results**] To maximize the number of ambiguities recognized in interviews, this paper proposes a protocol to conduct reviews of requirements elicitation interviews. In the proposed protocol, the interviews are audio recorded and the recordings are inspected by both the analyst who performed the interview and another reviewer. The idea is to use the identified cases of ambiguity to create questions for the follow-up interviews. Our empirical evaluation of this protocol involves 42 students from Kennesaw State University and University of Technology Sydney. The study shows that, during the review, the analyst and the other reviewer identify 68% of the total number of ambiguities discovered, while 32% were identified during the interviews. Furthermore, the ambiguities identified by analysts and other reviewers during the review significantly differ from each other. [**Contribution**] Our results indicate that interview reviews allow the identification of a considerable number of undetected ambiguities, and can potentially be highly beneficial to discover unexpressed information in future interviews.

Keywords: Requirements elicitation · Interviews · Ambiguities
Tacit knowledge · Reviews

© Springer International Publishing AG, part of Springer Nature 2018
E. Kamsties et al. (Eds.): REFSQ 2018, LNCS 10753, pp. 101–118, 2018.
https://doi.org/10.1007/978-3-319-77243-1_7

1   Introduction

Requirements elicitation interviews are often used as starting point of the requirements elicitation process [1–4]. Interviews are often perceived by students and novice analysts as an easy tool to use, but they can be affected by several factors, that can prevent the analyst to elicit all the relevant knowledge – including *tacit knowledge* [5] – during the elicitation process. Tacit knowledge is system relevant information that remains unexpressed often because it belongs to the unconscious level of processing of the customer or is too difficult to be properly described, and it therefore remains undocumented. Techniques were developed to facilitate the disclosure of tacit knowledge [6–9]. However, its detection is still an open problem in requirements engineering [6], and specific techniques are required to elicit it.

In our previous work [7], we have highlighted the relationship between ambiguity and tacit knowledge in requirements elicitation interviews. More precisely, we have shown that, differently from what happens in written requirements where ambiguity is a threat to the quality of requirements, ambiguity could be a powerful tool in oral synchronous communication. Indeed, when an ambiguity is detected in the words of a customer *during* an interview, the analyst asks additional follow-up questions that may lead to the identification of unexpressed, system-relevant aspects [10]. Unfortunately, given the highly interactive nature of requirements elicitation interviews, it is not always easy to recognize ambiguous statements during the interview, that are likely to be identified in second hearing of the interview.

This observation suggests conducting reviews at requirements elicitation interview process. Such a proposal would be a step forward in addressing the challenge highlighted by Salger: *"Software requirements are based on flawed 'upstream' requirements and reviews on requirements specifications are thus in vain"* [11]. Indeed, currently reviews of software process artifacts do not include any artifact before requirements documents [12]. Even if reviews are considered an effective practice to improve the quality of products [13–16], and the benefits of requirements reviews have been highlighted by several studies, especially for what concerns the identification of defects in requirements specifications [14,17,18], challenges remain for their widespread application [11,19].

For these reasons, we propose to add a review of the recording of the elicitation interviews. In our proposal, we include two types of reviews: one performed by the analyst, to give her the possibility to more carefully listen to the interview, and a second one conducted by another analyst, called *reviewer*, who will analyze the interview from an additional perspective. The rationale behind the proposal is that ambiguities in the words of a customer can be perceived in different ways by different analysts, as has already been observed for ambiguities in written requirements [20,21]. In the proposed method, the analyst performs the interview with the customer, and audio records the dialogue. The recording is then reviewed by the analyst and an external reviewer, who annotate the identified ambiguities, together with the fragment of conversation that generated it, and list the questions that they would have asked in the interview to disambiguate the annotated situation. The questions are used for further clarifications in future interactions with the customer. In [22], we have explored the feasibility and the benefits of this idea through an exploratory study that gave encouraging results. In this paper we aim at clearly defining the review protocol and assess its effectiveness through a controlled experiment performed with two independent groups of students from University of Technology Sydney (UTS) and Kennesaw State University (KSU).

The remainder of the paper is structured as follows. In Sect. 2, we summarize related works concerning ambiguity in RE with particular focus on their classification in oral communication, and review techniques, including a brief description of the result from our exploratory study. In Sect. 3, the controlled experiment is presented together with the developed review protocol. Sections 4 and 5 present the results of the controlled experiment and a discussion on its limitations. In Sect. 6, we provide final remarks and we describe the next planned step in our research.

2   Background

This section provides background information on topics relevant to our study. More precisely, Sects. 2.1 and 2.2 describe the related work on ambiguities in RE in general, and in interviews in particular. Section 2.3 describes the existing work on reviews in requirements engineering, and, finally, Sect. 2.4 briefly presents our work on interview reviews, including encouraging results from an exploratory study.

2.1   Ambiguities in Requirements

The problem of ambiguity in RE has been widely studied over the years, with particular focus on written requirements. The existing work can be roughly separated into two groups: strategies to *prevent* ambiguities, and approaches to *detect* ambiguities in (already written) requirements.

The first set of approaches can be divided into two categories: strategies which rely on formal approaches [23–25], and strategies based on constrained natural languages [26–28]. Looking into the first sub-category, the works of Kof [23] promotes ambiguity prevention by transforming requirements into formal/semiformal models, which are easier to analyze and constrain. The approaches implemented by tools like Circe-Cico [24] and LOLITA [25] also follow a similar rationale. The second sub-category is focused on the use of constrained natural languages, which should limit the possibility of introducing ambiguity and is also easier to be analyzed. Examples of well known constrained formats for editing requirements are EARS [26] and the Rupp's template [27]. Arora *et al.* [28] defined an approach to check the conformance of requirements to these templates.

Other approaches aim to *detect* ambiguities in requirements. Most of these works stem from the typically defective terms and constructions classified in the ambiguity handbook of Berry *et al.* [29]. Based on these studies, tools such as QuARS [30], SREE [31] and the tool of Gleich *et al.* [32] were developed. More recently, industrial applications of these approaches were studied by Femmer *et al.* [33] and by Rosadini *et al.* [20]. As shown also in these studies, rule-based approaches tend to produce a high number of false positive cases – i.e., linguistic ambiguities that have one single reading in practice. Hence, *statistical* approaches were proposed by Chantree *et al.* [34] and Yang *et al.* [35], to reduce the number of false positive cases, referred to as *innocuous ambiguities*.

All these works, with the exception of Chantree *et al.* [34] and Yang *et al.* [35], focus on the *objective* facet of ambiguity, assuming that the majority of the ambiguities could be identified by focusing on a set of typically dangerous expressions. In [7,10], we observed that this is not the most common case in requirements elicitation interviews, in which the *subjective* and contextual facets become dominant.

2.2   Ambiguity in Interviews

Differently from the ambiguity in written documents, the term ambiguity in interviews (i.e., synchronous oral communication), covers a larger set of situations. Indeed, an ambiguity can occur not only because the words used by the speaker are meaningless for the listener or are combined in a difficult to interpret structure, but also because the information delivered by the speaker is in contrast with the knowledge that the listener already built. Other ambiguities can be generated by the fact that new information acquired in a conversation can change the knowledge on a previously acquired concept. In particular, it is possible to identify the following categories of ambiguities in requirements elicitation interviews [10]:

- *interpretation unclarity*: The fragment of the speaker's speech cannot be understood;
- *acceptance unclarity*: The fragment uttered by the speaker is understandable and there is no reason to doubt that what can be understood from it matches with the intended meaning of the customer. However, the fragment appears *incomplete* to the listener or it has some form of *inconsistency* with what previously understood, or previous knowledge of the listener.
- *multiple understanding*: multiple interpretations of the fragment uttered by the speaker are possible, and each interpretation makes sense to the listener.
- *detected incorrect disambiguation*: previously the listener perceived an acceptance unclarity, and, later in the interview, she understands that the given interpretation was not correct (i.e., it did not match with the intended meaning of the speaker).
- *undetected incorrect disambiguation*: the listener did not perceive an acceptance unclarity, but, at a certain point of the interview, she understands that her interpretation of a certain fragment of the speaker was not correct.

Notice that since during a conversation the originator of a misunderstanding situation is present, the listener – the analyst in our case – can follow up with additional questions, which not only allows for disambiguating the situation, but also for finding additional knowledge that can be relevant for the analyst.

2.3 Requirements Review

IEEE Std 1028-2008 [12] defines the standards for the review of software products and categorizes them in five types: management reviews, technical reviews, inspections, walk-throughs and audits. In our work, we focus on *inspections*, which are *systematic peer-examinations that [...] verify that the software product exhibits specified quality attributes [...]* and *collect software engineering data*. Katasonov and Sakkinen [36] provide a categorization for reading techniques to be applied in inspection reviews, distinguishing between ad-hoc, checklist-based, defect-based, perspective-based, scenario-based and pattern-based. The technique proposed in our work is *defect-based*, since it focuses on a particular type of defect, namely ambiguity.

Inspections have been already successfully used in RE. In particular, Fagan [17] and Shull *et al.* [14] provide early and successful techniques for requirements inspection. A survey on the topic was published by Arum *et al.* [37]. More recent works on requirements review are those by Salger [11] and by Femmer *et al.* [19], which focuses on the *challenges* that requirements review faces in practice. The list of challenges include aspects such as the long time required for its implementation [19] and the need to have more effective elicitation techniques [11]. This latter goal is pursued by Karras *et al.* [38], who developed a tool for video inspection of requirements workshops. Notice that the majority of related work on requirements reviews focuses on reviews applied to specifications, while our goal is to analyze the audio recording of interviews. Our work differs also from that of Karras *et al.* [38], since we suggest to analyze only the audio recording of interviews, and we focus on ambiguity, a communication defect that is not considered by this previous study.

2.4 Interview Review: An Exploratory Study

The idea of moving the review at the level of requirements elicitation interviews to detect ambiguities was first presented in [22] together with our research plan and an exploratory study. The goal was understanding whether the idea that different ambiguities may emerge when an interview is listened by different subjects is actually grounded.

Our exploratory study used a preliminary version of the review method, and had two expert analysts applying it on a set of 10 *unstructured* interviews [4] performed by KSU undergraduate students. The reviewers were a researcher in requirements elicitation, and a professional analyst, respectively. The two reviewers were required to independently listen to the recording of each interview and to report ambiguous situations in a spreadsheet. They were requested to identify situations that they thought the analysts found ambiguous and situations that they found ambiguous but were not followed up by the analyst. The initial results showed not only that the reviews are very helpful in detecting ambiguities – the reviewers together found 46% that were not detected during the interview –, but also that the review process can benefit from the perspectives of different reviewers.

3   Experiment Design

The goal of our research is to analyze if reviewing requirements elicitation interviews allows the identification of additional ambiguities that were not identified during the interview by the requirements analyst. To investigate this problem in a systematic way, we set the following research questions:

RQ1: Is there a difference between ambiguities explicitly revealed by an analyst during an interview, and ambiguities identified by the analyst or by a reviewer when listening to the interview recording?

RQ2: Is there a difference between ambiguities identified by the analyst when listening to the interview recording, and ambiguities identified by a reviewer who listens to the interview recording?

RQ1 aims at exploring the contribution of the review phase in terms of ambiguities, considering the case in which the analyst performs the review and the case in which an external reviewer performs it. RQ2 focuses on the different contributions that the analyst, who performed the interview, and an external reviewer, who listens to the interview for the first time during the review, can give in the review phase. To answer these questions, we perform an experiment in which the same interview recording is reviewed by the analyst, and by an external reviewer. To provide the information to answer the questions, during the review the analyst explicitly distinguishes between ambiguities previously identified during the interview, and ambiguities found when listening. More details are given in Sect. 3.4.

3.1   Variables and Hypotheses

Variables. In our study, the *independent* variable is the *perspective*, which is a combination of the *role* of the person who is working in identifying ambiguities, i.e., the analyst or an external reviewer, and the *moment* in which the identification occurs, i.e., "during the interview" or "during the review". The perspective can assume four values: analyst in the interview (AI); reviewer in the review (RR); analyst in the review (AR). Notice that the perspective value "reviewer in the interview" (RI) is not applicable, since the reviewer does not participate to the interview.

The *dependent* variables are the *performance* in identifying ambiguities ($perf$, in the following) of the three identified perspectives. The performance of the generic perspective X (with $X \in \{AI, AR, RR\}$) is measured as the combination of the description and the numbers of ambiguities identified by X. To formally define $perf_X$, we introduce the following sets:

- a_{AI}: the set of ambiguities explicitly detected by the analyst during the interview;
- a_{AR}: the set of ambiguities detected by the analyst during the review;
- a_{RR}: the set of ambiguities detected by the reviewer during the review.

So, the performance of a generic perspective X (with $X \in \{AI, AR, RR\}$) is characterized by the content and the cardinality of the correspondent a_X, i.e., $perf_X = \langle a_X, |a_X| \rangle$.

Hypotheses. From **RQ1** we have derived two different null hypotheses:

H1.1$_0$: The reviewer's performance during the review is irrelevant with respect to the analyst's performance during the interview;

H1.2$_0$: The analyst's performance during the review is irrelevant with respect to the analyst's performance during the interview.

In H1.1$_0$, the perspective can assume the values AI and RR. In the light of these variables, H1.1$_0$ can be defined as $\mu_{|a_{RR}-a_{AI}|} = 0$, i.e., the mean of the number of ambiguities found in the review by the reviewer (RR) which were not found in the interview by the analyst (AI) is 0. Informally, if H1.1$_0$ cannot be rejected, it means that the ambiguities found in the review by the reviewer (RR), which were not found in the interview by the analyst (AI), were found by chance.

In H1.2$_0$, the perspective can assume the values AI and AR. Analogously, formalizing H1.2$_0$ can be defined as $\mu_{|a_{AR}-a_{AI}|} = 0$ i.e., the mean of the number of ambiguities found in the review by the analyst (AR) which were not found in the interview by the analyst (AI) is 0. Informally, if H1.2$_0$ cannot be rejected, it means that the ambiguities found in the review by the analyst (AR) which were not found in the interview by the analyst (AI) were found by chance.

From **RQ2**, we derive the following null hypothesis: **H2$_0$:** The reviewer's performance during the review and the analyst's performance during the review are equivalent. The independent variable assumes the values AR and RR. The dependent variable is still the performance in identifying ambiguities and can be measured in terms of found ambiguities. Notice that saying that the performance are equivalent means that the two sets of identified ambiguities are about the same not just in terms of cardinality, but also in terms of content. This hypothesis would be very difficult to analyze, so it can be reformulated in the following sub-hypotheses:

H2.1$_0$: The analyst's performance during the review is irrelevant with respect to the reviewer's performance during the review;

H2.2$_0$: The reviewer's performance during the review is irrelevant with respect to the analyst's performance during the review.

Indeed, if both the reviews are irrelevant one with respect to the other, the two reviews are equivalent.

So, H2.1$_0$ is formalized as $\mu_{|a_{AR}-a_{RR}|} = 0$, i.e., the additional ambiguities found by the analyst in the review (AR) with respect to those found by the reviewer during the review (RR) were found by chance. H2.2$_0$ is formalized as $\mu_{|a_{RR}-a_{AR}-a_{AI}|} = 0$, i.e., the additional ambiguities found by the reviewer in the review (RR) with respect to those found by the analyst during the review (AR) without considering the ones already found in the interview (AI) were found by chance. Note that in H2.2$_0$ we have to explicitly exclude the ambiguities found by the AI perspective: if the reviewer founds an ambiguity that was already found by the analyst during the interview, this is not taken into account in the computation. In H2.1$_0$ this is not needed, since a_{AR} and a_{AI} are disjoint sets.

In order to analyze the stated hypotheses, we designed and conducted a controlled experimental study which will be described in the remainder of this section.

3.2   Participants

Our controlled experiment was performed with two equivalent independent groups of participants, namely students of KSU and students of UTS. It consists of two phases: in the first phase participants performed a set of role-play require-ments elicitation interviews, and in the second phase, participants reviewed the interviews. In the following we will describe the participants from both insti-tutions and the main characteristic of the protocol. The complete protocol is available at https://goo.gl/PI2LLy.

The first group of participants consists of 30 students of KSU. The recruited students belonged to a User-Centered Design course, composed of undergraduate students of the 3rd and 4th year with major related to a computing discipline (software engineering, computer science, information technology, and computer game development and design). The students were provided with a two hours lecture on requirements elicitation interviews delivered by the 1st author, in which they received an introduction on different types of interviews and general guidelines on how to conduct each of the main types. The class used a reference book [39] and additional lecture notes. While the participation to the study was on a voluntary basis, students who participated were assessed and received additional marks for their final results.

The second group of participants consists of 12 students of UTS. They were Master of Information Technology students, a two years full time postgraduate degree[1], and almost all of them were in their 1st year. The students belonged to the Enterprise Business Requirements course. To prepare for the experiment, the students attended an introductory lecture on requirements elicitation that included how to run interviews, delivered by the 4th author, and were advised to take a (Lynda.com) course online on requirements elicitation interviews. Stu-dents participated in this activity as volunteers and were not assessed for it.

3.3   Interviews

In both locations, the students were divided into 2 groups, namely analysts and customers. The creation of the two groups and the association between customers and analysts were performed randomly. One week before the interview was planned, customers were told: "Take a week to think about a mobile app for smart-phones you would like to have developed. You have a $ 30,000 budget

---

[1] A full description of the degree can found at http://www.handbook.uts.edu.au/courses/c04295.html.

and your idea should be feasible within your budget. If the ideas you have seems not doable with this budget look at the apps you have on your phone and try to think how you would like to modify one of them."

For both the participants groups, the interviews took place simultaneously at the reference institution, and the time slot allocated was 30 min in addition to the time required for setting up the experiment. The interviews were recorded at KSU in Fall 2016 and at UTS in Spring 2017. Before starting the interviews both the customers and the analysts were required to fill out a demographic questionnaires, one specific for the analyst and one specific for the customer, with the goal of knowing the proficiency of the participant with the language used in the interview (in both institution, English) and their previous experience in the role they were acting.

The students conducted *unstructured* interviews [4], which is the most suitable approach in this context. Indeed, in the experiment, the students analysts are exploring ideas for new products for which they have no background information. The interviews were audio recorded.

In order to help the students to focus, the analysts were given the goal of collecting an initial list of requirements after the interview was performed. The requirements had to be listed in the form of user stories, detailed enough to estimate the required amount of work in terms of needed time and number of developers.

3.4 Reviews

After the interviews the participants were requested to work on the review of the interviews with the following rationale. Each student who acted as customer was requested to review an interview performed by another group. The interview to review was assigned to the customer randomly when the groups were created. Instead, analysts were requested to review the interview they conducted. This allows for two reviews: one internal, performed by the same analyst who performed the interview, one external, performed by a reviewer, who did not know anything about the interview and the product described in it before the review.

The main steps of the review protocol the reviewers were assigned are as follows:

1. Create a spreadsheet with the columns: *Time, Fragment, Question.*
2. Start the reproduction of the audio recording, start a timer, and start listening. If any external factor interrupt your work, please stop the timer and restart it when you resume your review.
3. Stop the audio when you perceive an ambiguity in the words of the customer.
4. Whenever you stop the audio for the listed cases, add a line to the spreadsheet with the following content:
   - **Time:** the moment in which the customer produces the fragment;
   - **Fragment:** the fragment of speech that triggered the ambiguity;
   - **Question:** the question that you would ask to the customer to clarify.

5. When you have finished listening, stop the timer and annotate the time that passed from the beginning of your activity. This will serve to estimate the time that you employed to perform the whole activity.

As guidelines to identify the ambiguities, participants were suggested the following: "As a rule of thumb, stop the reproduction in any case in which, if you were the analyst, you would have asked the customer one or more questions of the form:"

- *What does it mean [...]?* (You have not understood the meaning of what you heard)
- *What is the purpose of [...]?* (You have not understood the purpose of what you heard)
- *Can you discuss in more detail about [...]?* (What you heard is too general)
- *You mentioned that [...], but [...]?* (What you heard contradicts what you heard before, or your vision of the problem)
- *Do you mean <A> or <B>?* (What you heard can mean different things)
- *I thought that with [...] you meant [...], was I wrong?* (You have doubts about a previous understanding of some concept)

This review protocol allows the identification of ambiguities perceived by the reviewer (perspective RR, see Sect. 3.1). The review protocol is slightly different for the analysts, since they had to annotate their own interview, distinguishing between ambiguities perceived during the interview and ambiguities perceived during the review of the recording of the interview. In particular, steps 3 and 4 were modified as follows:

6. Stop the recording whenever the customer says something that is unclear, ambiguous or does not make sense to you. As a rule of thumb, stop the recording in any of the following two cases:
   - you asked a clarification question to the customer during the interview;
   - a new question comes to your mind now, and you regret not to have asked the question to the customer during the interview.
7. Whenever you stop listening, add a row to the spreadsheet, and write: fragment, time, question, and moment ("I" if the question was asked during the interview and "L" if the question came to your mind during the review).

In this way, the review of the analyst allowed the identification of the moments that she perceived as ambiguous within the interview (perspective AI) and the detection of additional ambiguities during the review (perspective AR).

4   Evaluation

To evaluate the results of this study and answer to our research questions, we analyzed the spreadsheets of the analysts and of the reviewers, and we created a_{AI}, a_{AR}, and a_{RR}. From these sets, we derived other relevant sets that will be used in the following analyses:

- $both_{AI,RR} = a_{AI} \cap a_{RR}$: the set of detected ambiguities in common between the analyst during the interview and the reviewer;
- $both_{AR,RR} = a_{AR} \cap a_{RR}$: the set of detected ambiguities in common between the analyst during the review and the reviewer;
- $ao_{AI} = a_{AI} - both_{AI,RR}$: the set of ambiguities detected only by the analyst during the interview. Notice that $both_{AI,AR}$ is not considered since it is empty by construction;
- $ao_{AR} = a_{AR} - both_{AR,RR}$: the set of ambiguities detected only by the analyst during the review (again $both_{AI,AR}$ is not considered since it is empty by construction);
- $ao_{RR} = a_{RR} - both_{AI,RR} - both_{AR,RR}$: the set of ambiguities detected only by the reviewer during the review.

The sum of the cardinalities of these sets forms the total number of ambiguities identified in the whole process. In the following, the data of KSU and UTS are combined together. At the end of this section, we will briefly discuss them separately.

Overall Evaluation. In order to have an initial idea of the performance of each perspective, we have computed the classic descriptive statistics (minimum, maximum, mean, and median) for the number of ambiguities found by each perspective and for the number of ambiguities found only by a perspective. These values and the corresponding box plots are reported in Fig. 1. It is worth noting that each perspective contributes to the identification of ambiguities by identifying on average at least 4 ambiguities that were not found by any other perspective (Fig. 1, for each ao_X the Mean value is above 4).

To look at the distribution of the detected ambiguities on the different combinations of roles and situations, we can refer to Fig. 2a. The figure considers the following cases of detection: only during the interview ($|ao_{AI}|$), only during the review performed by the analyst ($|ao_{AR}|$), only during the review performed by the reviewer ($|ao_{RR}|$), common to the interview and the review performed by the reviewer ($|both_{AI,RR}|$), and common to the reviews ($|both_{AR,RR}|$). These numbers are evaluated with respect to the total number of ambiguities, which is the sum of all these contributions. The number of ambiguities detected *only* during the interview – blue area, ($|ao_{AI}|$) – is 30%, and increases only to 32% if we consider also the ones that were also detected in the review of the reviewer ($|both_{AI,RR}|$) – purple area. Hence, the overall review activity identified 68% of the total number of ambiguities. Analogously, Fig. 2b shows the distribution of the detection of ambiguities for the performed interviews separately. Analyzing the data from the figure, we can observe that in most of the cases the majority of ambiguities are detected during the reviews – red, green and light blue areas – rather than during the interview – blue area. Specifically, it is possible to observe that in more than 75% of the cases the ambiguities detected during the interview ($|a_{AI}|$) are less than 50% of the total number of detected ambiguities – i.e., the blue area plot is below 50% for 75% of the interviews. Moreover, in 50% of the cases this percentage drops below 30%. These data are an interesting result

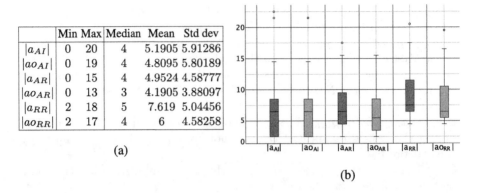

	Min	Max	Median	Mean	Std dev
$\|a_{AI}\|$	0	20	4	5.1905	5.91286
$\|ao_{AI}\|$	0	19	4	4.8095	5.80189
$\|a_{AR}\|$	0	15	4	4.9524	4.58777
$\|ao_{AR}\|$	0	13	3	4.1905	3.88097
$\|a_{RR}\|$	2	18	5	7.619	5.04456
$\|ao_{RR}\|$	2	17	4	6	4.58258

(a)

(b)

Fig. 1. Descriptive statistics and box plots for the main metrics of the performance

per se, because they highlight that there is a considerable number of ambiguities that is not identified during the interview and can be detected with a further analysis. Indeed, regardless of the subject who performs the review process – either the analyst or reviewer –, this analysis suggests that the review is useful to spot a significant number of ambiguities not identified during the interview.

RQ1: Contribution of the Review Activity. To answer **RQ1**, we look into the contribution of the review activity in detecting ambiguities with respect to the ones identified by the analyst during the interview. Looking at Fig. 2a, we see that the percentage of ambiguities that were common between the analyst (during the interview), and the reviewer is only 2% ($\|both_{AI,RR}\|$, purple area) of the total number of ambiguities identified in the whole process. It is also possible to notice that the reviewers contribute by identifying on average 37% ($\|ao_{RR}\|$, green area) of the total number of ambiguities. Looking only at the ambiguities detected by the analyst during the interview and by the analysts in the review ($\|a_{AI}\| + \|a_{AR}\|$ – notice that has pointed out at the beginning of Sect. 4 there is no overlapping between a_{AI} and a_{AR}), the contribution of the analyst's review in detecting ambiguities ($\|a_{AR}\|$) is on average more than 49% (not shown in the figures). Analogously, looking only at the ambiguities detected by the analyst during the interview and by the reviewer in the review ($\|a_{AI}\| + \|a_{RR}\| - \|both_{AI,RR}\|$), the contribution of the reviewer in detecting ambiguities ($\|a_{RR}\| - \|both_{AI,RR}\|$) is on average more than 56% (not shown in the figures). Among all the ambiguities detected by the reviewers only 4.45% ($\|both_{AI,RR}\|$, not shown) were identified also by the analysts during the interview. Notice that the reviewer's work always positive contributed to the detection of ambiguities. Indeed, in all the interviews the reviewer detected at least a couple of additional ambiguities with respect to those detected during the interview.

To more precisely answer to RQ1, we evaluate H1.1$_0$ and H1.2$_0$ by using the (student) paired t-test, which provides an hypothesis test of the difference between populations for pair of samples whose differences are approximately normally distributed. H1.1$_0$ is formalized as $\mu_{|a_{RR}-a_{AI}|} = 0$, where $|a_{RR} - a_{AI}|$

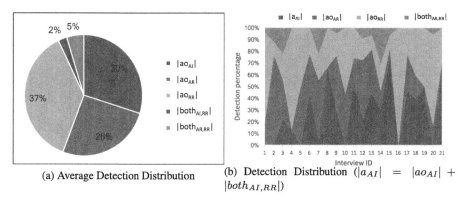

(a) Average Detection Distribution

(b) Detection Distribution ($|a_{AI}| = |ao_{AI}| + |both_{AI,RR}|$)

Fig. 2. Distribution of ambiguities (Color figure online)

is $|a_{RR}| - |both_{AI,RR}|$, and H1.2$_0$ is formalized as $\mu_{|a_{AR}-a_{AI}|} = 0$, where $|a_{AR} - a_{AI}|$ is $|a_{AR}| - |both_{AI,AR}| = |a_{AR}|$. The paired t-test is applicable in these cases since both $|a_{RR}| - |both_{AI,RR}|$ and $|a_{AR}|$ are normally distributed with a skewness of .958 (standard error $= 0.501$) and kurtosis of 0.01 (standard error $= 0.972$) and a skewness of 1.088 (standard error $= 0.501$) and kurtosis of -0.032 (standard error $= 0.972$), respectively. In both cases it is possible to reject the null hypotheses with significance level 5% since t_0 is greater than the tabular reference value. Indeed, we have 21 samples, which correspond to 20 degrees of freedom and a tabulated reference value $t_{0.025,20} = 2.086$, and, $S_d = 8.9944$ and $t_0 = 3.6877$ for $|a_{RR}| - |both_{AI,RR}|$ and $S_d = 5.0883$ and $t_0 = 6.5187$ for $|a_{AR}|$.

RQ2: Contribution of Different Reviews. To answer **RQ2**, we compare the ambiguities detected during the reviews performed by the analysts with those detected by the reviewers. Considering the ambiguities that were common between the analyst during the review and the reviewer, we have that these amount solely to 5% ($|both_{AR,RR}|$, light blue area in Fig. 2a) of the total number of ambiguities. On average the ambiguities that are common to both reviews is 7.14% (not shown in the figures) of the total number of ambiguities detected in the review phase ($|a_{AR}| + |a_{RR}| - |both_{AR,RR}|$). Furthermore, Fig. 2b shows that the set of ambiguities detected in both the reviews always contains less than 30% of the total number of detected ambiguities (the light blue area plot is always above 70%).

Analogously to what done for RQ1, to answer to RQ2, we evaluate H2.1$_0$ and H2.2$_0$ by using the (student) paired t-test. H1.1$_0$ is formalized as $\mu_{|a_{AR}-a_{RR}|} = 0$, where $|a_{AR} - a_{RR}|$ is $|ao_{AR}|$, and H2.2$_0$ is formalized as $\mu_{|a_{RR}-a_{AR}-a_{AI}|} = 0$, where $|a_{RR} - a_{AR} - a_{AI}|$ is $|ao_{RR}|$. Both $|ao_{AR}|$ and $|ao_{RR}|$ are normally distributed with a skewness of .902 (standard error $= 0.501$) and kurtosis of 0.01 (standard error $= 0.971$) and a skewness of 1.14 (standard error $= 0.501$) and kurtosis of 0.2 (standard error $= 0.971$), respectively. In both cases it is possible to reject the null hypotheses with significance level 5% since t_0 is greater than the tabular reference value. Indeed, we have 21 samples, which correspond to

20 degrees of freedom and a tabulated reference value $t_{0.025,20} = 2.086$, and, $S_d = 5.269$ and $t_0 = 5.4968$ for $|ao_{AR}|$ and $S_d = 3.881$ and $t_0 = 4.8288$ for $|ao_{RR}|$.

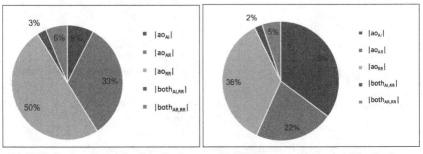

(a) UTS Average Detection Distribution   (b) KSU Average Detection Distribution

Fig. 3. Comparing UTS and KSU experiments (Color figure online)

KSU vs UTS Data. If we separate the data of UTS (Fig. 3a) and KSU (Fig. 3b), we can notice that while both cases suggest that there is a benefit in both the review performed by the analysts and the one performed by the external reviewers, there is a considerable discrepancy in the percentage of ambiguities detected only in the interview (8% in the case of UTS, 35% in the case of KSU – blue areas in the figures). This discrepancy might be caused by the fact that KSU students received a different training, with a higher focus on ambiguity, with respect to UTS students, and were therefore more focused on ambiguity detection already during the interview. However, this result does not change the validity of the above performed analysis, which focuses on the data regarding the *common* cases of ambiguity, which, on average, do not substantially vary among the two groups.

Another aspect that is relevant to our study and needs to be evaluated is the *time* employed by the reviewers for their task, with respect to the duration of the interviews. Unfortunately, the data collected by the students, especially the KSU ones, are incomplete. The 45% and the 18% of the data regarding the review time of analysts and reviewers, respectively, are missing. However, from the data collected, we observe that on average the reviews take about twice the time needed for the interviews. This is a reasonable time for an activity which contributes considerably to the detection of ambiguities.

5   Threats to Validity

In this section, we list the main threats to the validity of our study. Notice that this controlled study has been developed to overcome the limitations of the exploratory study presented in Sect. 2.4 and was designed preventing most of the problems of that experiment.

Internal Validity. The students participating in the experiments had slightly different backgrounds. In particular, UTS students were graduate students, while KSU students were undergraduate students. Even if their learning experience on requirements elicitation was similar, being at a different degree level could influence the attitude of the students towards the learning process. However, we argue that the fact that KSU students were mostly 3rd and 4th year students and they were evaluated, while the graduate students were not, may have mitigated this maturation threat. Furthermore, since UTS students were in the first semester of their first year of their degree, they can be considered nearly graduate. As collected in the survey that was distributed before the experiments, we noticed that a few of the students already experienced being part of an elicitation interview while others did not. This can represent an history threat. However, the participants with experience had in general a very limited experience, which classifies them all as unexperienced analysts, equivalent with respect to our experiment.

Construct Validity. We argue that there are no construct validity threats in our study. Indeed, our research questions (and consequently our hypotheses) maps very straightforwardly to the collected data: the questions are related to the number of detected ambiguities and we evaluated them directly using this measure, which represent the performance of the perspectives.

External Validity. The population validity is the major threat in this study, since we use students instead of practitioners to perform our interviews. Although according to Höst *et al.* [40] students with a good knowledge of computer science appear to perform as well as professionals, there is always a difference between the industrial world, and a role-playing settings. This limit will be addressed by our next research step with will be discussed in Sect. 6.

6   Conclusion and Future Work

In our previous work [22], we proposed to define a review method for requirements elicitation interviews, with the goal of identifying ambiguities in the conversation. Indeed, identified ambiguous situations can be used to suggest further clarifying questions, that can help in finding additional relevant (possibly *tacit*) knowledge. In this paper we presented a protocol to apply interview reviews in practice and a controlled experiment to evaluate the effectiveness of the protocol. The protocol consists in having both the analyst and an external reviewer to review performed interviews. The method aims to exploit both a more reflective attitude of the analyst during the review phase with respect to the interview phase, and the different perspective of the external analyst. Our experiment involved 42 students in two Higher Education Institutions, KSU and UTS, and measured the contribution of the reviews in detecting ambiguities. The experiment showed that reviews help to detect a considerable number of additional ambiguities and both the reviews were helping in different ways, suggesting the needs of both of them.

As a future work we aim to prove the correlation between the questions generated by detected ambiguities and the quality of the information that they allow to find. In particular, we want to address the following research question: Can the ambiguities identified during interview review be used to ask *useful* questions in future interviews? To answer to it, we plan to perform a case study in industry, in which the method will be applied, and the impact of the questions will be monitored along the development. The idea is to gather qualitative data about the *perceived* usefulness of the questions produced after the first interview, and their *actual* usefulness observable after the delivery of the products. It is worth mentioning that our approach can also help in requirements engineering education, since, by enabling students to listen to each others' interviews, can let them learn from the observed successful elicitation strategies and mistakes.

References

1. Davis, A., Dieste, O., Hickey, A., Juristo, N., Moreno, A.M.: Effectiveness of requirements elicitation techniques: empirical results derived from a systematic review. In: RE 2006, pp. 179–188. IEEE (2006)
2. Hadar, I., Soffer, P., Kenzi, K.: The role of domain knowledge in requirements elicitation via interviews: an exploratory study. REJ **19**(2), 143–159 (2014)
3. Coughlan, J., Macredie, R.D.: Effective communication in requirements elicitation: a comparison of methodologies. Requir. Eng. **7**(2), 47–60 (2002)
4. Zowghi, D., Coulin, C.: Requirements elicitation: a survey of techniques, approaches, and tools. In: Aurum, A., Wohlin, C. (eds.) Engineering and Managing Software Requirements, pp. 19–46. Springer, Heidelberg (2005). https://doi.org/10.1007/3-540-28244-0_2
5. Gervasi, V., Gacitua, R., Rouncefield, M., Sawyer, P., Kof, L., Ma, L., Piwek, P., De Roeck, A., Willis, A., Yang, H., et al.: Unpacking tacit knowledge for requirements engineering. In: Maalej, W., Thurimella, A. (eds.) Managing Requirements Knowledge, pp. 23–47. Springer, Heidelberg (2013). https://doi.org/10.1007/978-3-642-34419-0_2
6. Sutcliffe, A., Sawyer, P.: Requirements elicitation: towards the unknown unknowns. In: RE 2013, pp. 92–104. IEEE (2013)
7. Ferrari, A., Spoletini, P., Gnesi, S.: Ambiguity cues in requirements elicitation interviews. In: RE 2016, pp. 56–65. IEEE (2016)
8. Rugg, G., McGeorge, P., Maiden, N.: Method fragments. Expert Syst. **17**(5), 248–257 (2000)
9. Friedrich, W.R., Van Der Poll, J.A.: Towards a methodology to elicit tacit domain knowledge from users. IJIKM **2**(1), 179–193 (2007)
10. Ferrari, A., Spoletini, P., Gnesi, S.: Ambiguity as a resource to disclose tacit knowledge. In: RE 2015, pp. 26–35. IEEE (2015)
11. Salger, F.: Requirements reviews revisited: residual challenges and open research questions. In: RE 2013, pp. 250–255. IEEE (2013)
12. IEEE Std 1028–2008: IEEE Standard for Software Reviews and Audits (2008)
13. Laitenberger, O., DeBaud, J.M.: An encompassing life cycle centric survey of software inspection. JSS **50**(1), 5–31 (2000)
14. Shull, F., Rus, I., Basili, V.: How perspective-based reading can improve requirements inspections. Computer **33**(7), 73–79 (2000)
15. Bacchelli, A., Bird, C.: Expectations, outcomes, and challenges of modern code review. In: ICSE 2013, pp. 712–721. IEEE (2013)

16. Rigby, P.C., Bird, C.: Convergent contemporary software peer review practices. In: FSE 2013, pp. 202–212. ACM (2013)
17. Fagan, M.E.: Design and code inspections to reduce errors in program development. IBM Syst. J. **15**(3), 182–211 (1976)
18. Wohlin, C., Runeson, P., Höst, M., Ohlsson, M.C., Regnell, B., Wesslén, A.: Are the perspectives really different? Further experimentation on scenario-based reading of requirements. In: Experimentation in Software Engineering, pp. 175–200. Springer, Heidelberg (2012). https://doi.org/10.1007/978-3-642-29044-2_13
19. Femmer, H., Hauptmann, B., Eder, S., Moser, D.: Quality assurance of requirements artifacts in practice: a case study and a process proposal. In: Abrahamsson, P., Jedlitschka, A., Nguyen Duc, A., Felderer, M., Amasaki, S., Mikkonen, T. (eds.) PROFES 2016. LNCS, vol. 10027, pp. 506–516. Springer, Cham (2016). https://doi.org/10.1007/978-3-319-49094-6_36
20. Rosadini, B., Ferrari, A., Gori, G., Fantechi, A., Gnesi, S., Trotta, I., Bacherini, S.: Using NLP to detect requirements defects: an industrial experience in the railway domain. In: Grünbacher, P., Perini, A. (eds.) REFSQ 2017. LNCS, vol. 10153, pp. 344–360. Springer, Cham (2017). https://doi.org/10.1007/978-3-319-54045-0_24
21. Massey, A.K., Rutledge, R.L., Anton, A.I., Swire, P.P.: Identifying and classifying ambiguity for regulatory requirements. In: RE 2014, pp. 83–92. IEEE (2014)
22. Ferrari, A., Spoletini, P., Donati, B., Zowghi, D., Gnesi, S.: Interview review: detecting latent ambiguities to improve the requirements elicitation process. In: RE 2017, pp. 400–405. IEEE (2017)
23. Kof, L.: From requirements documents to system models: a tool for interactive semi-automatic translation. In: RE 2010 (2010)
24. Ambriola, V., Gervasi, V.: On the systematic analysis of natural language requirements with CIRCE. ASE **13**(1), 107–167 (2006)
25. Mich, L.: NL-OOPS: from natural language to object oriented requirements using the natural language processing system LOLITA. NLE **2**(2), 161–187 (1996)
26. Mavin, A., Wilkinson, P., Harwood, A., Novak, M.: Easy approach to requirements syntax (ears). In: RE 2009, pp. 317–322. IEEE (2009)
27. Pohl, K., Rupp, C.: Requirements Engineering Fundamentals. Rocky Nook Inc., Santa Barbara (2011)
28. Arora, C., Sabetzadeh, M., Briand, L., Zimmer, F.: Automated checking of conformance to requirements templates using natural language processing. TSE **41**(10), 944–968 (2015)
29. Berry, D.M., Kamsties, E., Krieger, M.M.: From contract drafting to software specification: linguistic sources of ambiguity (2003)
30. Gnesi, S., Lami, G., Trentanni, G.: An automatic tool for the analysis of natural language requirements. IJCSSE **20**(1), 53–62 (2005)
31. Tjong, S.F., Berry, D.M.: The design of SREE — a prototype potential ambiguity finder for requirements specifications and lessons learned. In: Doerr, J., Opdahl, A.L. (eds.) REFSQ 2013. LNCS, vol. 7830, pp. 80–95. Springer, Heidelberg (2013). https://doi.org/10.1007/978-3-642-37422-7_6
32. Gleich, B., Creighton, O., Kof, L.: Ambiguity detection: towards a tool explaining ambiguity sources. In: Wieringa, R., Persson, A. (eds.) REFSQ 2010. LNCS, vol. 6182, pp. 218–232. Springer, Heidelberg (2010). https://doi.org/10.1007/978-3-642-14192-8_20
33. Femmer, H., Fernández, D.M., Wagner, S., Eder, S.: Rapid quality assurance with requirements smells. JSS **123**, 190–213 (2017)
34. Chantree, F., Nuseibeh, B., de Roeck, A.N., Willis, A.: Identifying nocuous ambiguities in natural language requirements. In: RE 2006, pp. 56–65 (2006)

35. Yang, H., de Roeck, A.N., Gervasi, V., Willis, A., Nuseibeh, B.: Analysing anaphoric ambiguity in natural language requirements. Requir. Eng. **16**(3), 163–189 (2011)
36. Katasonov, A., Sakkinen, M.: Requirements quality control: a unifying framework. REJ **11**(1), 42–57 (2006)
37. Aurum, A., Petersson, H., Wohlin, C.: State-of-the-art: software inspections after 25 years. Softw. Testing Verification Reliab. **12**(3), 133–154 (2002)
38. Karras, O., Kiesling, S., Schneider, K.: Supporting requirements elicitation by tool-supported video analysis. In: RE 2016, pp. 146–155. IEEE (2016)
39. Sharp, H., Rogers, Y., Preece, J.: Interaction Design: Beyond Human Computer Interaction, 4th edn. Wiley, New York (2015)
40. Höst, M., Regnell, B., Wohlin, C.: Using students as subjects, a comparative study of students and professionals in lead-time impact assessment. ESE **5**(3), 201–214 (2000)

Pinpointing Ambiguity and Incompleteness in Requirements Engineering via Information Visualization and NLP

Fabiano Dalpiaz$^{(\boxtimes)}$ ⓘ, Ivor van der Schalk, and Garm Lucassen ⓘ

RE-Lab, Department of Information and Computing Sciences,
Utrecht University, Utrecht, Netherlands
{f.dalpiaz,i.l.vanderschalk,g.lucassen}@uu.nl

Abstract. [**Context and motivation**] Identifying requirements defects such as ambiguity and incompleteness is an important and challenging task in requirements engineering (RE). [**Question/Problem**] We investigate whether combining humans' cognitive and analytical capabilities with automated reasoning is a viable method to support the identification of requirements quality defects. [**Principal ideas/results**] We propose a tool-supported approach for pinpointing terminological ambiguities between viewpoints as well as missing requirements. To do so, we blend natural language processing (conceptual model extraction and semantic similarity) with information visualization techniques that help interpret the type of defect. [**Contribution**] Our approach is a step forward toward the identification of ambiguity and incompleteness in a set of requirements, still an open issue in RE. A quasi-experiment with students, aimed to assess whether our tool delivers higher accuracy than manual inspection, suggests a significantly higher recall but does not reveal significant differences in precision.

Keywords: Natural language processing · Requirements engineering
Information visualization · User stories · Ambiguity

1 Introduction

Defects in natural language (NL) such as ambiguity, unclarity, inconsistency, and incompleteness are common issues in requirements engineering (RE) [1–3], and they can lead to misunderstandings between stakeholders, overlooked requirements, and software systems that do not meet the stakeholders' needs.

The identification of requirements defects is no trivial task. Automated solutions are inhibited by the low maturity of NL processing (NLP) techniques—unable to gain a deep understanding of text [4]—and the necessary trade-offs between precision and recall [2,5,6]. On the other hand, manual approaches that rely on human intelligence and the application of inspection checklists, do not scale to large specification. Luckily, the two approaches are not incompatible.

© Springer International Publishing AG, part of Springer Nature 2018
E. Kamsties et al. (Eds.): REFSQ 2018, LNCS 10753, pp. 119–135, 2018.
https://doi.org/10.1007/978-3-319-77243-1_8

We make a step toward the synergistic use of NLP and human analysis as part of our research on user stories and agile RE. User stories are semi-structured notation for user requirements with a simple format [7]: *As a* student, *I want to* receive my grades via e-mail, *so that* I can quickly check them. We take as input the terms and relationships that are automatically extracted by our Visual Narrator tool [8] from a set of user stories. Unfortunately, despite its high extraction accuracy, Visual Narrator does not assist analysts to inspect the resulting graphical model, thereby making our approach impractical for large models.

In this paper, we modularize the models extracted from user story requirements by leveraging the viewpoints [9] that user stories natively express through their format (As a user . . . ; As a developer . . .). Such approach is embedded in a Web 2.0 tool that blends NLP and information visualization (InfoVis) techniques with the aim of identifying potential ambiguities and missing requirements.

We make four concrete contributions:

- We construct a framework that defines potential ambiguity and incompleteness based on the terminology and denotations used in different viewpoints.
- We build an algorithm for identifying (near-)synonyms that orchestrates state-of-the-art semantic similarity algorithms from the NLP domain.
- To help analysts explore potential defects, we propose a Venn diagram visualization that organizes the extracted terms according to the viewpoint(s), and emphasizes terminological ambiguity using colors.
- We report on a quasi-experiment that assesses whether pairs of analysts using the tool on a large interactive screen obtain higher precision and recall in identifying quality defects than analysts working pen-on-paper.

Organization. We explain our framework for identifying ambiguity and incompleteness starting from viewpoints in Sect. 2, then present the algorithm for detecting (near)-synonymy ambiguity in Sect. 3. We introduce our Venn diagram visualization in Sect. 4. We report on the evaluation in Sect. 5, discuss related work in Sect. 6, draw conclusions and present future directions in Sect. 7.

2   From Viewpoints to Ambiguity and Incompleteness

The different stakeholders of a software system are interested in distinct aspects. For example, website administrators care about content creation and structuring, while readers are mostly concerned in accessing existing content. According to Mullery [10], a *viewpoint* is a description of one stakeholder's perception of a system, and it consists of concepts and inter-relationships between them.

The existence of viewpoints inevitably leads to inconsistencies and conflicts in stakeholders' requirements. Recognizing and reconciling these issues are key tasks in RE [11], and they amount to (i) checking the consistency of the specification within one viewpoint (in-viewpoint checks), and (ii) checking the consistency of the specification among different viewpoints (inter-viewpoint checks) [9].

Viewpoints may also introduce ambiguity problems due to the use of different terminology and conceptual systems (how an expert assigns meaning to a term [12]). The descriptions of a domain by different experts lead to four types of relationships that depend on their chosen terminology (bank, car) and the distinctions (also known as *denotations*) in the domain that the terms refer to (a financial institution, a ground alongside a body of water, a road vehicle) [12]:

1. *Consensus*: same terminology, same distinction. Example: both experts use the term bank to refer to a financial institution.
2. *Correspondence*: different terminology, same distinction. Example: when referring to a road vehicle, one expert uses car and the other uses automobile.
3. *Conflict*: same terminology, different distinction. Example: both experts use bank, but one refers to a financial institution, while the other to a ground.
4. *Contrast*: different terminology, different distinction. Example: one viewpoint examines road vehicles, the other focuses on financial institutions.

A requirement is ambiguous when it has multiple valid interpretations [13]. We argue that when a collection of requirements contains terms related by correspondence or conflict, there is a possible ambiguity. Furthermore, possible missing requirements may arise due to contrast. Table 1 formalizes these concepts.

Table 1. Linking viewpoints' terminological and denotational relations [12] with possible ambiguity and incompleteness. Let t_1, t_2 be distinct terms, $[\![t]\!]^{V_1}$ be the denotation of term t according to the viewpoint V_1 (for simplicity, we assume that denotations refer to a single entity), and $\bot$ indicate absence of a denotation.

Relation [12]	Possible defect	Defect formalization	Example
Consensus	-	$[\![t_1]\!]^{V_1} = [\![t_1]\!]^{V_2}$	$[\![\text{bank}]\!]^{V_1} = $ financial institution
			$[\![\text{bank}]\!]^{V_2} = $ financial institution
Correspondence	(Near-)synonymy leading to ambiguity	$[\![t_1]\!]^{V_1} = [\![t_2]\!]^{V_2}$	$[\![\text{car}]\!]^{V_1} = $ road vehicle
			$[\![\text{automobile}]\!]^{V_2} = $ road vehicle
Conflict	Homonymy leading to ambiguity	$[\![t_1]\!]^{V_1} \neq [\![t_1]\!]^{V_2}$	$[\![\text{bank}]\!]^{V_1} = $ financial institution
			$[\![\text{bank}]\!]^{V_2} = $ land alongside river
Contrast	Incompleteness	$[\![t_1]\!]^{V_1} \neq \bot \wedge [\![t_1]\!]^{V_2} = \bot$	$[\![\text{bank}]\!]^{V_1} = $ financial institution
			$[\![\text{bank}]\!]^{V_2} = \bot$

Consider now an example: take the following four user stories from the WebCompany data set [8] (terms are emphasized in serif):

R_1. As a visitor, I am able to view the media gallery, so that I can see interesting photos about the event region.

R_2. As an administrator, I am able to edit existing media elements of a particular gallery, so that I can update the content.

R_3. As a user, I am able to add content to the selected profile.

R_4. As a visitor, I am able to use the contact form, so that I can contact the administrator.

Consensus does not lead to any ambiguity. For example, the term administrator has the same denotation both in R_2 and R_4 and it refers to the person managing the website and its users.

Ambiguity *may* occur with correspondence: distinct terms refer to the same denotation. The term media gallery in R_1 and the term gallery in R_2 do likely (but not necessarily) refer to the same denotation, a web gallery where photographs are displayed. The problem is that most synonyms are in fact near-synonyms (*plesionyms*), as they refer to similar yet not identical denotations [14].

Ambiguity *may* also occur in the conflict state: the same term is used for different denotations. This phenomenon is called *homonymy*. In R_2, the term content refers specifically to a media element, while in R_3 the term content may refer to either text, descriptions, images, videos or audio fragments.

Incompleteness (missing requirements) *may* occur in the contrast state, i.e., in the case in which one viewpoint refers to concepts that do not appear in another viewpoint. R_4 includes contact form that the visitor uses to get in touch with the administrator. However, there is no other user story in our short collection that specifies how the administrator can respond to this action.

3   NLP-Powered Identification of (Near)-Synonymy

To detect *(near)-synonymy* between terms that may lead to ambiguity (the *correspondence* relationship in Table 1), we develop an NLP-powered algorithm that integrates state-of-the-art semantic similarity techniques. This algorithm is used in Sect. 4 to set the terms' background color in the InfoVis approach.

Our NLP technique relies on algorithms that calculate the *semantic distance* between two terms: a numerical representation of the difference in meaning between two terms [15]. Current state-of-the-art NLP tools, such as Word2Vec, establish semantic similarity in the $[0.0, 1.0]$ range via word statistics that compare the contexts in which a term is used [16]. The higher the similarity score, the higher the chance that the two terms have the same denotation.

In this paper, we invoke the Cortical.io[1] tool that employs Semantic Folding Theory (SFT), a novel method that creates sparse distributed representations of terms (their semantic fingerprint [17]). Each activated bit of the semantic fingerprint represents a characteristic of that word. For example, some of the activated bits for the word *dog* may denote the concepts *fur, barking, omnivore*, while some activated bits for the word *moose* may represent *fur, herbivore, horn*. The higher the number of shared activated bits, the higher the similarity between two words.

Algorithm 1 takes a set of user story requirements and generates an ambiguity score for all couples of terms that appear in the use stories. In line 1, the Visual Narrator tool [8] extracts nouns (e.g., car, dog) and compound nouns (e.g., cable car, sledge dog) from the set *userStories*. Then (line 2), all combinations of term pairs are added to the variable *termPairs*. The algorithm constructs the context of each term (lines 3–5), i.e., the set of all user stories that contain such term.

---

[1] http://api.cortical.io/.

The loop of lines 6–12 takes care of computing the ambiguity score for each pair of terms $(t1, t2)$. The semantic similarity of the two terms is computed in line 7; we use the Cortical.io algorithm based on semantic folding and finger-prints. Then, the algorithm builds the context of each term pair: all and only the user stories where exactly one of the two terms occurs (lines 8–10). We exclude the user stories where both terms occur because we assume that the analyst who writes a story purposefully chooses the employed terms, and therefore two distinct terms in the same story are unlikely to be in a correspondence relation.

The similarity score can now be determined–again, via Cortical.io–for the contexts of each pair of terms (line 11). Finally, the ambiguity score (line 12) is computed as a linear combination of term similarity and context similarity. We currently assign a weight of 2 to former and a weight of 1 to the latter.

Algorithm 1. Computing the (near)-synonymy ambiguity score of term pairs

---

COMPUTEAMBIGSCORE(Set⟨UserStory⟩ *userStories*)
  1   Set⟨Term⟩ *usTerms* = VISUALNARRATOR(*userStories*)
  2   (Term,Term) *termPairs* = $(t1, t2)$. $t1, t2 \in usTerms \land t1 \neq t2$
  3   Set⟨US⟩ *ctxs* = ∅
  4   **for each** *term* ∈ *usTerms*
  5   **do** *ctxs*.ADD(*userStories*.FINDSTORIESTHATCONTAIN(*term*))
  6   **for each** $(t1, t2)$ ∈ *termPairs*
  7   **do** $sim_{t1,t2}$ = SEMANTICSIML($t1, t2$)
  8   int i = *usTerms*.INDEXOF($t1$)
  9   int j = *usTerms*.INDEXOF($t2$)
 10   (Set⟨US⟩, Set⟨US⟩) *pairContext* = (*ctxs*[i] \ *ctxs*[j], *ctxs*[j] \ *ctxs*[i])
 11    $simc_{t1,t2}$ = SEMANTICSIML(*pairContext*)
 12    $ambig_{t1,t2} = \dfrac{2 \cdot sim_{t1,t2} + simc_{t1,t2}}{3}$

Illustration. Consider the following set of user stories: {us1 = As a t_A, I want ..., us2 = As a t_A, I want to print t_C ..., us3 = As a t_B, I want ..., us4 = As a t_A, I want to save t_C and t_B ..., us5 = As a t_B, I want to load t_C ... }. Visual Narrator (line 1) extracts the terms t_A, t_B, and t_C, while line 2 computes all pairs: (t_A, t_B), (t_A, t_C), and (t_B, t_C).

Lines 3–5 build the contexts for each term. For example, the context for t_A is {us1, us2, us4}, i.e., {As a t_A, I want ..., As a t_A, I want to print t_C ..., As a t_A, I want to save t_C and t_B ...}.

Lines 6–11 calculate the ambiguity score for each pair of terms. Take (t_A, t_B), and assume that Cortical.io returns a similarity score between the terms (line 7) of 0.34. The pair of contexts for those terms (line 10) is ({us1, us2}, {us3, us5}). The semantic similarity algorithm is now launched between the two elements of the pair of contexts; assume this results in a context similarity of 0.66 (line 11). Finally, the ambiguity score is determined in line 12 as $(2 \cdot 0.34 + 0.66)/3 = 0.44$.

3.1   Validation of the Ambiguity Score

We determined the weights for sim_p and sim_c based on the outcomes of exploratory tuning attempts: we have analyzed and discussed the outputs of different weights on training data sets and examples, and we found such weights to lead to results we perceived as the most representative for our data sets.

While robust, large-scale experiments are necessary to identify optimal values for the similarity values, we tested the reliability of $ambig_p$ with our weights via a correlation study between the algorithm and human judgment. The details on the experimental design and data are available online [18].

We employed the *WebCompany* data set that consists of 98 user story requirements. From this, taking the algorithm's outputs, we randomly extracted 8 term pairs with a high ambiguity score ($\geq$0.6), 8 pairs with low ambiguity score ($\leq$0.4), and 8 pairs with medium ambiguity score (between 0.4 and 0.6).

Eight master's students in information science participated voluntarily. Each of them filled in a questionnaire that contained 12 term pairs with their contexts (4 with low ambiguity, 4 medium, 4 high), with the terms allocated in such a way that every term pair would obtain the same number of judgments. For each term pair, the participant had to indicate how likely they perceived the term pair to be ambiguous, using the scale "Impossible", "Unlikely", "Likely", "Certain" or "Don't know". In total, 24 term pairs were processed by the 8 participants.

A Pearson correlation on the data shows a *strong* and *significant positive correlation* between the scores of the algorithm and by the participants, r = .806, p = <.001. Although the data is not sufficient to draw definite conclusions about generality and sensitivity, the results are promising.

4   Pinpointing Ambiguity and Incompleteness via InfoVis

Building on the framework of Table 1, we design a novel InfoVis technique for analysts to explore multiple viewpoints and for helping them pinpoint possible ambiguity and incompleteness. Our approach, also thanks to Algorithm 1, helps identify defects concerning the *correspondence* (synonyms and near-synonyms) and *contrast* relations (missing requirements). The *conflict relation* (homonyms) is supported to a more limited extent, as explained in this section.

Our visualization is inspired by our previous work on the automated extraction of conceptual models from user story requirements (the Visual Narrator tool) [8]. However, despite the high precision and recall, those models become quickly too large and models for humans to grasp and analyze. This is especially true when conducting in-depth analyses such as searching for defects.

To improve the situation, we resort to visualizing viewpoints via a Venn diagram, which is a suitable means for displaying overlapping elements [19]. Figure 1 provides an example where the terms used from three viewpoints (by the stakeholders *Administrator*, *User* and *Visitor*) are shown alongside their overlap.

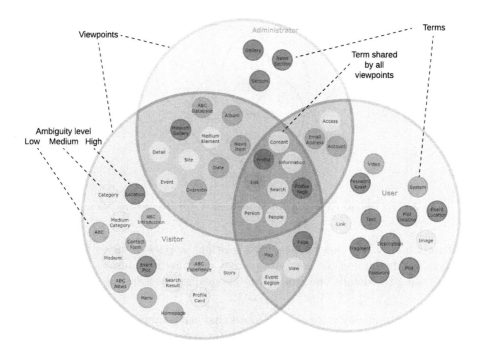

Fig. 1. Venn diagram visualization of three viewpoints and ambiguous terms.

Finding (near-)synonymy. The visualization outlines the possibly ambiguous terms by applying Algorithm 1. A term's background color is set depending on the highest level of ambiguity that term possesses with respect to another term. As explained below (details-on-demand), this high-level overview can be refined for more accurate results.

Missing requirements and homonymy. Our approach helps an analyst explore the relationships between the terms used by multiple stakeholders. Consider the Venn diagram in Fig. 2 that includes three viewpoints, and whose intersection produces 7 areas (A–G)[2]. There are interesting areas for the analyst to examine:

- Areas A, C, G include terms that appear in a single viewpoint. These are loci where missing requirements may be discovered, because they contain terms that appear in a single viewpoint. In Fig. 1, for example, the term Plot appears only in the *User* viewpoint, but presumably also the *Administrator* may have some requirements about this content type.
- Area E contains the terms that are shared by all three viewpoints, while areas B, D, F include the terms that appear in exactly two viewpoints. The instances of every term therein—one or more instances per viewpoint—are either in consensus (no problem) or conflict (possible homonymy) relation.

---

[2] Using triangular shapes, it is possible to show six viewpoints on a 2D space [20].

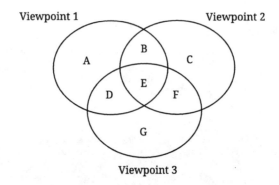

Fig. 2. The 7 areas (A–G) of our visualization applied to three viewpoints.

Determining which one of these two relations applies is up to the analyst, who should examine the user stories that contain those terms. This can be done using the details-on-demand zoom explained later in this section.

Filters. Our visualization comes with filters that can be applied to hide unwanted items from the display. We propose three filter types:

1. *Concept state filter* removes the concepts in a consensus/conflict state or those in a correspondence/contrast state from the display, so that the requirements engineer can focus on a given type of possible defects.
2. *Viewpoint filter* removes some viewpoints from the display, so that the analyst can focus on the remaining ones. This helps when more than three viewpoints exist; although it is possible to show six viewpoints without hiding any intersection [20], it is more practical to visualize two or three of them.
3. *Ambiguity filter* shows the elements within a given ambiguity score range. This can be useful to better examine the elements with high ambiguity score or to double check those with low-medium score. This is illustrated in Fig. 3.

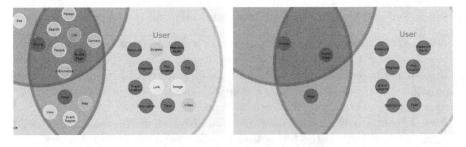

Fig. 3. Illustration of the ambiguity filter: on the right-hand side, only terms that are part of a term pair with an ambiguity score above 0.4 are shown.

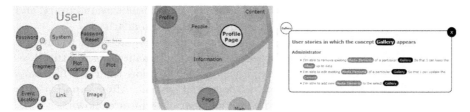

(a) Showing association relationships.   (b) Ambiguity for term profile page.   (c) User stories including term gallery.

Fig. 4. Illustration of details-on-demand.

Details-on-demand. These are features for retrieving additional details that are not visible through the main interface:

– *Association relationships* are the actions that a term refers to in the user stories. For example, in "As a user, I want to request a password reset", the association relationship of the term password reset is the verb request. When enabled, the association relationship is shown as a small icon next to the term. Each association relationship of a given term has a different color and is marked with the first character of the verb. Further details can be inspected by clicking on the icon, which opens a small pop-up window. Figure 4a shows the association relationships for nine terms, and provides details for the verb request of term password reset, and for the verb logout of term system.

– *Ambiguity inspection.* The ambiguity that a term shares with other terms can be inspected by clicking on it. Boldface font is applied to the term label and the background is set to white, while the color of all other terms is changed based on the ambiguity score they share with the selected term. Figure 4b shows high ambiguity between profile page and both profile and page.

– *User stories.* The user stories in which a term appears are shown in a pop-up window by double clicking on that term. The detailed term is given a black background, and other terms in those stories are given a blue background. Figure 4c shows these details for the term gallery.

5   Evaluation

In Sect. 5.1, we show feasibility by describing our implementation of the approach presented in the previous sections. In Sect. 5.2, we report results from our preliminary evaluation of the tool effectiveness with groups of students.

5.1   Proof-of-Concept Tool

We developed a proof-of-concept Web 2.0 tool that implements the visualization described in Sect. 4 and the algorithm for ambiguity detection of Sect. 3. The tool is built on the Bootstrap framework, relies on the D3.js visualization library, and calls the REST API of cortical.io to compute semantic similarity.

The tool can be accessed online[3]. The website provides quick links to two sets of real-world user stories that showcase the tool's functionality: besides the *Web-Company* data set already mentioned, it is possible to explore the *CMS-Company* data set [8] that refers to a content management system. After importing the data sets, the viewpoints with the highest number of terms are shown.

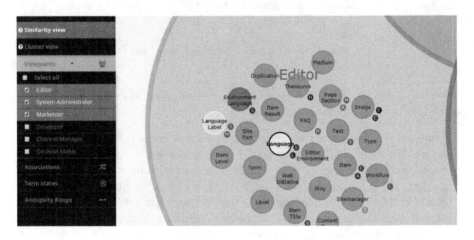

Fig. 5. Our tool showing an excerpt of the CMS-Company data set.

For example, in the CMS-Company data set, the three viewpoints shown by default are *Editor*, *System Administrator* and *Marketeer*, while the three less dense viewpoints are hidden: *Developer*, *Decision Maker* and *Channel Manager*. Figure 5 shows an excerpt of the CMS-Company data set where the three main viewpoints are selected, and the analyst focuses on the term Language within the viewpoint *Editor*: the tool shows that Environment Language is likely to be a (near)-synonym of Language, while Language Label is less likely to be so.

The tool is a proof-of-concept. Although most functionalities are implemented, it is not a product. Also, the Venn-inspired visualization currently works with up to 3 viewpoints, while the functionality to support more than three concurrent viewpoints (through different shapes) has not been implemented yet.

5.2   Quasi-Experiment with Students

We report on a controlled quasi-experiment we conducted with students that aimed to assess the effectiveness of our approach as implemented by the tool described in Sect. 5.1. Our report follows Wohlin *et al.*'s guidelines [21].

Goal Definition and Context Selection. The goal of our evaluation as well as a description of the context selection are presented in Table 2.

---

[3] http://www.staff.science.uu.nl/~dalpi001/revv/.

Table 2. Goal definition for our quasi-experiment.

Object of study	We study two objects: (i) Our tool-supported approach for identifying ambiguity and missing requirements supported by a wide 84" touch screen, and (ii) a manual, pen-on-paper inspection of the requirements
Purpose	Evaluate the relative effectiveness of our approach compared to the pen-and-paper inspection
Perspective	We take the point of view of RE researchers
Quality focus	We study the *precision* and *recall* of the approach in detecting *ambiguity* and *incompleteness*
Context	We involve voluntary master's students in Information Science from Utrecht University. We conduct a blocked subject-object study, for we have two objects and multiple subjects per object. Since we could not split the participants according to their background, we are conducting a quasi-experiment. The low number of students (n = 8) makes the results preliminary

Hypothesis Formulation. We derive four hypothesis by combining the two qualities we are interested in (precision and recall) with the two dependent variables: ambiguities and missing requirements. Therefore, our hypotheses unfold as follows: *Analysts who use our approach obtain a significantly higher X compared to analysts using a pen-and-paper inspection*, where X is as follows:

- *precision in finding ambiguities* (H1);
- *recall in finding ambiguities* (H2);
- *precision in finding missing requirements* (H3);
- *recall in finding missing requirements* (H4);

Based on extensive brainstorming among the authors, a pilot test, and the existing literature, we have constructed the following pragmatic definitions of missing user stories and ambiguous user stories to use in our quasi-experiment; these definitions reflect the type of support that our tool intends to deliver:

- A missing user story is one whose absence inhibits the realization of at least another user story;
- An ambiguity occurs when two user stories contain distinct terms that shares the same denotations.

Experiment Design and Operation. We divided our 8 participants into four groups of two members each; two groups used our tool, while two groups used the pen-and-paper inspection. The participants had to work with a set of user stories that we assembled from a Software Architecture course, which they had attended; those user stories were for an event ticketing system.

The experiment was repeated two times; in each instance, we involved one group using our tool run on the interactive screen (*treatment* group) and one group performing manual inspection (*control* group). We executed three steps:

1. *Briefing (20 min)*: all participants read a 1-page document that described the experiment's goals (investigating the effectiveness of a visualization technique for finding ambiguities and missing user stories), included instructions, and provided an example. Then, the second author gave a short presentation about ambiguity and missing requirements. Finally, the members of the treatment group were given a 5-min demo about our tool.
2. *Defect detection session (20 min)*: the two groups were assigned the task of finding ambiguities and missing user stories from the event ticketing system specification. They conducted their task in different rooms, with the second author unobtrusively observing the treatment group.
3. *Results evaluation (20 min)*: the groups collaborated toward identifying which of the identified ambiguities and missing requirements were true.

Validity Evaluation. We discuss the major threats to the validity of our study:

- *Internal validity.* The selection on participants based on their voluntary help made us unable to make a selection that evenly represents the entire population. While we tried to evenly balance the groups of participants based on our opinion on their skills and background knowledge, but we did not employ rigorous criteria to do so. Furthermore, relying on a discussion between group members to reach agreement on true ambiguities and missing requirements may suffer from social factors such as predominant personality and persuasion. Finally, the presence of an observer in the room with the treatment group may have affected the behavior exhibited by the participants.
- *Construct validity.* The pre-operational explication of constructs may have been unclear: ambiguity and incompleteness are difficult topics and, despite our attempt to use easily actionable definitions, the participants may have assigned different interpretations. Also, our treatment was influenced by a secondary factor, i.e., the use of an extra-large interactive screen, which could have affected the results. This threat is not extremely severe though, for this is the setting we designed our tool for. Furthermore, we did not study independently the effectiveness of the various features the tool embeds. Finally, it should be noted that the obtained results rely on the use of user story requirements; we cannot assess the generality for other notations.
- *Conclusion validity.* The small sample size implies low statistical power. Also, our study suffers from random heterogeneity of subjects, for it is likely that some individuals possessed significantly better analytical skills than others.
- *External validity.* The major threat in this category is that we chose students instead of professionals, for convenience reasons.

Analysis and Interpretation. The quantitative results of our quasi-experiment, obtained by running independent t-tests for H1–H4 based on the figures in Table 3, offer some interesting insights:

- *Precision (H1, H3):* we cannot find any significant difference between the groups. For ambiguity, $t(-1.106) = -1.208$, $p = .442$, and Cohen's effect size value ($d = 1.1$) suggests low practical significance. For missing requirements, $t(-.044) = 1.283$, $p = .971$, and Cohen's effect size $d = 0.04$ suggest low practical significance.
- *Recall (H2, H4):* we identify a significant difference in support of our hypotheses. For ambiguity, $t(-13.088) = 1.459$, $p = .017$, and $d = 13.2$, denoting high practical significance. For missing requirements, $t(-4.941) = 1.999$, $p = .039$, and $d = 4.999$, also suggesting high practical significance.

The results suggest to reject H1 and H3: our approach does not seem to increase precision in the identification of the stated defects. On the other hand, the results suggest to retain H2 and H4: our approach seems to lead to significantly higher recall compared to the pen-and-paper inspection. The validity of these results needs to be confirmed by replicating our study with more participants.

Table 3. Quantitative results of our quasi-experiment. TP and FP stand for true and false positives, respectively.

	Total TP	#TP	#FP	Precision	Recall
Session 1 – ambiguity					
Pen & paper	28	8	1	0.888	0.285
Tool		23	4	0.851	0.821
Session 2 – ambiguity					
Pen & paper	12	3	4	0.428	0.25
Tool		9	0	1	0.75
Session 1 – incompleteness					
Pen & paper	9	4	1	0.8	0.444
Tool		5	2	0.714	0.555
Session 2 – incompleteness					
Pen & paper	5	2	2	0.5	0.4
Tool		3	2	0.6	0.6

Qualitative results. We complement the results above with qualitative findings obtained from observation and via follow-up interviews with the participants:

- *Observations.* The two groups using the interactive screen behaved differently: while both members of the first group stood close to the screen and interacted with our tool, the second group had one person interacting with the screen and the other one standing at some distance to gain a more holistic viewpoint. The first group spent less time on identifying defects, perhaps due to the difficulty of obtaining a bird's eye view, and they also incurred in some conflicts, e.g., the tool interpreted as a pinch-to-zoom request the simultaneous drag-and-drop actions performed by the participants. In general, all the participants seemed confident with using either treatment even without an extensive training.

– *Interviews.* The participants provided suggestions that may help improve the tool. In particular, they identified some major missing features, such as a search field for quickly identifying the terms by name, a close-all button to hide all pop-up windows, and underlined association names in the details-on-demand window showing the user stories where a term appears in. Importantly, they indicated they would like to be able to change the elements in the visualization (rename and remove elements). They expressed appreciation for the tool, and found potential in terms of time saving thanks to the organization of the user stories around the viewpoints and the terms that occur in the stories.

6   Related Work

InfoVis for RE. A recent systematic literature review [22] classifies existing approaches along the RE activities they support, the involved stakeholders, and the focus on the problem or solution domain. According to that framework, our work supports the *requirements verification* activity, focuses on the *problem domain* (stakeholders' needs), and is intended for *decision-makers.*

Among existing visualization approaches, a similar approach to ours is taken by Savio *et al.* [23], who propose a 3D pyramidal visualization in which every face of the pyramid represents one stakeholder/viewpoint, and the pyramid is sliced along the z-axis to denote different levels of refinement of the requirements. Reddivari *et al.* [24]'s RecVisu+ tool organizes requirements graphically in clusters based on their similarity, it includes an algorithm for automated cluster label generation, and it supports manipulating the requirements during their elaboration. Orthogonally, the atomic elements in our approach are the terms (instead of the requirements), and the analyst can then inspect the corresponding requirements by requesting details (see Fig. 4c).

In our previous work [25], we proposed a cluster-based visualization of the terms extracted from user story requirements. Differently, in this paper the terms are not aggregated via clustering, but they are organized according to viewpoints, and ambiguity detection algorithms support the identification of possible defects.

Ambiguity in RE. Several studies on ambiguity in RE have been conducted so far. The seminal contribution of Berry and Kamsties [1] provides an excellent overview of the main categories of ambiguity and their relevant for RE, including lexical (investigated in this paper), syntactic or structural, semantic, and pragmatic. Since then, researchers have examined anaphoric ambiguity (pronouns) [26]; proposed dictionary-based approaches to detect ambiguous and weak terms [27]; introduced the notion of nocuous ambiguity [28] as opposed to harmless ambiguity; experimented what combinations of ambiguity metrics is more effective in practice [29]; and studied pragmatic ambiguity that depends on the background of the reader [30]. Our work adds another brick to this thread of research, as our techniques focus on pinpointing near-synonymy and homonymy.

7   Discussion

We have proposed an approach that combines InfoVis and NLP in order to help analysts identify some classes of ambiguity (near-synonymy and homonymy) and missing requirements. Our visualization represents the requirements graphically by highlighting the terms that are used and arranges those terms on a 2D space according to the viewpoint they belong to. Our preliminary evaluation suggests that our approach *may* lead to a significantly better recall than a pen & paper inspection, while no significant difference in precision could be detected.

Several research challenges need to be overcome. The effectiveness should be tested at a larger scale and possibly by isolating the effect of the individual tool functionalities. The algorithm for detecting ambiguity can be improved and tuned, while avoiding over-fitting. We also wish to study whether domain ontologies can lead to a deeper understanding of the requirements and their relationships. We would like to identify visualization mechanisms that avoid heavy reliance on colors, which are an obstacle for color-blinded people. Finally, we are interested in the use of InfoVis techniques to ease the transition from RE to architectural design.

More generally, this paper opens the doors for future work that combines InfoVis and NLP. While we examined incompleteness and ambiguity in user stories, other requirements notations and other defect types should be studied.

Acknowledgment. This project has received funding from the SESAR Joint Undertaking under grant agreement No 699306 under European Union's Horizon 2020 research and innovation programme.

References

1. Berry, D.M., Kamsties, E., Krieger, M.M.: From contract drafting to software specification: Linguistic sources of ambiguity. Technical report, School of Computer Science, University of Waterloo, Canada (2001)
2. Bano, M.: Addressing the challenges of requirements ambiguity: A review of empirical literature. In: Proceedings of the International Workshop on Empirical Requirements Engineering, pp. 21–24 (2015)
3. Rosadini, B., Ferrari, A., Gori, G., Fantechi, A., Gnesi, S., Trotta, I., Bacherini, S.: Using NLP to detect requirements defects: an industrial experience in the railway domain. In: Grünbacher, P., Perini, A. (eds.) REFSQ 2017. LNCS, vol. 10153, pp. 344–360. Springer, Cham (2017). https://doi.org/10.1007/978-3-319-54045-0_24

4. Cambria, E., White, B.: Jumping NLP curves: A review of natural language processing research. IEEE Comput. Intell. Mag. **9**(2), 48–57 (2014)

5. Berry, D., Gacitua, R., Sawyer, P., Tjong, S.F.: The case for dumb requirements engineering tools. In: Regnell, B., Damian, D. (eds.) REFSQ 2012. LNCS, vol. 7195, pp. 211–217. Springer, Heidelberg (2012). https://doi.org/10.1007/978-3-642-28714-5_18

6. Lucassen, G., Dalpiaz, F., van der Werf, J.M.E.M., Brinkkemper, S.: Improving agile requirements: the quality user story framework and tool. Requirements Eng. **21**(3), 383–403 (2016)

7. Cohn, M.: User Stories Applied: for Agile Software Development. Addison Wesley Professional, Redwood City (2004)

8. Robeer, M., Lucassen, G., Van der Werf, J.M., Dalpiaz, F., Brinkkemper, S.: Automated extraction of conceptual models from user stories via NLP. In: Proceedings of the International Requirements Engineering Conference (2016)

9. Finkelstein, A., Kramer, J., Nuseibeh, B., Finkelstein, L., Goedicke, M.: Viewpoints: A framework for integrating multiple perspectives in system development. Int. J. Softw. Eng. Knowl. Eng. **2**(1), 31–57 (1992)

10. Mullery, G.P.: CORE - a method for controlled requirement specification. In: Proceedings of the International Conference on Software Engineering, pp. 126–135 (1979)

11. Sommerville, I., Sawyer, P.: Viewpoints: principles, problems and a practical approach to requirements engineering. Ann. Softw. Eng. **3**(1), 101–130 (1997)

12. Shaw, M.L., Gaines, B.R.: Comparing conceptual structures: consensus, conflict, correspondence and contrast. Knowl. Acquisition **1**(4), 341–363 (1989)

13. Pohl, K.: Requirements Engineering: Fundamentals, Principles, and Techniques. Springer, Heidelberg (2010)

14. DiMarco, C., Hirst, G., Stede, M.: The semantic and stylistic differentiation of synonyms and near-synonyms. In: Proceedings of the AAAI Spring Symposium, pp. 114–121 (1993)

15. Rips, L.J., Shoben, E.J., Smith, E.E.: Semantic distance and the verification of semantic relations. J. Verbal Learn. Verbal Behav. **12**(1), 1–20 (1973)

16. Mikolov, T., Sutskever, I., Chen, K., Corrado, G.S., Dean, J.: Distributed representations of words and phrases and their compositionality. In: Proceedings of the Neural Information Processing Systems Conference, pp. 3111–3119 (2013)

17. De Sousa Webber, F.: Semantic folding theory and its application in semantic fingerprinting (2015). arXiv preprint arXiv:1511.08855

18. van der Schalk, I.: REVV: A tool to create a better understanding of software requirements through Information Visualization and NLP. Master's thesis, Utrecht University (2017)

19. Micallef, L.: Visualizing set relations and cardinalities using Venn and Euler diagrams. Ph.D. thesis, University of Kent (2013)

20. Carroll, J.J.: Drawing Venn triangles. HP Labs Technical Report (73) (2000)

21. Wohlin, C., Runeson, P., Höst, M., Ohlsson, M.C., Regnell, B., Wesslén, A.: Experimentation in Software Engineering. Springer, Heidelberg (2012). https://doi.org/10.1007/978-3-642-29044-2

22. Abad, Z.S.H., Ruhe, G., Noaeen, M.: Requirements engineering visualization: a systematic literature review. In: Proceedings of the International Requirements Engineering Conference (2016)

23. Savio, D., Anitha, P., Patil, A., Creighton, O.: Visualizing requirements in distributed system development. In: Proceedings of the Workshop on Requirements Engineering for Systems, Services and Systems-of-Systems, pp. 14–19. IEEE (2012)

24. Reddivari, S., Rad, S., Bhowmik, T., Cain, N., Niu, N.: Visual requirements analytics: A framework and case study. Requirements Eng. **19**(3), 257–279 (2014)
25. Lucassen, G., Dalpiaz, F., van der Werf, J.M.E.M., Brinkkemper, S.: Visualizing user story requirements at multiple granularity levels via semantic relatedness. In: Comyn-Wattiau, I., Tanaka, K., Song, I.-Y., Yamamoto, S., Saeki, M. (eds.) ER 2016. LNCS, vol. 9974, pp. 463–478. Springer, Cham (2016). https://doi.org/10.1007/978-3-319-46397-1_35
26. Yang, H., De Roeck, A., Gervasi, V., Willis, A., Nuseibeh, B.: Analysing anaphoric ambiguity in natural language requirements. Requirements Eng. **16**(3), 163 (2011)
27. Tjong, S.F., Berry, D.M.: The design of SREE: A prototype potential ambiguity finder for requirements specifications and lessons learned. In: Proceedings of the International Working Conference on Requirements Engineering: Foundation for Software Quality, vol. 7830, pp. 80–95 (2013)
28. Willis, A., Chantree, F., De Roeck, A.: Automatic identification of nocuous ambiguity. Res. Lang. Comput. **6**(3), 355–374 (2008)
29. Kiyavitskaya, N., Zeni, N., Mich, L., Berry, D.M.: Requirements for tools for ambiguity identification and measurement in natural language requirements specifications. Requirements Eng. **13**(3), 207–239 (2008)
30. Ferrari, A., Lipari, G., Gnesi, S., Spagnolo, G.O.: Pragmatic ambiguity detection in natural language requirements. In: Proceedings of the International Workshop on Artificial Intelligence for Requirements Engineering, pp. 1–8. IEEE (2014)

Large-Scale RE

Quality Requirements Challenges in the Context of Large-Scale Distributed Agile: An Empirical Study

Wasim Alsaqaf[(✉)], Maya Daneva, and Roel Wieringa

University of Twente, Enschede, The Netherlands
{w.h.a.alsaqaf,m.daneva,r.j.wieringa}@utwente.nl

Abstract. **[Context and Motivation]** Focusing single-mindedly on delivering functional requirements while neglecting quality requirements has been a point of criticism of Agile software development methods since their introduction. **[Question/problem]** Empirical evidence on the challenges that organizations currently face when dealing with quality requirements in Agile, is however scant. **[Principle ideas/results]** We performed a qualitative exploratory multiple case study in the context of real-life large-scale distributed Agile projects, in order to understand the challenges Agile teams face regarding quality requirements. Based on 17 semi-structured, open-ended, in-depth interviews with Agile practitioners from six organizations in the Netherlands, we collected and analysed data, revealing 13 quality requirements challenges classified in five categories: (1) team coordination and communication, (2) quality assurance, (3) quality requirements elicitation, (4) conceptual definitions, and (5) software architecture. We found an incongruity in the way QRs are conceptualized by Agile practitioners and in RE textbooks. **[Contribution]** The main contributions of the paper are the explication of the challenges from practitioners' perspective and the comparison of our findings with previously published results.

Keywords: Agile large-scale distributed projects · Requirements engineering
Quality requirements · Exploratory empirical research method · Interviews

1 Introduction

Agile and lean project delivery models are increasingly adopted or adapted in the context of large-scale and distributed project organizations. Moving away from the context for which it was originally conceived – small, co-located teams with actively-participating clients on board – problems attributable to the Agile approach more and more aggravate. One of those is the lack of attention for quality requirements (QRs). In a 2017 systematic literature review (SLR) [1] that we did on engineering QRs in Agile projects in general, we found twelve QR-specific challenges that could lead to a failure to meet user expectations. Our SLR also reported the lack of empirical evidence on how Agile projects handle QRs systematically in their entirety, particularly in Agile large-scale development (ALSD). This motivated us to do an empirical study on understanding the challenges distributed Agile teams in ALSD projects experience when engineering the QRs. We have interviewed 17 practitioners with different professional expertise (e.g. testers,

© Springer International Publishing AG, part of Springer Nature 2018
E. Kamsties et al. (Eds.): REFSQ 2018, LNCS 10753, pp. 139–154, 2018.
https://doi.org/10.1007/978-3-319-77243-1_9

architects, scrum master, managers) and from different domains (e.g. banking, public transportation, tax processing) working for Agile project organizations in the Netherlands. We set out to answer the following research question (RQ):

What challenges do Agile practitioners face when engineering the QRs in ALSD settings?

For the purpose of our research, we consider an Agile project 'distributed' if it consists of more than one team and its teams are distributed in terms of the distribution models described by Larman and Vodde [2], viz. multi-site teams - the teams work on different locations, but each team is single site, and dispersed teams - the teams work on different locations, and each team is multi-site.

The rest of this paper is structured as follows: Sect. 2 provides related work. Section 3 presents our research process, and Sect. 4 reports our results. Section 5 compares our results with those previously published and in Sect. 6 discusses validity threats. Section 7 discusses the results and Sect. 8 concludes.

2 Related Work

Table 1 lists studies reporting various RE challenges in Agile large-scale context. The first column describes the reported RE challenges and the second – the literature sources. Not all sources mention whether their studied projects were distributed or not. Also, not all indicate the size of the case study projects subjected to research. Regarding project size, Käpyaho et al. [3] classified the reported case study as large where approximately 30 Agile practitioners were involved. Paasivaara et al. [4] classified the case studies they included in their SLR as large. The median size of involved Agile practitioners was 300 participants. Kasauli et al. [5] illustrated the size of their case study projects by the number of sub-teams involved (e.g. one project had more than 30 sub-teams, each running its own scrum process). Petersen and Wohlin [6] used the number of involved participants per sub-team and the produced line of code (LOC) to denote the size of their case study projects. Each project had an average number of 37 team members and an average of 392,000 of LOC. Rolland [7] described his case study projects as large based on the involved teams and participants. The projects involved 13–14 teams and more than 200 participants. Sachdeva and Chung [8], Ramesh et al. [9] and Bjarnason et al. [10] did not indicate directly the size of the case studies in terms of numbers of participants. As it is hard to understand the relationships between the RE challenges C1-C15 (in Table 1) and the contextual settings in which these challenges were observed, we felt motivated to look closer into the ALSD context and do exploratory empirical work focused on QR-related challenges.

Table 1. Summary of RE challenges in ALSD reported in the literature. Requirements-related challenges are italicized.

ID	ALSD RE challenge	Source
C1	Minimal documentation and difficulties with getting the teams to document the requirement	[3, 5, 9, 10]
C2	*The non-availability of customers for requirements negotiation, clarification and feedback*	[3, 5, 7, 9, 10]
C3	Inappropriate architecture when new requirements arise	[6, 9]
C4	Difficulties with requirements-based effort estimation and planning	[4, 9, 10]
C5	*Requirements Prioritization based on a single dimension*	[6, 9, 10]
C6	*Weak quality assurance practices linked to requirements (e.g. testing of QRs, Automated and integration tests of the requirements)*	[3–7, 9, 10]
C7	Difficulty to discover dependencies between sub-systems in an early stage	[6, 7]
C8	*Neglect of QRs*	[3, 8, 9]
C9	Lack of customer's domain knowledge when creating user stores	[10]
C10	*Lack of a clear requirements picture early in de development cycle*	[3, 7, 8, 10]
C11	Ensuring sufficient competences within the teams	[10]
C12	Difficulties with including innovative ideas from the teams at the time of user story writing,	[10]
C13	Use of prototype code in production, to support requirements validation	[3]
C14	*Difficulties with the requirements refinement process*	[4, 5]
C15	*High-level requirements management largely missing in Agile*	[4, 5]

3   Our Exploratory Case Study Research Process

Agile development methods (ADMs) as well as RE depend in their application on human interactions and interpretations. Therefore, to understand how developers treat QRs in ADMs we have to study the subject in real-life settings. We designed a qualitative exploratory multi-case study by following the guidelines of Yin [11]. We conducted semi-structured, open-ended, in-depth interviews according to the guidelines of Boyce and Neale [12]: First, we made a plan describing (1) the kind of information we intended to collect, (2) the kind of practitioners who could provide us with the sought-after information and (3) the kind of project settings that would be an appropriate candidate to be included in the case study. To understand the challenges from different perspectives, we included practitioners with various backgrounds (e.g. different expertise and roles, e.g. architects, testers, different years of experience, different application domains). This is in line with research methodologists [11, 12].

Second, the first author developed an interview protocol, which was improved by feedback from the other two authors. We then conducted a pilot interview with an Agile practitioner to check the applicability of the questions in real-life context. No changes made to the interview questions after this stage[1]. The set of interview questions is composed of two parts. The interview starts with questions to understand the project context, and continues with questions about the practices the participants experienced in engineering the QRs in one particular project of their choice.

The interviews were conducted in Dutch by the first author. Our interviewees were 17 Agile practitioners from various organizations in the Netherlands. The term 'organization' used in this paper refers to the company that employs the participant and not the Agile project organization in which the participant worked. The organizations included in the case study all claimed to follow Agile development methodologies. The anonymized information about the organizations is summarized in Table 2. Three of the organizations (O2, O4, O6) have a long history in IT consultancy. They employ high skilled consultants and IT coaches specialized, among other things, in ADMs. One is a big government organization (O5) that has adopted an Agile large-scale framework for several years. Organizations O1 and O3 provide customized IT services. O1 is specialized in providing Transport services and O3 provides Administrative software (O3). Both O1 and O3 use an ADM to develop their software for several years. The second column of Table 2 indicates the approximate size of each organization, the third column shows how many projects from each organization we have included in our study, and the rightmost column shows how many participants from each organization joined our study.

Table 2. Case study organizations

Organization	Size in employee's number	# of projects	# of participants
O1	Middle (51–200)	2	4
O2	Middle (51–200)	1	2
O3	Big (200–500)	1	1
O4	Big (300–700)	3	3
O5	Big (10000–30000)	3	3
O6	Big (50.000–100.000)	4	4

Table 3 presents the studied projects' settings. All projects used Scrum as their ADM of choice. One project (P13) fell into the dispersed team category, while the other 13 projects (P1–P12 and P14) were composed of multi-site teams. The second column of Table 3 shows the total number of team members and the number of Agile teams in the respective project. For example, project P1 had 21 team members that formed 3 distributed teams. The third column shows which Agile scaled framework is used by each project. A cell with 'none' means that no particular framework was used for guidance. The rightmost column indicates the application domain.

---

[1] https://wasimalsaqaf.files.wordpress.com/2017/07/interview-questions.docx.

Table 3. Case study projects

Project	# members/teams	Use of a scaled-framework	Domain
P1	21/3	none	Public sector
P2	24/2	none	Public sector
P3	117/13	SAFe [13]	Government
P4	30/3	none	Commercial
P5	50/5	Scrum of Scrums [14]	Banking
P6	175/25	SAFe [13]	Commercial navigation
P7	56/7	none	Public sector
P8	12/2	none	Public sector
P9	28/4	none	Government
P10	40/6	none	Health care
P11	27/3	SAFe [13]	Government
P12	24/3	SAFe [13]	Government
P13	14/2	none	Insurance
P14	200/22	Spotify [15]	Telecom

Table 4 shows the years of work experience each participant has in general in the field of Software Engineering, and which role(s) (s)he performed in her/his projects which were described in Table 3. Some participants performed more than one role in the respective project, so the number of roles (20) is larger than the number of interviewees (17).

Table 4. Years of experience and roles of the participants

Participant	Years of experience	Project	Role
PA1	4	P1	Software Developer
PA2	20	P1	Software Developer & Software Architect
PA3	15	P2	Scrum Master
PA4	36	P2	Software Tester
PA5	21	P3	Scrum Master & Software Tester
PA6	6	P4	Scrum Master
PA7	20	P5	Agile Coach
PA8	22	P6	Agile Coach & Product Owner
PA9	10	P7	Software Architect
PA10	29	P8	Delivery Manager
PA11	25	P9	Software Architect
PA12	22	P10	DevOps Manager
PA13	17	P11	Scrum Master
PA14	15	P12	Software Designer
PA15	18	P7	Information Analyst
PA16	5	P13	Software Developer
PA17	7	P14	Agile Coach

The interviews happened between February and April 2017. The length of the interviews varied from 50 to 95 min. At the beginning of each interview, the research objective and the structure of the interview were explained. The researcher informed the participants further about their rights and responsibilities towards the research. All interviews were audio-recorded to avoid loss of data.

Our last step was the data analysis. The audio files were transcribed to a written version by a professional external organization. We chose not to do the transcription ourselves to avoid any interpretation bias that could be passed into the transcripts by the researchers involved in preparing and taking the interviews. The analysis process in this paper was done based on the grounded theory method described by Charmaz [16] which is suitable for qualitative exploratory research where theory should emerge from the data. Thereafter the first two researchers (Alsaqaf, Daneva) read the transcripts separately and inductively applied descriptive labels (called codes) to segments of texts of each transcript. Table 5 provides two examples of the process of coding a segment of text. In the next step, the researchers involved in the analysis stage came together and discussed the descriptive codes they applied. Similar descriptive codes were combined in higher-level categories. Different descriptive codes were resolved by conducting an argumentative discussion [17] between the researchers to reach a shared rationally supported position and then combined in higher-level categories. No unresolved different descriptive codes remained after this step.

Table 5. Texts and codes

Original text	Codes
PA1: *"The accuracy was mainly specified by the Product Owners and you also notice that there has been too little communication among the software developers. As a result, a number of bugs has emerged."*	Teams communication
PA10: *"A role that I missed in the beginning was such an overall architect who said: "hey, guys, if we do this, what shall it mean for the overall architecture? Do we really need another framework? If yes, what does that mean?" We have added this role later. However, we missed it at the beginning of the project."*	Teams organization

4   Results

Our qualitative analysis yielded 13 QRs challenges on team and project levels. We have divided those challenges into five categories as described in the next sub-sections. We illustrate our findings with quotations from the interview transcripts.

4.1   Teams Coordination and Communication Challenges

These challenges concern the sharing of information resources among the teams within a large Agile project team (e.g. in a Scrum of scrums setting) or among the development team and the client's organization. These are:

1. Late detection of QRs infeasibility. In the experience of our participants, inappro-priate work coordination and insufficient communication among distributed teams can result in figuring out too late that a needed QR is infeasible. This may cause expensive refactoring of the software architecture and re-implementing the delivered functions. Project P7 was supposed to deliver a web-based system for public use. The system should at all times (1) ensure the authentication and authorisation of the user (e.g. security), (2) ensure ease of use by providing the user with all needed in-formation and navigation options (e.g. usability) and (3) ensure high speed by loading the start web-page within 3 s (e.g. performance). The development team discovered at an advanced stage that collecting all the needed information after passing all the security filters will cause the start web-page to take at least 10 s to load. At this point a decision was made to drop the performance requirements since demanding these requirements will result in costly architectural rework. The team traced this issue to the fact that the QR conflicts were not apparent in the beginning and the Agile working process had no way to anticipate such conflicts.

2. Assumptions in inter-team collaboration. Our data indicate that QRs are rarely implemented in a single piece of code and can span the whole system. So they typically are the responsibility of different teams. These teams should establish an unambiguous interaction process to ensure the right implementation of the QRs that they share respon-sibility for. However, often teams make the assumption that every other team responsible for the implementation of a QR understands its part and will implement it correctly, so the resulting system would demonstrate the quality aspect demanded in the QR speci-fication. In the experience of our participants, this assumption however turns out unre-alistic. For example, in project P1, text documents had to be made available for end-users to search through. The documents were developed by one team and made available for end-users by another team. This is on the assumption that the documents are correct and accurate. PA1 reports: *"We had agreements about, for example, the validity of the documents. We agreed to put the word "expired" in the name of the document when a document is no longer valid. If the communication between the teams has not gone well – what actually happened- the end-users could consult document which did not reflect the reality at that moment"*. Another challenge that our practitioners found was that if a team accepts ownership over the correct implementation of a QR, then this team assumes to rely on the knowledge shared with other teams and also on their availability. Participant PA5 reports the following regarding teams' interactions: *"We want with pleasure to pay more attention to security tests. However, because we are a team among many teams, we have a lot of interactions with those teams. So, our work is still very disturbed by questions from other teams. It's just awkward. The same with performance tests, we just do not have time to do, or to collect knowledge about those tests. It is just very, yes, frustrating sometimes"*.

3. Uneven teams maturity. All our participants indicated that in their perception, the success of Agile projects relies on the tacit knowledge embedded in the teams, especially the knowledge related to architecturally significant requirements. They thought, expe-rienced developers are more likely to make better architectural decisions than junior developers [18]. However, when organizations form Agile teams, usually these include a mix of experienced and junior developers. In turn, they face the challenge of transferring the knowledge from the more experienced to the less experienced team members in a way that allows both sides to share the same knowledge of the system and enhance the overall quality of it by implementing the right QRs in the right way. Participant PA6 describes his experience: *"When we were a small company, we attracted only junior developers. Our senior developers made a strategic decision to build super libraries to deal with issues like security and performance. The novices could use the libraries without changing their internal structure. However, due to misunderstanding of some concepts or using the libraries in a wrong way by novices, performance problems have arisen which resulted in conflicts".*

4. Suboptimal inter-team organization. Large Agile projects that include multiple teams, face the challenge of organizing these teams around the so-called Product Backlog Items (PBIs). Our participants were well aware of multiple ways to organize the Agile teams in an ALSD project, however they did not know what way would work best in a particular context. They had no reliable way to predict the coordination costs associated with a particular organization of the teams around the PBI. The PBIs are all the desires that might be needed in the product and are listed in an ordered way in the "Product backlog" (PB) [19]. The PB is the single source of requirements for any change to be made to the product. Our participants used various approaches to this situation: (1) Component teams are organized around particular components of the system such as a database, user interface, etc. (2) Feature/Scenario teams are organized around particular product features such us login, log processing, etc. (3) Functional teams are organized around a single development function such as a test team or an architecture team. Depending on the context and the system to be implemented, one of the approaches or a combination of two or more could be used. However, since each of them has advantages as well as drawbacks, our participants thought that teams should be careful with their choice because a suboptimal choice could affect negatively the quality attributes of the system. Participant PA9 describing this challenge: *"When we started the project we divided the teams into scenario teams. Each team was responsible for the implementation of a whole scenario from the user interface through the database layer. We saw then that each component suffered from ambiguity and clear guidelines. Because each team had its own way of working and there was no ownership for the components, spaghetti code began to arise and it was difficult to understand the structure of the different components".*

4.2 Quality Assurance Challenges

These challenges concern the activities of verifying and validating the requirements. Our participants describes the challenges they face regarding quality assurance as follows:

1. Inadequate QRs test specification. According to our participants' observations, QRs are difficult to model and therefore identifying and designing acceptance tests for them may be difficult [20]. Besides, ADMs lack formal modelling of detailed require-ments [3] which makes the process of verifying the QRs more difficult. PA1 describes this challenge: *"At the end of the project an employee was added to the project to perform the acceptance test and he was responsible for data integration and accuracy tests. This tester did not find errors and gave a green light for accuracy, although we know that there are still potential problems"*. Participant PA4: *"There were no hard performance requirements. So, for example, if I'm doing a test and I feel it takes a very long time, I will give a warning. In principle, it would be good if we had all kinds of requirements on paper or just written somewhere, that is also a kind of a struggle for me, because sometimes I do not know what to test against"*.

2. Simulated integration tests. All participants perceived integration tests as critical to the verification of the implemented QRs. This was due to the fact that if QRs must be globally implemented, they impact the entire system and not only the components sepa-rately. Therefore, the work of the development teams should be merged at some point to perform integration tests. These tests could happen late in the development period. If these tests reveal QR defects, this could result in extremely costly re-work and refac-toring of the existing software architecture. For example, P3 was a large project that used SAFe [13] to coordinate the work among the distributed Agile teams. P3 had sprints of two weeks and shippable increments every six sprints. At the end of each six sprints, the whole set of all shippable increments delivered by the distributed teams was merged and went through an integration test by a devoted integration team (DIT). The DIT needed other four weeks to complete the needed integration tests. QRs related issues discovered by de DIT went back to the particular teams to be resolved. PA5 reported this challenge: *"So what we have done now is actually saving all the work of six sprints and offering it to the integration team at once, while you could actually do the tests in advance"*. The development teams do simulate integration test as part of their own unit tests. However, simulating an integration test is not the same thing as doing a real inte-gration test.

3. End user acceptance of QRs. Some of our participants use the so-called 'definition-of-done' (DoD) [19] to specify the related QR's. In Agile methods, DoD is the primary check mechanism for Agile team members [19] to have the same understanding of when to report a particular task (e.g. user story) as completed. As our participants wanted to include the QRs related to the user stories in development, they had to specify the conditions for deeming the QRs 'met' by the delivered product in the DoD. However, specifying QRs in the usual format of the DoD was far from straightforward and resulted in lengthy checklists which impact the development velocity negatively. Moreover, using a long DoD made end-user acceptance testing, and communication and coordi-nation related to QRs validation more complex. PA8 describes this: *"If you have legal or compliance matters, you will at all times comply with the compliance rules of the Dutch Bank or privacy laws, then you have to put them in the DoD, which results in a very long DoD. Every single item in the DoD has impact on the team velocity since you have to do a lot of work to finish one user story"*.

4.3 QRs Elicitation Challenges

These challenges refer to different aspects of identifying the right QRs from the right stakeholders. They are as follows:

1. Overlooking sources of QRs. Agile depends on the involvement of the stakeholders to iteratively collect the requirements. However, the scaled Agile frameworks deployed in our case study organizations provide no guidance for thorough stakeholder analysis. Indeed, face-to-face feedback sessions were planned to gather stakeholders' feedback on the implemented requirements and to let new stakeholder's requirements emerge. However, to collect those requirements, all stakeholders representing the different viewpoints of the system should be identified [21]. In the experience of our participants, as there was no stakeholder identification process, often Agile teams overlooked important stakeholders, leading to missing requirements and, in turn, increasing project cost. As PA7 reflected: *"If I look back at the whole project life cycle, I think identifying all the stakeholders and getting feedback from them as soon as possible is still the biggest threat to the success of the project"*. QRs are by nature cross-cutting requirements which means that they may influence other requirements of different viewpoints. Participant PA9 reports this issue: *"Identifying the QRs was a problem for us. Most QRs were not identified in advance and were discovered in a later stage. By that time it was very complex to implement them"*.

2. Lack of QRs visibility. QRs can be broken down into two categories External and Internal [22]. External QRs are visible to the stakeholders and describe how the system should perform the desired function to be of acceptable quality (e.g. security, performance, availability). The stakeholders of our case study organizations were very interested in those QRs and explicitly talked about them. Internal QRs describe the ease of understanding, maintaining and extending the system (e.g. maintainability, modifiability, extensibility) and contrary to external QRs are in the first instance barely visible to the stakeholders. In the end they are visible to stakeholders, namely by means of increased maintenance cost. Participant PA8: *"Internal QRs get attention only when it is really needed and when the system begins to crack"*.

4.4 Conceptual Challenges of QRs

These challenges refer to the conceptualization of QRs by the Agile teams. Specifically, we make a distinction between definitional challenges regarding the nature of QRs, and specification challenges regarding the ways to document them.

1. Conceptual definition of QRs. Participants differed in how they defined the nature of QRs and how they should be treated. Some (e.g. PA8, PA16) experience QRs as standalone requirements which should not be treated differently from FRs. Participant PA16 explained: *"Requirements of quality nature as well as those of functional nature can be placed on the Product backlog as well as the Definition of Done"*. Others (e.g. PA11, PA15) do not agree with this statement and emphasized the unique aspects of QRs. They see QRs as constraints on FRs. In their perception, QRs are not separate requirements and always specified in relation to some specific FRs. However, recognizing QRs as part of FRs could result in neglecting the QRs if the related FRs were of low priority and negatively impact the overall quality of the system [9]. For example, A new system with its own data storage process (DSP) was developed to replace the old one (i.e. project P2). However, the new system should operate within the same environment as the old one where the DSM is quite different. To guarantee data consistency and avoid future data errors Participant PA2 proposed to keep the old DSP intact. The product owner (PO) of the project however, did not recognize keeping the old DSP as high priority which resulted in putting the related QR (i.e. data consistency) on low priority.

2. Mixed specification approaches to QRs. Participants indicated that unclear conceptual understanding of QRs brings confusion regarding their recording in the DoD or in the user stories. In those projects that needed to comply with regulations, QRs were elaborated in much detail by using e.g. response time for characterizing performance requirements, but also cyclomatic complexity as a metric characterising the code that implemented the respective QRs (P6). This level of precision was in contrast with "more qualitative" expressions of the other QRs. This variety of specification formats created confusion of how to express which QRs and how to validate them.

4.5   Architecture Challenges

These challenges are concerned with linkages between the architecture processes that usually happen in a large project and the Agile development processes, and the architect's role and the Agile roles in a ALSD project:

1. Unmanaged architecture changes. Software architecture is intimately connected to the achievement of QRs [23]. Changes made to QRs at any time in the development cycle could result in costly changes in the software architecture because the earlier architecture becomes inappropriate for the new QRs [3]. Participant PA5 reports this issue: *"We have a number of developers who are already making changes closely to the architecture. Those developers who often have discussions with the software architect whenever he wants to make architectural changes which actually will undermine the overall performance. However, sometimes we choose for more performance and sometimes we do not"*. The many changes in the software architecture could lead to fragmentation of architectural knowledge. The architectural knowledge of a particular system component could be limited to the team responsible for implementing the system component and the overall system architectural knowledge to the role of the software architect. Besides, due to minimal documentation and fragmentation of knowledge, the knowledge about previous architectural decisions can be lost. This could cause the justification of QRs trade-offs already made to be lost, and the software to be less understandable and maintainable.

2. Misunderstanding the architecture drivers. Because Agile changes the way in which Agile team members interact with the software architect appointed to the large-scale project, our practitioners perceived that there was a lot of room for confusion in the prioritization of QRs for implementation. Our participants gave examples of cases in which there were conflicting ideas of which QRs drive the architecture and why architecture trade-offs are made in a particular way. Usually, in a project one or two QRs are the most important for the architecture and the other QRs are aligned with those. However, in a Scrum-of-scrums, there is no process to assure that teams maintain the same understanding of QRs' priorities from architecture standpoint. Participant PA8 indicated that in a very large project delivering a transportation navigation system, performance and usability were the two most important QRs and all other QRs were consistently checked for their possible effects on these two. PA8 explains: *"It was difficult to define all user experience (UX) items and share them among all distributed teams. Therefore we had a central UX club who monitor and assess all sub-products delivered by the teams based on face-to-face conversations. Besides, we had a dedicated quality tester who monitored the performance of the delivered products using perform-ance testing tools. Any issues reported by those parties propagated directly to the PB"*.

5   Comparison with Previously Published Results

We now compare our findings with the twelve challenges reported in our 2017 SLR [1]. Our 2017 SLR and the current study agree that ADMs do not provide any widely accepted technique for gathering QRs. Our present results also agree with the SLR findings in that the identification of stakeholders and their QRs at the right development stage is a challenge. Besides, Agile practitioners lack agreement on the nature of QRs and this makes the process of specifying the QRs unclear. However, more research needs to be done to investigate whether the lack of documenting the QRs is due to the inability of the user stories to document them (as reported in our SLR) or due to the lack of agreement about the nature of QRs (as reported above). Our results also overlap with other previously reported challenges [1], namely, (1) Inadequate QRs verification, (2) simulated integration tests and (3) unmanaged architecture changes However, we did not find any evidence about the challenges related to the product owner's role, e.g. issues, such as product owner's heavy workload and his/her insufficient availability [1], in no way threated the success of the projects in our case study.

We also compared our findings with the 15 challenges from literature reported in Table 1, Sect. 2. We use the identifiers C1-C15 to refer to the challenges from Table 1. Our findings overlap some, but not all of the challenges in Table 1: *(C1) Minimal docu-mentation and difficulties with getting the teams to document the requirement.* Our participants did not mention minimal documentation as a challenge by itself. However, they explained that minimal documentation could cause those architectural decisions and the justification of QRs trade-offs that were already made, to get lost, which in turn will make any further changes to the software a challenging task. *(C3) Inappropriate architecture when new requirements arise.* Our participants acknowledge that the emer-gence of QRs in a later stage of development makes the adjustment of the software architecture complex and could result in architectural rework. *(C6) Weak quality assur-ance practices.* Our findings reveal that distributed Agile projects struggle with quality assurance practices (e.g. Inadequate QRs verification, Integration tests), which could result in discovery of defects late in the software lifecycle. *(C7) Difficulty to discover dependencies between sub-systems in an early stage.* Our results did not mention this as a challenge. However, our study revealed that practitioners could overlook the consequences of such dependencies which could result in not delivering the demanded QRs. *(C8) Neglect of QRs.* The participants in our case study recognize these challenges (see Sects. 4.2 and 4.3). Due to complexity of identifying and verifying QRs at an early stage of the development cycle, a fast and non-elegant implementation of the QRs could be the result later in the development cycle. *(C10) Lack of a clear requirements picture early in de development cycle.* Our practitioners mentioned the late detection of QRs as a challenge for implementing them correctly (see Sect. 4.3). *(C11) Ensuring sufficient competence within the teams.* Our findings suggest that Agile teams face the challenge of transferring relevant knowledge from experienced team members to less experienced members, which could result in an insufficient distribution of competences among the distributed teams.

Our findings did not confirm the following challenges reported in Table 1: *(C2) The non-availability of customers for requirements negotiation, clarification and feedback, (C4) Difficulties with effort estimation and planning, (C5) Requirements Prioritization based on a single dimension (C9) Lack of customer's domain knowledge, (C12) Difficulties with including innovative ideas from the teams, (C13) Use of prototype code in production, (C14) Difficulties with the requirements refinement process and (C15) High-level requirements management largely missing in Agile.*

6   Threats to Validity

We evaluated the threats to validity by using the checklist of Yin [11]. We accounted for researchers' bias as the first two authors have extensive business experience. Specifically, the first author has an Agile software engineering background, therefore, some occupational bias [24] could be passed to the interview questions as well as the interviews themselves. This type of bias was reduced by (1) having the interview protocol and questions reviewed by experienced and senior researchers (the second and third authors); (2) conducting a pilot interview to ensure the applicability of the interview questions; (3) recording all the interviews and having the audio files reviewed by the senior researchers; and (4) having the audio files transcribed to a written version by a professional external organization. Following Adler [24], we considered that the purpose of our bias-reducing efforts was not to strip out the insider's status of the two authors regarding the interviewees (sharing the characteristic, role, or Agile experiences under study with the participants). Instead, the purpose was to make sure that our interview questions were thoughtfully posed and delivered in a way that allows our interviewees to reveal their true feelings without distortions. In line with this, we treated with special care the minimization of confirmation bias, specifically, the first two authors continually re-evaluated what we read in the transcripts and had the third researcher challenges any pre-existing assumptions and hypotheses.

Furthermore, King et al. [25] reported a lack of honesty that the participants could show in their answers to be possible a weakness in interview techniques. To reduce this threat we took the following measures (1) all the participants were volunteers and had the right to refuse answering any question at any time or even leave the interview at any stage without giving a reason; (2) All the participants were ensured that all information will be confidential and anonymous; (3) The interviewer started each interview by explaining the objective of the research to the participants and the importance of giving accurate and honest answers to the validity and reliability of the research; and (4) The participants had different backgrounds, disciplines and were of different application domains. This diversity allowed us to investigate and evaluate the same phenomena from different points of view. An another possible weakness of interview techniques is the tendency for the interviewer to ask leading questions [25]. However, this threat is minimal since we conducted a pilot interview to ensure the applicability of the interview questions after having the interview questions reviewed by the senior researchers.

Another very important concern is generalizability [11]: would our findings hold if we would interview other practitioners in other countries? We can only claim that the reported challenges occurred in the projects reported above by our subjects. In addition, seven challenges identified by us have also been identified by other researchers (C1, C3, C6, C7, C8, C10 and C11). We think that the desired generalization is not that the challenges we identified occur in all ALSD projects, but that they may occur more often in ALSD, and are important to understand, prevent and mitigate. Our research provides evidence that these challenges are important, because practitioners reported them as such; whether they occur more often requires more research.

7   Discussion

We found that practitioners perceived QRs as architectural requirements. They were concerned about the belated clarification of QRs in their projects and wanted QRs to be identified as early as possible and analysed for their architectural impact. This could be considered as a signal to clarify as early as possible the role of architecture in ALSD projects and its driving requirements. An open question remains regarding whether it makes sense in an ALSD project to define architectural requirements (e.g. QRs) up front. Our results make us think that this makes sense since the emergence of those require-ments in advanced stage results in re-architecting the software, leading to avoidable loss of time and resources.

Our consistent observation in the six organization was that Agile practitioners did not relate their user stories to QRs and to the requirements in general (be it FRs or QRs). Is the term 'requirements' that we know from RE textbooks (i.e. [26]) applicable to Agile projects? Or should we (researchers) forget this term and start talking about 'Agile customer desires'? As our Agile practitioners did not relate requirements to user stories, they also did not relate the properties of good requirements (that we know from text-books) to the user stories. When we asked our Agile practitioners to tell us about their understanding of the term 'requirements' in Agile, their collective experience was that in Agile projects, the requirements are equal to *"the user stories + the conversation about what is in the user stories + the acceptance criteria"*.

Our findings indicated a link between QR challenges and the way in which practitioners learn in Agile. Agile development is an ongoing learning process that involves tacit knowledge. Senior developers build a solid theoretical and practical knowledge that enable them to find their way easily in a dynamic environment and help them with making right decisions. Junior developers on the other hand do not have that tacit knowledge. The only knowledge they have is what they got at their educational institutes which does not include improvising in dynamic environments. Do we expect junior developers to make right decisions in dynamic environments based on their knowledge collected form educational institutes? If not, how to ensure they include QRs (which they get at universities) in dynamic environments (Agile) which does not recognise terms as requirements.

8   Conclusion

This paper identified, based on a qualitative exploratory case study, challenges that distributed Agile teams face regarding QRs. The contribution of the papers is twofold: (1) It identified 13 QRs challenges divided into 5 categories. (2) It compared the identified challenges to challenges found in previous studies. The paper shows that Agile practitioners do not agree on what QRs mean and how to deal with them. Agile practitioners use the concept of user stories to mean the customer desires which is − in the opinion of some of our participants, not equivalent to the concept of requirements. In addition, the paper indicates the lack of appropriate quality assurance practises to verify the right implementation of QRs. Our next step is to understand the problems in ALSD behind the identified challenges in Sect. 4 and the way practitioners cope with these problems in real-life projects (i.e. treatments). Then, we will map the identified treatments to the diagnosed problems to analyse which problems can be mitigated by which treatment. This will lead us to a set of treatments of which we will evaluate the effectiveness in mitigating the diagnosed problems.

References

1. Alsaqaf, W., Daneva, M., Wieringa, R.: Quality requirements in large scale distributed Agile projects – A systematic literature review- First submission
2. Larman, C., Vodde, B.: Large-Scale Scrum More with LeSS. Pearson Education (2016)
3. Käpyaho, M., Kauppinen, M.: Agile requirements engineering with prototyping: a case study. In: RE2015, pp. 334–343 (2015)
4. Dikert, K., Paasivaara, M., Lassenius, C.: Challenges and success factors for large-scale agile transformations: a systematic literature review. J. Syst. Softw. **119**, 87–108 (2016)
5. Kasauli, R., Liebel, G., Knauss, E., Gopakumar, S., Kanagwa, B.: Requirements engineering challenges in large-scale agile system development, pp. 6–8 (2017)
6. Petersen, K., Wohlin, C.: The effect of moving from a plan-driven to an incremental software development approach with agile practices: an industrial case study. Empirical Softw. Eng. **15**, 654–693 (2010)
7. Rolland, K.H.: "Desperately" seeking research on agile requirements in the context of large-scale agile projects. In: Proceedings of the XP 2015 (2015)

8. Sachdeva, V., Chung, L.: Handling non-functional requirements for big data and IOT projects in scrum. In: 2017 Proceedings of the 7th International Conference on Cloud Computing Data Science and Engineering Confluence, pp. 216–221 (2017)
9. Ramesh, B., Cao, L., Baskerville, R.: Agile requirements engineering practices and challenges: an empirical study. Inf. Syst. J. **20**, 449–480 (2010)
10. Bjarnason, E., Wnuk, K., Regnell, B.: A case study on benefits and side-effects of agile practices in large-scale requirements engineering. In: AREW, pp. 1–5 (2011)
11. Yin, R.K.: Case Study Research Design and Methods. Sage Publications Inc., Thousand Oaks (2013)
12. Boyce, C., Neale, P.: Conducting in-depth interviews: A guide for designing and conducting in-depth interviews. Evaluation **2**, 1–16 (2006)
13. Leffingwell, D., Knaster, R.: SAFe 4.0 Distilled: Applying the Scaled Agile Framework for Lean Software and Systems Engineering. Pearson Education (2017)
14. Larman, C., Vodde, B.: Practices for Scaling Lean & Agile Development. Addison-Wesley Professional, Upper Saddle River (2010)
15. Kniberg, H., Ivarsson, A.: Scaling Agile @ Spotify - with Tribes, Squads, Chapters & Guilds (2012)
16. Charmaz, K.: Constructing Grounded Theory: A Practical Guide Through Qualitative Analysis. SAGE Publications, London (2006)
17. Hitchcock, D.: The practice of argumentative discussion. Argumentation **16**, 287–298 (2002)
18. Boehm, B.: Get ready for agile methods, with care. Computer **35**(1), 64–69 (2002)
19. Schwaber, K., Sutherland, J.: The Scrum Guide (2016). http://www.scrumguides.org/index.html
20. Bourque, P., Fairley, R.E.D.: Guide to the Software Engineering Body of Knowledge, Version 3.0. IEEE Computer Society Press, Los Alamitos (2014)
21. Sommerville, I.: Software Engineering. Pearson Education (2011)
22. Mario, C.: Executable Specifications with Scrum. Pearson Education, Upper Saddle River (2013)
23. Kazman, R., Bass, L.: Toward deriving software architectures from quality attributes. Softw. Eng. Inst. 1–44 (1994)
24. Adler, P.N.: Membership Roles in Field Research. SAGE Publications Inc., Beverly Hills (1987)
25. King, N., Horrocks, C.: Interviews in Qualitative Research. SAGE Publications Ltd., London (2010)
26. Lauesen, S.: Software Requirements: Style and Techniques. Pearson Education, Upper Saddle River (2002)

The Problem of Consolidating RE Practices at Scale: An Ethnographic Study

Rebekka Wohlrab[1,2,3]([✉]) [ID], Patrizio Pelliccione[1,2] [ID], Eric Knauss[1,2] [ID], and Sarah C. Gregory[4]

[1] Chalmers University of Technology, Gothenburg, Sweden
wohlrab@chalmers.se, {patrizio.pelliccione,eric.knauss}@cse.gu.se
[2] University of Gothenburg, Gothenburg, Sweden
[3] Systemite AB, Gothenburg, Sweden
[4] Intel Corporation, Santa Clara, USA
sarah.c.gregory@ieee.org

Abstract. [**Context & Motivation**] Large-scale requirements engineering contexts often involve hundreds of experts that collaborate to specify the characteristics and functionality of an integrated product. As diverse disciplines and locations are involved, it is not uncommon that the understanding of processes and concepts differs between departments and teams. [**Question/problem**] In practice, it is challenging to allow for flexibility and diversity between organizational units and at the same time establish consistent practices and sufficient alignment among them. Yet, it is desirable to balance this tradeoff, so that short time to market at reasonable cost can be achieved. [**Principal ideas/results**] This paper presents an ethnographic study focusing on a three-year project in a large-scale industrial company that tried to consolidate requirements engineering practices and customize a tool solution to the company's needs while maintaining autonomy of individual units. [**Contribution**] We present challenges of the company's initiative and share mitigation strategies based on our lessons learned. Specifically, we give indications on when to consolidate and unify, and when to allow for diversity in RE practices.

Keywords: Large-scale requirements engineering
Ethnographic study · Industrial requirements engineering
Aligning requirements engineering practices

1 Introduction

Industrial requirements engineering faces the challenge of scale—both when it comes to the size of software systems and also because a large number of

---

Intel Corporation was not involved in the industrial case underlying this study.

© Springer International Publishing AG, part of Springer Nature 2018
E. Kamsties et al. (Eds.): REFSQ 2018, LNCS 10753, pp. 155–170, 2018.
https://doi.org/10.1007/978-3-319-77243-1_10

stakeholders from different disciplines and diverse organizational contexts are involved [1]. In these often globally distributed contexts, processes and tool differences are a common challenge [2]. Focusing on self-organizing teams that make local decisions has been observed to be successful [3] and it has been argued that this strategy allows software organizations to scale [4].

However, when trying to develop one integrated and aligned end product, it is challenging to deal with too heterogeneous systems engineering approaches. Especially with respect to requirements engineering and laying the foundations for development and testing, it is essential to find a trade-off between diversity and alignment of requirements engineering practices in organizations [5].

In order to explore this issue in a practical context, we conducted an ethnographic study [6,7]. We followed a three-year project in a large-scale industrial company that aimed to align requirements engineering practices and support this alignment by employing a systems engineering tool solution.

In this paper, we present experiences from the project and describe what changes in the tool solution and organizational context were made and for what reasons. Moreover, we share our lessons learned and mitigation strategies to counteract the challenges the project faced. We found that especially whenever communication with external stakeholders plays a role, it is necessary to have aligned practices. However, for activities like requirements elicitation, diverse methods should be supported. It is of central importance to carefully select stakeholders and document design rationales. Commitment from the top level of the organization and incentives for teams adapting practices are beneficial to successfully consolidate requirements engineering practices.

The remainder of the paper is structured as follows: In Sect. 2, we describe the industrial context of the company and the project to consolidate RE practices. Section 3 presents related work. Section 4 describes our research method. In Sect. 5, we elaborate on the findings of the initiative to consolidate requirements engineering practices. Section 6 presents a discussion of our findings and Sect. 7 concludes the paper.

2   Industrial Context

The main focus of this study lies on CompanyX, an automotive manufacturer with more than 10,000 employees. They are distributed across five countries. In the specific project that we focus on in this study, there were three locations involved. The organizational structure of CompanyX is characterized by departments related to the traditional architectural decomposition of a vehicle, e.g., powertrain, chassis, and electrics. Functional requirements, the focus of this paper, are specified in these departments. Moreover, there exists a department focusing on the vehicle as a complete system and specifying attributes for it.

Within CompanyX, we mostly interacted with Function Owners, a role responsible for the specification, development, and integration of user-visible functions in the system. These were typically engineers who had been involved in the development for many years before becoming responsible for the development of one or more functions in their area of expertise. Some of them additionally had the role of function developers who define the lower-level design of functionality and software components. The project was driven by a project manager with a background in requirements engineering and business processes. Another stakeholder was responsible for the configuration and user training related to the current and future use of the systems engineering tool within CompanyX.

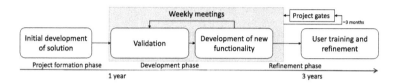

Fig. 1. The activities of the project

Figure 1 shows the activities of the project we focus on in this study. The project consists of a formation phase in which an initial solution is developed. Three application engineers from the tool vendor are involved, as well as the project manager and a stakeholder for the configuration of the systems engineering tool. After the formation phase, the stakeholders involve function owners from several departments, a responsible manager for the breakdown of functions, and another application engineer from the tool vendor for the iterative analysis, validation, and refinement of the proposed solution in weekly meetings. The initially-defined tool solution, decisions, and suggested changes gain maturity over the course of those weekly meetings. Project gates constitute an external mechanism to follow the project's progress. The project gates were evaluated by a steering group consisting of high-level managers. Once a sufficient level of maturity is reached, the project proceeds with user training and refinement. This is mostly driven by the project manager and a stakeholder for the configuration of the systems engineering tool.

CompanyX decided to collaborate with a tool vendor that develops, customizes, and supports the use of a configurable systems engineering tool. The tool is a customizable information management tool used mainly in the automotive domain for requirements engineering, architecture, design, and testing.

In CompanyX, initial requirements engineering approaches on the functional level differed significantly between departments. While the high-level processes are prescribed by the company, different practices are followed in different departments.

Figure 2 presents an abstraction of the organizational structure and various tools used for requirements engineering. In this figure, three departments are shown, two of which collaborate with suppliers, and one that does internal development. In some departments, the RE approach is based on textual documents, which is not unexpected due to these applications' pervasiveness across industry and the relative unfamiliarity with RE tools among those who do not possess a

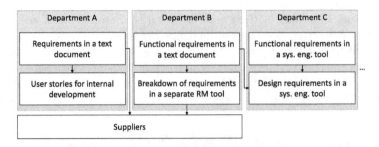

Fig. 2. Excerpt of organizational structure and tools used for requirements engineering

strong background in RE. Besides textual documents, also a requirements management tool and a systems engineering tool are used. The text documents are edited by function owners and stored in a document repository.

Depending on the department, different tools are used for the requirements engineering process. Some departments have an intense collaboration with third-party suppliers whereas others use more internal development (potentially across departmental borders, as in the case of Department B and C). Functional requirements are intended to be on an abstract level to describe system-level functionality that is later broken down in more detailed component-level requirements that trace back to the higher, system-level specification.

Functional requirements are typically on a high level, for instance, "when the driver opens the door, the interior lights should be turned on." However, some groups do not do a stepwise breakdown but rather use the functional requirements specification as the only requirements document (e.g., Department A). In this department, the requirements are used to create user stories for internal agile development. In Department C, the systems engineering tool was used already before the project to specify requirements on a functional level, and also analysis and design requirements and models. This is especially typical when the function owner also fulfills the role of a developer.

CompanyX is currently following the V model systems engineering process and data structure [8]. Some initiatives to implement agile practices have been started. In the current way of working, it is challenging to align the work of different groups to create an integrated product that facilitates development and testing activities. Requirements do not accurately represent the final product. Moreover, the departmental structure makes it difficult for individuals to see how their work fits into the overall system. As the company develops a product line of different systems, it is another challenge to actually see the final product and orient the own work towards it.

The project to change and align requirements engineering practices in different departments was initiated to counteract these issues. Later on, the project managers saw the necessity to establish a common tool supporting traceability between different development and testing phases. The goal was to start with the functional requirements and ensure that they explicitly capture the connections to final products and release dates.

3 Related Work

Carrillo de Gea et al. [9] assess 38 requirements engineering tools. Although the paper was published over five years ago, the challenges outlined reflect similar issues experienced by CompanyX, including those which influenced their decision to select and standardize on the chosen systems engineering tool. They found that insufficient support exists for requirements management, including baseline and project management features and "ensuring that the requirements actually reflect the product." Moreover, the authors discuss that in large organizations, critical requirements engineering data is often scattered across several systems and organizations. The complexity resulting from heterogeneous requirements management environments should be considered when selecting requirements engineering tools. Harmonizing requirements engineering practices by establishing a common tool, as in the case of CompanyX, alleviates the issue of scattered data and facilitates more disciplined requirements management and traceability.

Inayat et al. [10] state that agile RE helps overcome several challenges, for instance, integrating requirements engineering with development tasks and supporting collaboration between teams. While our study focuses on technical and organizational issues with a concrete project on the alignment of requirements engineering practices, we consider the aspect of agility a very interesting complementary perspective. CompanyX has started to use agile methods in parts of the organization, however, not for functional requirements engineering. We expect that the use of agile methods for this phase will impact the alignment-diversity perspective of requirements engineering practices.

Eliasson et al. [11] conducted a study on requirements engineering and information flows in automotive software development. Two challenges they discuss are dependencies between different research and development departments and the trade-off between under- and over-specification of product requirements. They proclaim the need to "bring cross-functional groups together to identify the right abstraction level for requirements." Our study focuses on bringing diverse groups together and find common requirements engineering practices.

Knauss et al. [12] present a case study dealing with an automotive OEM trying to implement more continuous integration practices. They arrive at the conclusion that more "unified, controlled, and consistent data" is needed in order to enable effective continuous integration. To align heterogeneous teams, it is important to also support unified data approaches and find an appropriate tool solution that can support these product development practices.

Weber and Weisbrod [13] describe how DaimlerChrysler established a generic requirements engineering process that was used in tailored forms across business units as they matured their own requirements engineering practices. They stressed the benefit of using a structure of atomic requirements and generating text documents from them. Weber and Weisbrod note that practitioners do not typically struggle with the actual requirements specification as functionality in automotive is often developed in an evolutionary manner. However, it is difficult to structure and present requirements in a comprehensive way. A more recent approach for Daimler's systems engineering is presented in [14]. They currently transition from text-based requirements engineering to model-based specifications. Haasis concludes that available tools do not address practitioners' needs, but organizational implications are not named. In this study, we describe organizational and tool aspects of a project related to requirements engineering.

In an analysis of industrial needs for requirements engineering in the embedded systems domain, Sikora et al. [15] conclude that the use of models for requirements engineering and different levels of abstractions for requirements would be beneficial. They motivate further studies in the areas of quality assurance and traceability between requirements and design. In contrast to our study, the authors of this paper also did not focus on tool or organizational aspects.

4   Research Method: An Ethnographic Study

We conducted an ethnographic study, a technique that originally stems from the areas of sociology and anthropology and that is particularly suitable to study human behavior in a specific context [6]. One common ethnographic approach involves the immersion of one or more researchers into the natural setting of a cultural group as a participant-observer and typically happens over an extended period of time [7]. The ethnographic researcher is acting both as an "outsider," gathering objective information about the context, artifacts, and interaction, but is also as an "insider," engaging in the same pursuits as those who are normally part of the environment under study.

We were interested in the study context as it allowed us to follow a large-scale industrial project aiming to find trade-offs between diversity and consolidation in requirements engineering. While we immersed ourselves in the study and did not aim to confirm a hypothesis, we specified guiding questions:

RQ1: What are challenges and their consequences when trying to consolidate RE practices in large-scale industrial systems engineering contexts?

RQ2: What are mitigation strategies when trying to consolidate RE practices in large-scale industrial systems engineering contexts?

4.1   Description of Research Method

The first author of this paper conducted this study as a participant during a period of 1.5 years. She works as an application engineer and business analyst at a tool vendor for a systems engineering tool and also pursues a PhD degree at Chalmers University of Technology. Besides the author, there were three other application engineers from the tool vendor involved during the course of the project. Whereas the first author was involved during the development and refinement phases, the other application engineers participated mostly in the project formation and development phases (see Fig. 1). To mitigate the risk of bias, long discussions with the other authors were used with the other authors (who were all external to the project). Moreover, in internal discussions to reflect on the progress of the project, all application engineers provided input with their own critical observations. Moreover, we discussed the findings presented in this paper with them as an opportunity to validate the analysis.

The activities of the observer included participating in weekly meetings at CompanyX's site with the project's stakeholders, presenting proposed solutions, configuring the metamodel and views of the systems engineering tool, joining the team for coffee breaks and lunches, and other activities, both related to the project work itself and of a more social focus. In ethnographic studies involving participant observation, it is encouraged that the observer engages in day-to-day activities with the others present ("informants"), rather than merely remaining a detached researcher. During the course of the study, the observer took notes of observations for future analysis, typically as a diary using notes hand-written on a notebook. The research questions were used as guiding questions for the note-keeping. For instance, decisions during the meetings were considered in the notes, but also other interesting points that emerged in discussions or breaks. Moreover, emails and meeting notes by the project leaders were recorded. The development and refinement phases were the periods in which data was collected by the observant. In order to mitigate threats to validity, we triangulated this data with notes, emails, and project documentation gathered over the course of the whole project. Additionally, to gather input after the study, two interviews of approximately one hour were conducted with the project manager and another participant of the project. In these interviews, we discussed lessons learned from the project and mitigation strategies to counteract the identified challenges.

The study took place directly at CompanyX. A consistent 2 h time slot was taken for the meetings and booked several weeks in advance. The weekly meetings typically took place in a meeting room with 12 seats around a larger table. Additional participants from two distributed sites joined via a video conferencing system. To facilitate this task, the project manager typically shared their computer screen.

During the first three months of the study, the observer focused on getting a good understanding of stakeholders and their viewpoints. Technical details and input for the creation of new solutions were other aspects that the field notes focused on. With time, the understanding of the project's context and dynamics increased. The data was analyzed in several iterations during which themes emerged, following a sequential analysis approach for ethnographic data [16]. We immersed ourselves in the project and started to identify the themes depicted in Fig. 4 during the development phase of the project. Over time, these themes were refined based on the notes, discussed, and renamed. We worked in an iterative fashion, both alone and in group discussions among. Two senior researchers and application engineers were involved in these discussions.

The themes were refined, grouped, and analyzed to arrive at connections and implications.

4.2 Threats to Validity

We consider several threats to validity in our ethnographic study [17].

The study was conducted by one researcher directly involved as an observant in the ethnographic study. Notes were taken to document incidents and activities which allowed us to analyze them. However, due to misconceptions and different understandings of terminology, there exist threats to *descriptive and interpretative validity*. We discussed our findings with fellow researchers and also conducted two one-hour interviews with participants of the project. This validation also helped to mitigate *theoretical validity* threats, especially the critical discussions of potential biases with fellow researchers.

Any qualitative study is influenced by researchers' backgrounds and preconceptions and therefore subject to *researcher bias*. The primary researcher in our study was employed at the tool vendor. While it is desirable that the ethnographic researcher is also an insider, it has an influence on how observations are interpreted. As described in Sect. 4.1, the remaining authors were external to the project and we used discussions with them and with internal project members to critically discuss and reflect on the findings during the course of the study. To further mitigate the threat, the paper was reviewed by an industry RE professional who cannot identify the company nor the tool. However, the industry RE professional attests to the generalizability of the findings and consistency with her own experience. Besides the experience with requirements engineering, she has worked extensively with ethnographers and anthropologists at her company for many years. She was involved in their Usage to Platform Requirements effort, and helped develop and conduct training on Usage Models, as well as ethnography-based requirements elicitation.

The review conducted by an industry RE professional mentioned in the last paragraph helped to mitigate threats to *generalizability*. However, in most contexts, tool vendors do NOT deploy trained personnel along with the tool. Other companies might select and use a tool, but would not have representatives from that vendor on-site participating in project meetings and helping with deployment. In our ethnographic study, the observer played the role of an active agent. This could have influenced the results and constitute a threat to *reactivity*.

The sample size of the study and the scope of the project were limited. However, the general research method might be fruitfully employed elsewhere (as it is described in detail in this section). This can help to analyze the replicability of our results.

5   An Initiative to Consolidate RE Practices

As presented in Shahrokni et al.'s work [18], development organizations occasionally reorganize themselves, which can be supported by tools or tool chains that are customizable to different processes and organizations. Figure 3 depicts how the reorganization of processes or organizations can be supported and is strongly intertwined with changes related to employed tools.

For the initiative to consolidate requirements engineering practices in CompanyX, both organizational and tool aspects turned out to bring their own challenges. The processes on a large scale did not undergo significant change (and were not the scope of the project), but the concrete methods changed supported by the tool. In this section, we present the high-level vision and scope of the project in Sect. 5.1, then technical and method challenges (Sect. 5.2), and organizational challenges (Sect. 5.3).

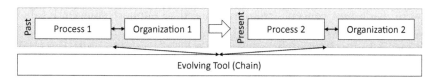

Fig. 3. Evolution of processes and organizations supported by a tool, adapted from [18]

5.1 Initial Vision and Scope of the Project

When the ethnographic study began, the project formation phase had already been completed. The project managers had already evaluated tool solutions and decided to collaborate with the tool vendor. The justification was that CompanyX saw the flexibility of the systems engineering tool and its adaptability to different processes as an advantage. Another application engineer from the tool vendor had created an initial conceptual model of general functional requirements. Functional requirements are used to describe the high-level functionality of a system and are used both for subsequent phases of analysis and design, and finally for functional testing.

In the first phase of the project, the tool vendor aimed to get an understanding of the customer's needs and find ways to formalize relevant information in a metamodel. In discussions with the project manager and other stakeholders, the goal was described to align functional requirements engineering practices by stressing the perspective of the final products and concrete release dates. The idea was to structure functional requirements specifications not according to each product function, but rather use the concrete products and release dates as the high-level structure. Requirements would be organized in "containers" related to products and their release dates. This facilitates the testing process, as testing is always directly connected to a final product. Also the idea of a "common container" for requirements for all products was discussed.

However, with time, this approach was discarded. As the function owners have a traditionally stronger focus on their own functions and requirements, it is a bigger effort to rewrite the functions and their structure to instead reflect the focus on products with release dates. Testing and development stakeholders were underrepresented in the weekly project meetings and their information needs were neglected. Related aspects are presented in Sect. 5.3.

5.2 Technical and Method Aspects

The project established the systems engineering tool as a common tool for functional requirements engineering. Today, it is accessible for all function owners—however, the project has not been closed yet and some users are still in the process of transitioning from their old way of working. Key decisions in the project have been made and key milestones have been reached, but work is still in progress for the widespread adaptation of the tool. Several changes in the tool were made and concepts were introduced to support sufficiently aligned requirements engineering practices:

To facilitate variability management on a lower level, the project worked on the integration of the systems engineering tool with a variant database using an API. This allows that a standard way of describing low-level variants for requirements is supported.

Another decision was to support use case modeling [19] on two levels. On one hand, casual use cases or use case summaries can be specified for initial elicitation of requirements. This involves describing the high-level purpose of a use case and the actors, but no formal scenario description. These use cases are often included in functional requirements specifications to make the function's purpose and structure clearer. On the other hand, formal specifications of use cases with basic course of events ("BCE") are supported which also encompass alternate paths. Typically, these ways of specifying are not combined: In some departments, casual use cases are more common, whereas others use formal specifications to a larger extent. It should be noted that some function owners also specify "situations" or "use conditions" regarding the weather or traffic to describe different modes of the function. They are commonly required by test teams as well as quality and reliability engineers.

Functional safety analysis is supported as well with a solution for hazard analysis and risk assessment. It allows function owners and other safety experts to specify hazards in a grid, deduce ASIL levels, derive safety requirements, and enable traceability. The feature of safety analysis was not considered from the very beginning, but plays an important role when eliciting requirements for functions. As safety is an essential concern for automotive companies, it must be considered already on the highest level of requirements specification.

There were common discussions regarding IDs of requirements. After a long discussion, a standard way of defining requirements IDs was achieved, using a common prefix and a sequential number. Especially for the collaboration with suppliers, it is essential to have unique and persistent requirements IDs to ensure traceability between the specification and their deliveries. For in-house development, it is not as central, especially if the systems engineering tool is used. The tool assigns unique and persistent IDs to all artifacts entered and supports traceability between all artifacts.

There was a change in the data presentation to support different stakeholders' concerns. For instance, functionality was added to provide a top-level overview of functions and responsibilities in a grid. Approximately ten different views and reports for variability and safety concerns were created. For instance, a grid view can be generated to show all requirements of a function with the relevant variants they are valid for. These views facilitate the function owners' work so that they can get an overview of their function and evaluate the correctness of the specified information. Moreover, application engineers from the tool vendor supported the company with the automatic generation of functional requirement specifications as PDF documents. These documents are both required for safety certification and are the traditional interface to suppliers. The need for document generation features has been voiced by practitioners in the past [13].

To summarize, the technical features that were implemented cover different areas: The specification of variants, both casual and formal use cases, safety analysis, requirements IDs, a higher level overview of functions and responsibilities, and several views, grids, and reports. The project decided to allow for diversity (e.g., when it comes to use cases), but in some areas also enforced commonality (e.g., when discussing requirements IDs and the need to find a consistent way of specifying them to collaborate with suppliers).

5.3   Organizational Aspects

Many participants in our project articulated a feeling that they are unable to change processes or organizational structures. The project originated from the middle of the organization. A project manager noted that it was challenging to get support for decisions from both the management organization and engineers who specify, design, and develop a system. We found relevant organizational aspects in both the high-level management organization and the system development organization.

Several issues were identified related to how the project was handled at the management level: The steering group (consisting of higher-level managers) did not have a full understanding of systems and software engineering concerns, in part because core stakeholders' background is in mechanical engineering. The different backgrounds and understandings, e.g., related to how terms like "function" are used, was challenging for the project. The project leaders observed the widely shared assumption that everybody in CompanyX could follow the same methods in detail. However, this assumption does not generally hold, as results depend a lot on the nature of the individual function compared to the individual's own area of expertise, e.g., how much software or mechanics is involved. Due to this lack of understanding, the steering group's vision was unclear and they did not aim to change things at a larger scale. Moreover, there were a few leadership changes during the improvement program that impacted the scope of the project. For instance, new concerns were raised when a manager with a background from a different department joined the project who suggested that different views on the data would be beneficial.

On the other hand, it was also challenging to convince the system development organization to adopt new practices. One of the issues was that people did not share the same vision of aligning traceability practices. They had become comfortable with their ways of working within their own area of responsibility and did not see the lack of a "big picture" as a crucial issue. The project managers' approach to align the ways of working was to try to find function owners who support the project to influence others to adopt it as well. Following this approach and trying to consider everybody's needs made it difficult to actually have an impact. However, it allowed motivated individuals to influence the scope of the project and question decisions. As a consequence, ideas were discarded (e.g., the approach of structuring requirements according to release dates) and new ideas came in. Sometimes new people questioned decisions made prior to their arrival after rationales behind those decisions had been forgotten. As a consequence of this lack of organizational memory, about a year after the initial decision had been taken, it was discussed whether the way of modeling casual and formal use cases should be discarded again. Ultimately, not many stakeholders actually stood behind the earlier decisions. This lack of alignment around earlier decisions impacted the level of trust stakeholders had in future decisions.

A test database was used to try out different metamodels and configurations in the systems engineering tool, but few people actually found the motivation to write specifications there. They saw the changing nature of the project and decided they did not have time to model their functions in a database that could potentially be discarded later on. CompanyX rewards project management milestones (e.g., opened project gates), but there was a lack of incentives for teams and leaders to adapt aligned practices and use the systems engineering tool for requirements engineering.

Core stakeholders were only temporarily involved in the process of defining the systems engineering framework and changes in RE practices, although they might have had important information needs that should have been considered. For instance, project managers (who would be interested in tracking how a project is proceeding and how many requirements of the vehicle with release date X are specified and implemented) were not involved. Also testers were only temporarily involved and did not influence the course of the project.

6   Summary and Discussion

This section presents a summary and discussion of our findings. Section 6.1 discusses challenges and consequences and Sect. 6.2 discusses solution candidates to deal with the challenges.

6.1   Challenges and Their Consequences (RQ1)

This section discusses the identified challenges and consequences and answers RQ1: What are challenges and their consequences when trying to consolidate RE practices in large-scale industrial systems engineering contexts?

Figure 4 shows an overview of the findings. The project tried to find a trade-off between diversity and alignment by supporting several tool features and methods. In some areas, alignment is of central importance, especially when it comes to requirements IDs that constitute an external boundary to suppliers. In the case of use case modeling, which is used for elicitation and to structure the specification document of a particular function, more diverse methods and tool solutions are supported.

Both the management and the system development organizations came with particular characteristics. The management organization underwent several leadership changes, core stakeholders had different professional backgrounds and understandings of the project, and the vision of the project was unclear. The system development organization felt comfortable with the existing practices,

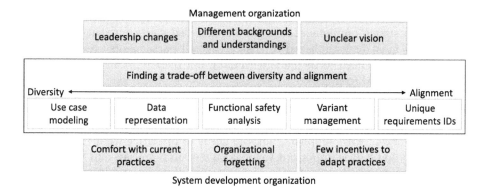

Fig. 4. An overview of the findings related to challenges and their consequences

suffered organizational forgetting as design decisions were not recorded, and did not perceive many incentives to adopt the project's practices.

Based on the experiences of this project and the interviews, we present potential mitigation strategies in the following section and give improvement ideas for practitioners that are involved in similar programs.

6.2 Mitigation Strategies (RQ2)

Based on our analysis of challenges, we discussed mitigation strategies in two interviews with project participants. This section presents the discussion of mitigation strategies and lessons learned from our study. We give answers to RQ2: What are mitigation strategies when trying to consolidate RE practices in large-scale industrial systems engineering contexts?

Involve the right stakeholders. The project in CompanyX struggled with finding a suitable team for the improvement program. At the beginning of a project, a careful analysis of stakeholders should be conducted to identify which roles and individuals should be represented. While there exist standard methods for this step, it can be challenging in practice. For instance, in this study we found that it is important to consider both the management and system development perspectives. If neither the top-level managers believe in the project's vision nor does the system development organization support and execute the practices, it is impossible to have an actual positive impact. For projects improving requirements engineering practices and their alignment, the consumers of the written requirements are the most important ones to include and have on board.

Engage all participants and make decisions with data. Some of the solutions in the project arose from situations in which individuals' opinions resulted in unmanaged changes to project plans or abandonment of previously-established commitments. This should be considered when selecting stakeholders for a project and when taking decisions based on what attitudes are voiced. Stakeholders with strong opinions should not be excluded solely on that basis, but ground rules must be established to ensure that all participants are able to be engaged. Decisions need to be made with data, not merely because of a participants' strongly-held feelings.

Focus on a final vision. We observed a tendency to work with details—e.g., in the case of long discussions on requirements IDs. Requirements IDs are important when working with suppliers, but one needs to prioritize what the focus of meetings should be. It is important to focus on measurable goals and relate decisions to those goals. The scope of a project can easily drift and it is important to keep a final vision in mind.

Try to enforce aligned practices only if you have good reasons. We found that it is desirable to align practices to a certain extent, especially when they are relevant to collaborate with external groups or stakeholders (as in the case of requirements IDs). However, it is of vast importance to understand required boundaries where alignment is necessary, but to allow for diversity otherwise. Especially for requirements elicitation, as in the case of use case modeling in CompanyX, diverse methods are beneficial to foster creativity and arrive at a complete set of requirements. It should be possible to periodically reassess and adapt the boundaries of alignment.

Carefully assess what to change (and when to change back to an initial solution). A reoccurring issue in the project was that solutions were discarded after some time and it was decided to go back to an initial state. We learned that one should not underestimate that the current solution might actually be the best. However, when discarding solutions, one should document why they did not work. Document rationales for decisions to counteract "organizational forgetting." We recommend to keep these rationales as first class entities also in the tool, and link them to relevant requirements or design elements related to those decisions.

Discuss a concrete tool solution to make people formalize their concerns. Whenever abstract process issues or general questions regarding the way of working were discussed, it was harder to arrive at conclusions. Talking about the systems engineering tool and its metamodel made discussions a lot more concrete and helped people formalize their concerns. The iterative process of the project (presenting a solution and gathering feedback in weekly meetings) made it easier to arrive at concrete conclusions and find ideas for improvement.

Keep traceability in mind: How can artifacts be connected? What other areas and phases need this information? When trying to find a common requirements engineering approach, it is important to keep in mind how these artifacts will be used in the future, and how the alignment with subsequent phases can be facilitated. For this reason, it is beneficial to keep opportunities to extend the methods and tools in mind. Ensuring traceability between different artifacts can be a strong enabler to support system-level thinking in the future.

Add incentives to teams and leaders who support and meet objectives in the organizational transformation. Although the systems engineering tool was configured and accessible early in the project, few stakeholders decided to actually work with it. It would have been beneficial to create actual incentives to support the project and encourage others to follow their footsteps. Organizations planning a similar program should assess what incentives or bonuses are valuable and show their appreciation for stakeholders supporting the program's objectives.

7   Conclusion

In this ethnographic study, we explored the issue of aligning diverse requirements engineering practices in a practical context. Focusing on a three-year project in an automotive company, we analyzed technical and organizational aspects of the project and supported the establishment of a systems engineering tool supporting requirements engineering.

We found that it is not desirable to find generic solutions and expect all methods to be alignable in detail, but that diverse practices are desirable especially for requirements elicitation, as in the case of use case modeling. For other concerns, especially the communication with external customers or suppliers, alignment (e.g., using requirements IDs) and traceability are needed. Organizations need to have an alignment between senior leadership and the people working in tactical roles. Stakeholders should be carefully selected for RE initiatives and decision rationales need to be recorded for the project's change-management practices and to counteract organizational forgetting. Continued and visible commitment from leadership and incentives for the team as a whole are required to successfully consolidate requirements engineering practices.

Our findings can be used by practitioners in similar programs and by researchers who work towards facilitating organizational alignment and diversity in requirements engineering contexts. Future work can compare the experiences and mitigation strategies to other projects and companies and suggest actionable guidelines for practitioners. We also consider the alignment of RE practices in agile requirements engineering an interesting area of future work.

Acknowledgments. We are grateful the support of participants in the case projects and we thank for all the clarifications provided when needed. This work was partly funded by Software Center Project 27 on RE for Large-Scale Agile System Development and the Wallenberg Autonomous Systems and Software Program (WASP).

References

1. Cheng, B.H., Atlee, J.M.: Research directions in requirements engineering. In: Future of Software Engineering (FOSE 2007), pp. 285–303. IEEE, May 2007
2. Damian, D.: Stakeholders in global requirements engineering: lessons learned from practice. IEEE Softw. **24**(2), 21–27 (2007)

3. Fricker, S.: Requirements value chains: stakeholder management and requirements engineering in software ecosystems. In: REFSQ 2010, Essen, Germany, pp. 60–66 (2010)

4. Feiler, P., Gabriel, R.P., Goodenough, J., et al.: Ultra-Large-Scale Systems: The Software Challenge of the Future. Software Engineering Institute (2006)

5. Knauss, E., Yussuf, A., Blincoe, K., Damian, D., Knauss, A.: Continuous clarification and emergent requirements flows in open-commercial software ecosystems. Requirements Eng. J. (REEN), 1–21 (2016).

6. Sim, S.E.: Evaluating the evidence: lessons from ethnography. In: Workshop on Empirical Studies of Software Maintenance, pp. 66–70 (1999)

7. Creswell, J.W.: Research Design: Qualitative, Quantitative, and Mixed Methods Approaches, 3rd edn. Sage Publications Ltd., Thousand Oaks (2008)

8. Walden, D.D., Roedler, G.J., Forsberg, K., Hamelin, R.D., Shortell, T.M. (eds.): Systems Engineering Handbook: A Guide for System Life Cycle Processes and Activities, 4th edn. Wiley, Hoboken (2015)

9. Carrillo de Gea, J.M., Nicolás, J., Fernández Alemán, J.L., Toval, A., Ebert, C., Vizcaíno, A.: Requirements engineering tools: capabilities, survey and assessment. Inf. Softw. Technol. **54**(10), 1142–1157 (2012)

10. Inayat, I., Salim, S.S., Marczak, S., Daneva, M., Shamshirband, S.: A systematic literature review on agile requirements engineering practices and challenges. Comput. Hum. Behav. **51**, 915–929 (2015)

11. Eliasson, U., Heldal, R., Knauss, E., Pelliccione, P.: The need of complementing plan-driven requirements engineering with emerging communication: experiences from Volvo Car Group. In: RE 2015, pp. 372–381. IEEE, August 2015

12. Knauss, E., Pelliccione, P., Heldal, R., Ågren, M., Hellman, S., Maniette, D.: Continuous integration beyond the team: a tooling perspective on challenges in the automotive industry. In: ESEM 2016 (2016)

13. Weber, M., Weisbrod, J.: Requirements engineering in automotive development: experiences and challenges. IEEE Softw. **20**(1), 16–24 (2003)

14. Haasis, S.: Systems engineering for future mobility. In: REConf. (2016). https://www.hood-group.com/fileadmin/projects/hood-group/upload/Images/REConf/2016/vortraege/mittwoch/auditorium/Keynote-Systems_Engineering_for_future_mobility.pdf

15. Sikora, E., Tenbergen, B., Pohl, K.: Requirements engineering for embedded systems: an investigation of industry needs. In: REFSQ 2011, pp. 151–165, March 2011

16. Fielding, N.: Ethnography. In: Gilbert, N. (ed.) Researching Social Life, pp. 266–284. SAGE Publications (2008)

17. Maxwell, J.: Qualitative Research Design: An Interactive Approach. Applied Social Research Methods. SAGE Publications, Thousand Oaks (2012)

18. Shahrokni, A., Söderberg, J., Gergely, P., Pelliccione, P., Söderberg, J., Pelliccione, P.: Organic evolution of development organizations - an experience report. In: SAE World Congress and Exhibition - Model-Based Controls and Software Development, pp. 1–9 (2016)

19. Adolph, S., Cockburn, A., Bramble, P.: Patterns for Effective Use Cases. Addison-Wesley Longman Publishing Co., Inc., Boston (2002)

Quality Requirements

QREME – Quality Requirements Management Model for Supporting Decision-Making

Thomas Olsson[1(✉)] ⓘ and Krzysztof Wnuk[2]

[1] RISE SICS AB, Lund, Sweden
thomas.olsson@ri.se
[2] DIPT, BTH, Karlskrona, Sweden
krzysztof.wnuk@bth.se

Abstract. **[Context and motivation]** Quality requirements (QRs) are inherently difficult to manage as they are often subjective, context-dependent and hard to fully grasp by various stakeholders. Furthermore, there are many sources that can provide input on important QRs and suitable levels. Responding timely to customer needs and realizing them in product portfolio and product scope decisions remain the main challenge.

[Question/problem] Data-driven methodologies based on product usage data analysis gain popularity and enable new (bottom-up, feedback-driven) ways of planning and evaluating QRs in product development. Can these be efficiently combined with established top-down, forward-driven management of QRs?

[Principal idea/Results] We propose a model for how to handle decisions about QRs at a strategic and operational level, encompassing product decisions as well as business intelligence and usage data. We inferred the model from an extensive empirical investigation of five years of decision making history at a large B2C company. We illustrate the model by assessing two industrial case studies from different domains.

[Contribution] We believe that utilizing the right approach in the right situation will be key for handling QRs, as both different groups of QRs and domains have their special characteristics.

Keywords: Requirements engineering · Quality requirements
Non-functional requirements · Requirements scoping

1 Introduction

Quality Requirements (QRs, a.k.a. non-functional requirements, NFRs), defined as "attributes of or constraints on a system." [1], are ever-increasingly important [2, 3] but also challenging to handle. There are many challenges associated with QRs, e.g., insufficient product usability [4], project overruns, increased time-to-market [5], poor cost estimation or lower priority of quality compared to functionality [6] and poor validation of QRs [7, 8].

Extensive research was conducted in eliciting [2] representing and modeling QRs [7], leaving the areas of their realization and release planning greatly unexplored. At the same time, our previous work brings evidence that realizing QRs puts new demands on

© Springer International Publishing AG, part of Springer Nature 2018
E. Kamsties et al. (Eds.): REFSQ 2018, LNCS 10753, pp. 173–188, 2018.
https://doi.org/10.1007/978-3-319-77243-1_11

scoping and release planning [2, 9, 10], e.g., QRs often require more than one software release to be realized, top-down planning is not sufficient in many cases and there is a lack of support for executing product strategies based on QRs. Making decisions about what requirements to focus on is often called scoping. Scoping is usually performed by a product manager at a product level [11] and impacts portfolio strategy and product success [12]. Requirements scoping is a continuous activity that supports in translating the product strategies into a series of software releases [11].

Several researchers studied QRs and challenges associated with them. In our previous work, QRs appear to be unequally distributed within the same specification and the same company [10]. Ernst and Mylopoulos analyzed open source projects and concluded that there are large differences among projects and no clear correlation to the project age [13]. Concerning release planning, Ameller et al. report that most models provide "simple output for which requirements to implement in the next release" [14]. Others have identified an under-emphasis of product quality and difficulties in handling cross-cutting concerns across teams with agile methodologies [15].

In this work, we present QREME – Quality Requirements Management model for supporting decision-making about QRs. QRs are changing over time (even if you do not actively make decisions on them), QRs are always present in the software whether you have made explicit decisions on them or not and scoping is a continuous activity, scoping for QRs is different from traditional scoping. The main parts of QREME are: (1) the prominent roles and their responsibilities when making decisions on QRs, (2) the decision forums and how they are related, and (3) the strategic and operational levels for both product-related decisions and business intelligence related decisions. We focus on the following research question: ***How can we support portfolio and product decision makers with respects to QRs?*** The benefit of using QREME is a combination of more effective scoping decisions (making the right decisions) and a quicker response to changes in the marketplace and to software quality issues. It will also be easier to plan the improvement of QRs over several releases. As QREME is addressing the scoping of QRs, the specific way in which QRs are modeled and documented are as such impacting the use of QREME.

The paper is organized as follows: Sect. 2 introduces background and relevant related work. The research methodology is described in Sect. 3. The proposed model with relevant descriptions is found in Sect. 4 and two cases using the model is elaborated on in Sect. 5. Section 6 concludes the paper, including future work.

2   Background and Related Work

There are several definitions of QRs [1]. One implication of the definition we use in this paper of QRs as "attributes or constraints on a system" is that a QRs cannot exist without a corresponding functional requirement or (sub-) system. This, in turn, implies that a requirement or a system will always exhibit the attribute or constraint even if it is not explicitly specified. For example, a system always has a startup-time even if it is not explicitly expressed with a QR. In this paper, we use the term Quality Attribute (QA) as the abstraction of a specific QR., For example, start-up time is a QA and "the system should start in 2 s" a QR. Furthermore, we use the term Quality Level (QL) for the measurable level of a QR, in alignment with our previous work [2]. From the example, "2 s" is the QL.

The continuous nature of requirements scoping plays a vital role in bridging strategic product portfolio planning and associated release planning with operational scope decisions that need to be taken to adapt to unexpected changes [16]. However, linking business strategy to detailed planning is non-trivial [17]. The software product management literature [18] recognizes the strategic importance of QRs in setting the product strategy [19] but does not consider its particular nature during the product and release planning processes. Our previous empirical work shows that QRs should be incrementally delivered and the scoping process stretches over several product releases [9].

Traditional software development is typically done in a forward feeding and top-down manner, typified by the waterfall model [20]. In a forward feeding process, ideas or goals are the starting point and are broken down into requirements, later to be implemented and verified. In the end, the resulting product is evaluated against the original ideas and goals. Today, feedback-driven or bottom-up approaches are gaining momentum, often supported by data-driven approaches [21] or crowd-based approaches [22]. Objective data usage can remove subjectivity from the product managers [23]. In a feedback-inspired process, ideas and goals emerge from the actual usage, mostly through experimentation on alternatives to improve the product, and lastly evaluated against requirements and strategies whether the product is evolving in the right direction. However, for feedback driven approaches, is not clear which type of information is needed for scoping and how to achieve alignment among stakeholders. In our previous work, we saw a need to combine both forward and feedback processes [9].

Agile approaches such as Scrum [24] or the ideas with DevOps [25] end up somewhere in-between. This transition has substantial implications for software product strategies, product requirements engineering and product scoping. Increased flexibility in decision making that the above transformations bring puts more pressure on the synergy between strategic planning, product scoping, requirements management and realization. Incremental delivery of software gains importance and impacts release planning methods and processes [26].

Scoping decisions are often interdependent [27], continuously made [11] during different steps in the development process [27], in different forums [12], at several abstraction levels [28] and often not in a top-down fashion [9]. We studied release planning for QRs [2] while Carlshamre et al. focused on interdependencies among requirements in software release planning [29]. Berntsson-Svensson re-used the interdependency types suggested by Carlshamre et al. to study dependencies between QRs but without an apparent release planning angle [6]. Our work focuses on how to plan and deliver QRs across many releases, with each release taking the software closer to the fulfillment of the complete QR and desired QL.

3   Research Methodology

We used Canonical Action Research (CAR) to develop the framework presented in this paper [30]. The focal point of CAR is a real-word problem that researchers attempt to address by combining scholarly observations with practical interventions using mostly interpretivist epistemology [30]. During one cycle, we continuously interacted with the environment under research and the subjects in this environment to reflect on the needs supported by the model.

Problem investigation. Previous work on analyzing decision patterns for quality requirements [9] have shaped the scope and goals of the current research. We have studied 4444 features from a period of 5 years from the beginning of a new product portfolio across many product and software releases. We combined decision history and document analysis with the interviews with key stakeholders involved in the decision-making process. Our main findings are: (1) QRs require planning across several releases, as they tend to require long lead-time and effort planning (2) some quality aspects (e.g. efficiency) were handled in a bottom-up fashion while other aspects (e.g. security) were driven from a top-down strategic process and (3) multiple strategies are required to have a responsive and aligned organization. The strong need for improved decision making about QRs was expressed during the interviews with the key stakeholders involved in the decision-making process.

Treatment design. During the development of QREME, we focused on creating QREME as "instrumental theory" that helps in generating coherent explanations and achieving understanding for decision making about QRs [30]. A clear need emerged early in the design process to handle both strategic and operational decision-making levels [27] as decisions on these levels are often interconnected. Moreover, the observations made from the in-depth analysis of 5 years of decision making about QRs confirmed that both feedback-loop and forward-loop are unsystematically used and needed to properly handle decision about QRs [9].

QREME was incrementally designed in a series of meetings where the authors discussed the versions and made changes and updates. Each new version of the model was critically evaluated and discussed in a workshop session among the researchers. Changes and updates were documented to enable traceability. The first version of QREME contained only the portfolio strategy and the product scope elements, based on empirical data [9] and related work [27]. After evaluations, it was decided that the core element of the feedback-loop is the product usage data that decision-makers need to continuously analyze and filter. Therefore, the analytics scope element was added to QREME. Next, the three decision forums were identified we named the input and output for each of the forums. Finally, in the last iteration, the roles involved in each decision forum were detailed.

Treatment Implementation and Evaluation. We evaluated QREME on two exploratory case studies from two companies developing software-intensive products but having different QR profiles. The evaluation consists of an assessment based on expert opinion on the companies' ways of working and which elements of QREME they are compliant with and would benefit from.

Company A focuses on user experience, performance and security as it develops software-intensive products of daily use for consumers. Company B, on the other hand, develops software-intensive products for B2B and is mainly concerned with performance, security, and maintainability. The products that company B develops have no user interface that the customers can interact with but collect digital images that can be analyzed in the software that combines it from several devices.

In the next phase, we will evaluate with companies and practitioners the underlying findings from [9] in other companies to ensure this is not unique the company used in that study. Furthermore, we will validate that QREME addresses the findings and is usable in a practical context.

3.1   Threats to Validity

We discuss the validity threats according to the four perspectives on validity proposed by Yin [31] and some of the guidelines provided by Runeson and Höst [32].

Construct validity is concerned with establishing appropriate methods and measures for the studied phenomena or concepts. The empirical evidence that the framework is based on was collected from both the analysis of the decision-making logs and in interviews. This multiple-source evidence provides trustful catalog of observations that impacted the design decisions for the framework. Moreover, we worked inspired by CAR [30] where a theory is the focal point of generating coherent explanations of the studied phenomena and QREME can be considered as an instrumental theory of decision making about QRs.

Internal validity is concerned with uncontrolled confounding factors that may affect the studied causal relationships. The relationships between the selected decision strategies were anchored in the empirical data obtained in our previous study [9]. Still, a threat remains that when QREME is put into operation at other than studies industrial contexts, we may discover additional confounding factors that may affect the decision processes and therefore should be further incorporated into the framework.

Reliability is concerned with the degree of repeatability of the study. The framework creation process was continuously documented to enable traceability and analysis. The QREME creation process was inspired by CAR guidelines to ensure rigor during the iteration and collaboration between researchers and practitioners [30]. However, reliability of the interpretations made during QREME development could be questioned as this step of the process remains highly subjective. We took precautions to minimize subjectivity by discussing our interpretations with industry practitioners and between the authors and seeking most reliable explanations.

External validity remains the main concern of this work. QREME is based on an in-depth analysis of five years of decision making about QRs at a large company. Still, we cannot claim that this is a representative case of how all software-intensive product development companies deal with QRs. Therefore, the suitability of QREME must be further validated outside the two contexts described in the case studies to bring supporting evidence that the foundations of the theoretical framework remain strong for other contexts, product types, and requirements engineering processes.

4 Quality Requirements Management Model (QREME) Supporting Decision-Making for Quality Requirements

The goal of QREME is to provide decision support for managing quality requirements, incorporating two highly interconnected processes: a top-down forward driven, and a bottom-up feedback process. QREME can be applied as an assessment instrument as well as to plan improvement activities for scoping of quality requirements.

4.1 The Anatomy of QREME

QREME has two abstraction levels for decisions: a strategic level and an operational level [9, 27], see Fig. 1. At the strategic level, strategic product decisions are handled, such as deciding which quality aspect (QA) to address and what customer segments to focus on. At the operational level, decisions for individual products are handled, such as quality level (QL) for a specific QR for a specific release or analysis of usage data in a specific context. For example, a QR can be start-up time from powering on a device and the QL can be 10 s. The operational decisions are usually short-term and consider individual products and releases.

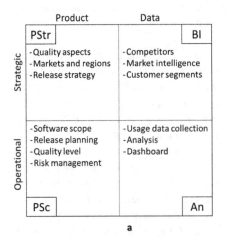
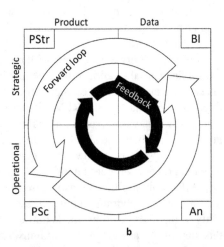

Fig. 1. The conceptual overview of QREME, with PStr = Portfolio Strategy, PSc = Product Scope, BI = Business Intelligence and An = Analytics. Figure 1a summarizes types of decisions in the different areas of QREME and Fig. 1b illustrates the two loops.

Furthermore, QREME separates scoping decisions on the products from decisions on data analysis. Product decisions are about what the products should realize and what data to utilize in the experiments.

This results in four scope decision areas: Product portfolio strategy (PStr), Product Scope (PSc), Business intelligence (BI) and Analytics (An), see Fig. 1a. QREME also distinguishes between (product-)planning-driven decisions (forward-loop) and data-driven decisions (feedback-loop), see Fig. 1b. For the two highly interconnected loops, the feedback-loop is usually faster than the forward-loop. Both loops traverse the four scope decision areas in opposite directions and at different speeds.

4.2 Scope Decision Areas

To achieve both a structured process in refining a long-term roadmap as well as an agile and short response-time to changes in the market, all four decision areas need to have a certain level of autonomy, independent input and possibility to influence each other.

The PStr area concerns strategic product decisions such as quality aspects, markets and release strategy. The decisions are on a strategic level [27] and should embody a company's strategy for the product(s) or portfolio. A **portfolio manager** is typically the main decision maker [33]. Decisions will outline portfolio-wide direction regarding which QAs to focus on and how individual products show relate to this. PStr decisions should be reviewed on a quarterly or half-year interval. The main decision forum is **the product portfolio strategy forum**. The decisions are typically summarized in informal natural language as a presentation file or a short document. The portfolio manager mainly interacts with the product manager and the business intelligence manager for scope decisions, cf. Fig. 2. Besides the roles directly involved in the decisions, the portfolio manager takes input from executive management, marketing manager, key account managers, etc.

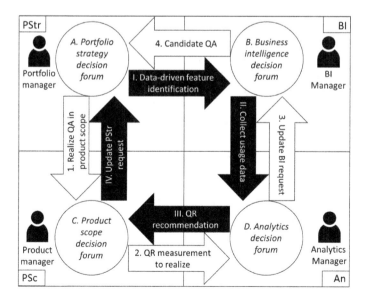

Fig. 2. Interactions among the four scope decision areas in the forward- and feedback-loops.

The BI area is also on the strategic level. BI decisions concern which competitors to monitor, which market data to collect and how to divide the customers into the relevant customer groups, etc. It can also be areas where the company wants to experiment (e.g., through A/B testing) rather than performing a (traditional) upfront requirements analysis. A **business intelligence manager** is the main decision maker for BI. Decisions should outline relevant BI data to ensure adequate coverage. Similar to PStr decisions, BI decisions should be reviewed and updated on a quarterly or half-year interval. The main decision forum is **the business intelligence decision forum**. The BI data is presented with graphs and numbers but in informal documents or presentations. Besides interacting with PStr and An regarding scope decisions, input comes from marketing manager, competitive intelligence, sales, etc.

The BI manager interacts with the portfolio manager on the strategic level and the analytics manager on the operational level (cf. Fig. 2). The BI manager also interacts much with, e.g., marketing managers, customer services and external companies to collect competitive intelligence.

The PSc area operational decisions (see Fig. 1a) target QL for a specific QR and the realization strategy in the coming releases. A **Product Manager** is responsible for PSc decisions [33]. Depending on the development context and release interval, PSc decisions could be made a weekly or monthly interval, or continuously. The main decision forum is the **product scope decision forum**. In an agile context, a more informal continuous dialogue in the team replaces the formal product scope decision forum. PSc decisions are on an operational level and in a semi-structured format e.g. in an issue handling tool, decision database or spreadsheet backlog. The product manager receives the portfolio strategy from the portfolio manager and product usage data from the Analytics manager (see Fig. 2). The product manager also interacts with key account managers, internal stakeholders, such as subject area experts and the development organization, and external stakeholders, such as customers and key account managers.

The **An area** decisions concern the product usage data collection and analysis. If a company is utilizing experimentation or beta-testing, decisions on how many experiments to run and how closely to monitor the product usage is an decision. Especially important is to be wary of the amount of data generated, as collecting usage data can result in the copious amount of data. An **Analytics manager** oversees the **An area** decisions. Analytics consists of one part focused on instrumentation and the actual usage data collection and one part of the analysis and presentation of the data. Decisions on which usage data to collect are made daily or weekly. Decisions are made either in centralized **Analytics decision forums** or distributed in different development teams. Analytics decisions are presented alongside with the rich and highly structured data. The analytics manager receives the product scope from the product manager as well as a usage data scope from the BI manager (see Fig. 2). The analytics team also interacts closely with the development team for the instrumentation and actual data collection. Competitor devices can also be used to compare specific measurements with.

4.3   The Interaction Between Roles and Decision Forums in QREME

The four scope decision areas are connected and impact each other through the two loops, as outlined in the previous section. Figure 2 outlines how decisions from different decision forums are connected to each other.

The forward-loop (counter-clockwise in the figure) is characterized by top-down flow where PStr decisions and extracted into PSc decisions that are realized in software [19]. Customer sentiment and sales data are reported back to the portfolio management. The forward-loop is often exercised by bespoke or MDRE (Market-Driven Requirements Engineering) companies where the development is either performed in-house or regulated by a contract. In these situations, it is possible to work with our framework to create systematic information exchange among the different decision processes.

The feedback-loop (clock-wise) is constructed based on the assumption that a software-intensive company has access to product usage data [21]. As a result, instead of having upfront investments to analyze and synthesize a scope, inspiration is taken from the product usage or other sources (e.g., social media), though both understanding as well as exploring changes. Based on product usage data analysis, improvements are identified and made part of the product scope for implementation. The resulting product scope is evaluated in the portfolio strategy.

We assume that no organization uses only forward- or feedback-loop. Rather, they tend to favor one of the loops without sufficient synergy between them. For example, information flow between the An and PSc need to be efficient. Low efficiency of this information flow may result in long lead-times, e.g., when the product usage data is not promptly integrated into the PStr forum via either PSc or BI. Moreover, if a QA is not considered to be relevant in PStr, the information night never reaches PSc.

There are four interactions in the forward-loop (labelled 1–4) and four interactions in the feedback-loop (labelled I–IV) among the decision forums (labelled A–D), see Fig. 2. We make two assumptions:

1. Decisions (and development) are made in all the forums continuously.
2. Decisions are made individually.

Hence, we are not considering the situation, e.g. where a requirements specification is prepared and finalized and then sent onwards in the process. Furthermore, there is no explicit beginning or end in the loops as most software-intensive companies work with existing portfolios and products and seldom create new portfolios. Table 1 outlines a guideline to choose whether to use the forward- or feedback-loop.

4.4   Tailoring QREME

The ideal model of QREME as described in the previous sections need to be adapted to the specific organization and their needs. In tailoring QREME, the central aspect to consider is to cater for the two loops and leverage from the different characteristics; the forward-loop with long-term planning and the feedback-loop with shorter lead-time to changes in the market and the software. However, the specific roles or decision forums are not crucial to have as in the ideal model. Instead, the critical aspect is to be aware of the different types of decisions and map the roles to the ones in the organization.

Table 1. Alternatives for scope decisions for the different forums

Forum	Forward-loop	Feedback-loop
A	**1. Realize QA in product scope** – The PStr can decide to have the PSc refine the decisions. This is a typical refinement of a QA to QRs, suitable when the market needs are well understood or when there is no comparable experience to learn from (e.g. radical innovation)	**I. Data-driven feature identification** – The PStr can decide to have BI analyze the actual needs. Instead of upfront QAs refinement, experiments determine the appropriate QLs. This is suitable when it is difficult to upfront estimate QLs or there is an opportunity to incrementally improve a QA in a data-driven manner without any change to QAs as such
B	**4. Candidate QA** – The decisions which QAs to improve as identified by BI can be send to PStr as a candidate QAs included in PStr. It can be market trends or QLs in the existing software which stands out in BI and it not represented in the PStr. The forward-loop is suitable when the product QLs are known and there is an identified gap in the PStr	**II. Collect usage data** – Decisions on which is the relevant QAs to collect refined data can be request of An. Based on market and competitor analysis and input from PStr, the BI identifies QAs which need clarification on regarding QLs in the software. This is appropriate when the QLs in the software are unknown and the QAs are part of the PStr
C	**2. QR measurement to realize** – PSc decides which QRs to implement. In the forward-loop, PSc requests An to collect usage data for the relevant QRs being implemented. This is a kind of refinement in terms of collecting data for defined QLs. The forward-loop from PSc to An for scoped decisions is appropriate when the QRs and their QL is in line with the portfolio strategy	**IV. Update PStr request** – If the product manager finds gaps in what they want to highlight to PSc, then the product manager can decide to send a QR to request PStr to update PStr with respect to the QR. This can happen when there is feedback from An on gaps or input from other stakeholders which PSc would like to include in the scope. The feedback-loop usage is appropriate when there is a discrepancy from the needs of the PSc and the PStr
D	**3. Update BI request** – Based on usage data analysis, An can request to update BI. This can be if QLs and QRs are identified as relevant for An but this is not in line with the current BI scope. Utilizing the forward-loop from An to BI is appropriate when the BI need to include product usage data currently not covered by the BI strategy, as a result of the forward-loop from PSc	**III. QR recommendation** –The An decision forum provides recommendations to the product manager on suitable QLs for different QRs as well as if there are specific QRs which need attention. The QAs might be identified in BI in the feedback-loop or be a feedback on QLs coming from PSc. The analytics manager should use the feedback-loop QAs in the strategy or when the customers express their strong dissatisfaction about QRs

5   Two Exploratory Case Studies

In this section, we present two case studies that provide experiences from applying QREME. The application consists of using QREME in an expert assessment on the companies' current decision processes related to scoping of QRs.

5.1   Case A: Consumer Device Products for a Global Market

Company A develops software-intensive products for B2C for a global market. Development is performed in a cooperative manner with other companies, sometimes called Software Ecosystems (SECO) [34]. Substantial investment is made in the software developed for the dedicated hardware. QAs play a crucial role in product success as well as customer purchase decisions. We performed an extensive longitudinal study of the decision patterns [9], which lay the underlying rationale for QREME.

Case: One of the observations was an issue with battery performance. The company releases several products per year. The software is updated several times over the life-cycle and up to 2 years after the product first reaches the market. Even though software today is a significant part of the engineering efforts, the underlying hardware platform brings substantial opportunities and limitations regarding the possible quality aspects. This "hardware legacy" is still visible regarding processes and culture, leading to a prevalence of the forward-loop.

Portfolio strategy. In the portfolio strategy decision forum, it was decided an overall target for battery performance and it had been the same for several product generations. However, despite reports of not meeting the target level, there were no actions on a portfolio level. Given the legacy of hardware development, there is a strong focus on the hardware side of the portfolio for the new products to reach the market and less focus on the software updates for existing products. The software product managers are not represented (cf. Fig. 2). Furthermore, the BI manager role is not present. Instead, the software organization undertakes ad-hoc measurements of the product usage. Albeit product managers repeatedly highlighting battery problems, the portfolio strategy decision forum failed to timely and appropriately react.

   When assessing this case using the framework, the feedback-loop, mainly with IV. In Fig. 2, is the most prominent problem in the portfolio strategy decision forum causing a delayed updated of the portfolio strategy. Furthermore, once the portfolio strategy was updated, there was still a focus on the forward-loop. We believe that it might have been more effective to employ a feedback-loop, see interaction I in Fig. 2, as the setting of an unrealistic QLs in the portfolio strategy, had previously shown to be ineffective. Hence, instead of using a feedback-loop, the battery performance should be improved until there is a positive sentiment rather than fulfilling a somewhat random number.

Product scope. The product manager got input from the portfolio manager to achieve a specific target QL for battery performance. However, it was one of many aspects needed fulfillment and was when the problems started to occur not prioritized among other features and QRs. There was also a strong focus on the products' introduction to the market and less focus on the software updates, limiting the ability to work with the product scope for later releases. This is further complicated by the fact that both the users' behavior (what they are doing) as well as the execution environment (the network) influence QAs. Hence, setting appropriate QLs upfront is challenging.

The feedback-loop from development to product scope work well regarding the framework (cf. III in Fig. 2). In the product scope decision forum, the product manager and representatives from the development organization are present. This creates a strong relationship and quite well working forward-loop and relative well feedback-loop. However, the product manager had difficulty to act on feedback, as the portfolio manager expected the portfolio strategy to be prioritized and as so often it caused an over-scoping. Furthermore, there was no explicit data scope role and no strong tradition to experiment. Because the forward-loop preference from the portfolio and focus on the first release of the products to the market, this also caused an over-scoping for the first release and down-prioritizing of software updates.

Analytics scope. There was no explicit analytics manager role as intended in our framework. Instead, the development organization, through the project manager performed some of the usage data collection tasks. However, there was no tradition or explicit ambition to experiment or test improvements on parts of the consumer base and form the analytics decision forum either.

BI scope. The BI is much focused on external input such as market and competitor data and less on internal data such as usage and customer services data. There is a strong focus on pre-release of new products and their perception as they are first introduced to the market. There is much less focus on monitoring the perception of the (software) products during the whole lifecycle.

There is a gap in the feedback-loop in that the communication in I and II (cf. Fig. 2) are mostly missing. Even if the portfolio strategy is used for BI in general, it is not used to understand specific QAs in the products. Furthermore, there is little or no direction from BI to the teams collecting usage data and performing analysis thereof. This case a fragmented picture and lack of actionable intelligence in a strategic level.

To summarize, there is a strong focus on the forward-loop, i.e., 1–4 in Fig. 2. The main information presented to the portfolio manager is related to general performance of the products including specific QRs. Specific suggestions were communicated from the analytics team to the product manager (III in Fig. 2). However, the feedback-loop from the portfolio manager to BI was effectively non-existent. Hence, there was no ambition to experiment and measure on software and incrementally update it in a data-driven way. Instead, it was expected that analytics is driven in a forward-loop manner.

The main benefit of improving the feedback-loop is expected to be a significantly shorter lead-time to adapt to customer expectations and changes in the market. Furthermore, sometimes decisions are made early in the process without real data. By introducing a clearer feedback-loop and daring to leave details to a later stage, more appropriate QLs will be implemented (neither too conservative nor over-shooting the target) which will in the end mean more effective use of development resources.

5.2   Case B: B2B Product Developing Company

Company B develops software-intensive products for B2B contexts for a global market in a market-driven manner. In this case, we analyze performance requirements just as in Case A. This illustrates a different approach to handling the QRs and how QREME can support it.

Case: Company B is one of the world's leaders in its market segment despite having no official requirements database and only lightweight and informal requirements management processes. The requirements are often expressed in a comparative way as "benchmarking", e.g., "Product x should be as Product y, but better" and "The new version of the software must not be worse than the last version". This way of expressing requirements combined with test-driven development methods created a very strong feedback-loop based on continuous validation of the product behaviors by engineers.

Portfolio strategy.   The portfolio strategy forum decision mainly focuses on new functionality and associated technical novelties. QRs and expected QLs are well understood and acknowledged but rarely quantified or explicitly documented. The leading requirements specification technique is to express the requirements about current or previous software capabilities. This creates issues in translating the strategy into objective QRs and the product scope.

Despite the best efforts, the forward-loop (1 in Fig. 2) is not sufficiently established to perform refinement into features with sufficient QRs and QLs and to later assess strategy fulfillment. On the other hand, the data-driven feature identification (II) works well when customers signal insufficient QLs that are escalated into the portfolio strategy decision forum. The role of the portfolio manager is not present in the organization as the responsibility falls between the executive management and product managers who have a limited responsibility for their products.

Product scope.   The refine of functional features in the product scope decision forum worked well but not for QRs. Due to lack of strategic guidelines and "benchmarking as requirements", the product manager could not effectively communicate with experts and developers. The "benchmarking as requirements" had to be combined with feature/product usage data. However, in this case, usage data was replaced by test data obtained from the lab. Software developers or testers ran the previous products on example use cases and measured the current QLs for performance and other quality aspects. No additional product testing and product usage data was generated leaving little guideline or support for scoping decisions. Regarding QREME, the feedback from analytics team to product manager (III in Fig. 2) works well. However, the forward communication (2) is mostly lacking, which makes analytics mostly reactive.

Data scope.   Developers, testers and often requirements engineers perform product tests to obtain reliable QLs. The product usage data arriving from the customers is only analyzed from the functional requirements viewpoint. The analytics manager role is not clearly established and clear data usage input challenges are not maintained. Upon incoming feature requests, this forum can only answer by providing QLs of previous products that can form a baseline for improvement suggestions. Potential feature recommendations are mostly functionality centered and lack clear QLs.

BI scope. The BI is much focused on external input from the market and competitors and direct customer data channels are not available for the company. The company sells its products via retailers who take the responsibility for hardware and software installations. Moreover, data is often secured by the customers and special permissions or legal documents are required to obtain it, e.g. by authorities. The company runs various products and software versions in the lab to obtain product usage data and to measure performance levels for products sold to the customers.

QREME highlights a need for an explicit role for the analytics manager. Furthermore, since there is no culture of experimenting or collecting product usage data, there is a need for education and training. QREME also emphasizes the need for more explicit channels and roles for portfolio management, to be able to quicker make changes relevant for the customers and markets.

The main benefit from applying QREME in this case is improving the forward-loop and increasing the synchronization effect between the feedback- and the forward-loop. Establishing the forward-loop and associated roles should mitigate the issues in translating the strategy into QRs and the product scope. Moreover, this should enable more proactive QRs definition rather than reactive response to customer dissatisfaction.

6   Conclusion and Future Work

In this paper, we addressed the research question for how to support decision-making for QRs. Based on related work and our empirical work on understanding the decision patterns for QRs, we propose a decision-making model to align roles and forums for QR decisions combining a forward-loop and feedback-loop on strategic and operational levels. The focal points of the QREME model introduced in this paper are the two loops and the group decision making forums.

We applied QREME into exploratory case studies where we performed two assessments of how two companies make decisions for QRs. Using QREME, we identify several challenges in handling QRs that the companies should focus on addressing; namely an over-emphasis on a forward-loop and lack of common direction for QRs. We see a potential to shorten lead-times to react to changes in the market and customer expectations as well as a more efficient use of development resources with more accurate setting of QLs and therefore not wasting resources.

QREME has not yet been rolled out for daily operational work at any of the studied companies. Therefore, we plan to integrate QREME into the daily requirements operations and decision making at the partner companies and measure the long-term impact of it. Besides that, we also see a need to understand in more detail the contextual factors influencing the choice of the forward-loop and the feedback-loop, especially for innovation and the strategic portfolio decisions but also product lifecycle and market maturity. Finally, we plan to integrate various requirements abstraction levels of requirements into the model and detailed requirement levels for the decision forums.

We believe that the improved understanding of QRs, specifically regarding the feedback-loop, can have a positive influence on getting companies to emphasize on QRs. In our experience, the development organization is often aware of the QRs, but at the same time, portfolio and product management typically do not drive improvement of QRs. By introducing a clearer feedback-loop and thus making the QRs explicit, both the understanding that addressing the QRs in the software takes up development resources and user experience of the product is improved. This, we speculate, can help to create a foundation for an overall clearer prioritization of QRs at all levels and both in the forward-loop as well as the feedback-loop.

Acknowledgements. We want to thank all the participants in the interviews. This work is supported by the IKNOWDM project (20150033) from the Knowledge Foundation in Sweden.

References

1. Glinz, M.: On non-functional requirements. In: IEEE International Conference on Requirements Engineering, Piscataway, NJ, USA, pp. 21–26 (2007)
2. Regnell, B., Berntsson-Svensson, R., Olsson, T.: Supporting roadmapping of quality requirements. IEEE Softw. **25**, 42–47 (2008)
3. Regnell, B., Berntsson-Svensson, R., Wnuk, K.: Can we beat the complexity of very large-scale requirements engineering? In: Requirements Engineering: Foundation for Software Quality, Montpellier, France, pp. 123–128 (2008)
4. Ebert, C.: Putting requirement management into praxis: dealing with nonfunctional requirements. Inf. Softw. Technol. **40**, 175–185 (1998)
5. Cysneiros, L.M.: Leite, J.C.S.D.P.: Nonfunctional requirements: from elicitation to conceptual models. IEEE Trans. Softw. Eng. **30**, 328–350 (2004)
6. Svensson, R.B., Gorschek, T., Regnell, B., Torkar, R., Shahrokni, A., Feldt, R.: Quality requirements in industrial practice - an extended interview study at eleven companies. IEEE Trans. Softw. Eng. **38**, 923–935 (2012)
7. Chung, L., Nixon, B.A., Yu, E., Mylopoulos, J.: Non-Functional Requirements in Software Engineering. Springer, USA (2000). https://doi.org/10.1007/978-1-4615-5269-7
8. Mylopoulos, J., Chung, L., Nixon, B.: Representing and using nonfunctional requirements: a process-oriented approach. IEEE Trans. Softw. Eng. **18**, 483–497 (1992)
9. Olsson, T., Wnuk, K., Gorschek, T.: Decision patterns for quality requirements: an empirical study. Submitted to J. Syst. Softw.
10. Berntsson-Svensson, R., Olsson, T., Regnell, B.: An investigation of how quality requirements are specified in industrial practice. Inf. Softw. Technol. **55**, 1224–1236 (2013)
11. Wnuk, K., Kollu, R.K.: A systematic mapping study on requirements scoping. In: Proceedings of the 20th International Conference on Evaluation and Assessment in Software Engineering, Limerick, Ireland (2016)
12. Regnell, B., Brinkkemper, S.: Market-driven requirements engineering for software products. In: Aurum, A., Wohlin, C. (eds.) Engineering and Managing Software Requirements, pp. 287–308. Springer, Berlin (2005). https://doi.org/10.1007/3-540-28244-0_13
13. Ernst, N.A., Mylopoulos, J.: On the perception of software quality requirements during the project lifecycle. In: Wieringa, R., Persson, A. (eds.) REFSQ 2010. LNCS, vol. 6182, pp. 143–157. Springer, Heidelberg (2010). https://doi.org/10.1007/978-3-642-14192-8_15

14. Ameller, D., Farré, C., Franch, X., Rufian, G.: A survey on software release planning models. In: Abrahamsson, P., Jedlitschka, A., Nguyen Duc, A., Felderer, M., Amasaki, S., Mikkonen, T. (eds.) PROFES 2016. LNCS, vol. 10027, pp. 48–65. Springer, Cham (2016). https://doi.org/10.1007/978-3-319-49094-6_4

15. Mohagheghi, P., Aparicio, M.E.: An industry experience report on managing product quality requirements in a large organization. Inf. Softw. Technol. **88**, 96–109 (2017)

16. Wnuk, K., Gorschek, T., Callele, D., Karlsson, E.A., Åhlin, E., Regnell, B.: Supporting scope tracking and visualization for very large-scale requirements engineering-utilizing FSC+, decision patterns, and atomic decision visualizations. IEEE Trans. Softw. Eng. **42**, 47–74 (2016)

17. Komssi, M., Kauppinen, M., Töhönen, H., Lehtola, L., Davis, A.M.: Roadmapping problems in practice: value creation from the perspective of the customers. Requir. Eng. **20**, 45–69 (2015)

18. Kittlaus, H.B., Clough, P.N.: Software Product Management and Pricing. Springer, Berlin (2009). https://doi.org/10.1007/978-3-540-76987-3

19. ISPMA: Software Product Management - Foundation Level v.1.2., pp. 1–39 (2014)

20. Royce, W.: Managing the development of large software systems. In: Proceedings of the IEEE WESCON, pp. 1–9 (1970)

21. Bosch, J.: Speed, data, and ecosystems: the future of software engineering. IEEE Softw. **33**, 82–88 (2016)

22. Groen, E.C., Doerr, J., Adam, S.: Towards crowd-based requirements engineering a research preview. In: Fricker, S.A., Schneider, K. (eds.) REFSQ 2015. LNCS, vol. 9013, pp. 247–253. Springer, Cham (2015). https://doi.org/10.1007/978-3-319-16101-3_16

23. Johansson, E., Bergdahl, D., Bosch, J., Holmström Olsson, H.: Requirement prioritization with quantitative data - a case study. In: Abrahamsson, P., Corral, L., Oivo, M., Russo, B. (eds.) PROFES 2015. LNCS, vol. 9459, pp. 89–104. Springer, Cham (2015). https://doi.org/10.1007/978-3-319-26844-6_7

24. Schwaber, K.: Agile Project Management with Scrum. Microsoft Press, Redmond (2004)

25. Hüttermann, M.: DevOps for Developers. Springer, New York (2012). https://doi.org/10.1007/978-1-4302-4570-4

26. Ruhe, G., Saliu, M.O.: The art and science of software release planning. IEEE Softw. **22**, 47–53 (2005)

27. Aurum, A., Wohlin, C.: The fundamental nature of requirements engineering activities as a decision-making process. Inf. Softw. Technol. **45**, 945–954 (2003)

28. Gorschek, T., Wohlin, C.: Requirements abstraction model. Requir. Eng. **11**, 79–101 (2006)

29. Carlshamre, P., Sandahl, K., Lindvall, M., Regnell, B., Nattoch Dag, J.: An industrial survey of requirements interdependencies in software product release planning. In: Proceedings of the Fifth IEEE International Symposium on Requirements Engineering, pp. 84–92 (2001)

30. Davison, R.M., Martinsons, M.G., Ou, C.X.J.: The roles of theory in canonical action research. MIS Q. **36**, 763–786 (2012)

31. Yin, R.K.: Case Study Research. Design and Methods. Sage Publications, Thousand Oaks (2003)

32. Runeson, P., Höst, M.: Guidelines for conducting and reporting case study research in software engineering. Empir. Softw. Eng. **14**, 131–164 (2009)

33. Kittlaus, H.-B., Fricker, S.A.: Software Product Management: The ISPMA-Compliant Study Guide and Handbook. Springer, Berlin (2017). https://doi.org/10.1007/978-3-642-55140-6

34. Jansen, S., Cusumano, M.A., Brinkkemper, S.: Software Ecosystems: Analyzing and Managing Business Networks in the Software Industry. Edward Elgar Publishing, Cheltenham (2013)

The Influence of Green Strategies Design onto Quality Requirements Prioritization

Nelly Condori Fernandez[1,2]([✉]) and Patricia Lago[2]([✉])

[1] Universidade da Coruña, A Coruña, Spain
n.condori.fernandez@udc.es, n.condori-fernandez@vu.nl
[2] Vrije Universiteit Amsterdam, Amsterdam, The Netherlands
p.lago@vu.nl

Abstract. [**Context and Motivation**] Modern society is facing important challenges that are critical to improve its environmental performance. The literature reports on many green strategies aimed at reducing energy consumption. However, little research has been carried out so far on including green strategies in software design.

[**Question/problem**] In this paper, we investigate how green software strategies can contribute to, and influence, quality requirements prioritization performed iteratively throughout a service-oriented software design process.

[**Methodology**] In collaboration with a Dutch industry partner, an empirical study was carried out with 19 student teams playing the role of software designers, who completed the design of a real-life project through 7 weekly deliverables.

[**Principle ideas/results**] We identified a list of quality requirements (QRs) that were considered by the teams as part of their architectural decisions when green strategies were introduced. By analyzing relations between QRs and green strategies, our study confirms usability as the most used QR for addressing green strategies that allow to create people awareness. Qualities like reliability, performance, interoperability, scalability and availability emerged as the most relevant for addressing service-awareness green strategies.

[**Contribution**] If used at the beginning of a green software project, our results help including the most relevant QRs for addressing those green software strategies that are e.g. the most domain-generic (like increase carbon footprint awareness, paperless service provisioning, virtualization).

Keywords: Green software design · Quality requirements
Prioritization

1 Introduction

In the last decade, a number of green strategies have been discussed in the literature to achieve the goal of reducing energy consumption (e.g. [1,2]). However, few are the approaches that assist the inclusion of green strategies into the software development process. This has been corroborated by a recent qualitative

© Springer International Publishing AG, part of Springer Nature 2018
E. Kamsties et al. (Eds.): REFSQ 2018, LNCS 10753, pp. 189–205, 2018.
https://doi.org/10.1007/978-3-319-77243-1_12

study [3], where most of the interviewed practitioners confirmed their inability to practice sustainability design within software engineering due to the lack of methodological- and tool support. In requirements engineering it is generally acknowledged that Quality Requirement (QR) prioritization is an important and difficult activity of the requirements management process [4]. The situation is even more complex in a services-oriented development environment, because software services are engineered with multiple sets of functional requirements to fulfill different groups of potential consumers with different QRs. Moreover, if environmental sustainability is targeted, new trade-offs emerge between environmental sustainability criteria (e.g. energy efficiency) and traditional quality requirements (e.g. usability, maintainability).

In an empirical study investigating the evolution of quality requirements prioritization during a service design process, Condori-Fernandez and Lago [5] identified *stable* quality requirements that can be considered as such from the beginning of a project, and *unstable* quality requirements that hence demand special attention throughout the project. In this paper, we investigate how the inclusion of green software strategies into a service design process can influence quality requirements prioritization. In order to assist the inclusion of green strategies into the design activities of the service-oriented design method proposed by Lago et al. [6], we adapted the service design process by adding the "design space refinement" activity. To this aim, our research was conducted in the context of the Computer Science Master Track in 'Software Engineering and Green IT' [7] at the Vrije Universitiet Amsterdam in close collaboration with an IT company in the Netherlands. The study involved 19 teams of master students playing the role of software designers/architects, and who completed the design of a real-life green software project.

In this paper, we focus on green strategies that address the two targets of green software engineering: (i) *Green in software*, where the goal is to reduce the energy consumption and the resources used by the software itself, and (ii) *Green by software*, where the goal is on using software to deliver environmental-friendly systems in other domains.

The rest of this paper provides a detailed account of our study. Section 2 describes the extended green software model and service design process on which our work is based. Section 3 presents design of the empirical study. Then, data collection and preparation is described in Sect. 4. Section 5 reports our analysis on influence of green strategies on QR prioritization. Sections 6 and 7 discuss the validity threats and conclude the paper, respectively.

2   Background

2.1   Extended Green Strategy Model

Gu et al. [8] proposed a green strategy model, which consists of a green goal that is realized by a number of green actions (see Fig. 1). In turn, each green action has a description explaining what the green action entails. Further, a green action typically belongs to one sub-category, which is a sub-set of category.

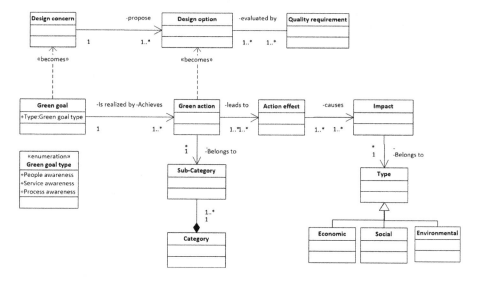

Fig. 1. Extended green strategy model, adapted from Gu et al. [8]

A green action leads to at least one action effect, which causes a certain impact. A green strategy is a plan of green actions intended to accomplish a specific green goal. In order to assist the inclusion of green strategies into the design space specification, we have extended the green strategy model. As shown in Fig. 1, the original model was extended by (i) mapping a green strategy (made of a green goal and a set of green actions) on the main elements of our design space (i.e. design concern, design option); (ii) adding the entity "quality requirement", which is used in the selection of design options; (iii) considering not only an economic impact, but also social and environmental impacts; (iv) making explicit the fact that a green goal can regard one or more of the following three types of green problems in service-oriented software engineering [9]:

– People awareness: the use of the services and/or Service-Based Applications (SBAs) makes the users realize their sustainability footprint. The services/SBAs may further propose the users tips/alternatives that help them comply with some green strategy.
– Service awareness: the services/SBAs are designed in such way that their execution is environmental friendly (e.g. energy efficient). These types of systems implement strategies that enable their green execution.
– Process awareness: the services/SBAs are especially conceived to create or support a more sustainable development process.

2.2   A Service-Oriented Design Process

In service-oriented design, the delivered software may come in two flavors: (i) as an inventory of services that deliver independent functionality (in the form of

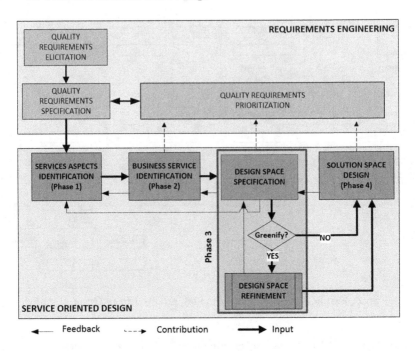

Fig. 2. QR prioritization supported by the service-oriented design method adapted from [5]

software services) of some business value (e.g. for internal reuse or for provisioning to third-parties); (ii) as a SBA reusing (i.e. composing) software services.

Moreover, while in the first case the developer makes service inventories available after they have been developed, in the second case developing the SBA demands for composed services to be already available for the application to be specified, designed, and tested. If such services are not there, assumptions about their interfaces and delivered functionality are to be made. While designing SBAs resembles in many ways traditional software development where e.g. components are being reused, designing service inventories is much more challenging. This is why we focused for many years on teaching this second aspect of service orientation. Related challenges include identifying those functionalities that deliver stand-alone business-relevant services; and evaluating designed services against QRs that must be ensured once the services are composed in a third-party software system or SBA. To address these challenges and provide our students with the necessary competencies in service-oriented software design, we defined the service-oriented design method explained in [6,10]. It consists of the following four phases (see also lower part of Fig. 2).

Services aspects identification is grounded in the definition of service aspects as "those QRs that are especially relevant for service-oriented software" and that must be therefore addressed in a service-oriented software design [10]. Starting from the application domain of a selected software project, service aspects identification aims at selecting the QRs that are especially critical to achieve via services and for that domain.

Business service identification. Starting from the description of usage scenarios, functional- and quality requirements, business process models and conceptual data models are used to identify business services by clustering service-relevant functionality within a business process. The elements of the business process models (e.g. activities and decision points) are examined as candidate business services. In turn, the elements of the conceptual data models (e.g. data entities and their dependencies) are examined as candidate business services that will complement or complete the business services previously identified with the necessary data management features.

Design space specification explores the most important issues influencing the design of a software solution (e.g. in services for charging electric cars, an issue is "How to minimize idle time of charging points over night when demand is low?"). Possible design solutions for the identified issues (e.g. "allowing variable pricing", or "elastically shutting down charging points") are evaluated against relevant QRs (e.g. availability vs. energy efficiency), and design decisions are made by means of trade-offs. This phase is supported by a template capturing quality-driven design decisions and developed in [11] (see Table 1). Design space specification hence addresses issues, possible alternative design solutions, and (among them) the decided-upon solutions (or design decisions).

Design space refinement. To include the green strategies, the specification of the design space must be refined. This refinement can take two main forms:

- Extending the design space: the green strategies may lead to new design issues, options or criteria. Here the green goal is mapped onto the corresponding design concern; and the green actions are mapped onto design options, or new design concerns if large in scope.
- Challenging the already existing design decisions: in this case, introducing a green strategy causes changes in the decisions addressing pre-existing design issues. E.g., the green strategy might introduce a new green-related criterion, like energy efficiency, that in turn might lead to new trade-offs in favor of alternative design decisions.
  The redefined design space is captured by using the template for a green strategy description [12], the template shown in Table 1, and the Question-Options-Criteria (QOC) notation [13].

Solution space design takes as input the set of candidate business services and design decisions made during design space exploration. It identifies which candidate services must be designed as software services to support the initial usage scenarios. Then, it defines views that show how they can be composed in SBAs and how they should interact to deliver the target functionality and QRs.

As shown Fig. 2, QR prioritization is an activity that is carried out throughout the whole service design process. Naturally, the outcomes of this process (e.g. identified design issues, design alternatives, trade-offs) contribute to a better requirements prioritization, too [5]. In this paper, our study focuses mainly

Table 1. Capturing the knowledge about Quality-driven Design Decisions [11]

Concern (Identifier: Description)		*Con#<number>: What, is the concern that needs to be solved (by taking a decision)? The description has to be in a form of a question)*
Ranking criteria (Identification: Name)		*What quality requirements have been used as criteria to take the decision based on the available options? (List the ranking criteria) Cr#<number>:*
Options (Repeat for each option)	Identifier: Name	*Con#<number> − Opt#<number> : Name of the option*
	Description	*Short description of the option*
	Status	*Has this option been **selected** or **rejected**?*
	Relationship(s)	*Indicate relationship with other options (by using their Identifiers): {forbids, conflicts with, enables, subsumes, is related to}*
	Evaluation	*Cr#<numberN>: To which extent does this option support ranking criterion Cr#<numberN>?*
	Rationale of decision	*Why has this option been selected or rejected? (use the ranking criteria identifiers in the argumentation)*

on the outcomes of the design space specification and refinement, as well as the solution space design.

3   Empirical Study Design

This research is carried out with the purpose of empirically investigating how Green Strategies influence on Quality Requirements prioritization in the domain of smart transportation from the viewpoint of a software designer. The following specific research questions were formulated:

RQ1: Which are the most Quality Requirements used by designers when green strategies are included into the design process?

RQ2: How do Green Strategies influence on Quality Requirements prioritization?

3.1   Research Context

The study has been carried out in the context of a master-level course in Service Oriented Design (SOD) taught for over a decade [14]. It requires modeling and reasoning competencies. The course deals with how to analyze business and domain requirements to identify and design a satisfactory software services' offer for the identified requirements. Contents revolve around the service-oriented design methodology described in Sect. 2.2.

About 20% of the 95 students participating in this course come from the Computer Science Master program with specialization in Software Engineering and Green IT [7], and 80% from Information Sciences Master program with specialization in Business Information Systems.

Table 2. Assignments of the EV-mobility project

Week	Phase	Assignment goal
1	Phase 1	A1: Identify quality requirements that are especially relevant for service-oriented applications
2	Phase 2	A2: Identify a set of relevant business services
3	Phase 3	A3: Document the design space according to the design space template shown in Table 1
4	Phase 3	A4: Reflect on and identify green strategies that facilitate accomplishing a specific environmental goal
5	Phase 3	A5: Refine the design space by adding the set of green strategies
6, 7	Phase 4	A6: Document the design solution for your business services and address your design decisions

In the reported study, all participants were randomly grouped in 5-member teams, resulting in 19 groups. Each group was assigned to one of the 3 tutors in the course. All teams address the same real-life case project in parallel and independently. Students put theory into practice by collaboratively working in the project. As shown in Table 2, several assignments were distributed along 7 weeks. Each week all teams receive a review and feedback by the respective tutor. Moreover, an industrial stakeholder is invited to the students' progress presentations and gives feedback based on his or her expectations on the final product. Students are encouraged to present the least understood requirements and/or discuss issues encountered during the week.

3.2   Case Project: EV-Mobility

The EV-mobility project (the case used in this study) focused on designing new software services on top of an existing charging point management platform, with the goal to facilitate the adoption of electric vehicles (EVs) in the Dutch private market. The project is proposed by one of our Green IT industrial partners.

Project-related concerns included: how electric cars can harmonize with people lifestyle, and how software services can create incentives for individuals to switch to electric cars, hence lowering their carbon footprint.

The main stakeholders of the EV-mobility project were:

EV Driver: early adopter driving an EV. Different motivation to do this: sustainability, new technology, marketing/image, low cost driving, etc.
Fleet Owner: The owner of the car can be the EV driver, a Lease company or the driver's Employer. Risk for this stakeholder is battery lifetime, which is currently unpredictable. To monitor this risk, Fleet owners are interested in gathering battery-related statistics.
Charging Point Service Provider (CPSP): It is operating a charging point network and providing services to EV drivers to increase utilization of the charging points and make life easier for EV drivers.

Distribution Service Operator (DSO): It is responsible to connect charging points to the electricity grid and may have a challenge, in the future, when EV's use will increase and peaks will grow.

Energy Suppliers: supply energy to charging points.

4   Data Collection and Preparation

In order to answer our two research questions, we carried out a manual text analysis of the deliverables produced in the third and fourth phases of the service-oriented design process, namely Design space and solution space, which correspond to deliverables of the assignments A3, A4, A5 and A6. Table 3 shows the average page length per deliverable as well as the areas of interest (AoI) considered as relevant for our study. The data collection was carried out in two steps: extracting Green software strategies, and identifying Quality Requirements.

Regarding the first step, 16 clusters of green strategies were identified from all teams' Deliverables D4 and D5. The type of green strategies that were considered as relevant for the EV-Mobility project are shown in the Appendix A (Table 6). Ten clusters were identified as domain generic strategies, whereas 6 clusters were considered as domain-specific strategies. More details of the green strategies extraction can be found in [12].

Regarding the Quality Requirements Identification, in this step we proceeded to identify: (1) QRs that were kept or added when a green strategy was integrated in the design space phase (Deliverables D3 and D5); and (2) QRs that were added at the solution space design phase after including the green strategy (Final report).

Firstly, we analyzed deliverable D3 (i.e. design decisions tables, QOC) in order to identify which quality requirements (service aspect) were considered as relevant for deciding on any of the options identified for each concern specified in the design space. Then, by analyzing the deliverable D5 (mappings between design space and green strategies), we located the new design concerns or existing ones that could have been added or modified as consequence of including a green strategy. Their respective design decision tables and QOCs were then analyzed to extract the corresponding QRs that were used as ranking criteria for evaluating

Table 3. Data sources: areas of interest per deliverable.

Deliverable	Area of interest	Average page length
D3: Design space	Design Decisions Tables[a], QOC	15
D4: Green strategies	Strategies descriptions, Graphical representation	10
D5: Design space with green strategies	Design Decisions Tables[a], QOC, Mappings	35
Final report	Quality Requirements list	4

[a]Design Decision Tables follow the template presented in Table 1.

the respective design options. During this extraction, synonyms were verified by reviewing the QR definitions and respective justifications given by the teams. By means of this analysis, we discarded two deliverables. This is because one of the teams did not consider QRs as design criteria (e.g. cost, behavioral impact). A second team focused only on describing green strategies without making a mapping to design concerns of sufficient quality. In the similar way, we proceed with the last deliverable (final report) to extract the corresponding new QRs that were considered at the design solution phase.

Nominal data was collected (yes $= 1$; no $= 0$), by assigning 1 when (i) the QR was considered as a ranking criterion for the selection of design options introduced by the green strategies; (ii) a new QR was added in the solution space design phase due to the introduction of a green strategy. In order to collect this data from the projects developed by the 19 teams, we created an Excel sheet template as shown in Appendix B (Fig. 4).

5   Results and Discussion

5.1   Most Used QRs When Green Strategies Are Included into the Design Process (RQ1)

With the purpose of identifying first which QRs were considered by design teams when green strategies were involved in the service design process, we calculated the frequency distribution of all QRs used in design space specification, design space refinement, and solution space design across all the projects. As shown in Fig. 3, 20 different QRs were used for designing the EV-mobility project. We observed that some QRs, like performance, privacy, accuracy, and efficiency, were consistently used before-, during- and after including a green strategy. The stability of these QRs can be explained due to the functionality required by the project (e.g. EV battery should be charged every time the service is requested). However, some others QRs like usability, reliability, availability, security, interoperability, and scalability were also considered as relevant during the design process but with lower stability. We also identified some QRs that were less frequently used by the teams throughout the design process. These QRs are auditability, portability, flexibility, maintainability, and testability. What is surprising is that according to our sustainability definition (cf. [15,16]), most of these QRs contribute to software longevity (i.e. the technical sustainability dimension). This result can be due to the nature of the specific green software project, which aims to primarily address social and environmental issues.

In order to understand more clearly how the most used QRs can contribute to prioritization when green strategies were included into the design process, our analysis focused on the QRs that were considered in the design space refinement at least by 3 teams. Table 4 shows the number of QRs that were added during the refinement or after (solution space design phase); and QRs that were already identified earlier (design space specification), but kept still as important during the refinement as a consequence of including green strategies. From this data, we found that the most-used QRs, except environmental sustainability

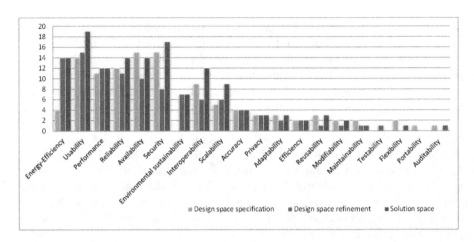

Fig. 3. Frequency distribution of influenced quality requirements used at design space specification, Design space refinement and solution space design

Table 4. Quality requirements added and/or kept during and after design refinement

	During design space refinement					
	Kept from		Added at		Added at	
	Design space specification		Design space refinement		Solution space design	
Energy-Efficiency	4	29%	10	71%	0	%
Usability	10	67%	5	33%	4	21%
Performance	10	83%	2	17%	0	0%
Reliability	9	82%	2	18%	3	21%
Availability	11	100%	0	0%	4	29%
Security	6	75%	2	25%	10	59%
Env Sustainability	0	0%	7	100%	0	0%
Interoperability	6	100%	0	0%	6	50%
Scalability	4	67%	2	33%	4	44%
Accuracy	4	100%	0	0%	0	0%
Privacy	2	67%	1	33%	1	33%

and energy efficiency, were kept as relevant from the design space specification. These results could have important positive implications for the development of green software projects. For example, reusing these technical QRs, that had been already considered as relevant before including green strategies at design space, can be economically beneficial for the software project. Only security and interoperability (see grayed rows) were added after the refinement by most of the design teams, followed by scalability.

Next, we analyze and discuss main results on the influence relation between green strategies and QRs considered as the most important in the design of a green software project.

5.2 Green Strategies Influence on Quality Requirements Prioritization (RQ2)

We considered the first thirteen clusters of green strategies shown in Table 6. The last three clusters were excluded because of their size (1 strategy only). As a green strategy can have an influence on a QR only if such QR is used for the selection of a design option that introduces a green action, we first calculated the frequency distribution of the most used QRs per green strategy. In order to answer RQ2, we calculated (i) the total number of influenced QRs by the respective cluster of strategies (shown in the last row of Table 5), and (ii) the total number of clusters that influence on a QR (last column of Table 5).

From this data we can observe that all clusters of **people-awareness strategies** influence on Usability (e.g. G1, G4, G5, G8, G11). Due to the type of green problem that the project aims to solve (making users become more aware of their own sustainability footprint), this result confirms that designers took on the challenge of designing usable services not only to improve user experience and user acceptance (e.g. [17]), but also to foster awareness among potential service consumers (e.g. non EV-drivers). However, it is surprising that none of the teams considered persuasiveness as a ranking criteria of the design concerns, despite its importance in the design of interactive systems [18]. This can be due to the traditional software quality models (e.g., [19–21]) used by the teams, which did not include persuasion as QR. Another important observation is that people-awareness clusters G1 and G4 yield the highest number of dependencies with QRs. For instance, for G1 (Raise carbon footprint awareness), besides usability and environmental sustainability, designers considered also security, reliability, privacy, accuracy and availability as relevant qualities for evaluating different design options (e.g. rank users on carbon footprint, display tips). Moreover, as cluster G1 contains domain-generic green strategies, the probability of reusing these influenced QRs at any other domain can be high. In a similar way, this capability of reuse applies also to the five QRs influenced (i.e. usability,

Table 5. Green strategies and Quality requirements

| Qualities | People awareness | | | Process awareness | | | Service awareness | | | | | People awareness | | Count |
	G1	G5	G4	G9	G12	G13	G2	G6	G10	G3	G7	G8	G11	
Usability	11	3	3		1		3	2	1	1	1	2	2	11
Energy efficiency	4	2	2	2	1		5	2	1	2	3		1	11
Env Sustainability	5	2	2	1			1	1		3	1	2	1	10
Reliability	4		1	2			2	1		4	4		1	8
Performance	2		1	3		1	2		1	3	3	1		9
Interoperability	2		1				3		1	2	1	1		7
Availability	3		2	1			5		1	4	3			7
Scalability	1				1		2			1	2	1		6
Accuracy	3	1					2	1	1					5
Security	4		2	1						1	1			5
Privacy	3		2				1	1						4
Efficiency		1				1	1					1		4
Count	11	5	9	6	3	2	11	6	6	9	10	5	4	

environmental sustainability, performance, interoperability and scalability) by the cluster G8 (Paperless service).

Regarding **service-awareness strategies**, our results show that availability was the quality mostly influenced by green strategies of clusters G2, G3 and G7. Moreover, for these three clusters we observed a good number of dependencies with QRs (last row). For instance cluster G7 (reduce carbon footprint caused by databases) influence reliability, performance, availability, energy efficiency and scalability. The importance of some of these QRs (reliability, performance, availability) was also confirmed by other surveys-based studies on QR prioritization (e.g. [22]). Finally, from the last column of Table 5, we corroborated that energy efficiency and environmental sustainability were influenced by most of the green strategies (11 out of 13 clusters). Few clusters like G13 (Create a green cloud of energy) did not have any dependencies with these two QRs. However this observation may be limited by the design teams who proposed such strategies in cluster G13.

We also observed that for cluster G8 (Paperless service), designers considered only environmental sustainability as ranking criterion for their design decisions. This result may be explained by the fact that environmental sustainability is a broader topic that covers also energy efficiency.

Looking at the last row of Table 5 and considering only domain-generic strategies (text highlighted in blue), we identify: *Raise Carbon Footprint awareness (G1)* as the most influential people-awareness green strategy of the EV mobility project and *Reduce Carbon Footprint caused by DB (G7)* as the most influential service-awareness green strategy. This is because most of the qualities (11 QRs and 10 QRs respectively) were used during or after the design refinement as as a result of implementing both strategies.

Our results differ from our first empirical study [5] in the following way: (i) New requirements like energy-efficiency, environmental sustainability, and privacy emerged as important/relevant requirements during design space refinement and solution space design. This was a consequence of including green strategies (e.g. use most efficient charging points) into the design process. (ii) Security, scalability and interoperability are requirements that were considered as important/relevant by almost half of the design teams *after* the inclusion of green strategies (e.g. Reduce Carbon Footprint in EV)

On the other hand, requirements like usability, performance, reliability, and availability were considered as relevant since the design specification of the EV project. These results are consistent not only with the data obtained in our first study [5], but also with the top-five list identified by Ameller et al. [22]. This top list was derived from an empirical study (interviews with software architects) and consisted of the following quality requirements: Performance, usability, security, availability, interoperability.

6 Threats to Validity

The following discusses the threats to the validity of our results and provides rationale for our related design decisions.

Internal validity. As software design is a socially intensive activity, the study was organized in 19 teams clustered in 3 working groups with 3 different tutors. In this way, our threat of selection bias was partially mitigated by assigning the teams to the working groups randomly. Expertise level of tutors was similar. Maturation was another potential threat in our study because the data was collected in different phases. However, the effect that the subjects can react differently as time passes was mitigated by various mechanisms meant to keep the students motivated: (i) weekly feedback from industrial stakeholders, (ii) weekly competition among working groups, and (iii) a prize competition for the best project selected by the company that proposed the EV-mobility project. It is also important to notice that weekly competition helped avoiding plagiarism among teams. Moreover, with the purpose of not limiting the service aspects identification to a pre-defined quality standard model, the design teams freely choose QRs not only from a set of selected articles on the topic of quality attributes for SOA were used by the students (e.g., [19–21]) but also from "Web searched" electronically available papers. Although we consider this flexibility as very positive for stimulating design creativity in our students, the list of QRs that were identified in this study is limited to these different sources of qualities. Moreover, given some qualities might be named in different ways, synonyms were verified during data collection. In a possible future replication it would be interesting to use a reference quality model for services, like S-Cube[1].

Construct validity. Researchers can bias the results of a study both consciously and unconsciously. This threat was mitigated since tutors' feedback focused specifically on methodology issues (e.g. correct use of the template for capturing design decisions) without influencing on the decisions themselves required by the EV-mobility project. Our analysis for identifying QRs affected by the inclusion of green strategies may be threatened due to QRs removed during or after the design refinement were not considered in this study.

External validity. Although master students participated in this study, we think that our setting was representative since students had an industrial project featuring a real case. Besides, the project involved also a high number of domain-generic strategies. Regarding sample size, we had "only" 19 teams. This could have been easily mitigated by reducing the size of teams (e.g. 3 instead of 5 students per team). However, in our experience 5-person teams is more realistic yet necessary to deliver quality results in such large-scale industrial cases. Besides, it would have been unfeasible to tutor more teams with the three available tutors.

---

[1] http://www.s-cube-network.eu/km/qrm.

7   Conclusions and Further Work

The main goal of this study was to determine how green strategies can contribute to, and influence, QR prioritization performed iteratively throughout a service-oriented software design process.

Our study was conducted in an academic setting but with a real-life industrial project.

The study has shown that technical QRs like usability, performance, reliability, availability, interoperability, and scalability were identified before the refinement but considered still as important for designing green strategies. Instead, some other QRs like security and interoperability emerged after the refinement. This suggests that both QRs might require deeper understanding of the solution space before being able to determine their relevance in the green software design. Only green-related QRs (i.e. energy efficiency, environmental sustainability) were added during the design space refinement by most of the teams.

Another interesting result from our analysis of QRs and the most used green strategies is that usability emerged as the most relevant QR for addressing people-awareness green strategies, followed by reliability and security. Other QRs like privacy, availability and accuracy were also considered but with lower intensity.

For service-awareness green strategies, instead, availability was the most relevant QR. Our study has also found that certain clusters of service-awareness green strategies (e.g. reduce carbon footprint caused by databases) had a higher number of influenced QRs than others (e.g. reduce carbon footprint of charging points). This result implies that the implementation of such green strategies could become more complex due to the higher number of QR dependencies.

Our results help with QR prioritization by including since a project's inception, the most relevant QRs for addressing those green strategies that are domain-generic (e.g. reduce services' carbon footprint). Moreover, this research can serve as a basis for future replications in different domains: this would be beneficial to build empirical knowledge that can be reused for both developing green software, and modernizing legacy software to address environmental issues.

Acknowledgment. This work has received partial funding from the Netherlands Enterprise Agency, with the project GreenServe. It was also partially supported by the Spanish Ministry of Economy, Industry and Competitiveness with the Project: TIN2016-78011-C4-1-R, and Galician Government with the project: ED431C 2017/58.

Appendix A: Green Strategies

Table 6. Software green strategies for the EV-mobility project. (Gray rows = Domain-generic strategies; rows = Domain-specific strategies) [12]

Green problem type	Green Software Strategy	Code	Size
People awareness	Raise Carbon Footprint awareness	G1	17
Service/Process awareness	Use most efficient charging points	G2	10
Service awareness	Reduce Service's Carbon Footprint	G3	9
People awareness	Eco-friendly driving awareness	G5	8
People/process awareness	Reduce Carbon Footprint in EV	G4	7
People/service awareness	Paperless service	G8	4
Service awareness	Reduce Carbon Footprint caused by DB	G7	4
Service/process awareness	Reduce Carbon Footprint of charging points	G6	4
Process awareness	Virtualization	G9	3
Process awareness	Renewable energy resource	G12	2
Process awareness	Create a green cloud of energy	G13	2
Service/people awareness	Battery Sustainability	G11	2
Service/process awareness	Smart battery charger	G10	2
Service awareness	Optimizing network traffic	G14	1
Service awareness	Green Computing	G15	1
Service awareness	Data monitoring	G16	1

Appendix B: Data collection template

Team ID	QR1			QR2			...	QRn		
	p1	p2	p3	p1	p2	p3		p1	p2	p3
T_1	0	1	1	0	0	0		0	0	1
.										
.										
T_{19}										
Total										

Fig. 4. Excel template for data collection (p1 = design space specification; p2 = design space refinement; p3 = solution space design)

References

1. John, J.: Green computing strategies for improving energy efficiency in IT systems. Int. J. Sci. Eng. Technol. **3**(6), 715–717 (2014). ISSN 2277-1581
2. Murugesan, S.: Harnessing green IT: principles and practices. IT Prof. **10**(1), 24–33 (2008). https://doi.org/10.1109/MITP.2008.10
3. Chitchyan, R., Becker, C., Betz, S., Duboc, L., Penzenstadler, B., Seyff, N., Venters, C.C.: Sustainability design in requirements engineering: state of practice. In: Proceedings of the 38th International Conference on Software Engineering Companion, ICSE 2016, pp. 533–542. ACM, New York (2016)
4. Cheng, B.H.C., Atlee, J.M.: Research directions in requirements engineering. In: Future of Software Engineering, FOSE 2007, pp. 285–303 (2007)
5. Condori-Fernández, N., Lago, P.: Can we know upfront how to prioritize quality requirements? In: IEEE Fifth International Workshop on Empirical Requirements Engineering, EmpiRE 2015, Ottawa, ON, Canada, pp. 33–40, 24 August 2015
6. Lago, P., Razavian, M.: A pragmatic approach for analysis and design of service inventories. In: Pallis, G., et al. (eds.) ICSOC 2011. LNCS, vol. 7221, pp. 44–53. Springer, Heidelberg (2012). https://doi.org/10.1007/978-3-642-31875-7_6
7. Lago, P.: A master program on engineering energy-aware software. In: 28th International Conference on Informatics for Environmental Protection: ICT for Energy Efficiency (EnviroInfo), pp. 469–476 (2014)
8. Gu, Q., Lago, P., Potenza, S.: Aligning economic impact with environmental benefits: a green strategy model. In: First International Workshop on Green and Sustainable Software (GREENS), pp. 62–68 (2012). https://doi.org/10.1109/GREENS.2012.6224258
9. Lago, P., Jansen, T.: Creating environmental awareness in service oriented software engineering. In: Maximilien, E.M., Rossi, G., Yuan, S.-T., Ludwig, H., Fantinato, M. (eds.) ICSOC 2010. LNCS, vol. 6568, pp. 181–186. Springer, Heidelberg (2011). https://doi.org/10.1007/978-3-642-19394-1_19
10. Gu, Q., Lago, P., Di Nitto, E.: Guiding the service engineering process: the importance of service aspects. In: Poler, R., van Sinderen, M., Sanchis, R. (eds.) IWEI 2009. LNBIP, vol. 38, pp. 80–93. Springer, Heidelberg (2009). https://doi.org/10.1007/978-3-642-04750-3_7
11. Gu, Q., Lago, P., van Vliet, H.: A template for SOA design decision making in an educational setting. In: Proceedings of the 2010 36th EUROMICRO Conference on Software Engineering and Advanced Applications, SEAA, pp. 175–182. IEEE Computer Society, Washington, DC (2010)
12. Condori-Fernandez, N., Lago, P.: Analyzing green software strategies within a service design process. In: Otjacques, B., Hitzelberger, P., Naumann, S., Wohlgemuth, V. (eds.) EnviroInfo Conference: From Science to Society: The Bridge Provided by Environmental Informatics, 31st edn., pp. 101–110. Shaker Verlag, Luxembourg (2017)
13. Moran, T.P.: Design Rationale: Concepts, Techniques, and Use. L. Erlbaum Associates Inc., Hillsdale (1996)
14. Lago, P., Muccini, H., Babar, M.A.: Developing a course on designing software in globally distributed teams. In: International Conference on Global Software Engineering, pp. 249–253. IEEE Computer Society, Los Alamitos (2008)
15. Lago, P., Koçak, S.A., Crnkovic, I., Penzenstadler, B.: Framing sustainability as a property of software quality. Commun. ACM **58**(10), 70–78 (2015)

16. Condori-Fernandez, N., Lago, P.: Characterizing the contribution of quality requirements to software sustainability. J. Syst. Softw. **137**, 289–305 (2018). https://doi.org/10.1016/j.jss.2017.12.005

17. Condori-Fernandez, N.: Happyness: an emotion-aware QoS assurance framework for enhancing user experience. In: Proceedings of the 39th International Conference on Software Engineering Companion, ICSE-C 2017, pp. 235–237. IEEE Press, Piscataway (2017)

18. Freeney, D.: Usability versus Persuasion in an Application Interface Design. Mälardalen University (2014)

19. O'Brien, L., Merson, P., Bass, L.: Quality attributes for service-oriented architectures. In: Proceedings of the International Workshop on Systems Development in SOA Environments, SDSOA 2007, p. 3. IEEE Computer Society, Washington, DC (2007). https://doi.org/10.1109/SDSOA.2007.10

20. Kounev, S., Brosig, F., Huber, N., Reussner, R.H.: Towards self-aware performance and resource management in modern service-oriented systems. In: 2010 IEEE International Conference on Services Computing, SCC 2010, Miami, Florida, USA, 5–10 July 2010, pp. 621–624 (2010). https://doi.org/10.1109/SCC.2010.94

21. Lewis, G.A., Morris, E., Simanta, S., Wrage, L.: Common misconceptions about service-oriented architecture. In: Proceedings of the Sixth International IEEE Conference on Commercial-off-the-Shelf (COTS)-Based Software Systems, ICCBSS 2007, pp. 123–130. IEEE Computer Society, Washington, DC (2007)

22. Ameller, D., Ayala, C., Cabot, J., Franch, X.: How do software architects consider non-functional requirements: an exploratory study. In: 2012 20th IEEE International Requirements Engineering Conference (RE), pp. 41–50 (2012)

User and Job Stories

On Modelers Ability to Build a Visual Diagram from a User Story Set: A Goal-Oriented Approach

Yves Wautelet[1]([⊠])(iD), Mattijs Velghe[1], Samedi Heng[2], Stephan Poelmans[1], and Manuel Kolp[2]

[1] KU Leuven, Leuven, Belgium
{yves.wautelet,stephan.poelmans}@kuleuven.be
[2] Université catholique de Louvain, Louvain-la-Neuve, Belgium
{samedi.heng,manuel.kolp}@uclouvain.be

Abstract. [**Context and Motivation**] User Stories (US) are often used as requirement representation artifacts within agile projects. Within US sets, the nature, granularity and inter-dependencies of the elements constituting each US is not or poorly represented. To deal with these drawbacks, previous research allowed to build a unified model for tagging the elements of the WHO, WHAT and WHY dimensions of a US; each tag representing a concept with an inherent nature and defined granularity. Once tagged, the US elements can be graphically represented with an icon and the modeler can define the inter-dependencies between the elements to build one or more so-called Rationale Trees (RT). [**Question/Problem**] RT and their benefits have been illustrated on case studies but the ability to easily build a RT in a genuine case for software modelers not familiar with the concepts needs to be evaluated. [**Principal ideas/results**] This paper presents the result of a double exercise aimed to evaluate how well novice and experienced modelers were able to build a RT out of an existing US set. The experiment explicitly forces the test subjects to attribute a concept to US elements and to link these together. [**Contribution**] On the basis of the conducted experiment, we highlight the encountered difficulties that the lambda modeler faces when building a RT with basic support. Overall, the test subjects have produced models of satisfying quality. Also, we highlight these necessary conditions that need to be provided to the lambda modeler to build a consistent RT.

Keywords: User Story · Rationale Tree · Modeling experiment
Granularity

1 Introduction

In agile methods, requirements are often written through *User Stories (US)*. *User stories are short, simple descriptions of a feature told from the perspective of the person who desires the new capability, usually a user or customer of the*

© Springer International Publishing AG, part of Springer Nature 2018
E. Kamsties et al. (Eds.): REFSQ 2018, LNCS 10753, pp. 209–226, 2018.
https://doi.org/10.1007/978-3-319-77243-1_13

system. US are generally presented in a flat list which makes the nature of the elements constituting them as well as their hierarchy and interdependence(s) difficult to evaluate [3].

The general US pattern relates a WHO, a WHAT and possibly a WHY dimension but, in practice, different keywords are used to describe these dimensions (e.g. Mike Cohn's *As a <type of user>, I want <some goal> so that <some reason>* [3]). Moreover, in the literature, no semantics has ever been associated to these keywords. Thus, Wautelet et al. [10] conducted research to find the majority of templates used in practice, sort them and associate semantics to each keyword. The key idea behind of [10] is that, using a unified and consistent set of US templates, the tags associated to each element of the US set provide information about both its nature and granularity. Such information could be used for software analysis, e.g., structuring the problem and solution, identifying missing requirements, etc. [5]. Most of the concepts of [10] are related to the i* framework [12], and a visual *Goal-Oriented Requirements Engineering (GORE)* model, the Rationale Tree (*RT*), has been formalized for graphical representation of US sets in [11]. Alternatively, a graphical representation using the use-case model based on the same concepts is proposed in [8].

A consistent RT allows its reader to identify the hierarchy of elements and their interdependence(s). This also provides a global view of the system to be developed. A RT is constructed from a tagged US set which is based on the US unified model proposed in [10]; of course a real life US set is seldom fully consistent so that when building a RT, the US set is sorted, cleaned, updated, etc. Concretely, the modeler, supported by a *Computer-Aided Software Engineering (CASE)* tool, should associate the tags to each US element and, in a visual window, link these US elements through means-end or traditional decompositions. When doing this, the modeler makes an assumption on (i) the nature of the US element (functional or not, coarse-grained or fine-grained) and (ii) how the US element needs to be fulfilled (immediately or by fulfilling other US elements found in other US or added to the set to ensure consistency). In terms of transformation of elements to a software design, the benefits of using the RT to build an agent-oriented architecture in [9].

This paper presents the results of an experiment where novice (students) and experienced (researchers) modelers are required to build RT out of two different US sets (cases). It is part of further validation of the applicability of the previously evoked research. The experiment has been designed in order to answer two main research questions. The first and main one is to see if, *starting from a US set, a lambda modeler is able to easily build a consistent RT.* The second is a side one and concerns *what are the necessary conditions to provide a lambda modeler the ability to build a consistent RT.*

2   Related Work

The need to test different decomposition techniques US with different agile methods and kind of stakeholders has been identified in [6]. We nevertheless only consider US as structured in the evoked form, independently of the agile method and evaluate the perspective of the modeler only. Trkman et al. [7] propose an approach for mapping US to process models in order to understand US dependencies. Their approach is oriented to building an operational sequence of activities which is a dynamic approach not targeted to multiple granularity level representation. We, however, aim to build a rationale analysis of US elements which is a static approach allowing to represent and identify at once multiple granularity levels. Finally, as identified by [2], the representation symbols in a visual notation have an impact on the modelers understanding. We by default used the symbols of i* but this parameter should be further studied.

3   Research Method: Designing the Modeling Experiment

The experimentation uses two cases: (Case 1) the carpooling system and (Case 2) the Book Factory. Due to the lack of space, we only expose Case 2 here. The description of the Case 1 can be found on p. 1 in an Appendix document placed online[1].

The Book Factory is a small Belgian retailer specialized in selling books, CD's and DVD's. The management has decided to invest in an online shopping environment for their customers in order to increase the customer-friendliness of their services. Within this online shopping environment, a user should have the possibility to place their orders online. Before an order is complete, a client should fill his online cart with products.

Secondly, the client should has to pay the invoice using an online payment. In order to be able to execute the payment, the system should calculate the invoice amount. Furthermore, the online payments are processed via the Ogone payment platform in order to increase the safety and security of the payment.

The related US set is provided within Table 1. A concept of the unified model has been associated to each US element; the interested reader can refer to [10] for their full definition. The type RT solution is provided in Fig. 1. This example is also the second exercise given to test subjects for the experiment. Let us note that, in US 5, *I need to calculate the total amount of the order* has been modeled as a *Capability* because it is seen as atomic while all the other elements tagged as *Tasks* are seen a being further decomposable. The choice can nevertheless be seen as arbitrary and as long as all of the elements we just referred to are tagged as *Task* or *Capability* the tagging can be seen as valid. Section 5 further discusses the interpretation and use of *Tasks* and *Capabilities*.

Process for Building the Modeling Experiment. As a first step in the research process, the different exercises (i.e. US sets to be tagged and transformed into a RT) used for the modeling experiment have been designed. In order to compare the output of the experiment subjects a *type solution* was built by a junior and 2 senior researchers (all part of the authors of the paper). Also, a theoretical part – to explain subjects the theory about the RT – has been built;

---

[1] https://goo.gl/8ZT5tD (this document is refereed to several times in the rest of this paper).

Table 1. US set in Case 2 of the feasibility study.

US ID	Dimension	User Story	Descriptive Concept Type
US 1	WHO	*As an owner*	Role
	WHAT	*I want my clients to be able to place orders online*	Hard-goal
	WHY	*So that the customer-friendliness of our services increases*	Soft-goal
US 2	WHO	*As a client*	Role
	WHAT	*I have to complete an order*	Task
	WHY	*So that I can place it online*	Hard-goal
US 3	WHO	*As a client*	Role
	WHAT	*I need to fill my 'online cart' with products*	Task
US 4	WHO	*As a client*	Role
	WHAT	*I need to pay my invoice*	Task
	WHY	*So that I can complete an online order*	Hard-goal
US 5	WHO	*As system component*	Role
	WHAT	*I need to calculate the total amount of the order*	Capability
	WHY	*So that the invoice can be paid*	Hard-goal
US 6	WHO	*As system component*	Role
	WHAT	*I want to pay my order online*	Task
	WHY	*So that my invoice is paid*	Hard-goal
US 7	WHO	*As a system component*	Role
	WHAT	*I need to process payments on the Ogone-payment platform*	Task
	WHY	*So that the payment is secured*	Soft-goal

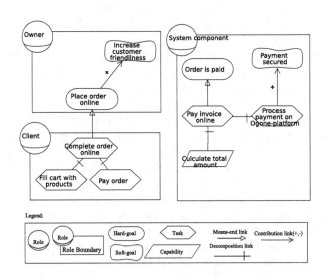

Fig. 1. Possible solution of Case 2 in the feasibility study.

it has been included in the set of papers given to test subjects. Finally, questions to measure some additional variables have been defined.

To evaluate the practical feasibility of the experiment, a primary evaluation/simulation with a group of researchers (PhD students and postdocs) at *Université catholique de Louvain (UCL)* has been done. Based on this test feedback, some aspects in the layout of the modeling experiment have been changed/adapted. No content-related aspects have nevertheless been changed whereby the integrity of the evaluation basis between the first and second version of the modeling experiment has not been affected. Therefore, we also considered the data collected from this experimentation for analysis. The final version of the modeling experiment has been placed online[2].

Assignment and Measured Variables. Test subjects were asked to produce two separate US models based on two cases. These cases respectively consisted of a set of 4 and 7 US. The first US set was less complex than the second one in that the RT to build up was less complex. Since US and the production of a US-based model was new to the test subjects, the assignment has been split up in 5 steps, i.e.:

1. Identification of all elements within the WHO dimension of the US;
2. Identification of all elements within the WHAT and WHY dimension of the US;
3. Identification of the appropriate concept or tag (i.e., *Capability*, *Task*, *Hard-goal* or *Soft-goal*) for each element within the WHAT and WHY dimension of the US;
4. Graphical representation (and linking) of the US' WHAT and WHY elements;
5. Identification and representation of other links between the US elements.

Throughout the modeling experiment, additional questions have been asked in order to gather *additional variables* concerning the educational background, the tacit knowledge and the perception on difficulty of the different test subjects, i.e.:

- Their educational background (i.e., obtained diplomas);
- Their primary occupation (i.e., student, researcher, assistant, etc.);
- Their modeling knowledge (i.e., the modeling languages they already worked with);
- Whether or not they were familiar with GORE;
- Based on rating-scales, their knowledge on the i* framework and their knowledge concerning US as requirements artefacts within agile methods have been measured.

In between the different assignment steps (i.e., steps 1 to 5 as described above), the test subjects were asked to indicate their experience and perception concerning the understandability of the theory and concerning the difficulty of the steps to be executed. Latter elements have been measured using a rating-scale. At the end of the modeling experiment, some additional questions were asked in order to find out the global perceived experience of the test subjects when modeling the two cases. More specifically, they were asked to indicate which case was perceived as most difficult and, based on rating-scales, the global understandability of the proposed approach was measured.

---

[2] https://goo.gl/i8GmJM.

4   Data Collection and Participants' Modeling Knowledge

The experiments have been conducted with *three groups* of expertise. The first group consists of business students with a major in IT (known as *Business Students* in this paper). The second group consists of students in IT (known as *IT Students* in this paper). For the two former groups, the experiment has been done in class in the context of a special session of a compulsory course. The third group of expertise is made by the researchers of the pre-test (known as *Researchers* in this paper). For this last group, the experiment has been done in a single class room during working hours. The researchers participated on a voluntary basis; all of the researchers of the department were invited. These researchers all hold (at least) a master diploma with a major in IT. The use of three different groups of population notably allows us to *analyze the difference in execution of the assignment* and to study whether or not there are significant differences between these groups of various modeling experience. We nevertheless point out that all of the participants have chosen for a strong IT component in their present or past curriculum.

Since a concrete sample framework is lacking within the context of this modeling experiment, a non-stochastic sample method is used to compose the different samples. More precisely, the strategy of convenience samples has been used. Ultimately, three different samples have been composed. For the group of *Business Students*, the modeling experiment has been executed by 21 students within the master in Business Administration at KU Leuven campus Brussels. For the group of *IT Students*, the modeling experiment has been conducted with 35 students within the second bachelor Applied Informatics at Odisee campus Brussels. Finally, for the group of *Researchers*, the experiments have been conducted with 13 members of the academic staff of UCL.

The questions on background in Business Analysis shows that nearly the entirety of the participants have some preliminary knowledge in modeling. Indeed, only 2 out of 69 participants do not have such specific experience (i.e., 1 *IT Student* and 1 *Business Student*). They are able to model, at least one model, with the *Unified Modeling Language (UML)*, *Business Process Modeling Notation (BPMN)* or others modeling languages; but not GORE (only 2 *Researchers* have knowledge on GORE frameworks).

Concerning the question about knowledge of the i* framework by participants, results showed that none of them is an expert with the framework. Some students received a specific 2 h presentation on i* during another course. Nevertheless, over 50% never heard about it (but most are unaware that i* is GORE). Meanwhile, two thirds of the participants know what US are and some of them are experts in using them.

5   Tagging of User Story Elements

According to the US meta-model presented in [10], the US elements of WHO dimension can only be tagged as *Role*. No interpretation aspect need to be

Table 2. Tagging of the US elements in Case 1 and 2.

	Business Students					IT Students					Researchers				
	Task	Capability	Hard-goal	Soft-goal	Not present	Task	Capability	Hard-goal	Soft-goal	Not present	Task	Capability	Hard-goal	Soft-goal	Not present
Case1															
US2															
WHAT	**42.9%**	33.3%	23.8%			31.4%	**51.5%**	11.4%	5.7%		**53.8%**	30.8%	15.4%		
WHY				9.5%	**90.5%**			2.9%		**97.1%**		30.8%	7.7%		**51.5%**
US3															
WHAT	**85.7%**	14.3%				**94.3%**	5.7%				**84.5%**	15.4%			
WHY	9.5%	4.8%	**75.2%**	9.5%		2.8%	8.5%	**71.4%**	14.3%	2.9%			**76.9%**	23.1%	
US4															
WHAT	23.8%	**76.2%**				34.3%	**62.8%**	2.9%			30.8%	**69.2%**			
WHY	38.1%	4.8%	**47.6%**	9.5%		**48.6%**	2.9%	37.1%	11.4%		**46.2%**	15.3%	15.4%	23.1%	
Case2															
US2															
WHAT	**85.7%**	14.3%				**66.7%**	27.2%	6.1%			**75.0%**	8.3%	16.7%		
WHY	4.8%	4.7%	**81.0%**		9.5%	9.0%	3.0%	**66.7%**	6.1%	15.2%		9.1%	**90.9%**		
US3															
WHAT	**52.4%**	42.8%		4.8%		**42.4%**	36.4%	9.1%	12.1%		**58.3%**	25.0%	16.7%		
WHY	4.7%		4.8%		**90.5%**					**100%**	8.4%		8.3%		**83.3%**
US4															
WHAT	**66.7%**	28.5%	4.6%			**75.0%**	18.8%	6.2%			**91.7%**	8.3%			
WHY	**52.4%**	4.7%	42.9%			25.0%	18.8%	**50.0%**	6.2%		**50.0%**		16.7%	33.3%	
US5															
WHAT	**52.4%**	47.6%				**71.9%**	25.0%	3.1%			41.7%	**50.0%**		6.3%	
WHY	23.8%		**76.2%**			19.4%	29.0%	**41.9%**	6.5%	3.2%	27.3%	9.1%	**36.4%**	27.3%	
US6															
WHAT	**47.6%**	42.9%	9.5%			**57.6%**	36.3%	6.1%			**63.6%**	27.3%	9.1%		
WHY	14.2%	9.5%	**66.7%**	4.8%	4.8%	15.6%	12.5%	**65.6%**	6.3%		18.2%	9.1%	**36.4%**	**36.4%**	
US7															
WHAT	**47.6%**	42.9%	9.5%			**50.0%**	37.5%	9.4%			45.5%	**54.5%**			
WHY					**100%**				3.1%	**100%**					**100%**

legend: [ ] Highest occurrence within the sample in question

discussed here. US elements in the WHAT and WHY dimensions can nevertheless be tagged as *Capability*, *Task*, *Hard-goal* or *Soft-goal* and need to be discussed.

The results of US elements tagging for the WHAT and WHY dimensions of Case 1 and Case 2 are represented in Table 2. Since a valid interpretation for the first US of both cases was given as illustration they have been left out of the results.

Based on the information provided in Table 2, we can draw the conclusion that the tagging of the different US elements of both cases differs *within* as well as *between* the different samples. In other words, tagging of a US element as being *Capability*, *Task*, *Hard-goal* or *Soft-goal* cannot be characterized as being univocal (similar results have been highlighted by [1,4] in the context of i* modeling). Also between the different samples, there are a lot of tagging discords; a few observations can be made:

- The tagging discords within the sample of *Business Students* is mainly between the tagging of a US element as being a *Task* or *Capability*. A higher variability in tagging of US elements can be observed within the samples of *IT Students* and *Researchers* especially within the Case 2;

- There exists some discords in what some US elements are. The confusion is mainly about the difference between a *Capability*, *Task* or *Hard-goal*;
- Despite this, test subjects unanimously agreed upon that the provided concepts (i.e., *Capability*, *Task*, *Hard-goal* and *Soft-goal*) were sufficient to model the different US sets. In other words, they did not witness having the need for additional concepts to accurately tag some US elements when performing the exercise.

As part of the modeling experiment, test subjects have been asked to indicate on a rating-scale whether or not the difference between the modeling concepts— i.e., respectively *Task* versus *Capability*, *Task* versus *Goal* (*Hard-goal* and *Soft-goal*) and *Goal* versus *Capability*—were clear. Within this rating-scale, the value 1 reflects the fact that the difference between the two modeling concepts was *not clear at all*. Conversely, the value 10 reflects a *complete awareness of the differences* between both modeling concepts. The descriptive statistics of these elements are provided in Table 3. Based on this data, we can draw the conclusion that, especially, the difference between *Task* and *Capability* was not completely clear for test subjects. Furthermore, the data indicates that *Task* and *Capability* were perceived as easier to differentiate from *Goal*.

Latter observation of the unclear difference between *Task* and *Capability* is confirmed by an analysis of the main modeling errors that have been made by the different test subjects. These modeling errors notably revealed that the atomic characteristic of *Capability* (i.e., the key feature that distinguishes *Capability* from *Task*) was not clear at all since a tremendous amount of test subjects graphically decomposed *Capability* elements into multiple sub-elements (using *decomposition-links*). This is not valid with respect to the presented base model. It, however, does not necessarily mean that the interpretation of element's granularity is necessarily incorrect (this is evaluated through the quality of the RT in the next section).

Table 3. Understandability of the difference between the elements.

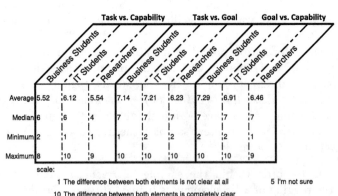

| | Task vs. Capability | | | Task vs. Goal | | | Goal vs. Capability | | |
	Business Students	IT Students	Researchers	Business Students	IT Students	Researchers	Business Students	IT Students	Researchers
Average	5.52	6.12	5.54	7.14	7.21	6.23	7.29	6.91	6.46
Median	6	6	4	7	7	7	7	7	7
Minimum	2	1	1	1	2	2	2	2	1
Maximum	8	10	9	10	10	10	10	10	9

scale:

1 The difference between both elements is not clear at all   5 I'm not sure

10 The difference between both elements is completely clear

Next to this, a statistical test has been performed in order to test whether or not there exist significant differences within the samples in the test subject's *'understandability scores'*. More specifically, the non-parametric Kruskal-Wallis test has been executed since the normality test (i.e., Kolmogorov-Smirnov) indicated that none of the variables involved were normally distributed. Latter non-parametric test verifies if multiple population variables have the same distribution. Based on the results of this test (not represented due to a lack of space, see the Appendix on p. 6) the conclusion can be drawn that no significant differences exist between the scores of *Business Students*, *IT Students* and *Researchers*[3].

6 Analyzing the User Story Model with Rationale Tree

6.1 Global Evaluation of the User Story Model: Qualitative Approach

Business Students. The sample of students with an economical background succeeded rather well in producing a RT. However, the results showed that a few test subjects within this first sample tended at modeling each US separately instead of producing a global model for the complete US set in the cases. They failed in identifying corresponding elements within different US and they consequently modeled the same elements multiple times (i.e., one time per occurrence in a US). Latter observation nevertheless has to be put in some perspective in that it could possibly be correlated with one of the limitations of the modeling experiment. More precisely, since test subjects only received the minimal required amount of information for executing the assignment within the modeling experiment, one could argue that more information concerning the ultimate purpose of the graphical representation should have been depicted in more detail within the theory part of the modeling experiment. This probably could have resulted in a higher understanding of the primary rationale behind modeling US and could consequently have resulted in a higher ability to produce a RT of a US set. Another tendency that could be identified within the *Business Students* is that test subjects with a (basic) knowledge of US were able to make up a higher-quality hierarchical structure within their RT. Furthermore, analysis of the different models produced by the test subjects in all three samples revealed that, together with *IT Students*, *Business Students* tend to put a stronger emphasis on the process-related aspect of the US set in their model. Latter phenomenon could clearly be observed within the Case 2. For example, US3 and US4 respectively consist of the elements Fill online cart and Pay invoice. Both elements can be seen as sub-elements of the WHAT dimension in US2: Complete an order. Many students tried to model latter two elements (i.e., fill cart and payment) in such a way that the process-related sequence of these elements was represented in their model; i.e. that the result reflects the constraint that the online cart should be filled with products before the invoice

---

can be paid. Adjoining it, many test subjects within this first sample made the remark that some modeling elements were missing in order to represent `sequential conditions` between elements in the model.

IT Students. More than *Business Students*, *IT Students* failed in overviewing the 'global model' and tended to model each US separately. This resulted in the fact that their models consisted multiple 'isolated' elements without any link to another element. As a consequence, it is impossible to trace the dependency and hierarchy relationships between the different elements within the RT. One can thus state that *IT Students* were less able to produce a high-quality RT from a US set. A second observation that could be done is that the 'technical' background of the *IT Students* reveals itself within their different models. A few students namely modeled elements that were not part of the US set that has been included in the cases. These elements could commonly be categorized as more 'technical' elements that are part of the actual development of the systems. For example, some students represented an element `show ride` within their model of the `Case 1`. Others included the element `verify payment` within the boundaries of their model of the `Case 2`.

Researchers. Only taking into account the ability to produce a RT of a US set, one can state that *Researchers* produced higher-quality RT compared to students. In other words, *Researchers* were able to produce a better global model where the complete US set was represented in the RT. Within the models produced by the different test subjects in this sample, a tendency of modeling more elements than present in the US could be observed (i.e., elements that were not present in the US set). Furthermore, a lot of *Researchers* decomposed existing elements into (smaller) sub-elements. As an example, the WHAT dimension within US2 of the `Case 1` consists of the element `propose a ride from A to B with the price, location and time of departure, and number of seats available`. Instead of modeling this element as being one *Task*, many *Researchers* used 4 different elements to model this (i.e., one for `price`, one for `location`, one for `time of departure` and one for the `number of seats available`). Secondly, the different test subjects within this sample tended at identifying and modeling links that were outside the scope and boundaries of the definition that had been provided in the theory. More specifically, they used the broader definition of the links as present within the i* framework.

Modeling Errors. Within the US models of the different test subjects, various modeling errors have been made. A frequently occurring modeling error concerned the decomposition of *Capabilities* into subcomponents. A second common error made by subjects of all three samples concerned the fact that the different roles (through boundaries) were not represented in the graphical US model.

Next to these modeling errors, nearly all US models of all test subjects contained one or multiple link errors (i.e., use of a faulty link). As an example, many test subjects in all samples used a *means-end link* between two *Tasks* while latter link has theoretically been defined as a link that is used between a *Task* and a *Hard-goal* if the former furnishes a realization scenario for the latter.

Table 4. Descriptive statistics of the number of elements and links modeled.

	Case1 Elements modeled			Case1 Links identified			Case2 Elements modeled			Case2 Links identified		
	Business Students	IT Students	Researchers	Business Students	IT Students	Researchers	Business Students	IT Students	Researchers	Business Students	IT Students	Researchers
Average	6.1	6.1	7.7	4.9	4.6	5.7	10.1	10.5	9.2	7.9	7.9	8.2
Median	6	6	6.5	5	4	4.5	10	9.5	9.5	8	8	9
Minimum	4	5	5	3	3	3	7	4	4	3	4	4
Maximum	11	9	17	10	8	13	13	13	13	11	13	10

The tremendous amount of linkage errors allows to draw the conclusion that some theoretical aspects concerning the different links have not been understood completely. This conclusion can directly be associated with the limited amount of information that has been given to test subjects.

Quantitative Evaluation of the US Models. Table 4 contains the data of the quantitative analysis of RTs. It allows to make a comparison between the US models made by the test subjects in the three different samples. Based on the results of the Kruskal-Wallis test (not represented here due to a lack of space, see the Appendix on p. 7), one can conclude that there are no significant differences between the number of elements and links modeled by the different test subjects in the three different samples. Latter non-parametric test has been executed since the Kolmogorov-Smirnov test has indicated that none of the variables involved are normally distributed.

6.2 Quoting the Performance in Modeling User Stories: Quantitative Approach

In order to be able to evaluate the individual performance of the test subjects in modeling the US sets in both cases, a score has been allocated to each US model. This score is notably based on three different evaluation criteria: *completeness*, *conformity* and *accuracy*.

Completeness has been used to verify whether or not all elements present in the different dimensions of the US set have been represented within the US model. For each element in the WHAT and WHY dimensions of a US that has been represented in the US model, 1 point was given.

In combination with completeness, the models have been evaluated with respect to conformity. During the exercises of the modeling experiment, the test subjects were asked to identify all elements in the WHAT and WHY dimension of the different US and classify each element as a *Task, Capability, Hard-goal* or *Soft-goal* (i.e., respectively steps 2 and 3 in the modeling experiment). In order to verify if the appropriate modeling concepts have been used in accordance with the classification of the elements, the evaluation criterion of conformity has been used. More precisely, if there was conformity between the classification of an element and the modeling concept that has been used to represent that element, 0.5 points (per element) were given.

Based on the type solution of both cases, the fundamental links that should be present in the US models have been identified. More precisely, 4 fundamental links have been identified in the Case 1 and 8 links in the Case 2. If one of the fundamental links was present in the US model of the test subjects, 4 points were given. If the link between the elements had been identified but the wrong type of link was used, only 1 point was given. This quotation of the ability of subjects to identify the links between the elements is the accuracy criterion.

Next to the scores on each evaluation criterion, a score on the global quality of the US models has been given. More specifically, an additional score on 10 was given for the Case 1 and a score on 20 for the Case 2. The score on the global quality has been based on a general comparison of the US models with the type solution. Furthermore, additional factors have influenced the individual score of the global quality. More specifically, the fact that all *Roles* were correctly represented, the number of modeling errors and the quality of the RT were factors that have been taken into consideration in allocating the score on global quality. An overview of the different evaluation criteria and the allocated scores are provided in Table 5. Ultimately, a total mark on each case has been calculated based on the scores of the individual evaluation criteria. More precisely, a total score on 38 was given for the Case 1 and a score on 73 was given on the second one. Both scores have eventually been reduced to a score on 10.

In order to get an overview of the 'general performance' of the test subjects in modeling the different US, a global score on 10 has been calculated. This score was based on the individual scores for Case 1 and Case 2. Within the calculation of latter global score a weight of 30% has been allocated to the Case 1 and a weight of 70% to the Case 2. The allocation of a different weight to both cases has been done since one could argue that a kind of 'learning-effect'

Table 5. Evaluation criteria in quoting the US models.

Evaluation criterion	Allocated scores	Maximum score	
		Case 1 (4 US)	Case 2 (7 US)
Completeness	1 point per modeled element	8 points	14 points
Consistency	0.5 points per consistently modeled element	4 points	7 points
Accuracy	4 points per correct link (only 1 point if the wrong type of link is used)	16 points	32 points
Global quality	–	10 points	20 points

Table 6. General performance of modelers.

(a) Descriptive statistics of the global score.

	Business Students	IT Students	Researchers
Average	6.20	5.50	6.60
Median	6.60	5.30	6.50
Minimum	2.90	3.60	4.40
Maximum	8.30	7.40	8.60

(b) Averages Scores on Case 1 and 2.

Sample Groupe	Case 1	Case 2
Business Students	6.30	6.20
IT Students	5.60	5.40
Researchers	7.20	6.30

could have occurred after the execution of the Case 1. The Case 2 furthermore consisted of a higher number of US, what implies that a bigger RT.

Table 6a consists of the descriptive statistics of the global score (on 10) that measures the performance of the test subjects in modeling a set of related US. The normal distribution of this global performance score[4] allows to perform the ANOVA-test in order to verify if there exists some significant differences between the scores of the different samples (i.e., *Business Students*, *IT Students* and *Researchers*). Based on the results of this test (not represented here due to a lack of space, see the Appendix on p. 8), the conclusion can be drawn that there indeed exist significant differences between the scores of the different test subjects in the three samples. More precisely, the results of the post-hoc test of Bonferroni (not represented here due to a lack of space, see the Appendix on p. 9) learn that, with a reliability of 95%, a significant difference can be found between the scores of the *IT Students* and those of the *Researchers*. There is no significant difference between the scores of *Business Students* and *IT Students* and between those of *Business Students* and *Researchers*.

Next to the differences in the global score between the three samples, one could question whether there exists a significant difference in the individual performance of modeling both cases. Table 6b represents the average score on both cases per sample. In order to test for significant differences in the score of Case 1 compared to the score Case 2, the paired samples t-test is performed on the different scores of each particular sample. The results of these tests (not represented here, see the Appendix on p. 10) show that no significant differences can be identified in the performance of *Business Student* and *IT Students* in modeling the US sets in both cases. This contrary to the sample of *Researchers*, where can be concluded (with a reliability of 95%), that the scores on Case 1 significantly differ from those of Case 2.

7 Analyzing the Experience of Test Subjects

7.1 Evaluating the Understandability of the Theory

In order to measure the understandability of the theory, four questions have been asked to test subjects. These questions were to be answered using a rating-scale

---

[4] Both the Kolmogorov-Smirnov test as well as the Shapiro-Wilk test indicated that the variable of the global score was normally distributed.

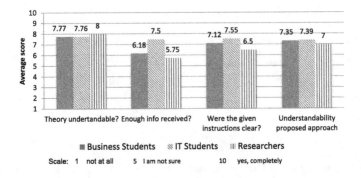

Fig. 2. Understandability of the theory.

going from 1 for *not at all* to 10 for *completely*. A first question concerned the understandability of the introductory theory part of the modeling experiment. Secondly, test subjects were asked if they received enough information to produce the models. Thirdly, they were also asked if the given instructions to model the US sets were clear. The fourth question concerned the understandability of the proposed approach for producing a US model using a RT. The average score of these questions are represented within Fig. 2.

Analysis of the results of these additional questions reveals that, despite the fuzzy differentiation between *Task* and *Capability*, the theory was rather understandable for most test subjects. However, an evaluation of the most common modeling error shows that not all aspects within the theory have been understood completely. In all three samples, a considerable amount of test subjects made particular modeling errors from which latter conclusion can be derived. As stated within Subsect. 6.1, a tremendous amount of modeling errors concerned the fact that *Capabilities* have been graphically decomposed into multiple subelements. This shows that the atomic characteristic of a *Capability* (i.e., the key feature that distinguishes it from a *Task*) has not always been understood. Another common modeling error – several elements were linked to a *Hard-goal* by means of a *means-end link* – allows to draw the conclusion that the theoretical definition of this type of link has not always been understood properly.

7.2 Evaluation of the Perceived Difficulty

A last component within the analysis of the results the modeling experiment concerns an evaluation of the perceived difficulty by the different test subjects in the three samples. Within the modeling experiment, several variables have been included in order to be able to measure the perception of the test subjects on the difficulty. The perceived difficulty has in fact been measured on three different levels. On a first level, the test subjects were asked to indicate on a rating-scale their perceived degree of difficulty in modeling the two cases. Secondly, the test subjects have been asked for their experience in executing the different steps (i.e., steps 1 to 5, see Sect. 3). On a third level, they were asked to indicate if Case 1

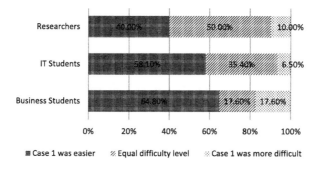

Fig. 3. Graph difficulty Case 1 versus Case 2.

was easier, of an equal difficulty level or more difficult to model compared to
Case 2 (as can be seen in Fig. 3).

Perceived Difficulty to Model both Cases. The first variable that has been
used to measure the perceived difficulty concerned the perception on the global
difficulty to model the US sets in Case 1 and 2. More precisely, the test subjects
were asked to answer the question '*was it difficult to model both cases?*' on a
rating-scale. On this scale, the value 1 represented the answer *not at all* and
the value 10 represented the answer *yes, completely.* The average score given by
the different test subjects on this question is 4.76 for Business Students, 5.52 for
IT Students and 5.75 for Researchers. In order to be able to provide an answer
to the question if there exist some significant differences between the perceived
difficulty by *Researchers, IT Students* and *Business Students*, the non-parametric
Kruskal-Wallis test has been performed. The results of this test (not represented
here due to a lack of space, see the Appendix on p. 12) indicate that there exists
no significant difference between the global perceived difficulty to model the US
in both cases.

8   Lessons Learned and (CASE Tool) Enhanced Support

As a second research objective, we want to identify the necessary conditions
that need to be provided to the lambda modeler to build a consistent RT. We
have, indeed, modified the CASE tool (see [9] for an explanation of the different
available views, all views are always kept consistent) that has been built to
support the creation of RT in order to better support the RT modeling activities.
This way, we aim to help the modeler in the modeling process and avoid him to
make some mistakes.

RT Validity. In order to deal with the ambiguity between the *Task* and *Capability* elements, we have included a model checker functionality that, when loaded
(clicked upon), evaluates if all the leaf nodes of the RT and only these are tagged
as *Capabilities*. If it is not the case, the modeler receives a warning together with
some theoretical explanations and is invited to modify the associated tag. If the

element's tag is modified, the icon is updated. He nevertheless still have the ability to refuse the change (it can indeed be that the element is a Task but its decomposition has not been done yet).

Completeness Aspect. One of the aims of a RT is to be able to study the completeness of requirements depicted in the US set through decomposition. As seen, the modeler as a natural tendency to try to add missing elements to complete the requirements model. Missing elements can be easily added in the RT. When using the model checker the modeler is explicitly shown dependencies with one leaf to invite him completing missing elements. Also a process view has been included allowing to model elements in a sequential order using BPMN; *Task* elements can be included as BPMN *sub-processes* and *Capability* elements as *activities*. This however remains an option.

Constraint Checking. Finally, to deal with the difficulty some modelers may have to link elements, we are developing an algorithm that automatically builds clusters of US elements in function of their semantic relatedness. Then, the modeler can make use of these clusters to link elements. The effectiveness of this method nevertheless still needs to be studied/validated.

9   Threats to Validity, Limitations and Conclusion

The first and main threat to validity comes from the quoting system itself. The latter has been built through an analysis of type solutions with the aim to define the criteria making these models of high quality. While we have justified the importance of the used criteria for the overall model evaluation, others could have been included but, more importantly, their balance – determined by the involved researchers themselves – can be seen as arbitrary. This issue could be further investigated in two ways. Firstly, we can make an independent study to (re)determine the evaluation criteria and their balance by, for example, asking the opinion of agile experts and practitioners. Concretely we can submit to experts RT built out of sets of US from cases they are familiar with. Then, we can ask them about their quality to determine what criteria they consider/use for evaluation and the relative importance of these criteria. With this new evaluation framework we can then reexamine the scores and results. A second way can be to use the criteria we have already used but to make variations in their relative weights to see how it impacts the overall scores and results.

A second threat to validity comes from the relatively small size of the US samples; respectively 4 and 8 US. One could not immediately generalize the results to a case with a significantly higher number of US. Another modeling experiment will be conducted to evaluate the capacity to build a RT out of a large US sample (over 20 US). Variants in the experiment will also include missing elements in requirements from the US set to evaluate if the RT helps with their identification.

The first limitation concerns the fact that the different test subjects only received a limited amount of information concerning the proposed approach of modeling US. To keep the time required to complete the modeling experiment within acceptable boundaries, only the minimal required information on modeling constructs (i.e., *Task*, *Capability*, *Hard-goal* and *Soft-goal*) and the different links between these elements have been included within the theory section of the experiment. In an ideal situation, more information/details on US and on the graphical notation should have been given.

The second limitation concerns the size of the different samples. There has been a large difference between the number of test subjects within each individual sample. Furthermore, the size of the samples (especially the sample of *Researchers*) is rather small what limits the ability to reflect the results from the study towards the scope of the complete population with an acceptable reliability level. The lack of professionals very familiar with US as test subjects is a third limitation that can be identified.

An evaluation of the interpretation of the different elements in the WHAT and WHY dimension of a US set has shown that there existed some discord in the classification of the elements. Two possible reasons for latter discord can be identified. Firstly, particular elements allow by nature to be interpreted in several ways. On a second level, the interpretation discords are a direct consequence of the lack in understanding the theoretical differences between the various elements. This is primarily the case for a *Task* and a *Capability*. These conclusions are confirmed by analyzing the most common modeling errors, where a tremendous amount of test subjects graphically decomposed a *Capability* into multiple sub-elements. Despite the interpretation differences in the modeling experiment, the large majority of test subjects agreed upon the fact that no additional concepts (next to the ones of a *Task*, a *Capability*, a *Hard-goal* and a *Soft-goal*) are required to represent the US elements.

Concerning the ability to build up a RT, most of the test subjects were able to produce an acceptable model out of a US set. The different students however tended at modeling each US separately. This notably resulted in a model with multiple 'isolated' elements that have not been linked to other ones. Students furthermore have put a stronger emphasis on the process related sequence of the elements. Some of them argued that the model should contain specific modeling elements to represent process-related sequence of the different elements. *Researchers* by contrast tended at modeling additional elements that were not represented within the set US.

Even if the assignment of modeling two US sets has been perceived as quite difficult by the different test subjects, we showed that with minimal or no knowledge of GORE, people have been able to build a visual representation of a US set through a RT with minimal theoretical explanations. The identification of the different links has been perceived by the test subjects in all three samples as being the most difficult; this is nevertheless more related to domain knowledge and further analysis than to the transformation of the US set in the RT as such. The application of the method on a large US set in a professional IT context has since then also been realized. The application/interpretation of theory has there not been reported as an issue and multiple new benefits of the RT in an agile context have been identified.

References

1. Abad, K., Pérez, W., Carvallo, J.P., Franch, X.: i* in practice: identifying frequent problems in its application. In: Proceedings of the 32nd ACM Symposium on Applied Computing (2017)
2. Caire, P., Genon, N., Heymans, P., Moody, D.L.: Visual notation design 2.0: towards user comprehensible requirements engineering notations. In: 21st IEEE International RE Conference, Rio de Janeiro-RJ, Brazil, pp. 115–124. IEEE Computer Society (2013)
3. Cohn, M.: Succeeding with Agile: Software Development Using Scrum, 1st edn. Addison-Wesley Professional, Boston (2009)
4. Dalpiaz, F.: Teaching goal modeling in undergraduate education. In: Proceedings of the 1st International iStar Teaching Workshop, CEUR Workshop Proceedings, vol. 1370, pp. 1–6 (2015)
5. Liskin, O., Pham, R., Kiesling, S., Schneider, K.: Why we need a granularity concept for user stories. In: Cantone, G., Marchesi, M. (eds.) XP 2014. LNBIP, vol. 179, pp. 110–125. Springer, Cham (2014). https://doi.org/10.1007/978-3-319-06862-6_8
6. Taibi, D., Lenarduzzi, V., Janes, A., Liukkunen, K., Ahmad, M.O.: Comparing requirements decomposition within the scrum, scrum with kanban, XP, and banana development processes. In: Baumeister, H., Lichter, H., Riebisch, M. (eds.) XP 2017. LNBIP, vol. 283, pp. 68–83. Springer, Cham (2017). https://doi.org/10.1007/978-3-319-57633-6_5
7. Trkman, M., Mendling, J., Krisper, M.: Using business process models to better understand the dependencies among user stories. Inf. Softw. Technol. **71**, 58–76 (2016)
8. Wautelet, Y., Heng, S., Hintea, D., Kolp, M., Poelmans, S.: Bridging user story sets with the use case model. In: Link, S., Trujillo, J.C. (eds.) ER 2016. LNCS, vol. 9975, pp. 127–138. Springer, Cham (2016). https://doi.org/10.1007/978-3-319-47717-6_11
9. Wautelet, Y., Heng, S., Kiv, S., Kolp, M.: User-story driven development of multi-agent systems: a process fragment for agile methods. Comput. Lang. Syst. Struct. **50**, 159–176 (2017)
10. Wautelet, Y., Heng, S., Kolp, M., Mirbel, I.: Unifying and extending user story models. In: Jarke, M., Mylopoulos, J., Quix, C., Rolland, C., Manolopoulos, Y., Mouratidis, H., Horkoff, J. (eds.) CAiSE 2014. LNCS, vol. 8484, pp. 211–225. Springer, Cham (2014). https://doi.org/10.1007/978-3-319-07881-6_15
11. Wautelet, Y., Heng, S., Kolp, M., Mirbel, I., Poelmans, S.: Building a rationale diagram for evaluating user story sets. In: 10th IEEE International Conference on Research Challenges in Information Science, RCIS 2016, Grenoble, France, 1–3 June 2016, pp. 477–488 (2016)
12. Yu, E., Giorgini, P., Maiden, N., Mylopoulos, J.: Social Modeling for Requirements Engineering. MIT Press, Cambridge (2011)

Jobs-to-be-Done Oriented Requirements Engineering: A Method for Defining Job Stories

Garm Lucassen[1] , Maxim van de Keuken[1], Fabiano Dalpiaz[1(✉)] ,
Sjaak Brinkkemper[1] , Gijs Willem Sloof[2], and Johan Schlingmann[2]

[1] RE-Lab, Department of Information and Computing Sciences,
Utrecht University, Utrecht, The Netherlands
{g.lucassen,m.a.r.vandekeuken,f.dalpiaz,s.brinkkemper}@uu.nl
[2] Stabiplan, Bodegraven, The Netherlands
{g.w.sloof,j.schlingmann}@stabiplan.com

Abstract. [**Context and motivation**] Goal orientation is an unrealized promise in the practice of requirements engineering (RE). Conversely, lightweight approaches such as user stories have gained substantial adoption. As critics highlight the limitations of user stories, *Job Stories* are emerging as an alternative that embeds goal-oriented principles by emphasizing situation, motivation and expected outcome. This new approach has not been studied in research yet. [**Question/Problem**] Scientific foundations are lacking for the job story artifact and there are no actionable methods for effectively applying job stories. Thus, practitioners may end up creating their own flavor of job stories that may fail to deliver the promised value of the Jobs-to-be-Done theory. [**Principal ideas/results**] We integrate multiple approaches based on job stories to create a conceptual model of job stories and to construct a generic method for Jobs-to-be-Done Oriented RE. Applying our job story method to an industry case study, we highlight benefits and limitations. [**Contribution**] Our method aims to bring job stories from craft to discipline, and to provide systematic means for applying Jobs-to-be-Done orientation in practice and for assessing its effectiveness.

Keywords: Job stories · Requirements engineering
Agile development · Jobs-to-be-Done · Problem orientation
Case study

1 Introduction

In Requirements Engineering (RE), problem orientation is a long-standing research domain that emphasizes the importance of defining problems and capturing the 'why' as opposed to defining solutions that only capture the 'what' and 'how' [1–5]. With the rise of agile software development, user stories have become increasingly popular with adoption up to 55% [6]. Although intended

© Springer International Publishing AG, part of Springer Nature 2018
E. Kamsties et al. (Eds.): REFSQ 2018, LNCS 10753, pp. 227–243, 2018.
https://doi.org/10.1007/978-3-319-77243-1_14

to focus on the problem space and not the solution space [7,8], user stories are often formulated with a specific solution in mind [9], also because some authors suggest their use for describing *features* [10].

Recognizing this problem for the development of innovative software products, Alan Klement introduced a new paradigm for requirements formulation called Job Stories [11], which relies on the following template:

When <*situation*>, **I want (to)** <*motivation*>, **so that (I can)** <*expected outcome*>.

A job story is written from the perspective of a customer who, in a given *situation*, expresses a *motivation* for the requirement to exist, aiming to attain an *expected outcome*. For example [11]: *When an important new customer signs up* (situation), *I want to be notified* (motivation), *so I can start a conversation with them* (expected outcome).

Job stories are based on the ideas of the Disruptive Innovation Theory's method *Jobs-to-be-Done* (JTBD) by Christensen [12], a collection of principles that help discover and understand the interactions between customers, their motivations and the products they use [13]. Despite its recency, there are many authors who propose different approaches to JTBD [14–17]. This is confusing for practitioners, who are unsure how to apply this new approach in their own environment and struggle to formulate relevant and useful job stories. In particular, JTBD is difficult to apply in the context of software, for many of the examples are for physical products. To improve on this situation, this paper makes the following contributions:

1. We collect Jobs-to-be-Done literature and position job stories among its different approaches and best practices (Sect. 2);
2. We conceptualize the notion of job story and analyze the syntax and semantics of 131 job stories gathered from public sources in Sect. 3;
3. We introduce the Integrated Job Story Method that reconciles the different views on JTBD and job story literature in Sect. 4;
4. We evaluate the applicability of the Integrated Job Story Method on a case study about app development in the computer-aided design field (Sects. 5 and 6).

We review related literature in Sect. 7 and present conclusions and future work in Sect. 8

2   Background: Job Stories and Jobs-to-be-Done

Job stories originate from Jobs-to-be-Done (JTBD), and the major principles of Jobs-to-be-Done build upon a large body of literature from management science [12,13,18]. The most similar predecessor to JTBD is the 1996 Outcome-Driven Innovation method (ODI), which focuses on understanding customers' *Desired Outcome*, i.e., what they want to achieve, instead of giving customers what they think they want [15].

Ten years later, Christensen introduced the notion of Jobs-to-be-Done: *"When people find themselves needing to get a job done, they essentially <u>hire</u> products to do that job for them"* [19]. To design products that customer segments want to hire for their jobs, traditional methods for market segmentation based on customer type or product type are inappropriate because they do not explain the 'why' of customer behavior. This aligns with fundamental theories in RE on the importance of the 'why' for software (process) analysis [1,2]. To uncover the *real* driving force of customer behavior, innovators should investigate the jobs that customers are struggling to get done [12].

For example, fast food restaurant customers buy milkshakes to solve two distinct jobs: (i) to keep themselves occupied during a long early commute to work in the morning, or (ii) to satisfy their kids' appetite for sugar in the afternoon. To tailor the milkshakes to better satisfy these jobs, the fast food restaurant decided to differentiate the types of milkshakes they sell: thicker, longer-lasting milkshakes to commuters in the morning, and a thinner, easier-to-consume milkshake for kids in the afternoon [14].

The milkshake example shows the suitability of Jobs-to-be-Done for physical products with straightforward functionality [12,14,15,19,20]. Through a series of blog posts and a self-published free book, Alan Klement and Intercom Inc. propose a new paradigm for JTBD-based requirements called *Job Stories* [11,21]. Building upon Christensen's rejection of demographic segmentation, Klement argues that user stories' emphasis on roles and their actions inhibit the discovery of the 'why' due to the many assumptions a personified role implies. Instead of putting the role central, job stories emphasize the motivational and situational context that drive customer behavior:

> *"**When** I am ready to have estimators bid on my game, **I want to** create a game in a format estimators can understand, **so that** the estimators can find my game and know what they are about to bid on."* [11]

Despite the initial idea of job stories as an alternative to user stories, practitioners have started adopting job stories alongside user stories. As Klement reports: *"You can write a job story to define a problem and then write user stories as potential solutions to that job story"* [16]. However, a study of the relationship between user stories and job stories is beyond the purpose of this paper.

3 Conceptualizing Job Stories

The original template for job stories [11] has been customized by practitioners in different ways (see the collection of job stories in our dataset for an overview[1]), yet they all comprise three main parts: (i) the triggering event or *situation* in which a problem arises, (ii) the *motivation* and goal to make a change to the

---

[1] The dataset of this paper is available at http://dx.doi.org/10.17632/xpcv3jb6b4.1.

situation and (iii) the resulting *expected outcome* that improves the situation [13]. Consider the following illustrative examples of job stories (labeled JS1–JS3) that we use throughout this section:

JS1. When I am looking for a new task on the task board, **I want to** filter tasks to only see those associated with my skills, **so I can** see open tasks that I am able to complete.

JS2. When an item does not have an estimate or has an estimate I'm not happy with, **I want to** be able to restart the estimation process and notify everyone, **so that** the team knows a particular item needs to be estimated upon.

JS3. When my friend tags me in an unflattering photo, **I want** my Facebook colleagues to not see me in that photo, **so that** I can maintain my professional reputation.

We attempt to build solid foundations for this RE artifact by performing a theory building exercise [22] resulting in a conceptual model of job stories. To do so, we conducted a thorough analysis of 131 job stories (available in the dataset) that we have identified through search engines in publicly accessible sources that include blogs, presentations, project code, theses, and books. Based on such analysis, and relying on frequency of occurrence and the authors' experience in conceptual modeling, we built a conceptual model of job stories (see Fig. 1).

We elaborate on the story components and discuss the adherence of the job stories with our conceptual model. The fully-fledged analysis is available in the dataset.

3.1 Template

A job story should roughly follow the original job story template (when... I want to... so that...) proposed by Klement [11]. For example, the *I* can be replaced with a different stakeholder or omitted entirely. This template is the syntactic structure within which the situation, motivation and expected outcome are interspersed.

Analysis: 113 of the 131 job stories adhere to the template. Out of the non-compliant stories, 6 added a role before the situation (resembling user stories), 6 did not include an expected outcome, 4 did not use a template, 2 did not include a motivation indicator.

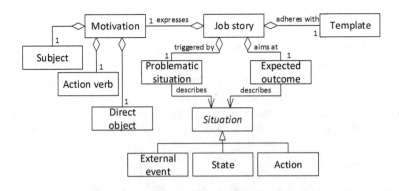

Fig. 1. Conceptual model of job stories

3.2   Problematic Situation

The first part of a job story provides the contextual starting point for the reader to understand why the actor has a motivation and a goal. It should describe a situation which confronts the actor with a concrete problem [13]. This may be a generic need such as wanting something to eat, or a specific problem in the context of a product such as JS2. In our job story analysis, we identified three variants of a well-formed situation that correspond to one example job story each:

- **Action.** The problem lies in the action that an actor is executing as part of her job. This case is exemplified by JS1.
- **State.** An actor or an object may be in a problematic situation (state) because of their attributes. This can take the form of an object property such as in JS2, but can also be an human emotional state such as being bored or unfamiliar with something.
- **External Event.** The problematic situation is experienced because of an external event, i.e., an action conducted by some other actor. Exemplified by JS3.

Analysis: Analyzing the 113 job stories that fit the job story template, two things stand out. First, most job stories (65) capture the situation as an action, 40 use a state and just 8 include an external event. Note that as an action or external event completes, the result is a new state. Second, only 36 job stories define a *problematic* situation. The other 77 job stories only describe a situation such as: "When I'm adding or deleting users" or "When I have multiple workspaces". While the original articles on job stories do not require the situation to be problematic [11,21], follow-up blog posts by Klement himself explain the importance of defining a concrete struggle and its context [13,23].

3.3   Motivation

The second part of a job story is its central element of motivation. Capturing the change that needs to occur in order to reach the expected outcome, the motivation generally already implies a solution to alleviate the problematic situation. Theoretically, motivations can have different structures, for they can be used to represent different types of requirements. The majority of motivations, however, adhere to the same basic grammatical structure as the means part of a user story [9]: (1) they contain a subject with an intent verb such as "want" or "am able", (2) followed by an action verb that expresses the action related to the problem to resolve, and (3) a direct object on which the subject of (1) executes the action. The motivations of JS1-3 adhere to the structure of a user story's means: <JS#, Subject+Intent, Verb, Direct Object> - <JS1, I want to, filter, tasks>, <JS2, I want to, restart, estimation process>, <JS3, I want, see, me>. Aside from these three parts, motivations are free form text and may contain any other linguistic construct such as adjectives and indirect objects.

Analysis: All 113 valid job stories adhere to the grammatical structure above to a greater or lesser extent: 83 job stories follow the structure exactly, including the *I* as the subject, 20 adhere to the user story structure but incorporate another actor as the subject as in "customers want to", and the remaining 10 do not include an action verb, but readers infer *to have* from the text structure like in "I want a filled in example".

3.4   Expected Outcome

While the first part of a job story presents the problematic as-is situation, the *expected outcome* sketches the desired to-be situation that the actor wants to achieve by satisfying the motivation. In this way, the expected outcome conveys additional context that is necessary to satisfy the motivation in the *right* way.

As the expected outcome also describes a situation, we encountered the same three possible variants in our job story analysis. Practitioners may define the expected outcome as: (1) an action the actor can now conduct as in JS1, (2) a desired state of an actor or non-sentient object such as *"so that proprietary intellectual property is secure"*, or (3) an external event for a different actor to conduct an action like JS2. The only difference is that the variants are often expressed in the negative form as in "so that there is no ambiguity" or "so that I don't have to refresh".

Analysis: The dominance of the action variety is less overwhelming with 51 job stories capturing the expected outcome with a new or improved action, while 42 define a state and 20 job stories refer to events.

4   Integrated Job Story Method

Multiple flavors of JTBD orientation exist. For example, the creators of ODI have embraced JTBD, but their method to capturing requirements starts from defining customers' desired outcomes [24]. Despite being advertised as a requirements engineering method based on JTBD, ODI differs from job stories. It is therefore hard for practitioners to understand which JTBD approach and format suits their situation best, resulting in various combinations of different methods [17,25].

We take a systematic approach to reconcile the existing methods based on JTBD, and thereby assist practitioners in operationalizing such paradigm. We do so by applying situational method engineering to construct a Process-Deliverable-Diagram (PDD) (see Fig. 2); the resulting PDD describes our integrated method in terms of JTBD and job story activities, as well as the utilized artifacts [26].

Our method, which is named *Integrated Job Story Method*, was assembled pragmatically: we studied the literature on JTBD, identified fragments that could be consistently combined, and determined feasibility based on an application to a real-world case, described below. Note that we propose *a* method for conducting RE based on JTBD, but other methods exist. Our method comprises five phases:

P1. Perform interviews: exploratory interviews are conducted with (prospective) customers in order to uncover their goals, their current way of achieving these goals, and the problems that exist in their as-is situation;

P2. Analysis phase: the workflow, context and motivations of the interviewees are analyzed to formulate initial jobs and job stories;

P3. Survey phase: in order to validate the results of the analysis phase, a survey is conducted with a larger sample of the target audience;

P4. Prioritization phase: the survey results are analyzed to determine which jobs present the largest opportunity for innovation, and;

P5. Project definition phase: the jobs and job stories for development are selected and a *project brief* is created that can facilitate the follow-up development project.

Case study. Stabiplan is a medium-sized (170 employees, 3,800+ clients) product software company in the market of computer-aided design (CAD) software. Stabiplan's products extend the AutoCAD and Revit products by AutoDesk for mechanical, electronics and plumbing (MEP) installations. We focus on a new addition to Stabiplan's product portfolio, i.e., independent products based on Revit called *apps* that have limited functionality and aim at new customer segments. Stabiplan's aims to use the method to determine what functionality, either existing or new, should be included in a highly specific Revit app for appliances and connectors to incite customers to adopt it. From here on, we refer to Stabiplan as *ModelComp* and Revit as *ModelPlatform*.

The Integrated Job Story Method incorporates two variants to accommodate two mainstream approaches to JTBD: a *quantitative* approach based on ODI— based on metrics—and a *qualitative* approach based on Klement's work. Our illustration adheres to the qualitative approach, but we also elaborate on the quantitative approach where possible. All jobs, desired outcomes and job stories are in the dataset; due to space limitations, we show only snippets in the paper.

4.1 Perform Interviews (P1)

This phase, which is not decomposed into activities due to its generic nature, involves arranging, performing, recording and transcribing interviews with suitable participants. This results in INTERVIEW TRANSCRIPTIONS for each interviewee including their INTERVIEWEE BACKGROUND, and the WORKFLOW they currently follow trying to reach their GOALS, in spite of the PROBLEMS they struggle with. The practice of interviewing customers as a part of JTBD is described both by Christensen [14] and Ulwick [15];

Case: We conducted and transcribed four extensive (1.5 h each) interviews with users of ModelComp working in appliances and connectors, the product's target market.

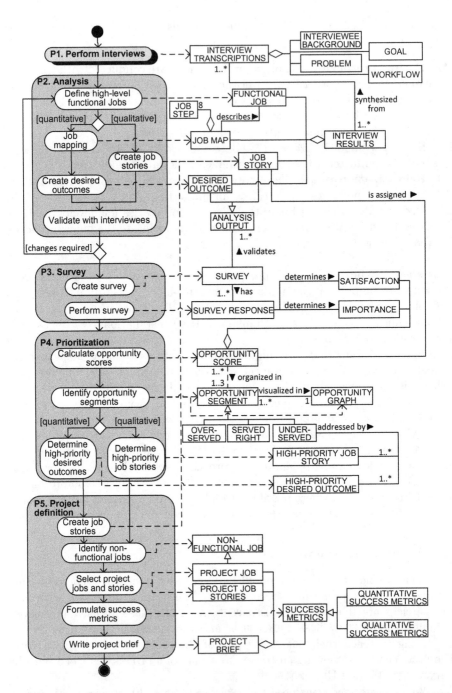

Fig. 2. Process-Deliverable Diagram [26] representing the activities (left-hand side) and the artifacts (right-hand side) of our integrated method for JTBD in software development.

4.2   Analysis Phase (P2)

Define high-level functional jobs. The interview transcriptions are analyzed, especially GOALS and WORKFLOWS; this results in a set of high-level FUNCTIONAL JOBS that the users are trying to get done. We use the term functional, drawing an analogy with the standard nomenclature in requirements engineering, to indicate that these jobs define *what* the user aims to achieve.

Case: Analyzing what the interviewees are trying to achieve when working with appliances in ModelPlatform, we formulate 4 high-level functional jobs for using ModelPlatform for appliances[2]:

J1 - Help me configure appliances.
J2 - Help me place appliances.
J3 - Help me model connector systems.
J4 - Help me create bills of materials.

Next, the method splits into its two main paths that reflect the ongoing discussion among JTBD practitioners: the quantitative approach that is inspired by ODI, and the qualitative approach that reflects way of working of job story practitioners.

Quantitative Approach

Job mapping. The identified JOBS are broken down into a series of JOB STEPS that are represented in a JOB MAP. Job mapping establishes what the entire job looks like for the customer from beginning to end, providing a perspective that is not limited to the scope of the product of interest [20]. This includes identifying new/innovative ways for the product to help the different customers get more of the job done.

Case: We applied the job mapping technique to analyze the customers' workflow and identify all the lower-level functional jobs the customers are trying to get done. Later in the project we created a fully fledged job map which is available in the dataset.

Create desired outcomes. Each job step in the job maps, alongside the interview transcriptions, is turned into DESIRED OUTCOMES: metrics that explain what success means to a customer for each JOB STEP. These statements describe a direction of improvement, a unit of measure, and provide contextual clarification and examples [20].

Case: Analyzing the interviewees' struggle when trying to get their jobs done, we defined 50 desired outcomes for the four jobs above. For J1, two examples are 'Minimize the chance that I need to check external documentation' and 'Minimize the chance that a fabrication specific thermostatic connector I need is not available'.

---

[2] We adopt Klement's syntax for the jobs: the customer hires a product to get jobs done.

Qualitative Approach

Create job stories. Each high-level functional job is refined into job stories; together, the stories should satisfy the interviewees' goals. The resulting JOB STORIES should provide context about the user's struggle to get the functional job done: the situation, motivation and expected outcome [13].

Case: Using the contextual information identified in the interviews, we created 21 job stories that relate to the jobs such as 'When I am configuring an appliance, I want the output power of the appliance to be accurately represented in the flow and return meters, so that my model will correctly represent the produced power.'

Validate with interviewees. The resulting desired outcomes or job stories of the analysis phase are checked to determine if they correspond to the stated problematic situation.

Case: We took an iterative approach to this activity by validating draft job stories based on the interviewee's input. The outcome was considered satisfactory and no substantial changes to the job stories were necessary.

4.3   Survey Phase (P3)

Create survey. This activity validates the output of the analysis phase with a larger group. The SURVEY asks the participants to rate each desired outcome or job story on two dimensions with a Likert scale: IMPORTANCE and SATISFACTION with current solutions [15]. This survey technique and the prioritization described in the next phase are based on Anthony Ulwick's ODI methodology [15];

Case: We created an online survey with 7-point Likert scale questions for each of the job stories which is available in our online materials.

Perform survey. This activity involves finding and reaching potential survey respondents as well as extracting the collected SURVEY RESPONSES for analysis.

Case: We distributed the survey and obtained 10 responses from the target audience.

4.4   Prioritization Phase (P4)

Calculate opportunity scores. For each of the job stories or desired outcomes, the following formula, taken from Ulwick's work [15], is applied to the survey response: OPPORTUNITY SCORE = IMPORTANCE + max(IMPORTANCE − SATISFACTION, 0).

Case: We calculated the mean opportunity score for all respondents for each job story.

Identify Opportunity Segments. This activity analyzes the opportunity scores to identify the job stories with a high rating for importance and a medium to low rating for satisfaction [20]. These are the job stories that are currently under-served and should present a significant opportunity for improvement. To do this, plot the job stories or desired outcomes on an OPPORTUNITY GRAPH, with the satisfaction on the y-axis and importance on the x-axis. Next, divide the OPPORTUNITY GRAPH in three OPPORTUNITY SEGMENTS to classify needs into UNDER-SERVED, SERVED-RIGHT, or OVER-SERVED. This approach is explained in [27].

Case: We plotted the job stories' Opportunity Scores on the Opportunity Graph in Fig. 3.

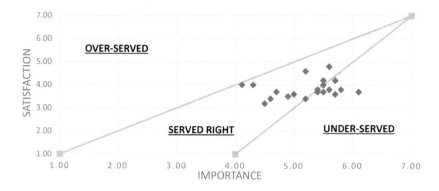

Fig. 3. Opportunity graph for ModelComp's job stories

Select high-priority job stories or desired outcomes. Analyze the opportunity segment to target and identify the HIGH-PRIORITY JOB STORIES or DESIRED OUTCOMES. Case: Based on the ratings of P3, none of the job stories in Fig. 3 are within the over-served segment, 10 job stories are served-right, 8 job stories are under-served and 3 are borderline cases. As ModelComp wants to improve upon an existing product, we select the 8 under-served job stories as well as the 3 borderline cases.

4.5 Project Definition Phase (P5)

This final phase of the method is based on the experiences reported by Alan Klement and the company Intercom, of working with job stories and creating project briefs [21]. We adapt those ideas for our integrated method.

Create job stories. In the quantitative approach, the requirements engineer formulates a set of job stories based on the selected high-priority desired outcomes.

Identify non-functional jobs that capture the fundamental problems the customer faces with her functional jobs. As fundamental problems are rarely about a straightforward, functional task [28], these NON-FUNCTIONAL JOBS are necessary to provide insight into the underlying forces that drive customer behavior [14]. Such non-functional jobs give insights on *how* the customer wants the function to be delivered.
Case: As no literature exists that explains how to categorize job stories based on the common non-functional jobs, a specific four step approach was defined for ModelComp:

1. Three high-level non-functional jobs are defined that drive customers to hire ModelComp to help their organization excel in business information modeling, the sub-field of CAD supported by ModelPlatform;
2. Each high-level non-functional job is decomposed into two or more medium-level sub-non-functional jobs;
3. All job stories are classified according to the medium-level non-functional job they belong to;
4. For each medium-level non-functional job, its associated job stories are classified in low-level non-functional jobs.

Select project jobs and stories. A subset of the non-functional jobs is assigned to the development project (PROJECT JOBS), alongside all or a sub-set of the high-priority job stories associated with the project jobs (PROJECT JOB STORIES). The selection may take into account synergies between jobs and job stories, e.g., stories that can be bundled in the same project because of their interdependencies at development time.

Case: We choose the low-level jobs whose job stories have the highest mean opportunity score. As the focus of this project is on improving *modeling* for appliances, we select low-level non-functional jobs 1 and 4: *"Help me ensure that I deliver high quality work"* and *"Help me save time"*. Together, these jobs comprise 10 job stories, out of which we select only those that are under-served, i.e., with an opportunity score of 7.0 or higher. This results in 8 job stories as shown in Fig. 4.

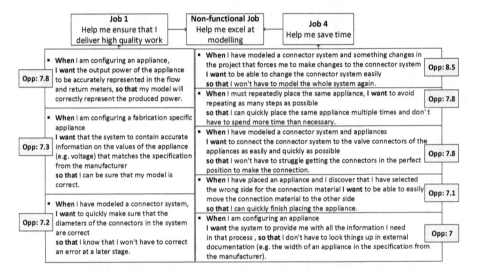

Fig. 4. Snippet of ModelComp job portfolio for appliances. The label "Opp." indicates the opportunity score for a given job story.

Formulate success metrics. To enable assessing whether the development is effective, QUALITATIVE- and/or QUANTITATIVE SUCCESS METRICS are establish that test whether the problem has been solved [21].

Case: We defined high-level success metrics that do not presuppose a solution, such as *'the solution helps the modeler feel confident that the appliances are configured correctly'* for Job 1 and *'the time it takes to change the types of appliances that are used in a piping system is reduced by X%'* for Job 2.

Write project brief. This artifact summarizes the results from all preceding phases. The resulting single-page PROJECT BRIEF includes a succinct description of the problem to be solved by the project, the relevant project jobs and project stories, as well as the success metrics to determine whether the problem has been solved [21]. The stakeholders can check the project brief to validate the requirements before starting the development.

Case: Using the jobs, job stories, problem and success metrics defined earlier, we wrote one project brief for each of the two jobs. To help tie the different elements together and provide more context, we also defined a high-level job story for each job.

Job 1: '**When** I am working on a complicated model for an important project and I cannot afford to make mistakes, **I want** to be able to identify and fix possible errors, **so that** I can be confident that the work I deliver is of high quality.'

Job 2: '**When** I have been working on a model for a while but suddenly the requirements change, **I want** to be able to quickly modify my existing model to address the new requirements, **so that** we can prevent major delays to the project.'

5   Evaluating the Integrated Job Story Method

Upon completing the project brief and delivering it to ModelComp stakeholders, we evaluated the utility of the method and its artifacts. We conducted an in-depth evaluation with the lead product manager, discussed the project brief with three marketeers and two developers. Below, we discuss the major findings and remarks by each stakeholder.

Lead Product Manager. He considers the process of interviewing customers and distilling requirements a useful and important practice. Although the project brief and job stories did not present revolutionary new insights to the product manager himself, he found them effective for scoping a project and conveying their customers' priorities to internal stakeholders. Even more interesting, however, are the supporting artifacts job portfolio and opportunity graph, which can help identify new high-level opportunities for apps that emphasize specific Jobs: *"Exploring what job stories are under-served, served right and over-served is very valuable to target apps to a specific country or market"*. Two major drawbacks of the method were identified. First, too many activities require active participation of (prospective) customers, who may be difficult to reach in a timely fashion. Second, the method is very time-consuming and the product manager considered the project to take too long by modern (agile) development standards.

Marketeers. JTBD fits well with this role, for marketing and sales should be convincing when it directly engages the jobs one is trying to complete [13,14]. Indeed, the marketeers found the project brief to be the most valuable artifact as it concretely defines a specific project that they can easily incorporate in their own work. In particular, they consider the contextual information in the project brief a more useful input for creating marketing material than a feature list. A feature list only shows the 'how' of a product, not the benefits for the customer (the 'why'): *"For our marketing strategy we assume that everyone uses a certain feature the same way. JTBD might help in finding out that this is not the case and that we should change our marketing in Germany or France."*

Developers. They consider the project brief and its associated job stories too high a level to be useful for actual software development. However, the developers considered the information in the project brief useful to familiarize new hires with the non-technical context of ModelComp's products: *"By showing how our work affects the customer, the project briefs could help new hires understand the context of our products and enable them to become more pro-active in the development process."*

6   Discussion

Since JTBD and job stories are young approaches, our work is still exploratory. Nevertheless, as part of our conceptualization, method construction and illustrative application in a real-world case, we could identify some interesting findings.

Balanced problematization of job stories. Although 113 job stories syntactically adhere to the job story template, only 31.9% (36) define a *problematic* situation. This may seem mostly harmless, but in fact often has a substantial negative impact: the problem definition shifts to another part of the job story, leaving no room for the expected outcome. Consider for example *"When I am searching for tools, I want Creatlr to filter the options to my demand, so I have less choice."*, here the problem, having too many tools to choose from, is implicitly captured in the expected outcome and the actual expected outcome is not captured: finding the right option quicker. A better way to write this job story is *"When a search for tools gives me too many options, I want Creatlr to filter the options to my demand, so I can quickly find the right tool"*. The practice of defining a job story poorly signifies the need for a more clear-cut definition of a job story and concrete guidelines for how to write a high-quality job story.

As a quality criterion, we propose that job stories should have a *balanced problematization*: the situation should be problematic, while the expected outcomes should *not* be problematic. Job stories can thus be in three states of *unbalanced problematization*:

1. Job stories whose situation is not problematic should either be *problematized*, or *discarded* when no problem can be identified. This is illustrated by the example about Creatlr above.
2. Job stories whose expected outcome is problematic should be *de-problematized*.
3. Job stories whose situation is not problematic and whose expected outcome is problematic should be *re-problematized*.

The variety of Jobs-to-be-Done approaches. Unfortunately, JTBD is not a unique and clear framework with delineated activities and deliverables. Instead, it is a 'set of principles' from which a wide variety of best practices, approaches and techniques have emerged [28]. As there are multiple, distinct approaches in literature, the Integrated Job Story Method integrates multiple sources that we selected based on our expertise. Additional validation and experimentation is necessary to establish the optimal approach.

Missing guidelines on how to write job stories. Despite the variety in Jobs-to-be-Done sources and approaches, there are no concrete guidelines for how to define jobs, job stories or desired outcomes from the goals, problems and workflows identified through the exploratory interviews. Similarly, there are no methods available to validate that the formulated job stories are appropriate and applicable.

7   Related Literature

The Jobs-to-be-Done theory is grounded in management and innovation science. A key input is Schumpter's theory on 'Creative Destruction': as firms grow and age, they lose some of their ability to innovate, and often end up losing their market share to radical innovations from new firms [29]. To avoid creative destruction, Levitt argues that companies should not define themselves by what they produced, but by what customer needs they are addressing [18]. Jobs-to-be-Done builds on these insights through its framing of the customer needs as the jobs that drive them to 'hire' products or services [19].

In the software industry, many different techniques are being used to perform RE, ranging from classical approaches such as use cases and scenarios to more recent techniques such as user stories [30]. Although not an entirely unique proposition, Jobs-to-be-Done is differentiated in its genuine problem orientation that is achieved through an understanding of the problematic context that drives customer behavior.

JTBD is similar to User-Centered Design (UCD), which involves focusing on usability throughout the entire development process and further throughout the system life cycle [31]. To do this, UCD advises designers to directly observe how users work [32], and use the insight to ensure that technology is organized around the user's goals, tasks, and abilities [33]. However, while UCD is a broad method focused on the whole process of software development, and focuses on usability [31], Jobs-to-be-Done focuses on the problem space and allows to consider multiple software qualities, not only usability.

A similar approach from the RE literature is Goal-Oriented Requirements Engineering (GORE), which revolves around the use of goals at different levels of abstraction, to capture the various objectives the system should achieve [34]. As such, like JTBD, GORE strives to uncover the 'why' behind software [2]. We consider JTBD as an industry-oriented adaptation of the principles behind goal orientation, which favors pragmatism (using text and simple diagrams) over conceptual soundness (e.g., the distinction between actor types, goals and tasks, goal types, and the distinctions that allow for formal reasoning over goal graphs).

Task oriented RE [4] proposes to express functional requirements as tasks that should be jointly achieved by humans and systems, but without assigning specific responsibilities. Job stories share the focus on the task/job, but focus on analyzing the motivations behind the job, rather than drilling down into the task details.

Job stories were conceived as a response to perceived problems with user stories and personas [11]. Experiences of Intercom illustrate that the implementation of job stories involves more than changing the template of the stories that are used. It also requires that processes are adopted to a JTBD mindset [21].

JTBD practitioners echo the concerns voiced by Christensen who argued that personas can not be used to explain why customers buy products [14], and Chapman and Millman, who argue that the validity of personas is impossible to verify [35]. JTBD posits that by focusing on the jobs that different 'types' of people have in common, these problems can be prevented [11].

8   Conclusion and Future Research

We have explored the notion of job stories: a new paradigm for agile RE based on Jobs-to-be-Done that focuses on capturing the motivational and situational context that drive customer behavior. Our constructed conceptual model and Integrated Job Story Method are a first theory building attempt, aimed at supporting practitioners apply this paradigm in a more systematic manner than the current ad-hoc practices.

Our work is exploratory and paves the way for future directions. Considering the varying quality of job stories created by practitioners, there is a need for concrete quality criteria for job stories. Similarly, we intend to develop problematization techniques for expressing problems in job stories and for coping with job stories that need to be (re-)problematized. Indeed, the lightweight template does not prevent practitioners from writing job stories that are highly solution-oriented.

Furthermore, because of job stories' similarity to user stories we would like to investigate how to extract concepts from job stories with natural language processing, similar to our earlier work on user stories [36]. Finally, we want to further validate, evaluate and improve the Integrated Job Story Method in order to establish a rigorous and reliable approach to working with JTBD and job stories in software development. This will require thorough empirical research to determine the usefulness of the various activities and artifacts. An interesting follow-up study concerns how practitioners use job stories—and our method—to express nonfunctional requirements.

References

1. Potts, C., Bruns, G.: Recording the reasons for design decisions. In: Proceedings of the International Conference on Software Engineering, pp. 418–427. IEEE Computer Society (1988)
2. Yu, E.S., Mylopoulos, J.: Understanding "why" in software process modelling, analysis, and design. In: Proceedings of the International Conference on Software Engineering, pp. 159–168. IEEE (1994)
3. Zave, P., Jackson, M.: Four dark corners of requirements engineering. ACM Trans. Softw. Eng. Methodol. **6**(1), 1–30 (1997)
4. Lauesen, S.: Task descriptions as functional requirements. IEEE Softw. **20**(2), 58–65 (2003)
5. Dalpiaz, F., Franch, X., Horkoff, J.: iStar 2.0 language guide (2016). arXiv:1605.07767 [cs.SE]
6. Kassab, M.: The changing landscape of requirements engineering practices over the past decade. In: Proceedings of the International Workshop on Empirical Requirements Engineering, pp. 1–8 (2015)
7. Jeffries, R.: Essential XP: card, conversation, and confirmation. XP Magazine, August 2001
8. Cohn, M.: User Stories Applied: For Agile Software Development. Addison-Wesley Professional, Boston (2004)
9. Lucassen, G., Dalpiaz, F., van der Werf, J.M.E.M., Brinkkemper, S.: Improving agile requirements: the Quality User Story framework and tool. Requir. Eng. **21**(3), 383–403 (2016)
10. Paetsch, F., Eberlein, A., Maurer, F.: Requirements engineering and agile software development. In: Proceedings of the IEEE International Workshop on Enabling Technologies: Infrastructure for Collaborative Enterprises, pp. 308–313. IEEE (2003)
11. Klement, A.: Replacing the user story with the job story (2013). goo.gl/fZ1iqe
12. Christensen, C.M., Hall, T., Dillon, K., Duncan, D.S.: Know your customers' "Jobs to Be Done". Harv. Bus. Rev. **94**(9), 54–62 (2016)
13. Klement, A.: When Coffee and Kale Compete. NYC Publishing, New York (2016)
14. Christensen, C.M., Anthony, S.D., Berstell, G., Nitterhouse, D.: Finding the right job for your product. MIT Sloan Manag. Rev. **48**(3), 38–47 (2007)
15. Ulwick, A.W.: Turn customer input into innovation. Harv. Bus. Rev. **80**(1), 91–97 (2002)
16. Klement, A.: Designing features using job stories (2013). goo.gl/NS889V

17. Johnson, L.: Jobs to be Done: a case study in the NHS, September 2017. goo.gl/gpaBpx
18. Levitt, T.: Marketing myopia. Harv. Bus. Rev. **38**(4), 24–47 (1960)
19. Christensen, C., Cook, S., Hall, T.: Marketing malpractice: the cause and the cure. Harv. Bus. Rev. **83**(12), 74–83 (2005)
20. Bettencourt, L.A., Ulwick, A.W.: The customer-centered innovation map. Harv. Bus. Rev. **86**(5), 109–114 (2008)
21. Intercom Inc.: Intercom on Jobs-to-be-Done (2017). ISBN 978-0-9861392-3-9
22. Eisenhardt, K.M., Graebner, M.E.: Theory building from cases: opportunities and challenges. Acad. Manag. J. **50**(1), 25–32 (2007)
23. Klement, A.: Your job story needs a struggling moment (2016). goo.gl/vsRC1d
24. Ulwick, A.W., Bettencourt, L.A.: Giving customers a fair hearing. MIT Sloan Manag. Rev. **49**(3), 62–68 (2008)
25. Carpenter, H.: A method for applying Jobs-to-be-Done to product and service design, January 2013. goo.gl/5NUVwh
26. van de Weerd, I., Brinkkemper, S.: Meta-modeling for situational analysis and design methods. In: Syed, M.R., Syed, S.N. (eds.) Handbook of Research on Modern Systems Analysis and Design Technologies and Applications, pp. 35–54. IGI Global, Hershey (2009)
27. Ulwick, A., Hamilton, P.: The Jobs-to-be-Done growth strategy matrix. Technical report, Strategyn (2016)
28. Christensen, C.M., Dillon, K., Hall, T., Duncan, D.S.: Competing Against Luck: The Story of Innovation and Customer Choice. Harper Business, New York (2016)
29. Schumpeter, J.A.: Socialism, Capitalism and Democracy. Harper and Brothers, New York (1942)
30. Lucassen, G., Dalpiaz, F., Werf, J.M.E.M., Brinkkemper, S.: The use and effectiveness of user stories in practice. In: Daneva, M., Pastor, O. (eds.) REFSQ 2016. LNCS, vol. 9619, pp. 205–222. Springer, Cham (2016). https://doi.org/10.1007/978-3-319-30282-9_14
31. Norman, D.A., Draper, S.W.: User-centered design. New perspectives on human-computer interaction (1986)
32. Dix, A.: Human-Computer Interaction. Pearson education, Prentice Hall Europe (1998). ISBN: 9780132398640. https://books.google.nl/books/about/Human_computer_Interaction.html?id=tNxQAAAAMAAJ&source=kp_cover&redir_esc=y
33. Endsley, M.R.: Designing for Situation Awareness: An Approach to User-Centered Design. CRC Press, Boca Raton (2016)
34. van Lamsweerde, A.: Goal-oriented requirements engineering: a guided tour. In: Proceedings of the IEEE International Requirements Engineering Conference, pp. 249–262. IEEE (2001)
35. Chapman, C.N., Milham, R.P.: The personas' new clothes: methodological and practical arguments against a popular method. Proc. Hum. Factors Ergon. Soc. Ann. Meet. **50**, 634–636 (2006)
36. Lucassen, G., Robeer, M., Dalpiaz, F., van der Werf, J.M.E.M., Brinkkemper, S.: Extracting conceptual models from user stories with visual narrator. Requir. Eng. **22**(3), 339–358 (2017)

Requirements Alignment

Keeping Evolving Requirements and Acceptance Tests Aligned with Automatically Generated Guidance

Sofija Hotomski[(✉)], Eya Ben Charrada[(✉)], and Martin Glinz[(✉)]

Department of Informatics, University of Zurich, Zurich, Switzerland
{hotomski,charrada,glinz}@ifi.uzh.ch

Abstract. [**Context and motivation**] When a software-based system evolves, its requirements continuously change. This affects the acceptance tests, which must be adapted accordingly in order to maintain the quality of the evolving system. [**Question/problem**] In practice, requirements and acceptance test documents are not always aligned with each other, nor with the actual system behavior. Such inconsistencies may introduce software quality problems, unintended costs and project delays. [**Principal ideas/results**] To keep evolving requirements and their associated acceptance tests aligned, we are developing an approach called GuideGen that automatically generates guidance in natural language on how to modify impacted acceptance tests when a requirement is changed. We evaluated GuideGen using real-world data from three companies. For 262 non-trivial changes of requirements, we generated guidance on how to change the affected acceptance tests and evaluated the quality of this guidance with seven experts. The correctness of the guidance produced by our approach ranged between 67 and 89% of all changes for the three evaluated data sets. We further found that our approach performed better for agile requirements than for traditional ones. [**Contribution**] Our approach facilitates the alignment of acceptance tests with the actual requirements and also improves the communication between requirements engineers and testers.

1 Introduction

When developing or evolving systems, requirements constantly change and, in most cases, these changes affect other documentation artifacts. In practice, however, impacted artifacts too often are not kept aligned with changing requirements. To a significant extent, this is due to the additional effort required and to insufficient communication of requirement changes [1,2]. Losing the alignment between requirements and other documentation artifacts increases the risk of discovering mismatches between stakeholders' expectations and the actual software behavior only late, leading to unintended costs, delivery delays and unsatisfied customers. For example, when acceptance tests are not kept aligned with changed requirements, testers will report bugs for actual features that were introduced in a change.

© Springer International Publishing AG, part of Springer Nature 2018
E. Kamsties et al. (Eds.): REFSQ 2018, LNCS 10753, pp. 247–264, 2018.
https://doi.org/10.1007/978-3-319-77243-1_15

In order to keep software documentation aligned and up-to-date when a system evolves, many researchers try to automatically identify which documents are related to each other and which of them are *impacted* by a change [3,4]. However, there is little research about how to actually *update* impacted documents, although it would be beneficial to have guidance about what actions to perform [5].

In our work, we contribute an approach for keeping acceptance tests aligned with evolving requirements, called GuideGen. GuideGen automatically generates guidance on how to modify impacted acceptance tests when requirements change. We take advantage of the fact that requirements and acceptance tests have much in common: both are usually written in natural language and contain information about what the system under development is expected to do: requirements specify what should be implemented [6] and acceptance tests validate whether the implementation satisfies the requirements of the stakeholders [7]. Due to this similarity, tracing from requirements to acceptance tests is not difficult. Our approach assumes that traces between every requirement and its associated acceptance test(s) exist. If this is not the case, automated trace generation techniques [4], [8] may be used for establishing such traces.

By analyzing changed sentences and words in a requirement, we derive guidance in form of a set of concrete suggestions about what should be changed in the acceptance test(s) associated with a changed requirement. Our tool also provides an easy way for communicating changes and the generated guidance to all interested parties. GuideGen aims at both reducing the effort for aligning acceptance tests with the actual requirements and improving the communication between requirements engineers and developers/testers.

In a previous paper [9] we presented the principal ideas of our approach together with some examples and a preliminary evaluation. In this paper we describe our method and the algorithms used in detail, give an overview of the GuideGen tool, and present the results of a thorough evaluation with real-world data.

The paper is organized as follows. In the next section we present our approach and its technical components. We then present our prototype tool in Sect. 3. Section 4 describes our evaluation. We discuss our results in Sect. 5. Related work is discussed in Sect. 6. Section 7 concludes the paper with a summary and outlook.

2 Our Approach

The goal of GuideGen is to identify all *relevant changes* in requirements that require the associated acceptance tests to be adapted and to *generate guidance* in natural language on how to adapt the acceptance tests based on these changes. An overview of our approach is shown in Fig. 1.

As soon as a requirements engineer applies changes to a requirement and saves them, our approach performs the following steps:

1. Identifying relevant change patterns: by comparing the old and the new version of the changed requirement we identify the elements that have been changed and their change types,

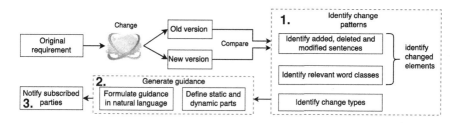

Fig. 1. Overview of the GuideGen approach

2. Generating guidance: in this step, we formulate suggestions in natural language on how to manage the changes,

3. Notifying subscribed parties: finally, the generated guidance and the changes can be communicated to the interested parties via e-mail.

In the remainder of this section, we present each of these steps in more detail.

2.1   Identifying Relevant Change Patterns

The goal of this step is to identify relevant patterns in the changes that are applied to a requirement. A *change pattern* is characterized by the change type (add, delete, or modify) and the changed element (a whole sentence or a word). If the changed element is a whole sentence, the change pattern is "Sentence is added" or "Sentence is deleted". If the changed element is a word, an example of a change pattern is "verb is deleted". *Relevant* change patterns are the ones whose changes require the acceptance tests to be adapted. In particular, relevant change patterns in our approach are the ones that directly or indirectly cause the change of some action, since acceptance tests contain a list of actions to be performed.

To identify the relevant change patterns, we first analyze the changes at a sentence level. Then we proceed by analyzing changes at a word level. Finally we classify each of the detected changes as relevant or irrelevant.

Analyzing changes at sentence level. In order to identify whether a whole sentence has been added, deleted or modified, we first split the old and the new version of the requirement into sentences using an implementation of the Stanford sentence splitting algorithm [10]. We get the list of old sentences (oldReq in further text) and the list of new sentences (newReq). Additionally, our tool transforms enumerated sentences into plain sentences. A plain sentence is a sentence without bullet points. An enumerated sentence contains the main part and at least two bullet points, e.g.
"A user can insert: - name,
                          - surname".

The sentence is transformed into: "A user can insert name" and "A user can insert surname". If a bullet point is added or deleted, the change is treated as an addition or deletion of a plain sentence. For instance, if we add "- e-mail", this change is treated as the addition of the sentence "A user can insert e-mail".

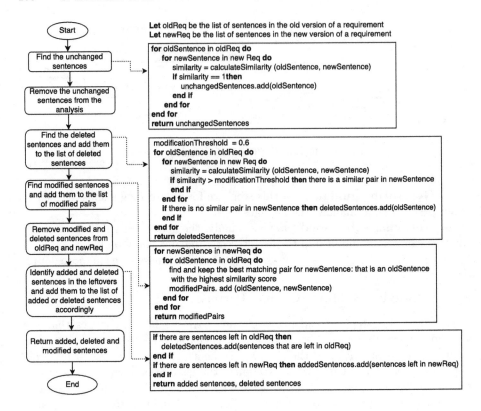

Fig. 2. The algorithm for identifying added, deleted and modified sentences

Otherwise, the addition of a noun that has no related verbs would be classified as an irrelevant change pattern.

We then compare all the sentences from oldReq with the sentences from newReq by calculating the similarity between them. Based on the similarity, we determine whether the sentence is unchanged, added, deleted or modified. The similarity is calculated using an existing semantic similarity toolkit [11]. In particular, we use greedy matching for word to word similarity that is based on WordNet. A flow diagram and the corresponding pseudo code of the algorithm are shown in Fig. 2.

If the similarity between a sentence in oldReq and one in newReq is equal to one, that sentence is considered to be unchanged. If a sentence in oldReq does not have a corresponding one in the newReq so that the similarity score between them is greater than the modification threshold of 0.6[1], then this sentence is deleted. When the similarity score between sentences is above the modification threshold, these sentences are candidates for modified sentences. We choose the best match – a pair of sentences whose similarity score is the highest among

---

[1] This is a heuristic value which yielded excellent performance in our evaluation, cf. Sect. 4.2.

other pair candidates. When we remove best matches, unchanged sentences and already identified deleted sentences from the oldReq and the newReq, there might be leftovers. The leftovers in newReq are added sentences and the leftovers in oldReq are deleted sentences. We illustrate this using the following example:

> A user can add new users to the group. ~~The addition of a new user must be first approved by the admin.~~ The admin <u>and the user</u> can modify personal data ~~and the status~~ of <u>that</u> ~~a~~ user. <u>Only user can modify its status. The admin must be logged-in in order to modify personal data of a user.</u>

Added words are green and underlined, removed words are red and struck through, while black words are unchanged.

Figure 3 shows the calculated similarities between the old and the new version of the changed requirement.

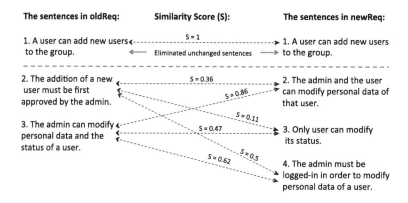

Fig. 3. Calculated similarity scores for the sentences in the example

The first sentence is eliminated from the further analysis because the similarity score is $S(1, 1) = 1$. Since all scores calculated for the second sentence, $S(2, 2) = 0.36$, $S(2, 3) = 0.11$ and $S(2, 4) = 0.5$, are below the modification threshold (0.6), the second sentence in the oldReq is found to be deleted. We defined the modification threshold based on experimentation: we calibrated it to the value that yielded the best results for identifying added, deleted and modified sentences. For the third sentence in old-Req we see that there are two matching sentences in the newReq so that the similarity is above the modification threshold: $S(3, 2) = 0.86$ and $S(3, 4) = 0.62$. We choose the best match in this case, i.e., $S(3, 2)$. Therefore, the third sentence in the oldReq is modified to the second sentence in the newReq. The third and the fourth sentence in the newReq become leftovers. Since they are both in the newReq we find that these two sentences have been added.

ID	TEXT	WORD CLASS	DEPENDENCY NUMBER	GRAMMATICAL FUNCTION
1	The	DET	2	det
2	admin	NOUN	4	nsubj
3	can	VERB	4	aux
4	modify	VERB	0	ROOT
5	personal	ADJ	6	amod
6	data	NOUN	4	dobj
7	and	CONJ	6	cc
8	the	DET	9	det
9	status	NOUN	6	conj
10	of	ADP	9	prep
11	a	DET	12	det
12	user	NOUN	10	pobj
13	.	PUNCT	0	punct

ID	TEXT	WORD CLASS	DEPENDENCY NUMBER	GRAMMATICAL FUNCTION
1	The	DET	2	det
2	admin	NOUN	7	nsubj
3	and	CONJ	2	cc
4	the	DET	5	det
5	user	NOUN	2	conj
6	can	VERB	7	aux
7	modify	VERB	0	ROOT
8	personal	ADJ	9	amod
9	data	NOUN	7	dobj
10	of	ADP	9	prep
11	that	DET	12	det
12	user	NOUN	10	pobj
13	.	PUNCT	0	punct

Fig. 4. The output of SyntaxNet for the old version (left) and the new version (right) of the sentence in the changed requirement

Analyzing Changes at Word Level. After identifying sentences that have been added, deleted and modified, we proceed to analyze what changes were applied to modified sentences. When a sentence has been modified, we identify word classes in the sentence and for each of these classes, we identify their change type. For identifying word classes we use Google's implementation of a globally normalized transition-based neural network model, called SyntaxNet [12]. SyntaxNet determines the word class (e.g., noun, verb) and the grammatical function (e.g., subject, object) for each word in a sentence. SyntaxNet also identifies dependencies between words and represents them with dependency numbers. We use these later when generating guidance (see Sect. 2.2). Figure 4 shows an example of the output of SyntaxNet.

In order to identify whether words have been added, deleted or modified, we adapted the algorithm implemented in a text-based diff engine, called Text_Diff [13]. Text_Diff detects changes at a phrase level. We process the output from Text_Diff so that we get the changes on a word level.

In the modified sentence from our example: "The admin and the user can modify personal data and the status of that a user", the original Text_Diff algorithm will detect the addition of the phrases "and the user" and "that" and the deletion of the phrases "and the status" and "a". We adapted the algorithm so that it detects additions and deletions of each word in these phrases, as presented in Fig. 5.

The   admin   <add>and   the user</add>   can modify per-sonal data <del>and the sta-tus</del> of <add>that</add> <del>a</del>   user.

The   admin   <add>and</add> <add>the</add>   <add>user</add>   can modify   personal   data   <del>and</del> <del>the</del>   <del>status</del>   of <add>that </add> <del>a</del> user.

Fig. 5. The original (left) and adapted (right) output of Text_Diff

Classify Identified Changes into Relevant and Irrelevant Changes. We consider a change to be relevant if it is likely to impact acceptance tests. Since acceptance tests contain a list of actions to be performed and as actions are generally expressed using verbs in English sentences, we consider verbs as the principal element of analysis in GuideGen. More concretely, we consider a change in a requirement to be relevant if it involves an addition, deletion or modification of a verb or of another word class that relates to a verb such as nouns and adjectives.

If a whole sentence has been added, it is considered to be relevant only if it contains at least one verb. Changes of determiners, adverbs and prepositions are not taken into consideration, since we assume that they do not influence any actions and, therefore, do not have an impact on acceptance tests.

In our example, the following change patterns are considered to be relevant: (1) deletion of the sentence "The addition of a new user must be first approved by the admin", (2) addition of the noun "user", (3) deletion of the noun "status", (4) addition of the sentence "Only user can modify its status" and (5) addition of the sentence "The admin must be logged-in in order to modify personal data of a user". Only these changes are processed in the next steps.

2.2   Generating Guidance

The goal of this step is to generate suggestions about how to modify the affected acceptance tests so that they stay aligned with the changed requirements. An example of a suggestion is *Add new steps or modify existing steps to verify that only user can modify its status*. Every suggestion contains static and dynamic parts.

The static parts of a suggestion differ according to the change patterns identified in the previous step. For instance, if a whole sentence has been added to a requirement, the static part of the suggestion is "Add new steps or modify existing steps to verify that". Accordingly, if a whole sentence has been deleted, the static part of the suggestion is "Delete the steps or their parts which verify that". If a sentence has been modified, the static parts are formulated according to the modification type: whether a verb, subject, object or adjective is added/deleted/modified or a noun is changed from singular to plural, etc.

Table 1. Words included in the dynamic part of a suggestion according to the changed element.

Changed element:	Sentence	Noun		Verb	Adjective
		Subject/conjunction	Object/conjunction		
Words included in the dynamic part:	Changed element (all words in that sentence)	Changed element with adjectives and determiners, related verb and all words that appear after that verb	Changed element, subjects with determiners and adjectives, verbs, prepositions with their objects	Changed element, subjects and objects with determiners and adjectives, prepositions with objects, adverbs	Changed element, related nouns

For instance, if a subject is added, the static parts of the suggestion are "Make sure that now +{*dynamic part*}" and "Add the steps which verify this activity".

The dynamic parts of a suggestion fill the gaps between the static parts. They differ according to the type of the changed element, as shown in Table 1. We defined the rules governing the dynamic parts with informal experimentation and by considering typical sentence structures in requirements documents.

If a whole sentence has been added or deleted, the dynamic part contains all words in that sentence. When a changed element is a subject, the dynamic part contains that subject with its determiners and adjectives, the first related verb and all the words that appear after that verb. We use the word index (ID in Fig. 4) to identify the position of the words. In our example, the following guidance is generated for the added subject "user": "Make sure that now the user can modify personal data of that user."

When the changed element is an object, a verb or an adjective, then the dynamic part contains that element plus its related words. We identify the related words by analyzing word classes, grammatical functions and dependency numbers of words in the modified sentence. Related words for an object are (1) a verb whose index corresponds to the dependency number of the object, (2) a subject whose dependency number refers to the index of the identified related verb and (3) prepositions whose dependency numbers refer to the changed object. We recursively include their related words in the dynamic part. Related words for verbs are (1) directly related subjects, (2) objects, (3) prepositions and (4) adverbs with their related words and corresponding indexes and dependency numbers, while related words for adjectives are the nouns that this adjective directly relates to.

If a subject/object is related to another, main subject/object by a conjunction, we identify the words that are related to the main subject/object. In our example, the deleted object "status" has a conjunction to the direct object "data" (see Fig. 4). Since the verb "modify" with its auxiliary verb "can" is directly related to the object "data", we consider them to be also related to

Table 2. The identified relevant change patterns with the corresponding guidance.

Relevant change patterns	Generated guidance
Change 1: deletion of the sentence "The addition of a new user must be first approved by the admin"	**Delete steps or their parts which verify that** *the addition of a new user must be first approved by the admin*
Change 4: addition of the subject "user"	**Make sure that now** *the user can modify personal data of that user.* **Add the steps which verify this activity**
Change 7: deletion of the object "status"	**Delete steps or their parts which verify that** *the admin can modify the status of a user*
Change 10: addition of the sentence "Only user can modify its status"	**Add new steps or modify existing steps to verify that** *only user can modify its status*
Change 11: addition of the sentence "The admin must be logged-in in order to modify personal data of a user"	**Add new steps or modify existing steps to verify that** *the admin must be logged-in in order to modify personal data of a user*

"status". The subject "admin" refers to the verb "modify" and has a related determiner "the", so they are both classified as related words of the deleted object. The preposition "of" directly refers to "status" and it has the related noun "user" with its determiner "a". The determiner "the" is directly related to "status". The words are ordered by the word index and the dynamic part is formulated as *the admin can modify the status of a user.*

Table 2 presents the guidance that is generated in our example. The guidance consists of one suggestion per change. Static parts are in boldface, while dynamic parts are italicized.

2.3 Notifying Subscribed Parties

In order to ease the communication of changes, we have implemented a notification mechanism that allows requirements engineers to send an automatically generated message to subscribed parties (in particular, testers) when a requirement has been changed. The message contains the summarized changes and the generated guidance. An example is given in Fig. 7 in the next section.

If requirements engineers consider a generated suggestion to be irrelevant, they can mark it so that the tool does not include it in the message. For example, if we add a new sentence: "This should be communicated to Tom.", then the generated suggestion "Add new steps or modify existing steps which verify that this should be communicated to Tom." is irrelevant and can be ignored.

3   Tool Support

We have implemented our approach in a *prototype tool*, a Java web application. The GuideGen tool allows users to upload the list of requirements from an external Excel file, make changes to each of them and notify subscribers (developers, testers, ...) about the changes and the guidance on how to modify the affected acceptance tests.

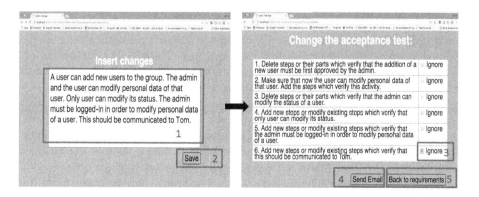

Fig. 6. User interface (UI) of the tool with highlighted process steps.

Figure 6 illustrates the steps taken when using the tool. The left screenshot shows how a user (typically a requirements engineer) can enter changes to a previously selected requirement (step 1) and save them (step 2). Within three seconds, the tool generates guidance consisting of a suggestion for each change and shows it to the user (right screenshot). Suggestions that the user considers to be irrelevant can easily be ignored (step 3). The result can be sent to the subscribed parties in an e-mail generated by the tool (step 4). The user can return to the list of requirements (step 5). Figure 7 shows the e-mail generated by the tool for the given example.

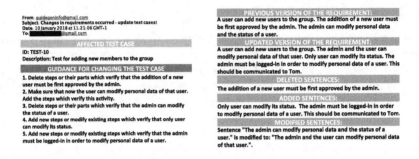

Fig. 7. The e-mail message generated for the example given in Fig. 6.

4   Evaluation

We evaluated GuideGen by applying it to real-world data sets with requirements changes provided by three companies. After pruning the data sets, we ran our tool with the requirements changes contained in the data sets and generated guidance for how to change the associated acceptance tests. The quality of the generated guidance was then assessed by experts from the three companies.

4.1   Study Design

Data collection and analysis. We obtained data sets containing information about changes of requirements from three companies (Table 3). For our evaluation, we needed data records containing the old and the changed version of a requirement and the associated acceptance tests. Table 4 characterizes the data sets.

We pruned the received data sets as follows: (1) We omitted all requirements that had not been changed at all or did not have acceptance tests associated with them. (2) We removed irrelevant changes such as added or deleted punctuation marks, spaces or empty lines. The pruning yielded a total of 448 changed requirements. Our tool filters out semantically irrelevant changes such as addition or deletion of determiners or corrections of typos. On the other hand, for several requirements there was more than one change. So we eventually could evaluate a total of 262 changes (28 for C1, 37 for C2 and 197 for C3).

Table 3. Characteristics of the companies that provided us data sets from one of their projects.

Company	Domain of activity	Software process model	# of employees in total	# of employees on the project	Country
C1	Access control and security solutions	Agile (Scrum)	≈16000	≈120	Switzerland
C2	IT integration, cloud services	Agile (Scrum)	≈500	≈100	Serbia/Germany
C3	Automation for warehouses and distribution centers	Waterfall	≈2500	≈500	Switzerland

Table 4. Characteristics of the data sets used in our evaluation study.

Company/Data set	Type of requirements	# of requirements in the data set	# of considered requirements	# of evaluated changes
C1/DS1	User story	157	20	28
C2/DS2	User story	30	30	37
C3/DS3	Classic textual requirement	5301	398	197

Running the tool. For every of the 262 evaluated changes, we generated guidance for how to change the associated acceptance tests using our tool prototype. We uploaded the old version of the requirements into the tool, replaced each of them with the new version, and recorded the generated guidance.

Assessing the quality of the generated guidance. The generated guidance was assessed by experts from the three companies. An overview of the experts and their experience is provided in Table 5.

95 changes were fully assessed by two or three experts. We created a questionnaire[2] in which, for every requirement, we presented the old and the changed requirement, the associated acceptance tests and the guidance for changing the acceptance tests generated by our tool. For each suggestion provided in the guidance, we asked six questions to assess the quality of the suggestion: (1) Is the suggestion correct in terms of actions that need to be performed? (2) Is it grammatically correct? (3) Is it complete? (4) Does the expert understand what has been suggested by the tool? (5) Would the expert be able to perform an update of the impacted acceptance test without any further clarifications? (6) Is the suggestion redundant or unnecessary? Finally, we asked whether there is anything missing from the guidance for a changed requirement (i.e., from the set of all suggestions generated for that requirement). Questions 1–3 and 5 had to

---

[2] https://docs.google.com/forms/d/1vLJYFIjmtLjzC60e2iT3JLbs9ST8LmOOhO9ko tfrBwo/edit. For confidentiality reasons, the file does not contain the real data from our data sets, but only the example shown in this paper.

Table 5. Characteristics of the experts who participated in the study.

Company	Participant	The role of participant	Years of experience in IT	Years on the current position
C1	P1	Requirements engineer	10	4
C1	P2	Senior test analyst	12	4
C2	P3	Requirements engineer	6	3
C2	P4	Senior test engineer	7	4
C3	P5	Requirements engineer	10	5
C3	P6	QA manager	12	6
C3	P7	Test engineer	4	4

be answered on a five-point Likert scale (from "strongly disagree" to "strongly agree"). In case of non-agreement, the expert was asked to provide an explaining text. Question 4 was a yes/no question, while Question 6 and the final question about missing suggestions were answered as free text.

In company C3, due to limited availability of the experts, only 30 suggestions could be thoroughly assessed by all three experts. The suggestions generated for the remaining 167 changes could only be assessed for correctness by a single expert.

When the experts had finished answering the questionnaire for all changed requirements assigned to them, we conducted a short interview where we asked them seven questions about the usefulness and applicability of our approach[3].

4.2 Results

In this sub-section we present the results of the assessment of the generated guidance by the experts and some key insights from the follow-up interviews.

All 262 changes were correctly identified in terms of the change type, showing that the algorithm for identifying added, deleted and modified sentences with a modification threshold of 0.6 performs accurately. Table 6 presents the results of the evaluation of the guidance generated for 95 changes in requirements by the experts.

For calculating the percentages in Table 6 for the questions answered on a Likert scale, we interpreted the values 4 ("Agree") and 5 ("Strongly agree") as "yes". Analogously, we interpreted 1 ("Strongly disagree") and 2 ("Disagree") as "no". 3 ("Neutral") was interpreted according to the textual explanation provided by the experts. From eleven such answers three were interpreted as "yes" and eight as "no".

Table 6 shows that in C1 and C2 the experts assessed more than 80% of the suggestions as correct in terms of actions. In C3 one expert was more negative

---

[3] https://docs.google.com/forms/d/1rk-P-m4sd8rpHk_umForPW6QebWRnoLBjfex hBqiVI4/edit.

Table 6. The quality of the generated suggestions based on an assessment by industrial experts.

Generated in total/ assessed	Company/ Partici- pant	Correct in terms of actions	Gramma- tically correct	Complete	Under- standable	Self- expla- natory	Redundant/ unnece- ssary	Missed changes
28/28	C1/P1	89.2%	82.1%	100%	100%	75%	7.1%	3.6%
	C1/P2	89.2%	82.1%	100%	100%	75%	7.1%	3.6%
37/37	C2/P3	81%	67.5%	94.6%	100%	75.6%	10%	5.4%
	C2/P4	81%	67.5%	94.6%	100%	75.6%	10%	5.4%
197/30	C3/P5	50%	86.6%	96.6%	93.3%	70%	50%	3.3%
	C3/P6	70%	80%	93.3%	100%	73.3%	30%	3.3%
	C3/P7	66.7%	86.6%	96.6%	93.3%	73.3%	33.3%	3.3%

than the other two, especially regarding the correctness in terms of actions. This is due to a misunderstanding: expert P5 classified all redundant suggestions as wrong in terms of actions, i.e., when they were actually correct, but unnecessary. So we can consider the correctness of our guidance for data set 3 to be at least 66.7%.

"- The section 3 contains:
   – Doctors' corner
   – Register your practice opens a form inline or a popup with:
      — Name of your practice (mandatory)
      — Contact phone (mandatory)
      — Contact e-mail (mandatory)
      — Give us your contact details and we will get back to you soon! "

Fig. 8. Example of a changed requirement from C2. Added text is in green and under-lined.

Figure 8 shows a change (in the acceptance criteria of a user story) where GuideGen does not work such well. According to the experts, the text means that Sect. 3 of a web page contains a label "Doctors' corner" and a button "Register your practice". When a user clicks on the button, a pop-up window is displayed. The change in the requirement is that an additional message shall be displayed in this window.

For this change, the GuideGen tool generated the following suggestion, which the experts considered to be wrong both in terms of actions and grammatically: "Add new steps or modify existing steps which verify that the Sect. 3 contains register your practice opens a form inline or a pop-up with give us your contact details and we will get back to you soon!". This result may indicate that our app-roach does not perform well on ill-structured texts (the experts confirmed that this text is not formulated well). However, it may also indicate that our treatment of enumerations (cf. sentence level analysis in Sect. 2.1) needs improvement.

The last column in Table 6 presents the number of changes that were relevant, but not detected by GuideGen. In C1 a noun without any related verbs was added. This was classified as an irrelevant change and hence no guidance was generated. Further, the current version of our tool does not consider the change of numerical values as a relevant change pattern. Hence, no guidance was generated for two such cases in C2 and one in C3. This problem will be fixed in the next release of the tool.

As stated above, the guidance for 167 changes in requirements from company C3 could not be evaluated fully due to limited availability of the experts. Table 7 shows the results of the assessment of the generated suggestions for these changes.

Table 7. Suggestions assessed for correctness in terms of actions by a single expert only.

Company/ Participant(role)	Assessed suggestions	Correct in terms of actions	Wrong (re-phrasing only)	Wrong (only clarifications or notes added or deleted)	Wrong (due to tool limitations)
C3/P6 (QA)	167	70.6%	10.2%	13.8%	5.4%

We found that 70.6% were correct in terms of actions, while 24% were incorrect because the changes only rephrased a requirement or added or deleted only clarifications or notes. A small percentage (5.4%) of wrong suggestions were due to limitations of our prototype tool (e.g., wrongly identified dependencies).

Next, we present the main findings from the follow-up interviews with the experts regarding the overall usability and usefulness of GuideGen. All experts stated that GuideGen can be helpful in communicating changes on time and with less effort, it can help test engineers to make a decision on how to update acceptance tests and they would be willing to slightly adapt their style of writing requirements in order to ensure better quality of guidance. Four experts emphasized that one of the reasons for wrongly generated guidance was the poor quality of the requirements. They stated that suggestions can be too general, but that this is directly related to the level of detail specified in the requirements. The experts from C1 stated that the approach would be even more useful if it could highlight the parts of the acceptance tests that should be changed directly in the acceptance test document. With respect to the usability of the tool, P1 and P2 suggested an improvement of the user interface so that the tool navigates directly to the steps that are suggested to be changed.

4.3   Threats to Validity

Internal and construct validity. Our evaluation strongly depends on the expertise of the people who assessed the guidance generated by GuideGen. In order to foster validity, we aimed at assessing each guidance by at least two experts. In company C3, due to limited availability of experts, we could assess only 30 cases this way, while the rest was evaluated only in terms of correctness by a single expert. We tried to mitigate this problem by including all types of changes in the fully evaluated sample from company C3. Even with this restriction, the workload for the experts was high, since they needed to answer six questions per 28 and more suggestions, which might impact the quality of their answers. Therefore, we provided an online access to the questionnaire, so that the experts could answer the questions in iterations.

External validity. The generalizability of our results is limited by the fact that our evaluation covers data sets from only three companies. We tried to improve generalizability by including both agile and traditional requirements artifacts as well as different types of changes in our data sets. Although the study involves only seven participants, we had at least two participants per data set and we tried to keep diversity in terms of roles, so that requirements engineers and test managers are included.

5   Discussion

The results presented in Table 6 show that the quality of the generated guidance differs from company to company. This is not surprising as the outcome of our natural language processing techniques depends on the type and quality of requirements artifacts and on the content that is being changed in these artifacts.

GuideGen performs better for user stories than for traditional requirements. This is probably due to the fact that user stories typically are more concise and describe features more precisely than traditional requirements do. Further, text changes in traditional requirements documents often do not bring any novelty to the feature that is being described, but only provide clarifications or simply rephrase the text.

The complexity of a sentence also affects the quality of the guidance generated. On the one hand, very short or incomplete sentences affect both the correctness and completeness of suggestions and may even cause the omission of relevant changes. On the other hand, long, complex sentences which contain one or more relative clauses or statements in parentheses may cause problems: word classes, their grammatical functions and dependencies between words in a sentence may be wrongly identified, which leads to wrongly generated guidance.

Our approach currently cannot recognize certain types of irrelevant changes, for example, when mere comments such as "This should be communicated to Tom" are added. Wrong suggestions are generated in this case. However, our tool allows a requirements engineer to remove such false positives easily before communicating changes and generated guidance to subscribers (cf. Fig. 7).

GuideGen needs only sets of old and changed requirements (and their associated acceptance tests) as input. This is both a strength and a limitation. It is a *strength* because with our tool, requirements engineers can easily communicate requirements changes together with guidance on how to change the acceptance tests that correspond to the changed requirements. On the other hand, it is a *limitation*, as our tool does not analyze which artifacts are impacted by a changed requirement. This problem is addressed by research on automated traceability and change impact analysis [4, 8, 14].

6   Related Work

Many researchers investigate requirements traceability for supporting change impact analysis. For example, Antoniol et al. [15], Marcus and Maletic [14], De Lucia et al. [4] and Hayes et al. [16] use information retrieval methods to ensure automated traceability for change impact analyses. Others employ natural language processing. For example, Arora et al. [8] analyze the impact of changes in a requirement on other requirements in a system using NLP methods. However, all these approaches focus on identifying which requirements or other artifacts are impacted by a change in a requirement, while we investigate how to manage the change and which actions to perform in order to keep requirements and acceptance tests aligned.

Bridging the communication gap among people involved in developing a system draws attention of researchers and practitioners. Sinha et al. [17] define and explain the communication problems when managing requirements in a distributed environment. Bjarnason and Sharp [18] and Adzic [19] emphasize the communication problems between requirements engineers, developers and testers in agile projects. By generating guidance in natural language that can be easily communicated to the interested parties via e-mail, our approach supports easy and timely communication of changes between requirements engineers and developers/testers.

7   Conclusions

Summary. We presented GuideGen, a tool-supported method for automatically generating guidance on how to align acceptance tests with evolving requirements. With a correctness score of more than 80% for real-world agile requirements and around 67% for traditional requirements, our approach provides useful guidance for maintaining acceptance tests and keeping them aligned with the evolving requirements.

Future Work. We will improve GuideGen based on the evaluation results and then perform a more thorough evaluation of its overall usefulness and usability.

Acknowledgements. We thank our experts and their companies for investing time and effort into the evaluation of our approach. This work was partially funded by the Swiss National Science Foundation under grant 200021-157004/1.

References

1. Bjarnason, E., Runeson, P., Borg, M., Unterkalmsteiner, M., Engström, E., Regnell, B., Sabaliauskaite, G., Loconsole, A., Gorschek, T., Feldt, R.: Challenges and practices in aligning requirements with verification and validation: a case study of six companies. Empir. Softw. Eng. **19**(6), 1809–1855 (2014)
2. Hotomski, S., Ben Charrada, E., Glinz, M.: An exploratory study on handling requirements and acceptance test documentation in industry. In: 24th IEEE International Requirements Engineering Conference (RE 2016), pp. 116–129. IEEE (2016)
3. Borg, M., Gotel, O.C., Wnuk, K.: Enabling traceability reuse for impact analyses: a feasibility study in a safety context. In: 7th International Workshop on Traceability in Emerging Forms of Software Engineering (TEFSE), pp. 72–78. IEEE (2013)
4. De Lucia, A., Marcus, A., Oliveto, R., Poshyvanyk, D.: Information retrieval methods for automated traceability recovery. In: Cleland-Huang, J., Gotel, O., Zisman, A. (eds.) Software and Systems Traceability, pp. 71–98. Springer, London (2012). https://doi.org/10.1007/978-1-4471-2239-5_4
5. Nair, S., de la Vara, J.L., Sen, S.: A review of traceability research at the requirements engineering conference[re@21]. In: 21st IEEE International Requirements Engineering Conference (RE 2013), pp. 222–229. IEEE (2013)
6. Sommerville, I., Sawyer, P.: Requirements Engineering: A Good Practice Guide. Wiley, New York (1997)
7. Myers, G.J., Sandler, C., Badgett, T.: The Art of Software Testing. Wiley, New York (2011)
8. Arora, C., Sabetzadeh, M., Goknil, A., Briand, L.C., Zimmer, F.: Change impact analysis for natural language requirements: an NLP approach. In: 23rd IEEE International Requirements Engineering Conference (RE 2015), pp. 6–15. IEEE (2015)
9. Hotomski, S., Ben Charrada, E., Glinz, M.: Aligning requirements and acceptance tests via automatically generated guidance. In: 4th Workshop on Requirements Engineering and Testing (RET) (2017)
10. Manning, C.D., Surdeanu, M., Bauer, J., Finkel, J.R., Bethard, S., McClosky, D.: The Stanford CoreNLP natural language processing toolkit. In: ACL (System Demonstrations), pp. 55–60 (2014)
11. Rus, V., Lintean, M.C., Banjade, R., Niraula, N.B., Stefanescu, D.: Semilar: the semantic similarity toolkit. In: ACL (Conference System Demonstrations), pp. 163–168 (2013)
12. Andor, D., Alberti, C., Weiss, D., Severyn, A., Presta, A., Ganchev, K., Petrov, S., Collins, M.: Globally normalized transition-based neural networks. arXiv preprint arXiv:1603.06042 (2016)
13. Hagenbuch, J.S.C.: Text_diff-engine for performing and rendering text diffs. https://pear.horde.org/
14. Marcus, A., Maletic, J.I., Sergeyev, A.: Recovery of traceability links between software documentation and source code. Int. J. Softw. Eng. Knowl. Eng. **15**(05), 811–836 (2005)
15. Antoniol, G., Canfora, G., Casazza, G., De Lucia, A., Merlo, E.: Recovering traceability links between code and documentation. IEEE Trans. Softw. Eng. **28**(10), 970–983 (2002)
16. Hayes, J.H., Dekhtyar, A., Sundaram, S.K.: Advancing candidate link generation for requirements tracing: the study of methods. IEEE Trans. Softw. Eng. **32**(1), 4–19 (2006)

17. Sinha, V., Sengupta, B., Chandra, S.: Enabling collaboration in distributed require-
    ments management. IEEE Softw. **23**(5), 52–61 (2006)
18. Bjarnason, E., Sharp, H.: The role of distances in requirements communication: a
    case study. Requir. Eng. **22**(1), 1–26 (2017)
19. Adzic, G.: Bridging the Communication Gap: Specification by Example and Agile
    Acceptance Testing. Neuri Limited, London (2009)

Coexisting Graphical and Structured Textual Representations of Requirements: Insights and Suggestions

Martin Beckmann[1(✉)], Christian Reuter[2], and Andreas Vogelsang[1]

[1] Technische Universität Berlin, Berlin, Germany
martin.beckmann@tu-berlin.de
[2] Daimler AG, Sindelfingen, Germany

Abstract. [**Context & motivation**] Many requirements documents contain graphical and textual representations of requirements side-by-side. These representations may be complementary but oftentimes they are strongly related or even express the same content. [**Question/problem**] Since both representation may be used on their own, we want to find out why and how a combination of them is used in practice. In consequence, we want to know what advantages such an approach provides and whether challenges arise from the coexistence. [**Principal ideas/results**] To get more insights into how graphical and textual representations are used in requirements documents, we conducted eight interviews with stakeholders at Daimler. These stakeholders work on a system that is specified by tabular textual descriptions and UML activity diagrams. The results indicate that the different representations are associated with different activities. [**Contribution**] Our study provides insights into a possible implementation of a specification approach using mixed representations of requirements. We use these insights to make suggestions on how to apply the approach in a way that profits from its advantages and mitigates potential weaknesses. While we draw our conclusions from a single use case, some aspects might be applicable in general.

Keywords: Model-driven software specification · Graphical models
Requirements documents · UML activity diagram

1 Introduction

Eliciting and specifying requirements by means of models is becoming more and more popular in the development of complex embedded systems [1]. However, these models usually accompany and complement textual requirements and do not replace them. Therefore, many requirements documents contain graphical and textual representations of requirements side-by-side. This combined use of graphical diagrams and textual descriptions is considered beneficial for the requirements management process [2,3].

© Springer International Publishing AG, part of Springer Nature 2018
E. Kamsties et al. (Eds.): REFSQ 2018, LNCS 10753, pp. 265–280, 2018.
https://doi.org/10.1007/978-3-319-77243-1_16

In practice, there are more substantial reasons why the same information may be expressed in a graphical model and also in an accompanying text. For example, industrial applications, tool support, and model exchange for graphical models are still not standardized [4] and, as a result, manufacturer/supplier handover is still performed by textual documents. This is especially important, since these textual documents often serve as the basis for legal considerations between the contractors [3,5]. Also, due to different backgrounds of the stakeholders, not everyone is capable of understanding the graphical models [6].

Maintaining and updating information in graphical and textual representations is often performed manually. In previous work, we have shown that this is a potential source for inconsistencies and quality issues in the requirements specifications [7]. Moreover, best practices and guidelines for when and how to use graphical or textual representations are missing. This leads to discussions about the validity of the representations, when deviating representations exist.

Without a deeper understanding of how the different representations are used and why they coexist, it is hard to come up with measures for ensuring consistency or to decide how content should be represented. Therefore, we are interested in how coexisting graphical and textual representations of requirements are used by stakeholders of the system. For this purpose we considered one particular instance of this case in practice, where a team at Daimler uses UML Activity Diagrams to provide a high-level overview of the activation conditions for a vehicle function. The information contained in this model is afterwards transferred into a tabular textual representation that is then further detailed.

We conducted eight interviews with practitioners at Daimler. Three interviewees have developed the specification approach described above. Five interviewees work with the resulting requirements document. From these interviews, we derive a model that describes for which activities stakeholders use graphical or textual representations. Also, we use the acquired data to provide suggestions on how graphical and textual representations should be used to leverage their potential and avoid pitfalls which would lead to quality issues.

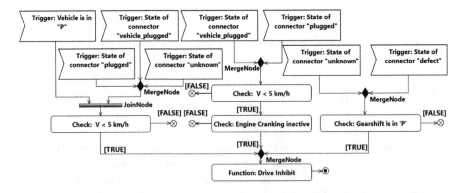

Fig. 1. Activity diagram of the function *Drive Inhibit*

2   Background

A team at Daimler employs UML activity diagrams [8] to specify functions of a system. The diagrams are used to get an early overview of the desired function behavior with a special focus on the activation of the function, execution conditions, functional paths, and deactivation. Figure 1 depicts a diagram of the system. The actual behavior of the activated function is described in the *Action* node labeled with *Drive Inhibit* (bottom of the diagram). The activation of the function is described by a combination of triggers and checks for conditions. This pattern to describe functions is also known for building textual requirements [9]. Activity diagrams are interpreted according to the requirements-level semantics of activities as defined by Eshuis and Wieringa [10]. As such, we assume that each node executes as soon as a token is placed on that node (by a transition or by occurrence of events). We also assume that the time required to execute a node is infinitely short. Control nodes have the usual semantics: *MergeNodes* (diamonds) and *JoinNodes* (bars) represent OR connections and AND connections, respectively. All the activity diagrams of the system are modeled in a similar way in regard to the used pattern, structure and layout.

The activity diagrams are then embedded in a textual requirements specification in two representations: (a) graphically as an image, (b) in a tabular, textual form which is supposed to reflect the same behavior as the activity diagram. The tabular representations may be refined and extended later.

Figure 2 shows the textual representation of the activity diagram in Fig. 1 as we found it in the specification document of our industry partner. The basic idea of the textual representation is to represent the triggers and checking conditions which govern the execution of a function as a kind of AND-OR table with postfix boolean operators. As such, the textual representation emphasizes the propositional logic aspect of the behavior. Each row represents an object, which is described by a set of attributes (columns). These attributes are needed to display the relevant information of the activity diagram in the requirements document. The *ID* attribute contains a unique identifier of the object. The *Text* attribute is a textual description of the object and is supposed to be equal to the text of the corresponding element in the activity diagram. It also contains the boolean operators which connect multiple elements within a cell or connect one row to the next row on the same *Level*. The *Level* is an attribute to structure the objects hierarchically. It is derived from the structure of the activity diagram. The *Type* attribute denotes whether an object is a function, a trigger or a condition to be checked. The object types in the table are derived from the types of the corresponding elements in the activity diagram.

Note that the activity diagram and the textual representation exhibit a number of differences with respect to both placement of elements and the specified behavior. E.g., the element *Check: Engine Cranking inactive* has the predecessor *Check: V < 5* km/h in the activity diagram, while in the textual representation the element *Vehicle Gear selector is in position "P"* is the predecessor. Besides, some rows in the textual representation mistakenly have a connector at their end (*ID 1113, 1233*), although there are no further rows on the same *Level*.

These issues may originate from the manual generation of the textual representation and changes over time. We have addressed these problems in a previous paper [7].

ID	Text	Level	Type
1000	**1.1.1.1.1.1 Drive Inhibit**	6	Function
1236	State of connector "unknown" OR State of connector "defect" OR	7	Trigger
1237	Vehicle Gear selector is in position "P" AND	8	Check
1113	Engine Cranking inactive OR	8	Check
1111	State of connector "plugged on vehicle side" ("VEH_PLUGGED") OR "plugged on vehicle and EVSE side" ("PLUGGED") OR	7	Trigger
1112	Vehicle velocity is below 5 km/h	8	Check
1114	Vehicle Gear selector is in position "P" OR	7	Trigger
1232	Vehicle velocity is below 5 km/h	8	Check
1233	State of connector "plugged on vehicle side" OR State of connector "plugged on vehicle and EVSE side" OR State of connector "unknown" AND	7	Trigger
1238	Vehicle velocity is below 5 km/h	8	Check

Fig. 2. Textual representation of the function *Drive Inhibit*

The sample in Fig. 2 only depicts the contents derived from the activity. Besides the mentioned attributes, the document may contain other attributes used for further development. Also, the textual document may contain more detailed information in the form of further requirements and descriptions. These entries may be both formal (e.g., parameter values) and in freely-written natural language.

3   Related Work

Graphical notations as a means to ease the understanding of complex systems have been used in different contexts [11,12]. Nevertheless, despite showing several advantages there are drawbacks such as end users' unfamiliarity with graphical notations and limits on the displayable details in visualizations. Moreover in requirements engineering, research has identified the need for different representations of requirements [13]. A possibility to tackle these issues is to use accompanying text for graphical models. Arlow et al. introduced an approach called *Literate Modelling* that works with this idea and employs UML models as the graphical models [6]. This concept of coexisting graphical models and textual descriptions was picked up and discussed for future tools in requirements engineering [14]. In addition the approach is supported by ideas using a graphical model as a basis to generate a structure for requirements documents and requirements itself [15].

However, to the best of our knowledge, there is only a small number of works on the topic of how to apply the approach and on its impact. Aside from computer science, it has been shown that the combined use of words (written and spoken) and pictures has a beneficial effect on a person's perception [16]. Still, it is also known that readers focus on the representation that takes the least effort to understand, in case they contain the same information [17].

A study of Burton-Jones et al. with student participants investigates whether a combination of representations is beneficial [18]. They report a positive impact for understanding a new system by using conceptual graphical models and a textual narrative, but do not give details on how to implement such an approach in practice. Our intent is to improve the understanding in this area by interviewing practitioners and to make suggestions on how to implement such a mixed representation approach in the best way possible.

4 Study Design

To gain a better understanding of how the approach is used and how the involved parties work with the activity diagrams and the textual parts, we conducted an interview study with stakeholders of one particular system. We designed the study along the recommendations of Runeson and Höst [19].

Research Objective: We want to know how the different stakeholders use the graphical models and the textual descriptions, how and where they make changes, and how they ensure consistency of the specification. Additionally, we are interested in the stakeholder's perception of advantages, challenges, and best practices of the application of the approach.

To reach this objective, we pursue three research questions (RQ):

RQ1: For which activities do the stakeholders use which representation? With this research question, we aim at getting insights about the use of different representations in order to be able to derive suggestions for working in a setting with coexisting representations.

RQ2: What are the reasons why stakeholders use one or the other representation for specific tasks? We want to find out why stakeholders use one of the representations for certain tasks. This is meant to provide insights on the benefits the graphical models offer and how the coexisting artifacts are used in the work of the involved persons.

RQ3: What challenges arise in the combined use of graphical models and text and how should they be addressed? We want to know what problems the stakeholders face. This gives us an idea on potentials for improvement. Also, this RQ is used to derive suggestions for the use of graphical models in combination with text for specifying functions.

Study Object: We conducted this study in the context of the development of one particular system. The system contains functions involved with charging the batteries of Plug-in Hybrid Electric Vehicles and Battery Electric Vehicles. As such, the system contains requirements that are relevant for safety as well as for usability. Overall, there are 14 functions in the system which are described by the approach mentioned in Sect. 2. These functions contain a total of 22 activity diagrams and almost 2,000 objects (including requirements, descriptions and headings). The additional activity diagrams result from the fact that some subfunctions of the functions are also described by activity diagrams and text.

Data Collection: We conducted interviews with eight stakeholders of one particular system. The majority of the interviewed stakeholders (five) either depend on the contents of the requirements document directly or on content which is derived thereof automatically or manually. The rest of the stakeholders (three) are concerned with the methods that are applied to specify systems and components at Daimler. We group the participants into three groups: those involved with the testing of the functions (in the following referred to by: T_1, T_2), those who use the specified functions to specify components (C_1, C_2, C_3), and those developing the applied methods (M_1, M_2, M_3).

The interviews were performed by following an interview guideline. The interview guideline was created in multiple iterations. In each iteration the structure and questions were refined by discussions with other researchers and practitioners of our industry partner to ensure that the research questions are properly addressed. However, the interviews were conducted as open interviews. In case the participants mentioned issues aside from the questions of the guideline, we did not interrupt and followed up on these issues in some cases. Also, insights gained during the interviews were considered in the following interviews.

The first part of each interview concerned the background of the interviewee. We asked questions on how long they have been working with the contents of the system, what their current role is, whether there was prior knowledge in dealing with graphical models, and what their general attitude is towards the use of graphical models.

The second part aimed at eliciting facts about their work. This question covered what the participants actually use the activity or text for as well as in what way the two artifacts provide different information for their tasks. Furthermore, we asked what purposes the activity diagram and the textual description respectively fulfill. As the participants M_1, M_2 and M_3 do not directly work on the contents we engaged them in a discussion about their idea how the artifacts are supposed to be used. In addition, we asked the participants for their general impression on the quality of the activity diagrams and the accompanying text.

The third part aimed at initiating a discussion with the participants. We wanted to know where they see advantages in the current approach, what challenges they face in applying it in their own work and how to possibly deal with them. We also wanted to find out how they perceive the influence of the approach on the contents they are provided with. Hence, we encouraged the participants to give their opinion on the way the system's functions are specified and what consequences they expect for their tasks. Furthermore, we wanted to find out whether they can imagine a different process for the specification of functions and how that would differ from the current approach.

The majority of the interviews (five) was conducted on site. The rest of the interviews (three) was conducted by telephone. We ensured that the statements of the participants were handled in an anonymous way to guarantee honest answers. The interviews were scheduled to last about an hour. In the end the shortest interview lasted 32 min, while the longest took almost 90 min. The interviews were recorded.

Data Analysis: The first author created transcripts of the interviews. These transcripts summarize the whole interview and contain the essential statements of the participants. Due to the open nature of the interviews the number of statements differ from participant to participant. We analyzed the transcripts by applying qualitative coding [20]. The analysis was performed by the first and the second author. Our first step was to read the interview transcripts to get an overall impression. This impression was used to extract a first set of concepts. These concepts were then discussed in regard to their relevance towards the research questions. The discussion resulted in a common set of concepts. We then checked the transcripts for information, which fit the identified concepts. This task was performed independently and afterwards the coding was compared. In case of deviations the results were discussed until we reached a mutual agreement. This mutual agreement led to the omission of a number of statements, since they did not directly address the research questions. It turned out that some of these omitted statements covered interesting aspects nonetheless. Hence, it was decided to repeat the process in the same manner with additional concepts in order to include these aspects. We deduced the relevance of these aspects by the fact that they were mentioned by multiple participants.

5   Study Results

5.1   Demographics and Background

The interviewed participants have been working for our industry partner for a time period between 2 and 28 years. All of the participants stated to have prior experience in working with graphical models. This encompassed statements between some familiarity with UML and similar graphical notations to expert knowledge in the application of graphical models in the development of systems. Also, all participants stated to have a positive attitude towards the use of graphical models. Those statements ranged between seeing minor benefits to the impression that graphical models are nowadays necessary to be able to comply with standards and to create high-quality requirements.

5.2   Benefits and Use of the Approach

To address RQ1 and RQ2, we considered the answers to the questions that concerned the activities the participants perform during their work as well as parts of the discussion revolving around the advantages they perceive.

The tasks the participants perform are shown in Fig. 3. Boxes denote activities, while ovals represent artifacts. The lines show the associations that the participants mentioned in the interviews. The arrow between the two artifacts indicates that the graphical model is the initial artifact which is used to derive the textual descriptions.

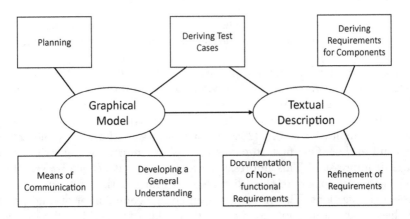

Fig. 3. Tasks associated with the artifacts

To use the graphical models as a means of communication and to develop a general understanding was identified as a task by almost all participants. Additionally, two participants (M_1, M_3) mentioned to use the graphical model during release planning. They use the relations between the elements of the diagram to gain insights into dependencies between underlying components, which in turn facilitates the planning. The only task associated with both representations is deriving test cases. In this matter, participant T_2 explicitly mentioned that the activity diagrams are the actual basis to create some of the test cases and not just a supporting alternative view of the text.

Nevertheless, the groups involved in testing and those responsible for components of the system both stated to rely mostly or even solely on the textual description to derive their own artifacts (test cases and components requirements). Furthermore the textual description was mentioned to be used to refine requirements and to provide more details on contexts and surrounding circumstances by all of the participants.

Aside from the performed activities, there seems to be confusion about the use of the approach itself. There was no common understanding between the participants on whether the textual or the graphical representation should be created first, which one is used in case of inconsistencies, and where changes are incorporated. Different statements were made on this topic. Some participants mentioned that they are unaware of how the artifacts are created and where to incorporate changes.

Moreover, the answers of the participants offered insights on what they think the artifacts are used for and what benefits the approach offers. Tables 1 and 2 show an overview of all statements the participants made about graphical models and textual descriptions, respectively. A ✓ denotes that the participant made that statement while a – denotes that the participants did not make mention of that fact.

Since all participants mentioned to have a positive attitude towards the use of graphical models, it is not surprising that their use is considered beneficial. Many even mentioned that they consider the use of graphical models as a necessity. As the associated tasks have shown, there is a lot of agreement that activity diagrams are used as a means of communication and a basis for discussion. Also, it was mentioned explicitly by almost all participants that the diagram improves the general understanding of a function.

For the textual descriptions, most participants mentioned that they see the text as the reference and it is used to provide details. The fact that the text is necessary because of legal considerations was only mentioned explicitly by participant T_2. The necessity to support stakeholders who are unfamiliar with the use of graphical models was stated by C_1, T_2 and M_2.

5.3   Challenges and Possible Improvements

To answer RQ3, we asked how they perceive the quality of the activity diagrams and their textual representation. More specifically, we wanted to know how they like the way the artifacts are structured and whether they face challenges by maintaining coexisting artifacts.

All participants emphasized that consistency is a major problem in the way the approach is currently applied. As a consequence, all participants would appreciate automatic support for deriving the textual description from the activity diagrams. They assume that this would have a positive impact on their work.

The textual representation was criticized with regard to its interpretation. Some participants said that they would prefer a different structure as the current one is not intuitively understandable. However, further inquiries on this issue revealed that the boolean operators without following rows on the same level (described in Sect. 2) are not perceived as a problem.

Many issues with the activity diagrams were mentioned. For instance, critique was expressed on the depiction of the activity diagrams. This critique focused most often on the fact that the diagrams are not uniformly designed using the same tool. Also, the pattern depicted in Fig. 1 is not strictly enforced. Furthermore, the contained information was criticized in regard to both the amount and level of detail. This point encompassed different opinions of the participants. Some of them stated that required information, such as signal names and values, are missing in the diagrams. Others stated that there are too many elements and details in some diagrams to understand a function properly. Yet, others said that the activity diagrams contain information (e.g., of other components) that is not relevant for them.

As the layout of a graphical model has a major impact on its understandability [21], we also wanted an opinion on the quality of the layout. All of the participants mentioned to be satisfied with the quality in that regard. Still, the way the activity diagrams are embedded in the tool was criticized. The diagram is included as a picture in a cell in the requirements document. Since the default size of such a cell does not allow for the display of the complete diagram, it is necessary to adjust its size manually in order to see the full diagram.

Table 1. Statements about the use of graphical models by participants

Participant	Considered beneficial	Considered necessary	Means of communication/Discussion	Improves understandability	Should be basis for text	Display architecture	Represents relations	Used for planning
C_1	✓	–	✓	✓	✓	✓	✓	–
C_2	✓	–	✓	✓	✓	–	✓	–
C_3	✓	–	✓	✓	✓	✓	✓	–
T_1	✓	–	✓	✓	✓	–	✓	–
T_2	–	✓	–	–	–	–	–	–
M_1	–	✓	–	✓	✓	✓	✓	✓
M_2	–	✓	✓	✓	✓	✓	✓	–
M_3	–	✓	✓	✓	–	–	✓	✓

Table 2. Statements about textual descriptions by participants

Participant	Acts as reference	Legal considerations	Contains details	Handover for supplier	Used for non-functional requirements	Support stakeholders unfamiliar with models
C_1	✓	–	✓	–	–	✓
C_2	✓	–	✓	–	–	–
C_3	✓	–	✓	✓	–	–
T_1	✓	–	–	–	–	–
T_2	–	✓	✓	✓	–	✓
M_1	–	–	✓	✓	–	–
M_2	–	–	✓	✓	✓	✓
M_3	–	–	✓	–	–	✓

5.4   Beyond the Research Questions

Since we designed the study as an open interview, many things were mentioned that did not directly address our research questions. Still, some of these statements are within the scope of our research objective.

Regarding the question what the graphical model is used for, the answer that appeared most often was an improved understandability. Further questions in that matter revealed that the understanding concerns mostly relations between the elements in the graphical representation. Aspects of activities such as independent executability of actions and asynchronous behavior were never mentioned. When we specifically asked for that, it was stated, that this is of no importance on that level of description.

As the automated generation of the textual description from the graphical models was mentioned, we wanted to know whether the capability of synchronization of the graphical and textual representation is needed. The participants answered that this capability would be nice-to-have, but all agreed that changes are best incorporated in the graphical model. M_1, C_2 and T_2 said, it should not be possible to change aspects of the graphical model in its textual description and hence a synchronization in the backwards direction should not be allowed.

Towards the end of the interviews, we challenged the approach as a whole and asked whether they could work without the textual representation. Because of the already mentioned uses of the text, about half the participants instantly stated that it does not seem possible. The rest was open to the idea, but had doubts, because of organizational considerations (e.g., handover to suppliers, legal issues) and also stated the necessary models would mitigate their main advantage — the capability of offering a clear overview. Participant T_2 said this would require major modifications in the company structure. It would be possible if all development tasks from suppliers are reintegrated to one place.

6   Discussion

6.1   Findings from Our Study

All in all, there seems to be a common understanding between the different stakeholders on why they use this approach and on what to use each artifact for. We derive this conclusion from the fact that all of the stakeholders consider the two coexisting artifacts to be at least beneficial. This is also reflected by the fact that there is a high-level of agreement towards the way the respective artifacts are used. Furthermore, the association of specific tasks with certain artifacts indicates that both the graphical representation and the textual representation are necessary to manage the complexity of today's systems and hence create high-quality requirements specifications.

The graphical representation is mainly seen as a means of communication and discussion and for improved understandability by almost all participants. Communication and discussions are necessary to make sure the behavior is as originally intended. A proper understanding of the function is mandatory for the stakeholders. These two purposes facilitate subsequent tasks such as deriving requirements for components and the manual generation of test cases. Thus, we see the diagram in a rather supportive role. These results also indicate that the graphic models are primarily used for the purpose of visualization and not for expressing precise semantics. In consequence it serves a wallpaper use [22].

The only aspect that was commented conflictingly about the graphical models regarded their depiction. Participant T_1 mentioned, that she would rather prefer more elements in a diagram than scrolling to a different diagram to get more information. Participant T_2 mentioned that the maximum number of elements in a diagram should be restricted to about seven elements and, if further elements are required, they should be nested into a linked diagram. In addition, some participants complained about information in the diagrams that is not relevant to them. This conflict cannot be resolved by using a single graphical representation of a function for all stakeholders (cf. [13]).

As for the textual representation, the results strongly suggest that it is in fact the preferable medium to accommodate refinements and details. Half of the participants mentioned the need to support stakeholders unfamiliar with graphic models. This is an issue that constantly appears in contexts where models are used. The coexistence of textual descriptions and graphical models appears to be a possible solution to this issue [23]. Nevertheless, there might be more fitting possibilities to arrange the textual representation than the one currently used (see [24] for a study on different textual representations of activity diagrams).

Although the graphical representation is created as a first step for the specification, its use is not restricted to the specification phase. As our participants perform a variety of tasks, we found out that the graphical model fulfills more purposes than just being a starting point for further specification. Amongst others it is used to derive test cases and to support understanding of the intended behavior. Hence, it proved to have been a good idea to consider participants outside the group of people who create the graphical models and textual descriptions. This selection of participants, on the other hand, also explains the lack of understanding which artifact is created at which step in the process, where changes are incorporated, and which artifact has to be used in case of inconsistencies. In hindsight, it turned out that the lack of a definition which artifact is used as the lead is also linked to the study object. Although half of the participants mentioned that the text is used as a handover and for legal considerations, this mainly applies to the derived component specifications. System specifications are mainly used internally and hence using the textual representation as the reference is not strictly enforced.

With regard to these insights we conclude that in our case using a textual and graphical representation on the same level of abstraction is an appropriate means in the development of systems since the artifacts serve different purposes. To make the most of the approach, we make suggestions that aim at mitigating the found weaknesses and taking advantages of the identified strengths.

6.2   Suggestions

Based on the insights we make suggestions on how to implement a mixed repre-sentations approach in order to leverage the potentials of the respective represen-tations. From the high level of agreement concerning that the activity diagram should be used as a basis for the text, we conclude that the activity diagram is indeed an adequate starting point for the specification process of our industry partner. This finding is largely in line with research on the use of graphical mod-els that emphasizes its use during the early stages of development [25]. Hence, this section starts with suggestions on the use of the activity diagrams and pro-ceeds with suggestions on the textual representation of our industry partner.

Use of the Activity Diagrams. One of the major factors to the success of graphical models is that it needs to be understood by as many stakeholders as possible. To achieve this, it is paramount to design the models according to a defined pattern. Also, we recommend to use a common tool for the modeling in order to ensure a uniform look, although this might be hard to enforce. Never-theless, access to the tool should be granted to all who make use of the activity diagram. This is required to address the problem with the handling of the dia-gram. From the different opinions on the contained information, we conclude that a mechanism is needed to tailor the models according to each individual's needs. This suggestion has been stated before [13] and is in line with established solutions on using textual requirements [26].

Use of the Text. Deriving the text from the activity diagram avoids incon-sistencies and hence ensures that the same behavior is described by both repre-sentations. Aside from the situation of our industry partner, there are already a number of approaches dealing with the generation of requirements specifications (or parts thereof) from models [15]. Following our participants the text can be used to incorporate refinements and details. As the complementary information may also be freely written in natural language, this representation may in fact be better suited for stakeholders unfamiliar with the notations of activities. Detailed information should only appear in the text to avoid further consistency issues and to guarantee the main purpose of the activity diagram is not impaired — to maintain a high-level overview.

Incorporation of Changes. As the appearance of changes is inevitable in the course of development, their incorporation in the artifacts must be considered. Changes to the relations of entities are easier to implement in the diagram. For textual changes it does not make much difference which representation is used. Nevertheless, to avoid inconsistencies only a single artifact should be used. Hence, the activity diagram should accommodate changes which affect both representations, although this might be hard to realize considering the fact that multiple persons work with the specification artifacts. The changes in the activity diagram are then propagated to the textual representation. It has to be noted that the additional textual content is not deleted or modified in the process.

Alternatively, changes could be automatically incorporated by using tools such as Projectional Editors, which automatically edit different projections of a common underlying model, in this case the activity diagram and its textual representation. However, this approach requires substantial efforts and accordingly trained developers [27]. Hence, a custom-made and lightweight solution to generate and update the textual representation might be better suited for the situation of our industry partner.

Further Related Tasks. As for the tasks of the respective artifacts, the situation displayed in Fig. 3 is already a good way of applying the strengths of the model and the text. The main concern of the graphical model is human-based analysis and the exchange of ideas between stakeholders. As such, the tasks of planning, improving understanding, and facilitating communication are prone to involve a visualization. Still, since the graphical representation provides a high-level overview, these tasks are restricted to early stages of development, when the required descriptions do not need to be detailed. Nonetheless, the defined syntax and semantics of a graphical model can also be used to automatically derive test cases [28].

6.3   Threats to Validity

The participating stakeholders were selected by the second author who is also actively participating in the development of the examined system. We did not follow specific selection criteria, except that participants must work actively on the examined system. However, the group of study participants only represent a subset of all people working actively with the requirements documents.

Furthermore we only had access to internal participants within one company. However, the activity diagrams and their textual descriptions must also be read and understood outside the company, such as legal authorities and suppliers. Their opinion is critical since inquiries on unclear issues require more effort between multiple organizations than inside a single company.

Also, our study examined the present situation of an approach using activity diagrams. The use of other graphical models might influence the proposed suggestions as well as the benefits and weaknesses we identified.

To answer our research questions, we only had access to a limited number of participants who actively work with this approach or are responsible for the applied methods. Also, we only gained insights into a single implementation of a mixed representation approach which uses activity diagrams and a very specific kind of textual representation. In conclusion, although our findings turned out to be consistent, our results can only be seen as a first step. Hence, further research is required to generalize our findings.

7   Conclusion and Future Work

In this paper, we present the results of a number of interviews we conducted to gain a better understanding of a specification approach that uses coexisting activity diagrams and tabular textual descriptions. The results incorporate an assessment of our participants on which artifact is suitable for which task as well as their opinion on the benefits of the respective artifacts. The use of graphical models for themselves as well as their use in coexistence with textual description on the same level of abstraction is perceived as beneficial. We use the insights gained by these results to derive suggestions. The suggestions serve the purpose of providing a guideline on how to implement such an approach in order to avoid inconsistencies and leverage its full potential.

Although we think that our results can be generally applied to approaches using coexisting graphical and textual artifacts, the results should be further validated by repeating the study with differing implementations of the approach. The differences might concern the type of graphical model and the pattern for textual description. Also, the extent to which practitioners benefit from our suggestions needs to be further examined. Moreover, the graphical and textual representations described in this paper are not the only artifacts. To handle the complexity of today's systems, further diagrams and associated documents might be needed. Ensuring the propagation of necessary changes to these artifacts is still not implemented in an acceptable manner and hence needs further investigation.

References

1. Broy, M.: Challenges in automotive software engineering. In: International Conference on Software Engineering (2006)
2. Davis, A.M.: Just Enough Requirements Management: Where Software Development Meets Marketing. Dorset House Publishing Co. Inc., New York (2005)
3. Sikora, E., Tenbergen, B., Pohl, K.: Industry needs and research directions in requirements engineering for embedded systems. Requirements Eng. **17**(1), 57–78 (2012)
4. Reuter, C.: Variant management as a cross-sectional approach for a continuous systems engineering environment. In: Grazer Symposium Virtual Vehicle (2015)
5. Maiden, N.A.M., Manning, S., Jones, S., Greenwood, J.: Generating requirements from systems models using patterns: a case study. Requirements Eng. **10**(4), 276–288 (2005)
6. Arlow, J., Emmerich, W., Quinn, J.: Literate modelling - capturing business knowledge with the UML. In: International Conference on the Unified Modeling Language (1998)
7. Beckmann, M., Vogelsang, A., Reuter, C.: A case study on a specification approach using activity diagrams in requirements documents. In: International Requirements Engineering Conference (2017)
8. Object Management Group (OMG): OMG Unified Modeling Language (OMG UML), Version 2.5 (2015). http://www.omg.org/spec/UML/2.5/

9. Firesmith, D.: Generating complete, unambiguous, and verifiable requirements from stories, scenarios, and use cases. J. Object Technol. **3**, 27–40 (2004)

10. Eshuis, R., Wieringa, R.: Tool support for verifying UML activity diagrams. IEEE Trans. Softw. Eng. **30**(7), 437–447 (2004)

11. Huff, A.S.: Mapping Strategic Thought. Wiley, Chichester (1990)

12. Pidd, M.: Tools for Thinking: Modelling in Management Science, 3rd edn. Wiley, Chichester (2009)

13. Gross, A., Doerr, J.: What you need is what you get! The vision of view-based requirements specifications. In: International Requirements Engineering Conference (2012)

14. Finkelstein, A., Emmerich, W.: The future of requirements management tools. In: Information Systems in Public Administration and Law. Österreichische Computer Gesellschaft (2000)

15. Nicolás, J., Toval, A.: On the generation of requirements specifications from software engineering models: a systematic literature review. Inf. Softw. Technol. **51**(9), 1291–1307 (2009)

16. Mayer, R.E.: The Cambridge Handbook of Multimedia Learning. Cambridge University Press, New York (2005)

17. Payne, J.W., Bettman, J.R., Johnson, E.J.: The Adaptive Decision Maker. Cambridge University Press, Cambridge (1993)

18. Burton-Jones, A., Meso, P.N.: The effects of decomposition quality and multiple forms of information on novices' understanding of a domain from a conceptual model. J. Assoc. Inf. Syst. **9**(12), 748–802 (2008)

19. Runeson, P., Höst, M.: Guidelines for conducting and reporting case study research in software engineering. Empirical Softw. Eng. **14**(2), 131–164 (2009)

20. Adolph, S., Hall, W., Kruchten, P.: Using grounded theory to study the experience of software development. Empirical Softw. Eng. **16**(4), 487–513 (2011)

21. Mendling, J., Reijers, H.A., Cardoso, J.: What makes process models understandable? In: Alonso, G., Dadam, P., Rosemann, M. (eds.) BPM 2007. LNCS, vol. 4714, pp. 48–63. Springer, Heidelberg (2007). https://doi.org/10.1007/978-3-540-75183-0_4

22. Drusinsky, D.: From UML activity diagrams to specification requirements. In: International Conference on System of Systems Engineering (2008)

23. van Oosterom, P., Lemmen, C., Ingvarsson, T., van der Molen, P., Ploeger, H., Quak, W., Stoter, J., Zevenbergen, J.: The core cadastral domain model. Comput. Environ. Urban Syst. **30**(5), 627–660 (2006)

24. Beckmann, M., Vogelsang, A.: What is a good textual representation of activity diagrams in requirements documents? In: International Model-Driven Requirements Engineering Workshop (2017)

25. Lindland, O.I., Sindre, G., Sølvberg, A.: Understanding quality in conceptual modeling. IEEE Softw. **11**(2), 42–49 (1994)

26. Weber, M., Weisbrod, J.: Requirements engineering in automotive development - experiences and challenges. In: Joint International Conference on Requirements Engineering (2002)

27. Berger, T., Völter, M., Jensen, H.P., Dangprasert, T., Siegmund, J.: Efficiency of projectional editing: a controlled experiment. In: International Symposium on Foundations of Software Engineering (FSE) (2016)

28. Beckmann, M., Karbe, T., Vogelsang, A.: Information extraction from high-level activity diagrams to support development tasks. In: International Conference on Model-Driven Engineering and Software Development (2018)

RE Previews and Visions

Security Requirements Elicitation
from Engineering Governance,
Risk Management and Compliance

Ana-Maria Ghiran[(✉)] [iD], Robert Andrei Buchmann[(✉)] [iD],
and Cristina-Claudia Osman[(✉)] [iD]

Business Informatics Research Center, Babeş-Bolyai University, Cluj-Napoca, Romania
{anamaria.ghiran,robert.buchmann,cristina.osman}@econ.ubbcluj.ro

Abstract. **[Context and motivation:]** There is a variety of sources from which security requirements may be derived, typically pertaining to fields such as software engineering, information systems risk assessment, security auditing, compliance management, IT governance etc. Several approaches, especially in the software engineering domain, have already investigated security requirements within a broader scope, including results from risk management. **[Question/ problem:]** Identifying security requirements according to just one of these fields might not suffice – opportunities of integration and enrichment must be investigated. **[Principal ideas/results:]** Our proposal advocates a convergence of different security requirements sources towards their richer specification, based on semantic technology. **[Contribution:]** Through this vision paper, we sketch the outline for a new perspective on eliciting security requirements, based on knowledge-driven integration of approaches from software engineering, risk assessment, governance and compliance.

Keywords: Security requirements · Risk assessment · Governance · Compliance
GRC framework · Resource Description Framework

1 Introduction

Security requirements can be encountered in a variety of situations: *business analysts propose requirements to develop software applications* (e.g., "the users of the application must be authenticated in order to use it"), *managers analyse requirements to create policies that mitigate risks* ("username and passwords must not be related" – e.g. corporate internal security policy), *executives check requirements* regarding the regulatory obligations (e.g.: appropriate safeguards should be in place to protect user data like login credentials – see General Data Protection Regulation (GDPR) (Regulation (EU) 2016/679), *auditors evaluate requirements against standards* ("users must change their passwords at least every 90 days"- see 8.5.9, Payment Card Industry (PCI) Data Security Standard, Requirements and Security Assessment Procedures, 2.0). All these requirements pertaining to *authentication* are engendered by different motivational sources (business objectives and strategies, business operation, contractual obligations, laws and regulations, standards and best practices,

© Springer International Publishing AG, part of Springer Nature 2018
E. Kamsties et al. (Eds.): REFSQ 2018, LNCS 10753, pp. 283–289, 2018.
https://doi.org/10.1007/978-3-319-77243-1_17

frameworks, implementation languages etc.) and their knowledge-driven integration must be considered in order to glean richer and comprehensive security requirements.

The security requirements elicitation process based on the integration of software engineering and governance, risk management and compliance (GRC) will demand participation of different stakeholders, possibly involving different methods for requirements and knowledge representation. This vision paper proposes semantic technology as an integration catalyst, to enable the convergence of various requirements sources and means of representation. The remainder of the paper is structured as follows: Sect. 2 provides background information over the proposed solution and presents related works. Section 3 details our approach for integrating requirements enabled by a common representation of both natural language and diagrammatic format of security requirements given by semantic technologies and a shared repository. The paper ends with conclusions.

2   Background and Related Work

Our proposal is motivated by the fact that each GRC discipline alone (Governance, Risk Management and Compliance) creates valuable information for the other two and repetitive tasks are done if they are treated separately, while risking to neglect their semantic connections. To enable their integration, we propose a knowledge repository of requirements that can be shared by stakeholders including analysts, executives, auditors, developers etc. *Requirements knowledge* is understood under the definition given by [1], as a means to externalize tacit knowledge into an explicit representation that can be subjected to various degrees of formalization. For this, we opt for the graph-based representation given by RDF – the Resource Description Framework [2].

RDF [2] offers, besides its initial XML dialect, some serializations that are more human readable (e.g., Turtle). At the same time, it supports graph-based, machine-readable representation based on linking the concepts/resources described in formal statements). RDF is used in our proposal as the underlying technology that enables semantic connections between the various requirements representations: *textual*, *visual* (diagrammatic) and *ontology-based* representations (as derived by requirements from the considered fields of practice).

Software engineering stressed the importance of security requirements as security for IT systems should be addressed from their inception rather than patched: a systematic review of security requirements engineering has been conducted by [3]. Tondel et al. [4] recommended that security requirements would describe what should be achieved rather than how it should be done. This relates to the emergence of a new perspective on security requirements based on goal-driven methodologies [5]. The security requirements elicitation started to incorporate requirements from information system risk assessments [6]. Vunk et al. [7] studied integration of GRC for the IT systems of an organization. Still, we could not found approaches that would integrate all four fields under a common semantic representation. This problem has also been identified by [8]. Most security modelling languages – e.g., UMLSec [9], SecureTropos [10] and its extensions [11] are offering *diagrammatic representations* that are easily interpretable by humans, while not being directly machine readable. This means that reasoning and integration possibilities are very limited.

Ontologies have been used in requirements engineering with several applications [12]: to explicitly model domain knowledge, to perform consistency analysis in requirements, to manage requirements knowledge and requirements changes. Dermeval et al. [12] conducted a review of the literature about the application of ontologies in requirements engineering and determined that in spite of the increased interest, still there is no clear understanding about their role in supporting different requirements engineering activities.

3   The Vision of GRC Security Requirements Engineering

The security requirements elicitation process can have multiple paths: (a) approaches rooted in software engineering (where elicitation of the security requirements will combine information gathered from business analysis and risk assessments) generating a semi-formal representation of the requirements; (b) approaches that are based on reports of risk assessments, guidelines and generate an informal representation of the requirements in natural language statements. We have divided security requirements based on their means of representation into three categories: *high level requirements* (human readable and abstract requirements), *intermediate level requirements* (employ some structured representation format) and *low level requirements* (provide formalized, explicit and concrete requirements for the assets of a particular organization). The overall proposed concept is depicted in Fig. 1.

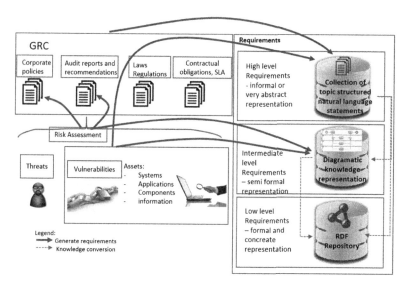

Fig. 1. Integrating different security requirements sources

Dividing the requirements based on their representation format reveals the dual methodology necessary to transform them into RDF knowledge graphs: (i) a manual approach to transform natural language requirements into graph-based formal representations and (ii) a semi-automated approach to convert diagrammatic representations into machine-readable descriptions. Later, we can categorize them into a taxonomy and separate them regarding the scope area or the problem space to be analysed, as proposed by [8].

As an automated method to construct RDF statements from natural language is still difficult to implement, we will manually include them. Also, we can reuse some of the already available knowledge expressed in other repositories or we can include some universally valid information in the form of OWL axioms (statements that are not found into requirements expressed in natural language but are relevant for reasoning and can be explicitly included in the knowledge repository to facilitate inferences). Figure 2 shows statements expressed in Turtle serialization format for RDF together with their graph representation and some sample queries. The inferred statements are written in italics and are represented with a dotted line.

Examples of RDF statements expressed in Turtle serialization format

:hasPassword rdfs:domain :User; rdfs:range :Password.
:UserX :hasPassword :UserXPasswordA, :UserXPasswordB, ...
=> *:UserX a :User. :UserXPasswordA a :Password. :UserXPasswordB a :Password.*

:WeakPassword owl:unionOf (:NoDigitsPassword :NoSymbolPassword :ShortPassword).
:NonCompliantUser owl:onProperty :hasPassword; owl:someValuesFrom :WeakPassword; rdfs:subClassOf :User.
:WeakPassword owl:onProperty :forAsset. owl:allValuesFrom :VulnerableAsset; rdfs:subClassOf :Password.
:VulnerableAsset rdfs:subClassOf :Asset.

:forAsset rdfs:domain :Password; rdfs:range :Asset.
:currentValue rdfs:domain :Password; rdfs:range xsd:string.
:UserXPasswordA :currentValue "abcdefgh"; :forAsset :AssetX.
=> *:AssetX a :Asset.*

:UserXPasswordA a :NoDigitsPassword.
=>*:UserXPasswordA a :WeakPassword.*
=> *:UserX a :NonCompliantUser. :AssetX a :VulnerableAsset.*

Natural Language

A user instance is linked to all its password instances; user and password instances are categorized based on their participation in hasPassword relations

A weak password is any password that has no digits or no symbols or is too short; a noncompliant user is one who has at least one weak password; a vulnerable asset is one for which a weak password was set

Password instances are linked to their instance values and the assets for which they facilitate access; passwords and assets are categorized based on their participation in forAsset relations

Because UserXPasswordA is a password without digits, it is inferred that it is a weak password, and from this it can be signalled that UserX is a noncompliant user and AssetX is vulnerable

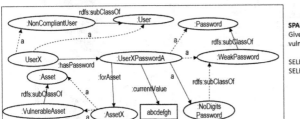

SPARQL Query:
Give me the noncompliant users and the vulnerable assets

SELECT ?x WHERE {?x a :NonCompliantUser}
SELECT ?x WHERE {?x a :VulnerableAsset}

Fig. 2. Expressing knowledge in RDF and sample query

Having the visual representation of a system in a diagrammatic form irrespective to the application domain, has proved to be valuable for both the analysis of the existing system and the development of new systems. The work at hand proposes an enhancement over the models used in describing security requirements expressed in diagrammatic forms by adding semantics.

The following example shows how diagrammatic knowledge can be extracted into a machine readable format, that is into RDF, by resorting to the knowledge conversion framework proposed by [13].

The main features of an internet banking system are reflected in an UML use case model in Fig. 3. The model shows the normal use cases for a customer together with two abuse cases for a hacker. The system should permit the authentication of the client. The example considers two types of authentication: One-Time Password, respectively using a Token. Moreover, the system should enable a series of financial operations like: Bank Transfer, Bill payment and Exchange money. Two of the possible abuse cases are Tampering and DDOS. The diagram is created with the BEE-UP tool [14, 15], which provides a modelling editor for UML with the possibility of exporting UML diagrams as RDF knowledge graphs. We can see the corresponding RDF statements that were generated: for each concept there is a unique identifier in the form of URI that was generated by concatenating a domain name (e.g. www.security.org/example#), the construct name (Use_Case_UML), the internal identifier and the name derived from the one given by the designer (Online_authentication). Its semantics is captured by assigning it to a certain type (predicate "a"), and for each relation it is explicitly stated its origin and destination using the properties "cv:from" and "cv:to".

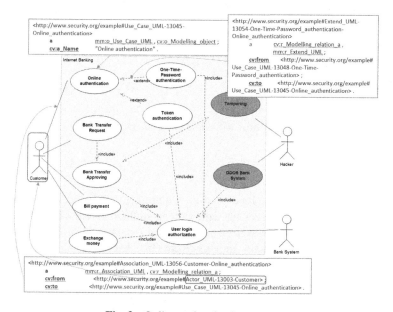

Fig. 3. Online authentication process

We could also employ models that describe the security requirements for certain business assets. Among the tools that could be used to visually describe the security requirements we selected Secure Tropos [16]. Figure 4 shows a simple example created with Secure Tropos that considers the previous described case regarding online authentication. To denote restrictions about actions or achieving goals like "Show account balance", it uses the concept of constraint "Only authorized users". Security constraints can be satisfied by security objectives like Authorization – used here (others can be Confidentiality, Integrity, Availability). For the chosen security objective, there can be more security mechanisms that can be used: Username and password, One time password and Secure Protocol. A Threat (stolen password) can impact the security mechanism and also can be linked to Attacks View where the attack's means exploiting a system's vulnerability are further described. The modelling tool for Secure Tropos was implemented on the ADOxx [17] metamodeling platform. A direct translation of the model content into RDF in not yet available for the ADOxx. But, we can employ the method described in [18], which allows any type of model created with ADOxx-based modelling tools to be converted to knowledge graphs. From this model, beside a DDOS threat (previously depicted), the knowledge base is enriched with another threat case: Stolen Password.

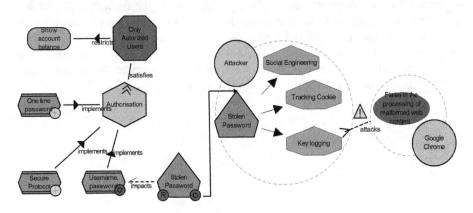

Fig. 4. Security modelling in secure Tropos [16]

4 Conclusions

Our paper advocates an approach for security requirements elicitation that is based on the integration of multiple sources for requirements, unified in terms of representation with the help of RDF. We showed how model based requirements engineering can be enhanced by security requirements gathered from GRC expressed in natural language, by relying on a requirements repository built with semantic technology. A requirements knowledge base will enable a shared, explicit and formal analysis of requirements, understanding, reusability and integration with other kind of requirements knowledge bases. Eliciting security requirements for software development would benefit from the analysis done for risk assessments as it could better incorporate corporate governance and regulatory compliance demands. A more comprehensible presentation of how security requirements are engendered from the integration of various sources could be achieved by an ontology of security requirements that would clarify the precise meaning of the concepts. The development of such an ontology is considered as the next step in our research.

Acknowledgments. The work presented in this paper is supported by the Romanian National Research Authority, UEFISCDI, grant PN-III-P2-2.1-PED-2016-1140.

References

1. Maalej, W., Thurimella, A.K. (eds.): Managing Requirements Knowledge. Springer, Heidelberg (2013). https://doi.org/10.1007/978-3-642-34419-0
2. W3C: RDF 1.1 concepts and abstract syntax (2014). https://www.w3.org/TR/rdf11-concepts/. Accessed 17 Sept 2017
3. Mellado, D., Blanco, C., Sánchez, L.E., Fernández-Medina, E.: A systematic review of security requirements engineering. Comput. Stand. Interfaces **32**(4), 153–165 (2010). https://doi.org/10.1016/j.csi.2010.01.006
4. Tondel, I.A., Jaatun, M.G., Meland, P.H.: Security requirements for the rest of us: a survey. IEEE Softw. **25**(1), 20–27 (2008). https://doi.org/10.1109/MS.2008.19
5. Dubois, E., Mouratidis, H.: Guest editorial: security requirements engineering: past, present and future. Requirements Eng. **15**(1), 1–5 (2010). https://doi.org/10.1007/s00766-009-0094-8. Special Issue on Security Requirements Engineering
6. Fabian, B., Gürses, S., Heisel, M., Santen, T., Schmidt, H.: A comparison of security requirements engineering methods. Requirements Eng. **15**(1), 7–40 (2010). https://doi.org/10.1007/s00766-009-0092-x
7. Vunk, M., Mayer, N., Matulevičius, R.: A framework for assessing organisational IT governance, risk and compliance. In: Mas, A., Mesquida, A., O'Connor, R.V., Rout, T., Dorling, A. (eds.) SPICE 2017. CCIS, vol. 770, pp. 337–350. Springer, Cham (2017). https://doi.org/10.1007/978-3-319-67383-7_25
8. Schmitt, C., Liggesmeyer, P.: A model for structuring and reusing security requirements sources and security requirements. In: REFSQ Workshops, pp. 34–43 (2015)
9. Jürjens, J.: UMLsec: extending UML for secure systems development. In: Jézéquel, J.-M., Hussmann, H., Cook, S. (eds.) UML 2002. LNCS, vol. 2460, pp. 412–425. Springer, Heidelberg (2002). https://doi.org/10.1007/3-540-45800-X_32
10. Mouratidis, H., Giorgini, P.: Secure Tropos: a security-oriented extension of the Tropos methodology. Int. J. Softw. Eng. Knowl. Eng. **17**(02), 285–309 (2007). https://doi.org/10.1142/S0218194007003240
11. Matulevicius, R., Mouratidis, H., Mayer, N., Dubois, E., Heymans, P.: Syntactic and semantic extensions to secure Tropos to support security risk management. J. Univ. Comput. Sci. **18**(6), 816–844 (2012). https://doi.org/10.3217/jucs-018-06-0816
12. Dermeval, D., Vilela, J., Bittencourt, I.I., Castro, J., Isotani, S., Brito, P., Silva, A.: Applications of ontologies in requirements engineering: a systematic review of the literature. Requirements Eng. **21**(4), 405–437 (2016)
13. Karagiannis, D., Buchmann, R.A., Walch, M.: How can diagrammatic conceptual modelling support knowledge management? In: Proceedings of the 25th European Conference on Information Systems (ECIS), AISel, pp. 1568–1583, Guimarães (2017)
14. OMiLAB: Bee-Up tool. http://austria.omilab.org/psm/content/bee-up/info. Accessed 17 Sept 2017
15. Karagiannis, D., Buchmann, R.A., Burzynski, P., Reimer, U., Walch, M.: Fundamental conceptual modeling languages in OMiLAB. Domain-Specific Conceptual Modeling, pp. 3–30. Springer, Cham (2016). https://doi.org/10.1007/978-3-319-39417-6_1
16. SecureTropos Modelling Toolkit. http://austria.omilab.org/psm/content/sectro/info. Accessed 17 Sept 2017
17. BOC-Group, ADOxx tool. http://www.adoxx.org/live/. Accessed 17 Sept 2017
18. Karagiannis, D., Buchmann, R.A.: Linked open models: extending linked open data with conceptual model information. Inf. Syst. **56**, 174–197 (2016). https://doi.org/10.1016/j.is.2015.10.001

On the Understanding of BDD Scenarios' Quality: Preliminary Practitioners' Opinions

Gabriel Oliveira$^{(\boxtimes)}$ and Sabrina Marczak$^{(\boxtimes)}$

Computer Science School, PUCRS, Porto Alegre, Brazil
gabriel.pimentel@acad.pucrs.br, sabrina.marczak@pucrs.br

Abstract. [**Context & Motivation**] In agile development, acceptance tests are written to express the details from the conversations between customers and developers. One of the formats to express those details is BDD (Behavior-Driven Development) scenarios, which use a ubiquitous language, one that business and technical people can understand, to build an executable specification that represents a system behavior. [**Question/Problem**] Problems caused by bad documentation are known to cause project failure and we believe those problems apply to documentation in the format of acceptance tests as well. Thus, in the long-term, we seek to understand what would be the definition of a good BDD scenario and the criteria to define it. [**Principal idea/results**] To achieve that, we previously identified known requirements' quality attributes that would be suitable to evaluate BDD scenarios' quality. Based on that list of attributes, we now aim to validate that list with practitioners, identify their interpretation of the listed attributes, and uncover general recommendations to write BDD scenarios. [**Contribution**] Preliminary results from our initial set of interviews revealed practitioners' interpretations for consistent, testable, valuable, understandable, and unambiguous attributes and some recommendations to write good BDD scenarios, such as the use of declarative form of writing.

Keywords: Documentation quality · Documentation evaluation
Behavior-Driven Development · Empirical study

1 Introduction

Most agile methodologies represent requirements using user stories. Cohn [1] states that a user story card is an expression of the essential elements of a requirement - it has just enough information to remind everyone what the story is about. A verbal conversation takes place to refine that customer requirement. When the conversation gets down to the details, the customer and the developer specify what needs to be done in the form of acceptance tests. Bjarnason et al. [2] clarify this agile approach of integrating requirements engineering with testing stating that the conceptual difficulty of specifying tests before implementation

© Springer International Publishing AG, part of Springer Nature 2018
E. Kamsties et al. (Eds.): REFSQ 2018, LNCS 10753, pp. 290–296, 2018.
https://doi.org/10.1007/978-3-319-77243-1_18

led to the conception of Behavior-Driven Development (BDD) – an approach that incorporates aspects of requirements analysis, requirements documentation and communication, and automated acceptance testing.

BDD is an agile practice which uses a language that business and technical people can understand to describe and model a system [3]. The model is formed by a series of textual scenarios, expressed in a format known as Gherkin, designed to be easily understandable for all stakeholders and easy to automate using dedicated tools. The scenarios related to a particular feature are grouped into a feature file, that contains a short description of the feature and the scenarios that compose it. Each scenario is made up of a number of steps, where each step starts with one of a small number of keywords. The natural order of a scenario is *Given... When... Then...*, where *Given* steps describe the preconditions for the scenario and prepares the test environment, *When* steps describe the action under test and *Then* steps describe the expected outcomes.

It is well known that bad requirements are one of many potential causes of a project failure [4] and that bad scenarios documentation can lead to misleading information that will negatively impact the tests ability to reflect the system coverage and the team confidence on them [5]. Therefore, we judge it necessary to better understand how we can prevent BDD textual scenarios to suffer from problems caused by bad documentation by proposing guidelines on how to write good BDD scenarios [6]. To the best of our knowledge, BDD scenarios practitioners can only rely on a few guidelines and examples of good and bad scenarios provided by Smart's experience reported on his book [3].

Requirements are evaluated by a set of quality attributes. The Business Analyst Body of Knowledge (BABOK) [7] brings nine attributes a traditional requirement must have in order to be a quality one, as follows: atomic, complete, consistent, concise, feasible, unambiguous, testable, prioritized, and understandable. Also, the INVEST (Independent-Negotiable-Valuable-Estimable-Scalable-Testable) framework described by Cohn [1] is often used to evaluate for user stories. Lucassen et al. [8] argue that qualitative metrics are not sufficient to evaluate user story quality employ highly. Due to that fact, they define additional criteria to evaluate user stories on their QUS Framework. We preferred to clarify the BABOK and INVEST attributes interpretation on BDD scenarios before using other frameworks such as QUS.

Our on-going research has the goal to uncover what a good BDD scenario is. The first steps of our on-going research on this topic were to acquire known quality attributes in a literature review and to use them on a pilot study with graduate students to understand how novice evaluators use those attributes to judge the quality of BDD scenarios [6]. Based on that list of filtered known quality attributes, we are now seeking to understand what are practitioner's interpretation of those attributes when reading BDD scenarios and their recommendations on how to write good BDD scenarios. To achieve that, we acquire practitioners personal criteria, tied to textual scenario's details, and ask them how each of their criteria map to our list of known quality criteria.

This paper aims to highlight our preliminary findings from the already conducted interviews, that partially fulfill our goal. Therefore, the following sections present our empirical study and results.

2   Research Method

Our long-term research has the goal to uncover the concept of quality in BDD textual scenarios, as summarized in Fig. 1, based on the opinion of practitioners involved in industry projects that have or had been using BDD scenarios. Their quality criteria, the rationale behind their opinions and their interpretation of known quality attributes will be used to consolidate our understanding of BDD scenarios quality. In order to aid us overcome the challenge of interpreting their different opinions, often phrased in different ways, we believe it would be best to guide the conversation with a set of known quality attributes and with real BDD scenario examples.

Therefore, our first step to achieve our goal, shown in Fig. 1 Step (A), was to discover the list of quality attributes used on agile requirements, which brought us the following attributes from the BABOK [7] and INVEST [1]: atomic, complete, consistent, concise, estimable, feasible, independent, negotiable, prioritized, small, testable, understandable, unambiguous, and valuable.

Our second step, shown in Fig. 1 Step (B), was to actively use those known quality attributes with BDD scenarios and better understand what would be the challenges on this process. To that end, we organized a pilot study with novice practitioners [6], that indicated that some attributes in the list may not be suited for BDD scenarios individually (like *complete* or *consistent*) or may be seen as a confusion source to the evaluator (like *atomic* or *independent*). Therefore, the refined list of attributes to use on BDD scenarios are: concise, estimable, feasible, negotiable, prioritized, small, testable, understandable, unambiguous, and valuable.

We are now using those attributes on the interviews with practitioners as shown in Fig. 1 Step (C). During the 8 already conducted interviews, notes were taken to summarize practitioners personal criteria, their recommendations on how to write good BDD scenarios, what they think about those known quality attributes, and how they interpret each one – mapping their personal criteria into those known quality attributes.

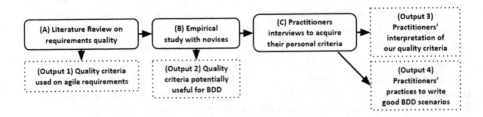

Fig. 1. Research design

Our subsequent analysis was guided by grounded theory procedures [9]. The interviewer conducted open-coding on the recording of each interview, just after they were finished, with the objective of identifying participants' rationale and summarize their personal quality criteria, recommendations on how to write good BDD scenarios, opinions about those known quality attributes, the interpretation of each one, and the mapping of their personal criteria into those known quality attributes. The interviewer codes were discussed with the second author and refined. That summary has been the input used to generate our preliminary results in Sect. 3.

Additionally, the pilot study have shown us the need to guide conversations with known examples to aid practitioners realize their own quality criteria. To avoid our own bias towards what would be a good or bad BDD scenario, we decided to not create the examples ourselves. Instead, we handed them real BDD scenarios, taken from an open source project that employ BDD scenarios to detail their applications' behavior. Our project of choice was Diaspora[1], a decentralized social network with a list of feature files mapping the behavior of the different application screens. To the best of our knowledge, Diaspora is Github's open source project with the most feature files available.

From the 8 interviewed practitioners (ranging from P1 to P8), some of them (P4, P8) are responsible for the scenarios' refinement, some (P1, P2, P5, P6, P7) are also responsible for the coding of automated checks, and one (P3) is responsible for the creation of scenarios and application code.

Some interviewees (P5, P6) had less than a year of experience using BDD scenarios, while others had up to 3 years (P1, P2, P4, P7) or up to 10 years (P8). Some of them (P1, P4) write scenarios after meetings with developers and product owners, but the majority (P2, P3, P5, P6, P7, P8) write scenarios themselves and validate later with the team. Regarding gender, we had a majority of male interviewees (P2, P3, P4, P6, P7, P8). Finally, almost half of the interviewees (P2, P6, P8) were self-employed consultants, while some (P4, P5) worked in big companies (more than 3000 employees). Others (P3, P7) worked in small companies (couple hundreds employees) and one (P1) worked at a startup (less than 50 employees).

One threat to the validity of our interview-based study is that the main analysis was done by a single researcher, the one doing the interviews. That researcher bias may have directed the observations in unexpected ways. To address this limitation, the generated codes were reviewed by the second author. Also, another threat to be acknowledged is the fact that the most of our 8 interviewees belonged to the same role. We plan to expand both the number of interviews and our role coverage in the following months.

3   Results

For the interviewed practitioners, each BDD scenario should: have a single goal – to validate a single business rule; achieve that goal using a few steps; and

---

[1] https://diasporafoundation.org/.

Table 1. Summary of quality attributes for BDD scenarios

Attribute	Interpretation	Bad patterns	Good patterns
Concise	"To the point", few and small steps	Unnecessary details Mixing steps order Data tables	Declarative writing Short statements Only essential details
Testable	Single and clear goal and clear outputs	Keyword repetition Mixing steps order	Declarative writing Title matching Then 1 or 2 Given Steps Only 1 Then step
Understandable	Consistent use of business terms	Technical jargon Mixing steps order Data tables	Declarative writing Data tables Fictional characters
Unambiguous	Single action, scenario cover one behavior	Mixing steps order Keyword repetition Weak words	Only 1 When step Fictional characters
Valuable	Why this scenario exist	Mixing steps order	Expressive feature and scenario description

express those steps in a domain specific language, natural to business people. Our summary from their collective quality attributes interpretations is represented in Table 1, along with their recommendations – separated into good writing patterns to be followed and bad writing patterns to avoid.

Estimable, feasible, negotiable and *prioritized* were judged not fit to evaluate scenarios by all practitioners, although P2 and P3 declared *prioritized* suited to conceptual features (often referred as an epic, a group of user stories). Also, all those attributes demand a domain knowledge of the product that cannot be found in a scenario's textual description.

For the majority of interviewees (P2, P4, P5, P6, P8) *valuable* attribute was on that category as well, as the value of a scenario depends on who one asks and the context it is being used. Others (P7, P3, P1) argued that scenarios titles and the feature description should indicate how valuable each scenario by stating "why" each should be there.

Ambiguity in scenarios was sometimes (P1, P7) referred to the understanding that two scenarios test the same thing - thus, making sure all scenarios test different aspects of the feature and that they together cover the entire feature would make scenarios *unambiguous*. For some others (P2, P3, P4, P8), using weak words such as "something good" mark a scenario as ambiguous. For P6, scenario's coverage of the feature should also be mapped into unambiguous attribute. Finally, P5 judged a scenario *unambiguous* if it was *understandable*.

Understandable attribute was often (P1, P2, P3, P5, P6, P7, P8) interpreted as the act of writing scenarios in a business language, using business terms in a consistent way between scenarios, leaving implementation details out of the textual descriptions. As scenarios are meant to be used by technical and business people, their description should not contain technical details such as HTTP response codes. For P4, an *understandable* scenario is a *small* one.

Testable attribute represent that the scenario intention should be clearly stated (P2, P4), only one behavior should be tested (P6) and the *Then* clause should be reflected on the title (P5). However, others (P3, P7, P8) do not see this attribute as applicable to BDD scenarios, as it's a product characteristic. P1 have stated that *testable* is the same as *understandable*

Differences between the *concise* and *small* attributes were not clear, thus we joined them in Table 1. Some interviewees (P2, P3, P7, P8) said they were supposed to be equal, others declared that *small* scenarios are those with few number of steps – between 4 or 5 steps (P1) – while *concise* is more related with "to the point" (P4, P5, P6) statements – short phrases, fitting into the reader screen, that does not carry unnecessary details.

Some bad patterns were identified by participants on Diaspora's feature files. The disregard for the natural order of steps (Given/When/Then) hurt *concise* (P2, P3, P6, P8), *testable* (P2, P7), *understandable* (P2, P4, P8), *unambiguous* (P3), and *valuable* (P3) attributes. The multiple use of a step affect each attribute differently: multiple *Given* steps show that the scenario may not be *testable* due to the many dependencies that need to be set up (P6, P7); multiple *When* steps makes a scenario purpose more *ambiguous* (P7); multiple *Then* steps gave the impression that more than one business rule was being tested at once, hurting the scenario' single goal represented by the *testable* (P3) attribute or even making it more *ambiguous* (P4). Also, representing input and output data into tables harm the scenario's *concise* (P1) and *understandable*(P7) attributes.

An identified good pattern was that writing scenarios into a declarative way would make it more *testable* (P1, P2, P5), *concise* (P8), and *understandable* (P7), preventing changes on the user interface to force a change on scenario's descriptions. Another good pattern is representing common user characteristics using fictional character names to represent a type of user or a role in the system. Referring to those fictional characters using third person speech would make the scenario more *understandable* (P3, P7) and *unambiguous* (P6).

Some interviewees had identified missing characteristics, such as complete (for P1, P4, and P6, scenarios on a feature file should cover all aspects under test), independent (for P6, scenarios should be read and executed in any order), atomic (for P6, scenarios should describe one thing), unique (for P3, it should group together *testable, understandable, unambiguous,* and *valuable*), modular (for P3, it should group together *small* and *testable*), and ubiquitous (per P8, having a consistent way of writing, is only partially covered by *understandable*). However, those characteristics occurrences were almost individual ones.

Finally, most of the interviewees (all, except P5) judged that having a list of attributes would be helpful, as those words make it easier to talk about scenarios quality, help express their informal criteria in a better way and work as a validation checklist to help a reviewer. P6 warned us that a long criteria is harmful - 5 or 6 should suffice. Another interviewee (P5) had not agreed that a list would be helpful - BDD technique require one to talk to people and make them agree upon some scenario descriptions, thus narrowing one's view to a limited set of quality attributes would cause more harm than good. Additionally, for P8, scenarios writing is a team exercise and represents a team consensus and there would be no need to have a perfect scenario – a good enough scenario, written by many hands, would reach the BDD technique goal of building a single system model shared by business and technical people.

4 Conclusion

This paper presents our preliminary findings to support our on-going research's goal, revealing practitioners' interpretations for and some recommendations to write good BDD scenarios taken from our initial set of interviews. We believe that our on-going effort will yield the necessary information to effective use those attributes on BDD scenarios. In addition to running more interviews to consolidate the presented results, another next step is to represent their interpretations in a series of questions, mixed with their recommendations, as an improved guide to identify how good a scenario is.

Acknowledgments. The results presented in this paper were achieved in cooperation with Hewlett Packard Brasil LTDA, using incentives of the Brazilian Informatics Law (Law no 8.2.48 of 1991).

References

1. Cohn, M.: User Stories Applied: For Agile Software Development. Addison Wesley Longman Publishing Co., Inc., Redwood City (2004)
2. Bjarnason, E., Unterkalmsteiner, M., Borg, M., Engström, E.: A multi-case study of agile requirements engineering and the use of test cases as requirements. Inf. Softw. Technol. **77**, 61–79 (2016)
3. Smart, J.: BDD in Action: Behavior-Driven Development for the Whole Software Lifecycle. Manning Publications, Shelter Island (2014)
4. Kamata, M.I., Tamai, T.: How does requirements quality relate to project success or failure? In: International Requirements Engineering Conference, New Delhi, India, pp. 69–78. IEEE (2007)
5. Neely, S., Stolt, S.: Continuous delivery? Easy! just change everything (well, maybe it is not that easy). In: Agile Conference, Nashville, USA, pp. 121–128 (2013)
6. Oliveira, G., Marczak, S.: On the empirical evaluation of BDD scenarios quality: preliminary findings of an empirical study. In: Workshop on Empirical Requirements Engineering in Conjunction with the International Requirements Engineering Conference, Lisbon, Portugal. IEEE (2017)
7. IIBA: A Guide to the Business Analysis Body of Knowledge (BABOK Guide), 3rd edn. International Institute of Business Analysis (2015)
8. Lucassen, G., Dalpiaz, F., Van Der Werf, J., Brinkkemper, S.: Forging high-quality user stories: towards a discipline for agile requirements. In: International Requirements Engineering Conference, Ottawa, Canada, pp. 126–135 (2015)
9. Corbin, J., Strauss, A.: Basics of Qualitative Research: Techniques and Procedures for Developing Grounded Theory. SAGE Publications, Inc., Thousand Oaks (2004)

Personal Recommendations in Requirements Engineering: The OpenReq Approach

Cristina Palomares[1(✉)], Xavier Franch[1], and Davide Fucci[2]

[1] Universitat Politècnica de Catalunya, Barcelona, Spain
cpalomares@essi.upc.edu
[2] University of Hamburg, Hamburg, Germany

Abstract. **[Context & motivation]** Requirements Engineering (RE) is considered as one of the most critical phases in software development but still many challenges remain open. **[Problem]** Recommender systems have been applied to solve open RE challenges like requirements and stakeholder discovery; however, the existent proposals focus on specific RE tasks and do not give a general coverage for the RE process. **[Principal ideas/results]** In this research preview, we present the OpenReq approach to the development of intelligent recommendation and decision technologies that support different phases of RE in software projects. For doing so, the OpenReq approach will be formed by different parts that will be integrated in a process. Specifically, we present in this paper the OpenReq part for personal recommendations for stakeholders, which takes place during requirements elicitation, specification and analysis stages. **[Contribution]** OpenReq aims to improve and speed up RE processes, especially in large and distributed systems, by incorporating intelligent recommendation and decision technologies.

Keywords: Recommender systems · Personal recommendations
Requirements Engineering

1 Introduction

Requirements Engineering (RE) is among the most critical phases for successful software development projects [1]. Because of its crucial role, RE should be performed at a high quality. However, some challenges still remain open in RE. Some of these challenges are related to software complexity: requirements and stakeholder discovery is difficult when thousands of requirements, stakeholders and feedback are involved in the process [2]. Moreover, reaching a decision is hard when stakeholders have too many alternatives available that need to be surveyed and evaluated [3]. Some other challenges are related to requirements quality, especially in terms of ambiguity, incompleteness, and inconsistency [4, 5].

One possible line of research to improve the overall quality of RE processes is the use of recommender systems (RSs) [6–8]. By using RSs, some of the tasks in these processes can be semi-automated and the amount of information shown to stakeholders can be reduced. RSs help stakeholders to find information and to make decisions in

E. Kamsties et al. (Eds.): REFSQ 2018, LNCS 10753, pp. 297–304, 2018.
https://doi.org/10.1007/978-3-319-77243-1_19

situations where they lack experience or cannot consider all the data at hand. These systems proactively tailor suggestions that meet the particular information needs and preferences of users. The current applications that use RSs in RE focus mostly on specific RE tasks and do not address the RE process as a whole.

We propose the OpenReq approach to overcome such limitation. The overall goal of the OpenReq project [9] is to develop intelligent recommendation and decision technologies that support different phases of RE, specifically elicitation, specification, analysis, management and negotiation. The project focuses on using artificial intelligence-based techniques that proactively support stakeholders—which act in the role of requirement analysts—, both as individuals and as groups, within the scope of RE. In a nutshell, OpenReq will support: (1) the automated identification of requirements from different knowledge sources (e.g., communities or natural language text documents); (2) the personal recommendation of requirements, requirements-related aspects (such as quality tips or requirement meta-data fields) and stakeholders; (3) the support of group decision making in release planning by providing a solution that fulfills all users preferences or indicates the conflicts that need to be solved to provide a solution; (4) the automated identification of (hidden) dependencies between requirements. This will help to overcome the challenges introduced in the first paragraph. OpenReq will provide an open source tool and a set of APIs that will integrate these innovative technologies applied to RE. Currently, a prototype version exists incorporating some functionalities related to points 3 and 4.

This paper focuses on the personal recommendations of OpenReq (i.e., point 2 above), and explains the initial considerations about these recommendations and the technological approaches that will be used to develop such system. By personal recommendations we mean recommendations that help stakeholders, as individuals, during the RE process. These have to be considered in contrast to the recommendations that are made to groups of stakeholders in RE, which take into account the preferences and needs of all the stakeholders in the group.

In the following, we will provide an overview of the existent recommender systems for RE (Sect. 2). Section 3 will present the OpenReq approach to personal recommendations. Finally, we conclude the paper in Sect. 4.

2 Recommender Systems in RE

Although recommender systems have been mostly applied to the Web (e.g., e-commerce, search engines), these systems have gained attention in different fields, one of them being Software Engineering (SE) [10]. Within SE, a prominent use case is related to bugs, from distinguishing bugs from enhancement requests [11] to assign bugs to the right developer [12]. Other recommender systems proposed for SE are used to predict defect priority [13], identify services that best suit the customer' needs [14], and give developers recommendations related to source code [15]. Accordingly, recommender systems are also used in RE to help in the early stages of SE [6, 16]. Table 1 highlights some of the representative approaches of recommender systems for RE according to the RE stage they tackle, the main focus of this stage, the types of requirements they handle, and if there is an implementation available.

Table 1. Recommender systems for RE

Id	RE stage	Focus	Req. types	Tool
[17]	E & S	Requirements discovery	Sustainability	Yes
[18]	E & S	Requirements discovery	Non-functional	NS
[19]	E & S	Requirements discovery	All	NS
[20]	E & S	Reqs. discovery, Stakeholders identification	All	NS
[21, 23, 25]	E & S, Management, Negotiation	Stakeholders identification, Feature requests clustering, Prioritization, Triage	All	Yes
[22]	E & S	Quality assurance	All	NS
[24]	Management	Feature requests changes	All	Yes
[26]	Negotiation	Group decision support	All	Yes
OpenReq	E & S, Analysis, Management, Negotiation	Requirements discovery, Stakeholders identification, Quality assurance, Group decision support	All	Yes

E & S = Elicitation and Specification, NA = Not Applicable, NS = Not Stated

Recommender systems have especially been applied to the elicitation and specification of requirements. Some approaches focus on recommending a specific type of requirement (e.g., sustainability requirements [17]) and, in a more general way, non-functional requirements [18], while others are applicable to any kind of requirement [19, 20]. Other approaches focus on identifying stakeholders that could help during the elicitation process [20, 21], whereas consistency assurance is undertaken in [22].

Other RE activities where recommender systems are used are requirements management and negotiation. Regarding requirements management, recommender systems complement feature requests systems in tasks such as grouping forums to avoid parallel discussions on the same topic [23] and managing changes [24]. In negotiation, recommendations are used to support prioritization and triaging of requirements [25], as well group decisions making [26].

As presented in Table 1, almost all the proposed approaches focus on a specific RE task but do not support the needs of stakeholders in different requirements-related tasks through the different RE stages. Only the approach composed by references [21, 23, 25] is dealing with more than one RE task, but it does not consider recommendations during the analysis of requirements. OpenReq aims to incorporate recommendation and decision technologies to support the stakeholders' needs in the different RE stages (including requirement analysis) by providing an open source tool and a set of APIs that will be available for requirements analysts.

3   OpenReq Approach to Personal Recommendations in RE

One of the goals of the OpenReq project is assisting stakeholders with personal recommendations during the RE process—specifically, during the requirements elicitation, specification and analysis stages. The types of recommendations for individual stakeholders are already stated in the OpenReq project. As shown in Fig. 1, they will be related to the screening and recommendation of relevant requirements, to the improvement of requirements quality, to the prediction of requirements properties, and to the identification of relevant stakeholders. These recommendations will be context-aware, meaning that the current context of the stakeholders will be taken into account when providing the recommendations.

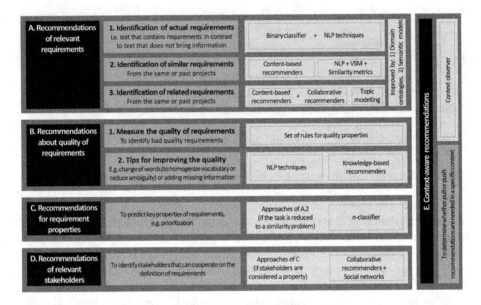

Fig. 1. Personal recommendations in OpenReq

A summary of how OpenReq will achieve each of the personal recommendation tasks is presented in Fig. 1. The approach for each one of the tasks has been selected by taking into account a state-of-the-art analysis done by the authors and the knowledge of the authors in the research field. A detailed explanation of the approach for each task follows.

A. Recommendations of relevant requirements. The recommendations in this group are related to the:

1. *Identification of actual requirements*, i.e., recognize text that contains "actual" requirements in contrast to the one that does not bring valuable information. From the technical perspective, a binary classifier [27] will be used in combination with some basic Natural Language Processing (NLP) techniques [28] (to identify actions expressing a need, such as "must", "have/has to", etc.).

2. *Identification of similar requirements*, in the same project or from previous ones. For this purpose, different approaches will be investigated. The first one is based on content-based recommenders [29] that, by taking into account the requirements and current project metadata, will be able to recommend requirements that have already

been defined in previous projects. The second approach is based on NLP techniques (such as tokenization, stemming, and stop words removal) that represent each requirement using a Vector Space Model (VSM) [30]—i.e., the text of a requirement is transformed into a vector in a multi-dimensional space, where each dimension of the space corresponds to a term. Therefore, we can compute the similarity among two requirements using measures like Cosine, Dice or Jaccard [30].

3. *Identification of related requirements.* Here, content-based (based on semantic and text-based similarities) and collaborative recommendation approaches (based on context information) will be used [29] taking into account the available requirement metadata. Another approach is based on Topic Modelling [31], which can be used to associate a label (i.e., a topic) to a requirement or a subset of them, and then cluster the requirements in groups of related ones. The clustering can be done at different level of granularities (e.g., a hierarchy of topics), achieving different levels of relatedness.

The previous identification task can be improved by the use of: (a) domain ontologies, especially to identify synonyms that are domain-specific, and (b) semantic models, to specify how requirements are semantically related among each other.

B. Recommendations for improving the quality of requirements. In this case, the recommendations are related to:

1. *Measure the quality of requirements* to identify bad quality requirements. A set of rules reflecting quality properties will be identified from existing related work (e.g., [32]) and adapted to OpenReq. These rules can then be used against requirements to check their quality, compounding them to calculate a quality score.

2. *Tips for improving the quality of requirements.* The goal of these tips will be related to reducing ambiguity and improving completeness and adherence to templates. Some examples of tips would be changing some wording (to standardize the vocabulary or reduce the ambiguity of requirements) or adding missing information. Simple word lists can be used to identify weak words (e.g., terms that are considered ambiguous, such as "sometimes" or "usually") and thesauruses can be used to identify alternative terms. For more complex tips, knowledge-based recommenders [29] can point out open tasks on the basis of previously defined rules. These tips can be, for instance *"additional meta-information needed", "text should be extended",* or *"additional users should review this requirement".*

C. Recommendations for requirement properties. The focus here is to predict key properties of requirements, such as priority. To this end, the recommender will match requirements at hand with those that have already been defined in past or ongoing projects. Therefore, this case is reduced to point A.2, where three approaches are possible: one based on content-based recommendations; one based on NLP techniques (VSM and similarity measures), and one based on topic modelling. Alternatively, the recommendation of each requirement property can be seen as a classification task with n classes where machine learning approaches can be used to assign a value to the specific property of a requirement. These three approaches can be combined with metrics to estimate specific properties (such as [33] for risk metrics). These metrics can either be adapted from existing work or created for OpenReq.

D. Recommendations of relevant stakeholders. Here, the recommendations aim at detecting stakeholders who can cooperate on the definition of requirements. The first approach is based on the assumption that stakeholders can be seen as one property of a requirement; therefore, the same approaches presented in item *C* could be used. The second approach is based on a collaborative filtering recommender that, by analysing existing social networks (e.g., typical roles of stakeholders in past software projects), individual strengths of stakeholders (e.g., topics the stakeholder has contributed to and related topics the stakeholder could be interested in), and personal availabilities, will create a user profile that will be used to match requirements to stakeholders. This collaborative filtering can be improved with weighting schemes [34] to requirements topics in which stakeholders have interest in or are experts on.

E. Context-aware recommendations. We aim to determine whether push recommendations (i.e., automatically delivered to stakeholders) or pull recommendations (i.e., stakeholders trigger them when needed) can be applied in a specific context. A *context observer* component, integrated in OpenReq, will take into account contextual information to take tailored decisions about when, what, and in which way recommendations will be delivered. For instance, we can use the history of a stakeholder's activities within OpenReq to know if she is too busy to receive notifications containing tips related to requirements quality.

4   Conclusions

In this paper, we provide an overview of the personal recommendations that will be supported by OpenReq to improve and speed-up the RE process, as well as the first considerations about how such recommendations can be implemented using a combination of state-of-the-art recommender systems and NLP techniques. Within the scope of OpenReq, we will focus on the development of a new RE solution for the systematic improvement of related development, maintenance, quality assurance, and decision processes, and also on integrating these improvements as extensions of existing RE tools. We expect to have a first prototype of the personal recommendations component by January 2018.

Acknowledgments. The work presented in this paper has been conducted within the scope of the Horizon 2020 project OpenReq, which is supported by the European Union under the Grant Nr. 732463.

References

1. Hofmann, H., Lehner, F.: Requirements engineering as a success factor in software projects. IEEE Softw. **18**(4), 58–66 (2001)

2. Johann, T., Maalej, W.: Democratic mass participation of users in requirements engineering? In: RE 2015 (2015)
3. Davis, A.M.: The art of requirements triage. J. Comput. **36**, 42–49 (2003)
4. Sikora, E., Tenbergen, B., Pohl, K.: Requirements engineering for embedded systems: an investigation of industry needs. In: Berry, D., Franch, X. (eds.) REFSQ 2011. LNCS, vol. 6606, pp. 151–165. Springer, Heidelberg (2011). https://doi.org/10.1007/978-3-642-19858-8_16
5. Méndez, D., Wagner, S.: Naming the pain in requirements engineering: a design for a global family of surveys and first results from Germany. In: IST (2015)
6. Mobasher, B., Cleland-Huang, J.: Recommender systems in requirements engineering. AI Mag. **32**(3), 81–89 (2011)
7. Hamza, M., Walker, R.J.: Recommending features and feature relationships from requirements documents for software product lines. In: RAISE 2015 (2015)
8. Elkamel, A., et al.: An UML class recommender system for software design. In: AICCSA 2016 (2016)
9. Intelligent Recommendation and Decision Technologies for Community-Driven Requirements Engineering (Horizon 2020 Project, https://www.openreq.org)
10. Robillard, M.P., Maalej, W., Walker, R.J., Zimmermann, T. (eds.): Recommendation Systems in Software Engineering. Springer, Heidelberg (2014). https://doi.org/10.1007/978-3-642-45135-5
11. Antoniol, G., Ayari, K., Di Penta, M., Khomh, F., Guéhéneuc, Y.-G.: Is it a bug or an enhancement?: a text-based approach to classify change requests. In: CASCON 2008 (2008)
12. Nagwani, N.K., Verma, S.: Predicting expert developers for newly reported bugs using frequent terms similarities of bug attributes. In: ICT-KE 2011 (2011)
13. Yu, L., Tsai, W.-T., Zhao, W., Wu, F.: Predicting defect priority based on neural networks. In: Cao, L., Zhong, J., Feng, Y. (eds.) ADMA 2010. LNCS (LNAI), vol. 6441, pp. 356–367. Springer, Heidelberg (2010). https://doi.org/10.1007/978-3-642-17313-4_35
14. Tu, Z., et al.: Gig services recommendation method for fuzzy requirement description. In: ICWS 2017 (2017)
15. Mens, K., Lozano, A.: Source code-based recommendation systems. In: Robillard, M.P., Maalej, W., Walker, R.J., Zimmermann, T. (eds.) Recommendation Systems in Software Engineering. LNCS (LNAI), pp. 93–130. Springer, Heidelberg (2014). https://doi.org/10.1007/978-3-642-45135-5_5
16. Felfernig, A., et al.: An overview of recommender systems in requirements engineering. In: Maalej, W., Thurimella, A.K. (eds.) Managing Requirements Knowledge, pp. 315–332. Springer, Heidelberg (2013). https://doi.org/10.1007/978-3-642-34419-0_14
17. Roher, K., Richardson, D.: A proposed recommender system for eliciting software sustainability requirements. In: USER 2013 (2013)
18. Danylenko, A., Löwe, W.: Context-aware recommender systems for non-functional requirements. In: RSSE 2012 (2012)
19. Kumar, M., Ajmeri, N., Ghaisas, S.: Towards knowledge assisted agile requirements evolution. In: RSSE 2010 (2010)
20. Finkelstein, A., et al.: StakeRare: using social networks and collaborative filtering for large-scale requirements elicitation. IEEE Trans. Softw. Eng. **38**, 707–735 (2012)
21. Castro-Herrera, C., Cleland-Huang, J.: Utilizing recommender systems to support software requirements elicitation. In: RSSE 2010 (2010)
22. Felfernig, A., Friedrich, G., Schubert, M., Mandl, M., Mairitsch, M., Teppan, E.: Plausible repairs for inconsistent requirements. In: IJCAI 2009 (2009)
23. Cleland-Huang, J., Dumitru, H., Duan, C., Castro-Herrera, C.: Automated support for managing feature requests in open forums. Commun. ACM **52**, 68–74 (2009)

24. Garcia, J.E., Paiva, A.C.R.: REQAnalytics: a recommender system for requirements maintenance. Int. J. Softw. Eng. Appl. **10**, 129–140 (2016)
25. Duan, C., Laurent, P., Cleland-Huang, J., Kwiatkowski, C.: Towards automated requirements prioritization and triage. Requirements Eng. **14**, 73–89 (2009)
26. Felfernig, A., Zehentner, C., Ninaus, G., Grabner, H., Maalej, W., Pagano, D., Weninger, L., Reinfrank, F.: Group decision support for requirements negotiation. In: Ardissono, L., Kuflik, T. (eds.) UMAP 2011. LNCS, vol. 7138, pp. 105–116. Springer, Heidelberg (2012). https://doi.org/10.1007/978-3-642-28509-7_11
27. Winkler, J., Vogelsang, A.: Automatic classification of requirements based on convolutional neural networks. In: REW 2016 (2016)
28. Manning, C.D., Surdeanu, M., Bauer, J., Finkel, J., Bethard, S.J., McClosky, D.: The Stanford CoreNLP natural language processing toolkit. In: Association for Computational Linguistics (ACL) System Demonstrations, pp. 55–60 (2014)
29. Jannach, D., Zanker, M., Felfernig, A., Friedrich, G.: Recommender Systems: An Introduction. Cambridge University Press, New York (2010)
30. Falessi, D., Cantone, G., Canfora, G.: A comprehensive characterization of NLP techniques for identifying equivalent requirements. In: ESEM 2010 (2010)
31. Chien, J.T.: Hierarchical Theme and Topic Modeling. IEEE Trans. Neural Networks Learn. Syst. **27**, 565–578 (2016)
32. Bucchiarone, A., Gnesi, S., Lami, G., Trentanni, G., Fantechi, A.: QuARS express - a tool demonstration. In: ASE 2008 (2008)
33. Rempel, P., Mäder, P.: Estimating the implementation risk of requirements in agile software development projects with traceability metrics. In: Fricker, S.A., Schneider, K. (eds.) REFSQ 2015. LNCS, vol. 9013, pp. 81–97. Springer, Cham (2015). https://doi.org/10.1007/978-3-319-16101-3_6
34. Said, A., Jain, B.J., Albayrak, S.: Analyzing weighting schemes in collaborative filtering: cold start, post cold start and power users. In: SAC 2012 (2012)

Big Data

State of Requirements Engineering Research in the Context of Big Data Applications

Darlan Arruda$^{(\boxtimes)}$ and Nazim H. Madhavji

Department of Computer Science,
University of Western Ontario, London, Canada
darruda3@uwo.ca, madhavji@gmail.com

Abstract. **[Context and Motivation]** Big Data applications, like traditional applications, serve end-user needs except that underlying the software system is Big Data which the system operates upon. In comparison to traditional software development where the development processes are usually well-established, the processes for the development of applications involving Big Data are not clear just yet from the scientific literature – given the nature of computing involved and data characteristics such as volume, variety, veracity, and velocity. **[Question/Problem]** This, uncertain situation, has given rise to new questions, that is: "What are the early signs of the ways Big Data applications is treated in requirements engineering (RE)? What new directions in RE research are envisaged to promulgate further research?" **[Principal ideas/Results]** This paper presents the state of the art of requirements engineering (RE) research involving Big Data applications. Initially, 311 papers were identified from numerous sources from which, after methodical selection, 14 papers were deemed relevant for use in this study. Our investigation centres around: (i) phases of the RE process, (ii) type of requirements, (iii) application domains, (iv) RE research challenges, and (v) solution proposals targeted by RE research. Our key observation is that there isn't a significant amount of research addressing: (a) aspects of RE in the context of Big Data applications; and (b) RE methods, tools and processes for the development of Big Data applications. Thus, this situation provides opportunities for research in this new area of RE. **[Contribution]** This paper presents the state-of-the-art of RE research in the context of Big Data applications, an analysis of the current research, and directions for further research.

Keywords: Big data applications · Requirements engineering
Systematic literature review · Research directions

1 Introduction

Big Data is a term applied to data sets whose size or type is beyond the ability of traditional relational databases to capture, manage, and process the data [1]. Big Data differs from traditional data because of its specific characteristics such as volume, velocity, variety, veracity and value - the well-known "V" characteristics. Volume means, with the generation and collection of masses of data, data scale becomes increasingly big [2]. Velocity means the speed of growth and transfer of data are really

© Springer International Publishing AG, part of Springer Nature 2018
E. Kamsties et al. (Eds.): REFSQ 2018, LNCS 10753, pp. 307–323, 2018.
https://doi.org/10.1007/978-3-319-77243-1_20

fast. Variety means that Big Data has many different forms of data. Veracity means the uncertainty of data [2]. Value refers to the opportunities and insights extracted from the analysis of Big Data that translate into business advantage [1].

Since its "boom", Big Data has caught the attention of industry and companies interested in its high potential, and many government agencies have announced plans to accelerate Big Data research and applications [3]. However, *Big Data system development* – also known as Big Data software engineering - has a relatively short history, starting a trend in 2011 when the term was presented by IBM [4]. Big Data system development refers to the development of systems that incorporate Big Data in serving the end-users, for example, through services with which users interact [5].

Notwithstanding, the development of Big Data applications faces more and greater risks than traditional small-data system development [4]. Not only because of its short history but also because of (i) the characteristics of Big Data (e.g., volume, velocity, variety, veracity, value) [5], (ii) the Rapid technology changes, (iii) the difficulty of selecting Big Data technologies, (iv) the complex integration of new and old systems, (v) the difficulty in matching available frameworks and technologies (e.g., Cassandra) with systems requirements [6], to name a few.

In exploring the scientific literature on Big Data Software Engineering, it is difficult to fail to notice that not much attention has been given to RE in the development of Big Data applications. This situation motivated us to formally conduct a systematic literature review (SLR) [7] of RE research in the context of Big Data applications and synthesise any insight for further research in this domain.

Following deliberations, we arrived at the following core points to be used in this investigation: (i) types of requirements and (ii) activities of the RE process addressed in Big Data RE research; (iii) RE research challenges identified in the literature; (iv) application domains covered; and (v) any advances made in the area (e.g., RE solutions proposed in the development of Big Data applications). The types of requirements would give an insight into where the emphasis lies (e.g., functionality, quality, data, etc.). The activities would give an idea of the extent of coverage of the RE process. The RE challenges highlight the documented dark alleys of this emerging field. The application domains give an insight into practical areas of foray with Big Data and RE. Finally, advances describe the knowledge and technology gains made to date by the research community.

While one may find complementary points to add to this core, in this investigation we felt that the listed set of core points cover a significant ground in the RE field. The implications of the results of this study are anticipated for research as the gained knowledge will be a step forward to a better understanding of the actual state of the RE research involving Big Data applications.

This rest of the paper is organised as follows: Sect. 2 discusses the research methodology. Section 3 presents the descriptive data. The results are discussed in Sect. 4. Section 5 gives some recommendations for further research. Section 6 discuss threats to validity of this study. Finally, Sect. 7 concludes this paper.

2   Research Methodology

In this section, we present the methodological procedures followed in this study. We adapted and followed the steps for conducting a SLR proposed in [7]. The following are described: (i) research questions, (ii) search strategy, (iii) selection criteria, (iv) data extraction and, (v) the selection process.

2.1   Research Questions

We ask the following main research question: **What are the early signs of the ways Big Data applications is treated in Requirements Engineering (RE)?** As described in the Introduction section, informal observations and exploration of the literature made it compelling to investigate further the state of RE research in this domain. We thus decomposed the overall question into the following constituent questions:

- Q1. What are the activities in the RE process, types of requirements and application domains targeted by the identified RE research involving the development Big Data applications?
- Q2. What are the RE research challenges in the context of Big Data applications?
- Q3. What solutions have been proposed in the domain of RE and Big Data applications?

In Sect. 4, the paper explores the answers to each of these questions.

2.2   Search Strategy

This study focused mainly on searches in electronic databases such as ACM Digital Library, Science Direct, IEEE Xplore and Scopus as they index a considerable amount of papers published in conferences, journals and workshops proceedings - including the Big Data and RE conferences (e.g., IEEE Big Data, Big Data Congress, RE conference, etc.).

In order to use the electronic databases in a way they would return relevant results we defined and used the search terms (e.g., big data, requirements engineering, elicitation, analysis, specification, validation, negotiation, prioritization, management) related to the research topic of this paper. We performed various searches using different combinations of search terms before deciding upon a final version of the search string. We observed that, when using the search string without the word "*requirements*" preceding each term, the number of irrelevant papers were greater. For example, many papers related to Big Data but not to Big Data software and requirements engineering, used terms such as analysis, validation and negotiation to convey different ideas (e.g., data analysis, Big Data negotiation, etc.) from the focus of this study - the Requirements Engineering aspect of it.

To ensure that the literature review adheres to the topic of this study – Requirements Engineering for Big Data Applications, we decided to add the term "*requirements*" preceding each search term in our search string. The final version of the search string used for this review is:

("Big Data" AND ("Requirements Engineering" OR "Requirements Elicitation" OR "Requirements Specification" OR "Requirements Analysis" OR "Requirements Validation" OR "Requirements Negotiation" OR "Requirements Prioritization" OR "Requirements Management"))

Moreover, while performing the search for relevant papers using the databases commented above, we kept (manually) searching for scientific works in specific Big Data and Software Engineering conferences proceedings (such as International Conference on Software Engineering, RE International conference) and journals (such as IEEE Transactions on Software Engineering, Empirical Software Engineering, Journal of Systems and Software, IEEE Transactions on Big Data, Journal of Big Data, Big Data Research, The Services Transactions on Big Data and the Requirements Engineering Journal). The manual search consisted of accessing specific journals and conferences proceedings so as to search for relevant results. If the venue (journal or conference) website provides a search engine, we then searched for specific terms such as "Big Data" in order to identify possible results. Otherwise, we checked the Table of Contents and abstracts with the aim to identify relevant papers.

2.3 Selection Criteria

For this review, we set the following selection criteria: (i) studies must be in paper/ article/chapter formats, (ii) must be written in English, and, (iii) must address any aspect of RE in the context of Big Data software applications.

2.4 Selection Process

The selection process - adapted from [7] - used in this study is composed of three steps. In step 1, the results were filtered by their title and abstract. The papers considered relevant for this study were selected, and in step 2 analysed by reading their introduction and conclusion sections. The papers deemed pertinent to the context of this research were potentially chosen for the next step (step 3), which consisted of reading the entire paper. Then, a final list of selected papers was created, and all the relevant information was logged into the appropriate data extraction documents.

2.5 Data Extraction

In order to better organise the selected papers included into the SLR, a document composed of the following attributes was used: study id, title, authors, source, year of publication, full reference and the designated questions they address as well as important statements to help to answer the defined questions. Also, we created and used a spreadsheet to log important information (such as types of requirements, type of research, contributions, venues of publication, etc.) that helped in the descriptive analysis.

3   Descriptive Data and Analysis

In this section, we present and discuss the descriptive results of this study.

3.1   Descriptive Data

During the automatic search, a total of 311 papers were identified. However, it is important to note that, as also pointed out by Kitchenham and Charters [7], initial SLR searches tend to result in many irrelevant papers. For example, in this study, numerous papers appeared in the search results because these papers contained terms such as "Requirements Engineering" or "Big Data" but they did not actually address any aspect of RE in the context of Big Data applications. After applying the selection criteria and reading the title and abstract (in step 1 – see Sect. 2.4 for the three-step process), only 24 papers were considered relevant. In step 2, the resultant papers were examined by reading their introduction and conclusion; thirteen papers were deemed relevant. Note that in these steps, if the cumulative information analysed till then in a paper was not decisive as for relevance, we then scanned internal sections of the paper to determine whether or not it addressed the topic of this SLR. Thus, we anticipate minimal false negative cases in the selection process.

Additionally, a total of five papers were selected during the manual search based on the selection criteria as well. These papers were carried out to the final step in the selection process (step 3) which consists of reading the entire paper. In the end of the selection process, 14 papers [4, 5, 9–20] were considered relevant to be used in our investigation. Figure 1 presents the selection process and the number of results for each step.

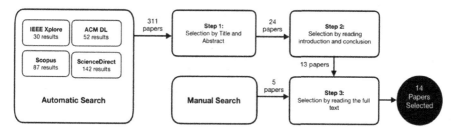

Fig. 1. Distribution of papers identified and selected organised by the phases in the selection process.

Figure 2 shows the number of selected papers by venue of publication. Table 1 shows their distribution by year. Most of the selected papers were published in 2015. Together, 2014 and 2016 represent six of the published papers. The years of 2013 and 2017, are represented by one and two papers, respectively. Regarding the venue of publication, the majority of the papers were published in workshops and conferences proceedings (four papers in each venue). Two studies were published as chapters in books and two other papers were published in journals. One study was published in a

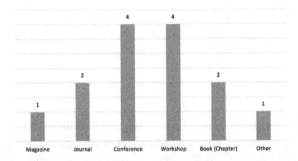

Fig. 2. Distribution of papers by venue of publication.

Table 1. Papers by year

2013	2014
1 ($\sim$ 7%)	3 ($\sim$ 21%)
2015	**2016**
5 ($\sim$ 37%)	3 ($\sim$ 21%)
2017	
2 ($\sim$ 14%)	

magazine (RE magazine by the International Requirements Engineering Board - IREB) and another study was published online in a report format by the NIST Big Data Public Working Group. The complete list of the venues of publication is presented in Table 2.

The papers selected were also classified with respect the type of research they present. For such classification, we used the classification for RE research proposed by Wieringa *et al.* [8] which consists of the following classes of papers:

1. *Evaluation Research:* refers to the investigation of a RE problem or the implementation of a RE technique in practice. In this case, the novelty of the technique is not a criterion by which the paper should be evaluated.
2. *Proposal of Solution:* refers to the proposal of solution technique that argues for its relevance, but without being validated.
3. *Validation Research:* in this type of research the properties of a solution that has not been implemented in practice is investigated and analysed.
4. *Philosophical Papers:* presents a new way of looking at existing things, a new conceptual framework, etc.
5. *Opinion papers:* These types of papers present the author's opinions regarding an existing problem/issue.
6. *Personal Experience Papers:* in these types of research, the emphasis is on what and may concern to multiple projects. It also must be the author's personal experience. It is also important that the paper provides the reader with a set of lessons learnt by the authors from their experience.

Table 2. Publication venue and number of papers from each venue

Publication venue	Issue, volume or year	Paper count
Conferences		
IEEE International Congress on Big Data	2013	1
International Conference on Data and Software Engineering	2014	1
International Conference on Cloud Computing, Data Science & Engineering	2017	1
IEEE International Conference on Big Data	2017	1
Workshops		
IEEE/ACM International Workshop on Big Data Software Engineering	2015	2
	2016	1
International Workshop on Quality-Aware DevOps	2016	1
Journals		
International Journal of Ambient Systems and Applications	Vol. 2, No. 2/2014	1
IEEE Intelligent Systems	Vol. 30/2015	1
Books and Magazine		
Studies in Big Data – Springer	Vol. 05/2014	1
New Trends in Databases and Information Systems - Springer	Vol. 539/2015	1
Requirements Engineering Magazine	Issue 2016-01	1
Online Publication		
NIST Special Publication	Vol. 3/2015	1
Total		**14**

The overall distribution of papers by type of research and their contribution is presented in Table 3. Also, we analysed the selected papers with respect to their contribution and research type organised by the RE activities they addressed (Fig. 3).

Table 3. Overall distribution of papers by type of research and contribution

Type of research	Paper citation	Paper count	Type of contribution	Paper citation	Paper count
Evaluation research	[4, 11, 19]	3	Method/Approach	[4, 12, 13]	3
Proposal solution	[13–16, 18, 20]	6	Model	[19, 20]	2
Validation research	[10, 12]	2	Tool	[10, 15]	2
Philosophical papers	[5, 9, 17]	3	Framework/Architecture	[11, 14, 16, 18]	4
Opinion papers	–	0	Processes and Methodologies	–	0
Experience papers	–	0	State-of-the-art	[5, 9, 17]	3

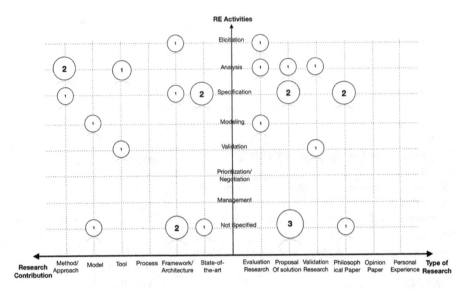

Fig. 3. Papers by contribution and type of research organised according to the RE activities they address.

3.2 Discussion

One observation from the results of this study is that, surprisingly, the RE conferences such as the RE Conference and the International Working conference on Requirements Engineering: Foundations for Software Quality (REFSQ) and the Requirements Engineering Journal haven't yet published papers on aspects of RE in context of the development of Big Data applications.

For instance, in conducting manual searches for Big Data related publications in the Requirements Engineering Journal, we found only one result matching with the term "Big Data". However, the resultant paper does not deal with RE for Big Data applications; it simply used the term "Big Data" within the paper. In regard to the searches of the RE and REFSQ conferences, we analysed proceedings (title and abstract) from 2009 to 2017, since Big Data was not widely known in previous years.

Regarding the REFSQ proceedings, we did not find any papers discussing Big Data.

For the RE Conference proceedings, we found one talk abstract from 2016, as well as a paper from 2017. However, the paper does not address any aspect of RE for the development of Big Data applications. Instead, as is the case with the RE Journal resultant paper, it used the term "Big Data" within the text. Thus, no papers were selected from these sources to be used in this SLR. It is important to note that (repeated from Sect. 3.1 for convenience), if the information analysed (title and abstract) in a paper was not decisive as for relevance, we then scanned internal sections of the paper to determine whether it should be included in this study.

Next section presents the results and discussion of this investigation.

4   Results and Discussion

Research aimed at addressing RE in the context of Big Data applications is currently at an early stage. In this section, we discuss the results of this study with the aim to provide the state of the art of RE research in the context of Big Data applications. To answer to the main question of this paper, we have taken a close look at the selected papers with respect to the secondary research questions represented by the following core points (repeated from Sect. 2.1 for convenience): (i) types of requirements, activities in the RE process and application domains they address, (ii) RE research challenges, and (iii) RE solutions that have been proposed in the context of Big Data applications. The subsections that follow discuss these core points.

4.1   (Q1). What Are the Activities in the RE Process, Types of Requirements and Application Domains Targeted by the Identified RE Research Involving the Development Big Data Applications?

As presented in Table 4, with regards to the activities in the RE process they discuss, most of the papers selected discussed either the analysis (three papers) or specification (four papers) phases. Elicitation, modelling and validation were discussed by only one study each. No papers were found discussing requirements negotiation, prioritization and management in the context of Big Data applications. Also, our analysis shows that the RE research involving Big Data applications fell into one of the domains listed in Table 4. Unfortunately, none of the selected papers actually discusses the applicability or details on how to deal with Big Data requirements for a specific domain. However, in [16], use case descriptions were collected from various contributors within different application domains and used to derive a set of generic requirements for Big Data applications. Overall, the selected papers discussed - to some extent - functional, quality and data requirements.

Table 4. Types of requirements, activities of the RE process and application domains targeted by available RE and Big Data Research

RE activities	Paper citation	Type of requirements	Paper citation	Application domains
Elicitation	[11]	Functional requirements	[5, 11, 17, 19, 20]	Healthcare
				Biomedical research
Analysis	[4, 12, 15]	Quality requirements	[5, 10–13, 15, 17–20]	Government
				Marketing
Specification	[5, 13, 14, 17]	Data requirements	[14, 16]	IT/Telecom
				Astronomy and
Modelling	[19]	Architecturally significant requirements	[4]	Physics
				Earth
Validation	[10]	Not specified	[9]	Environmental and Polar Science
Not specified	[9, 16, 18, 20]	**Note:** One paper could have discussed one or more types of requirements. Therefore, the sum of the papers in this table can be greater than the total number of papers selected.		Defense
				Commercial
				Social Media

Functional Requirements. As well-known in the literature, functional requirements (FR) describe what the system should do, how the system should react to particular inputs, and how the system should behave in particular situations [21]. That wouldn't be different in the RE research involving Big Data software applications. From our analysis, the selected papers discussed the importance of addressing functional requirements for Big Data software applications. However, very few studies (two papers) actually provided examples of functional requirements. Also, these examples relate to generic functional requirements any Big Data application should address. For instance, extracted from [16, 19]: (i) database capacity; (ii) data properties (e.g., system should check the completeness and accuracy of the data); (iii) backup routines; (iv) domain specific FRs (not discussed in detail); (v) data transformation (e.g., Needs to support batch and real-time analytic processing), (vi) data source (e.g., Needs to support slow, bursty, and high-throughput data transmission between data sources and computing clusters).

Quality Requirements. Basically, the selected papers discuss the following quality attributes a Big Data system must address: privacy and security [15, 16, 19] performance [12, 19]; availability [4, 13]; scalability, consistency, elasticity and low latency [4]. While some papers (10 papers) discuss the quality attributes for Big Data applications and others propose solutions to deal with quality requirements in the development of Big Data applications – only one study actually gave examples (e.g., "Req 1: System needs to protect and preserve security and privacy of sensitive data) of security and privacy requirements [16].

Data Requirements. Having the right specification of data requirements is important for defining some of the systems functional requirements (e.g., systems needs to support diversified output file formats for visualization, rendering, and reporting; systems needs to support legacy, large, and advanced distributed data storage [16], etc.). In our investigation, only two papers [9, 14] discussed the necessity of selecting the right type of data as well as the data properties that must be taken into consideration when eliciting and specifying data requirements (e.g., data size, data types, file formats, rate of growth, at rest or in motion). However, none of them actually provided concrete examples of what a data requirement looks like. In [9], two different templates that can be used to support the definition of data requirements are presented: (a) template for sourcing the data and, (b) a template to match the business problems with the data. In [14], a requirements specification framework for Big Data collection is proposed (Sect. 4.3).

In the next section, we present and discuss some of the RE research challenges identified in this review.

4.2 (Q2). What Are the RE Research Challenges in the Context of Big Data Applications?

Four papers were the source of the "research challenges" in the context of Big Data applications [5, 13, 17, 19]. Basically, the challenges identified in this review are related to the necessity to understand and take the Big Data specific characteristics (such as volume, velocity, variety, etc.) into consideration while dealing with the systems requirements. Examples of the challenges are presented below.

1. **Big Data Characteristics:** The need to properly address the Big Data V-characteristics in the *definition, analysis and specification* of both functional and quality requirements [5, 13, 19]. It is essential that while eliciting the scenarios of desirable system responses, the characteristics of Big Data are represented in requirements notations so that solution design can be created to meet the specifications [5]. Notwithstanding, it is also important that these data characteristics are defined along with the systems quality attributes (in the specification of quality requirements) as it is believed to be complementary set of properties. For example [13]: "the system shall use a stream-processing engine with a latency of 0.5 – 2.0 s (e.g., Storm, S4, Spark or Samza) to process data in real-time between global earthquake sensors and the data centre". This requirement addresses both velocity (*data characteristic*) and performance (*quality attribute*); two commonly discussed issues in the context of Big Data systems.
2. **Writing verifiable requirements:** The need to *specify* verifiable requirements. In [17], it is explained that Big Data Analytics applications faces concept drift, which means that statistical properties of the target variable, which the model is trying to predict, change over time in unforeseen ways, thus causing predictions to become less accurate as time passes. Therefore, one of RE problems for Big Data Analytics applications is to be able to define and specify verifiable (testable) requirements [17].

Intuitively, it appears that there are more challenges and issues related to the RE activities involving the development of Big Data applications than what might appear from our review. Further empirical studies are clearly needed to uncover more facts.

4.3 (Q3). What Solutions Have Been Proposed in the Domain of RE and Big Data Applications?

The technical solutions identified in our investigation are presented in Table 5 and discussed below. These solutions are organised into three groups: (a) Approaches, Methods and Models, (b) Architectures and Frameworks and, (c) tools.

With reference to Table 5, we present an overview of the solutions identified in this study.

Methods, Models, and Approaches. In [4], a Big Data System design method is proposed - an attempt to systematically combine architecture design with data modelling approaches in development of Big Data Systems. Even though this method is not specific for RE but for system design, it incorporates a RE step for requirements analysis which is composed of the following activities: (i) identification of business goals, (ii) identification of constraints, concerns and drivers, (iii) identification of quality attribute scenarios and, (iv) definition of Big Data architecture scenarios based on the quality attributes scenarios identified. Also, this method suggested a Big Data template for logging data information (e.g., data source quality, data variety, data volume, velocity, read/write frequency, time to live, queries, etc.). The resultant requirements should be used to drive the design of Big Data systems.

In [12], an approach composed of two processes for dealing with both privacy and performance requirements for IoT and Big Data projects in scrum is proposed. In the security side, the problems with dealing with security requirements is that they are

Table 5. Overview of the solutions proposed in RE and Big Data Research

Solutions proposed	Author (s)
Approaches, Methods and Models	
Big Data System Design method	Chen *et al.* [4]
Approach for handling non-functional requirements for Big Data projects in scrum	Sachdeva and Chung [12]
Approach for analysing and specifying Quality Requirements	Noorwali *et al.* [13]
RE Generic model based on I* and KAOS	Eridaputra *et al.* [19]
RE Artefact Model in the Context of Big Data Software Projects	Arruda and Madhavji [20]
Architectures and Frameworks	
Descriptive Architecture for Big Data Requirements Elicitation	Lau *et al.* [11]
Requirements Specification framework for Big Data Collection	Al-Najran and Dahanayake [14]
NIST Interoperability Framework*	NIST [16]
Framework with security constraints	Youssef [18]
Tools	
Verification Tool	Bersanini *et al.* [10]
UML extension for privacy requirements analysis	Jultla *et al.* [15]

commonly treated as soft goals and thereby there's no clear way of defining if they are met or not. In the performance side, the authors argue that the problem of handling performance requirements for IoT and Big Data applications is that it is treated as a qualitative measure rather than a quantitative one. To solve both problems, the use clear user stories acceptance criteria in scrum is proposed. The authors argue that this approach helped to introduce the quality requirements such as security and performance in early stage of the software development process and help to define clear parameters for the measurement of both security and performance requirements.

In [13] an approach for analysing and specifying quality requirements for Big Data Applications is proposed. The main idea is to intersect a Big Data characteristic with a quality attribute (e.g., variety × security). This approach incorporates three elements - Big Data characteristic, quality attributes, and quality requirement description and helps to ensure that the Big Data characteristics are addressed in the specification of quality requirements.

A Requirements specification generic model using i* framework and KAOS approach was described in [19]. In this work, the authors tried to elicit generic requirements for Big Data based on the data characteristics (e.g., Volume demands improved storage capacity; Velocity demands Database tools with high performance, etc.). Then, the elicited requirements were modelled using i* framework and the KAOS approach. The models resulting from i* and KAOS tools can then be used as references in the modelling of both functional and quality requirements for Big Data applications. These models were applied to a case study conducted at the Indonesian's government agency for development planning of West Java and, according to the authors, the results demonstrated that the models can be used to create valid software requirements specifications for Big Data applications.

In [20], a Requirements Engineering artefact model in the context of Big Data Software development projects is proposed. The model depicts the RE artefacts and inter-relationships involved in the development of Big Data Software applications. It is argued that this type of model can be used as a reference for the design of project-specific processes, software maintenance, and for supporting project decisions throughout the entire product life-cycle, currently bereft in the Big Data RE research.

Architectures and Frameworks. In [11], a conceptual descriptive architecture to help understand the user requirements and system characteristics of Big Data Analytics software is proposed. This architecture was developed as a high-level specification of how the numerous tools might work together in a Big Data Analytics platform. To develop this conceptual architecture, the authors applied sense-making models (e.g., iterative cognitive process that the human performs to build up a representation of an information space that is useful to achieve a goal) for Big Data analysis to help understand the cognitive complexity of Big Data Analytics as it is believed to consist of components that exploit both machine capability and human intelligence. In this work, the authors also presented two instantiations of the generic architecture of two use cases (social media and biomedical research domains) to provide examples of Big Data solutions related to situations in a specific organisation.

In [14] a requirements specification framework is proposed with the focus of identifying Big Data specific scenarios to be used in the data collection phase in the development of Big Data Analytics applications. In this framework, the scenario description governs the data collection process. Once the Big Data scenarios are elicited, they should be analysed with respect to: (i) the purpose (why, whereto, for when, for which reason); (ii) the sources (data provider, consumer, etc.); (iii) search patterns (determines which phrases and keywords correspond to the scenario at hand and must be contained within the data to be used); and (iv) the value (saving time by not collecting garbage but only needed data that is ready to use for more accurate real-time analysis). The authors claim that it helps to accelerate the analysis time by focusing on retrieving data from the source that meets the scenarios, thus improving the current processes of Big Data collection.

In [16] The NIST Big Data Interoperability Framework provides a discussion on security and privacy requirements with focus on the "fundamental concepts needed to understand the new paradigm for data applications, collectively known as Big Data, and the analytic processes collectively known as data science", and listed requirements extracted and summarised from 51 different use cases. These requirements are classified into seven different groups (e.g., data source requirements, data transformation requirements, etc.). Similarly, in [18] a framework based on Big Data Analytics in mobile cloud computing environments that applies security constraints and access control mechanisms that guarantee integrity, confidentiality and privacy in Big Data healthcare systems is presented.

Tools. In [10], a software verification tool – called DICE Verification Tool (D-VerT), - is proposed with the aim to allow designers to evaluate the system design against safety properties such as reachability of undesired configurations of the system. For example, this tool checks if a given topology reaches an unwanted configuration (e.g., whether it allows for bad executions that do not conform to some non-functional requirements). The verification is performed on annotated UML models which contain all the necessary information related to a topology. This tool supports two different types of verification based on logical formalisms: bounded satisfiability checking and the reachability checking. The bounded satisfiability checking has a topology property as input and checks whether there is an execution that violates this property. In the reachability checking type of verification, the topology is defined through an array-based system that undergoes verification of a safety problem. This approach uses a set of system transitions, an initial configuration and, a formula that defines the set of unsafe states. The result of this analysis is either safe or unsafe.

In [15], the authors proposed privacy extensions to UML use cases diagrams to help software engineers to visualize privacy requirements as well as to design privacy into Big Data applications. This solution is implemented as MS Visio extension ribbon in Visual Studio. The authors argued that these extensions to UML help software engineers to visually and quickly model privacy requirements in the analysis phase of the RE process. As a proof of concept, a prototype was created to show the usefulness of the extension and how it can be used to model the privacy requirements for Big Data systems in the domain of healthcare.

5   Recommendation for Further Research

In the RE area involving Big Data applications, as stated in [5], "a clearer understanding is needed, separating requirements for infrastructures, analytic tools and techniques, and end-user applications". Some papers in RE for Big Data applications describe either the challenges posed by the Big Data paradigm to Software Engineering (Sect. 4.2) or the quality attributes such a Big Data Software might address (e.g., security, performance, data consistency, etc.) (Sect. 4.1). Also, we note that these traditional quality attributes are orthogonal to the V-characteristics of Big Data. Thus, one of the research challenges is to be able to integrate these complementary set of attributes in the specification of system requirements. Moreover - from our analysis – we observe that, thus far, little scientific research has focused on RE in the context of Big Data applications and, no research was found addressing RE methods, tools and processes, for negotiation, validation, prioritization and management in the context of Big Data.

Finally, we noticed that little empirical studies have been conducted in this topic (Sect. 3.1). While some papers [13–15, 20] have proposed solutions, they lack validation just yet. Only five papers [4, 10–12, 19] actually have their proposals validated through empirical studies (e.g., case studies in industry). Therefore, it is important that more empirical studies in industry are performed to obtain an improved understanding of the RE activities in the development of Big Data applications. Also, empirical studies would add significantly to the meagre knowledge base on RE involving Big Data applications, which can improve processes and technologies and uncover more facts that could lead to further research in this area.

6   Threats to Validity

Concerning the threats to validity, the following threats were assessed.

Construct Validity: Regarding the search string used in this study, we used the terms we considered most suitable to make the string as comprehensive as possible to capture the relevant literature. We performed various searches using the identified terms (e.g., search strings with different combinations of terms) (Sect. 2.2) to decide upon the final version. Thus, we anticipate that this threat can be considered contained.

Internal Validity: Two major implications to be discussed are: (i) there might be bias in paper selection and (ii) the fact that we conducted manual searches. These issues were addressed by defining the steps for selecting the potential papers and establishing the selection criteria (Sects. 2.3 and 2.4) In addition, with respect to the manual searches, it is important to note that they were performed only in a limited set of sources (e.g., specific journals and conference proceedings).

External Validity: This threat is not considered relevant in this study because unlike in a case study or a scientific experiment where environment scopes (e.g., projects) are bounded, the scope of literature review data (selected papers) is universal.

Conclusion Validity: All the conclusions drawn in this paper are shown to have been rooted in specific core sections of this paper – thus there is traceability.

7   Conclusions

This paper describes the results of a systematic literature review on RE research involving Big Data applications. This review was conducted with the aim to answer the overall research question defined in this study ("What are the early signs of the ways Big Data applications is treated in requirements engineering (RE)?" See Sect. 2.1 where sub-questions Q1–Q4 are also described). The selection process used in this review was composed of three steps (Sect. 2.4). At the end of the selection process, 14 papers were deemed relevant for this review (Sect. 3.1).

Our findings are: (i) 11 papers discussed and proposed solutions (Sect. 4.3) to address specific areas of the RE process for Big Data applications (e.g., elicitation, specification and analysis of Big Data requirements). These solutions vary from RE methods, models and approaches to frameworks and architectures (see Table 5). Moreover, some of the selected papers [5, 13, 17, 19] also discussed RE research challenges in the context of Big Data (Sect. 4.2). From our analysis, we also noted the type of requirements and the activities in the RE process that are discussed in the papers selected for this study (Sect. 4.1).

While the findings may not be surprising to the esoteric few, the value of this paper to the wider audience is in setting the current baseline. An important observation, and conclusion, made is that, currently, there isn't a significant amount of research addressing: (a) RE in the context of Big Data applications; and (b) RE methods, tools and processes, for elicitation, negotiation, analysis, validation, prioritization and management in the context of Big Data. This thus presents the RE community with new opportunities for further research. Examples described in Sect. 5 are: (i) separation of requirements for infrastructures, analytic tools and techniques, and end-user applications; (ii) integration of quality attributes and V-characteristics of Big Data in the specification of system requirements; and (iii) need for new RE methods, tools, processes and methodologies for Big Data applications.

Acknowledgments. This research is supported by grants from CNPq, The National Council of Technological and Scientific Development – Brazil and NSERC, Natural Science and Engineering Research Council of Canada.

References

1. IBM homepage. https://www.ibm.com/analytics/hadoop/big-data-analytics. Accessed 22 Jan 2018
2. IBM Home page. http://www.ibmbigdatahub.com/sites/default/files/infographic_file/4-Vs-of-big-data.jpg. Accessed 22 Jan 2018
3. Chen, M., Mao, S., Liu, Y.: Big data: a survey. Mob. Netw. Appl. **19**, 171–209 (2014)
4. Chen, H.-M., Kazman, R., Haziyev, S., Hrytsay, O.: Big data system development: an embedded case study with a global outsourcing firm. In: 2015 IEEE/ACM 1st International Workshop on Big Data Software Engineering, pp. 44–50 (2015)
5. Madhavji, N.H., Miranskyy, A., Kontogiannis, K.: Big picture of big data software engineering: with example research challenges. In: Proceedings of the 1st International Workshop on Big Data Software Engineering, BIGDSE 2015, pp. 11–14 (2015)
6. Anderson, K.M.: Embrace the challenges: software engineering in a big data world. In: Proceedings of the 1st International Workshop on Big Data Software Engineering, BIGDSE 2015, pp. 19–25 (2015)
7. Kitchenham, B., Charters, S.: Guidelines for performing systematic literature reviews in software engineering version 2.3. Engineering **45**, 1051 (2007)
8. Wieringa, R., Maiden, N., Mead, N., Rolland, C.: Requirements engineering paper classification and evaluation criteria: a proposal and a discussion. Requirements Eng. **11**, 102–107 (2006)
9. Narayanan, R.: Evolving and improving the requirements approach to big data projects: a roadmap to implementing big data projects. Requirements Eng. Mag. 1–21 (2016)
10. Bersani, M.M., Marconi, F., Rossi, M., Erascu, M.: A tool for verification of big-data applications. In: Proceedings of the 2nd International Workshop on Quality DevOps, pp. 44–45 (2016)
11. Lau, L., Yang-Turner, F., Karacapilidis, N.: Requirements for big data analytics supporting decision making: a sensemaking perspective. In: Karacapilidis, N. (ed.) Mastering Data-Intensive Collaboration and Decision Making. SBD, vol. 5, pp. 49–70. Springer, Cham (2014). https://doi.org/10.1007/978-3-319-02612-1_3
12. Sachdeva, V., Chung, L.: Handling non-functional requirements for big data and IOT projects in scrum. In: 2017 Proceedings of the 7th International Conference on Cloud Computing Data Science Engineering Confluence, pp. 216–221 (2017)
13. Noorwali, I., Arruda, D., Madhavji, N.H.: Understanding quality requirements in the context of big data systems. In: Proceedings of the 2nd International Workshop on BIG Data Software Engineering - BIGDSE 2016, pp. 76–79 (2016)

14. Al-Najran, N., Dahanayake, A.: A requirements specification framework for big data collection and capture. In: Morzy, T., Valduriez, P., Bellatreche, L. (eds.) ADBIS 2015. CCIS, vol. 539, pp. 12–19. Springer, Cham (2015). https://doi.org/10.1007/978-3-319-23201-0_2

15. Jutla, D.N., Bodorik, P., Ali, S.: Engineering privacy for big data apps with the unified modeling language. In: 2013 Proceedings of the IEEE International Congress on Big Data, BigData 2013, pp. 38–45 (2013)

16. NIST Big Data Public Working Group: Use Cases and Requirements Subgroup: NIST Big Data Interoperability Framework: Volume 3, Use Cases and General Requirements 3, 260 (2015)

17. Otero, C.E., Peter, A.: Research directions for engineering big data analytics software. IEEE Intell. Syst. **30**, 13–19 (2015)

18. Youssef, A.E.: A framework for secure healthcare systems based on big data analytics in mobile cloud computing environments. Int. J. Ambient Syst. Appl. **2**, 1–11 (2014)

19. Eridaputra, H., Hendradjaya, B., Sunindyo, W.D.: Modeling the requirements for big data application using goal-oriented approach. In: 2014 International Conference on Data and Software Engineering, pp. 1–6 (2014)

20. Arruda, D., Madhavji, N.H.: Towards a requirements engineering artefact model in the context of big data software development projects. In: Proceedings of the IEEE International Conference on Big Data, pp. 2232–2237 (2017)

21. Sommerville, I.: Software Engineering, 9th edn. Pearson, Boston (2009)

Automatic User Preferences Elicitation:
A Data-Driven Approach

Tong Li[1(✉)] , Fan Zhang[2], and Dan Wang[1]

[1] Beijing University of Technology, Beijing, China
{litong,wangdan}@bjut.edu.cn
[2] Institute of Software Chinese Academy of Sciences, Beijing, China
zhangf@ios.ac.cn

Abstract. [**Context and motivation**] In the increasingly competitive software market, it is essential for software companies to have a comprehensive understanding of development progress and user preferences of their corresponding application domain. [**Question/problem**] However, given the huge number of existing software applications, it is impossible to gain such insights via manual inspection. [**Principal ideas/results**] In this paper, we present a research preview of automatic user preferences elicitation approach. Specifically, our approach first clusters software applications into different categories based on their descriptions, and then identifies features of each category. We then link such features to corresponding user reviews and automatically classify sentiments of each review In order to understand user preferences over such feature In addition, we have carefully planned evaluations that will be carried out to further polish our work. [**Contributions**] Our proposal aims to help software companies to identify features of applications in a particular domain, as well as user preferences with regard to those features. We argue such analysis is especially important for startup companies that have few knowledge about the domain.

Keywords: User preferences · Topic modeling · Sentiment analysis
Machine learning · Natural language processing

1 Introduction

In the increasingly competitive software market, startup software companies (or companies that plan to explore new software markets) should have a comprehensive understanding of the application domain they are working on. On one hand, they should be aware of main features that have been investigated in the application domain in order to avoid reinventing wheels. On the other hand, it is even more important for them to understand user preferences on different features so as to maximumly meet user needs.

Typical Requirements Engineering (RE) approaches for investigating application domains include questionnaires and interviews, which are time-consuming and comparatively expensive. Recently, more and more researchers are trying to

© Springer International Publishing AG, part of Springer Nature 2018
E. Kamsties et al. (Eds.): REFSQ 2018, LNCS 10753, pp. 324–331, 2018.
https://doi.org/10.1007/978-3-319-77243-1_21

mine useful information from public data sources to support RE activities [1]. In particular, user reviews are deemed as valuable sources that have been mostly investigated to elicit user requirements [2–4]. However, all such analysis is exclusively focusing on analyzing user reviews without linking them to descriptions of corresponding software applications. As a result, it is difficult to understand to which extent the designed features are liked or disliked by users.

In this paper, we present a research preview on automatically eliciting user preferences over features of software applications in a particular domain. The essential idea of this proposal is associating software features identified from software descriptions with user reviews, based on which user's preferences can be determined through sentiment analysis. Specifically, our approach first takes descriptions of software applications from a particular application domain as inputs, which are then clustered to identify different themes with corresponding functional keywords. Then, we train and adopt a word2vec model to link user reviews to functional keywords of corresponding applications. Finally, we leverage machine learning algorithms to train sentiment classifiers so as to automatically identify user preferences based on their sentiment.

Our approach focuses on features of a category of software applications rather than an individual application. We argue that such information is more valuable for software companies to comprehend the overall development of a particular area. Thus, companies can base their upcoming software products on the most popular set of features within that area.

2   Related Work

Guzman and Maalej propose a method to identify user preferences for specific features by mining user reviews [2]. This method extracts software features from the user's reviews based on the frequency of occurrence of words, and then determine user preferences by analyzing the sentiments of user reviews. Similarly, Carreno et al. analyze user reviews on particular system functionality in order to help software developers to determine the release of the next version [4]. Different from such methods, in this paper we argue that users do not necessarily be able to accurately describe software functions and user comments may contain a lot of redundant and meaningless information that is irrelevant to software functions. Therefore, we propose to identify functions from application descriptions and filter unrelated user comments that do not concern such functions.

In addition to analyzing user preferences, Hariri et al. propose a feature recommendation method based on association rule mining and clustering analysis [5]. Our approach shares the same idea with the first step of this approach, i.e., extracting features from application descriptions. However, their approach requires the software descriptions to be well-structured, i.e., having a dedicated product summary section and describing features in bulleted lists, which do not hold in many software repositories (e.g., Apple Store). Therefore, we opt not to base our proposal on their approach and investigate different solutions that will be detailed in the next section.

Chen et al. propose AR-Miner, aiming to find out user reviews with a larger amount of information [3]. To this end, they first use EM naive Bayesian to train non-information review classifiers in order to filter meaningless reviews. Then they propose a review ranking algorithm based on results of topic modeling analysis in order to find high-information reviews. This method is complementary to our propose in the sense that the review ranking algorithm can help us to better eliminate meaningless user reviews, and improve the performance of our approach. Zou et al. proposed to mine software quality from user reviews [6]. In particular, this method defines a series of grammatical patterns that may contain quality descriptions in order to identify software quality from user reviews. In addition, they uses SVM to train sentiment classifiers to analyze user preferences on such qualities.

3   A Data-Driven User Preferences Elicitation Approach

User preferences are typically associated with particular subjects, such as application features. In this work, we focus on eliciting user preferences on typical features of a category of software applications. We refine this goal into three sub-goals, each of which constitutes an indispensable part of our approach. In particular, our approach first identifies features of a category of software applications, and then links user reviews to the identified functions. Thus, by analyzing sentiment of user reviews, we are able to obtain user preferences over corresponding features.

3.1   Identifying Application Functions

Identifying features of a category of software applications can help software developers to efficiently understand the "state of the art" in the corresponding application domain. As application descriptions typically include functional information, we propose to mine functional keywords of applications in the same category to profile the main features of such applications. It is worth noting that the granularity of categories has a strong influence on this step of analysis. As a precursor to feature identification, we propose to cluster applications based on their descriptions to obtain sub-categories that are of proper granularity, based on which we can further identify features of that category. We have designed a topic modeling-based method and a clustering-based method, respectively, in order to optimally implement our proposal. Such two methods will be systematically compared in future experiments, design of which is detailed in Sect. 4.

Topic Modeling-Based Method. We propose to apply Latent Dirichlet Allocation (LDA) [7] to identify different topics from application descriptions. Specifically, we view the set of application descriptions as a mixture of various topics, each of which indicates a sub-category of the input applications. In addition, the topic model approach allows us to control the granularity of the obtained sub-categories by adjusting the number of topics that are to be identified. This is pragmatically useful, as our approach can take an arbitrary number of applications as input and adaptively create sub-categories with proper granularity. Note that such adaptation requires manual intervention.

As by products of LDA, each identified topic consists of a list of keywords. Keywords that have higher probability to be included in a topic are better representatives of this topic. We take such keywords as candidate components of features, which requires further manual inspection to determine features. It is worth noting that unstructured application descriptions (e.g., application descriptions in App Store) are likely to include contents that are irrelevant to application features. Thus, an iteratively updated list of stop words are used to exclude irrelevant terms. In addition, as we exclusively focus on features of applications which are typically described using nouns and verbs, we apply POS-tagging techniques to extract only nouns and verbs for training LDA models.

A Clustering-Based Method. Alternatively, we propose to apply clustering techniques to input applications with regard to their descriptions, and each generated cluster is then deemed as a sub-category. To this end, we first vectorizes each application's description using *doc2vec* [8], which can generate vectors for text of arbitrary length and has been empirically evaluated as effective and robust [9]. Then, we cluster applications based on their corresponding vectors using a simple and efficient clustering algorithm *density-peak* [10]. Note that the density-peak algorithm is better than classical clustering approaches, as it considers not only density of data points, but also distances between different density peaks. Thus, it is robust in the sense that it is able to discover clusters even with some noisy inputs. Once appropriate sub-categories are generated, for each sub-category, we then apply a collocation finding algorithm [11] to the descriptions of applications belong to the sub-category in order to identify features of such applications.

3.2   Associating Functionality with Reviews

Establishing connections between features and reviews is essential for comprehending user preferences. To this end, we intuitively propose to match the previously identified functional keywords with words of reviews. Because users are likely to use their own terms to describe application functions which can be different from application descriptions, strict text matching might not work well. Consequently, word semantics should be taken into account during such analysis. To this end, we propose to adopt *word2vec* to produce word embeddings, which can quantify and categorize semantic similarities between words [12]. *Word2vec* takes a large corpus of text and produces a vector space which typically consists of several hundred dimensions, and assigns each unique word in the corpus with a particular vector in the space. Typically, there are two types of model architectures that *word2vec* can use to produce a distributed representation of words, i.e., continuous bag-of-words (CBOW) and continuous skip-gram. We here adopt the latter one as it is much faster for training.

As for this step of analysis, we first train a *word2vec* model using both application descriptions and user reviews. Based on the obtained model, we then match user reviews with functional keywords of a particular application category, the output of which sheds light on not only how many user reviews comment application features but also which functional keywords are commented.

3.3   Classifying Reviews

Sentiment analysis of user reviews reflects users positive and negative emotions, and thus contributes to elicitation of user preferences. Typical sentiment analysis techniques rely on hard-coded dictionaries, which consist of a list of positive words and negative words, respectively. Such techniques examine words in isolation, giving positive points for positive words and negative points for negative words and then summing up these points. In this way, the order of words is ignored and important semantic information of sentences is lost. Recently, it has been recognized as a drawback from lexical sentiment analysis techniques that have been previously used for the analysis of application reviews [13].

To deal with the problem, we treat sentiment analysis as a binary-classification problem, i.e., a review is classified as either positive or negative, and propose to adopt a supervised machine learning approach to classify user reviews. In particular, we engineer features of user reviews by taking into account not only words but also syntactic structure and semantic dependencies of user reviews. We then leverage different machine learning algorithms to train classifiers and compare their performance, including Naive Bayes (NB), Fisher Kernel (FK), Support Vector Machine(SVM), and Logistic Regression (LR).

4   Evaluation Plan

The overall research goal of this work is to efficiently and comprehensively elicit user preferences on features of software applications within a particular category. We plan to evaluate the performance of our proposal by addressing the following questions:

- **RQ1.** To what extent can the topic modeling-based method and the clustering-based method respectively extract features of a category of software applications from their unstructured descriptions?
- **RQ2.** To what extent can the *word2vec* method accurately associate user reviews with previously identified features?
- **RQ3.** To what extent can our proposal accurately classify sentiments of user reviews?
- **RQ4.** Whether software companies can benefit from our approach and would like to adopt it?

Data Collection. We plan to evaluate our approach based on a significant number of applications from Apple Store, which currently has more than two million applications, and provides APIs for searching and downloading application information[1]. As our approach is supposed to assist software companies in developing software applications of a particular category, we plan to collect applications within the corresponding category. Specifically, we plan to collect 5,000 applications that are within the *finance* category and 200 user reviews for each of these applications (i.e., totally 1,000,000 user reviews) for analysis.

Analysis Process. According to the previous research questions, we include following analysis steps in our evaluation.

- We first plan to have two groups of participants to apply the topic modeling-based method and the clustering-based method, respectively, to identify features of different subcategories of the 5,000 applications. To assess such analysis results, we will randomly pick up three subcategories of applications, and manually identify their features as the *grounded truth*.
- Next, we automatically identify reviews that comment on the identified features. Among the one million user reviews, we will randomly choose 1,000 reviews and manually examining the performance of our approach.
- Once we have obtained all the user reviews that are associated with particular features, we then manually create a training dataset for sentiment analysis which consists of 10,000 reviews, and take all other reviews as the test dataset. We will use standard metrics in the field of information retrieval [14]., including *precision*, *recall*, and *f-measure* to evaluate the performance of the above analysis.
- In addition to the above laboratory experiments, we want to further evaluate our approach in a realistic industrial setting with practitioners who are going to develop financial software applications. Specifically, we will examine our approach against the Technology Acceptance Model [15].

Threats to Validity. There are a couple of threats to the validity of our evaluation. Firstly, the unbalanced samples post an internal threat to the validity of our sentiment analysis in our pilot test. Since we have planned to collect a huge set of user reviews (one million), we believe be able to find enough negative samples for training and thus mitigate this threat. Secondly, our evaluation focus on a particular category of software from one particular software repository, which could be an external threat to validity. Thus, subsequent evaluations are required to cover additional categories from different software repositories. Thirdly, we plan to perform manual analysis in order to create *grounded truth*, and the reliability of such analysis is essential for the validity of our evaluation. As a result, we plan to involve at least two domain experts in each manual analysis, in case there are conflicting opinions, a third one will be introduced.

---

[1] https://affiliate.itunes.apple.com/resources/documentation/itunes-store-web-service-search-api.

5   Conclusions

In this paper, we present a research preview about a data driven user preference elicitation approach. Our approach aims to help software companies, especially startup companies that has less experiences in the area, to efficiently understand not only which features have been developed in a particular application category but also to which extent user like or dislike them. Specifically, we divide our proposal into three parts, and have tentatively explored alternative technical solutions to implement each part. We have designed a suite of evaluation plans, which constitute the next step of our work.

Acknowledgements. The work is supported by National Natural Science Foundation of China (Grants No. 91546111 and No. 91646201), Beijing Natural Science Foundation P.R.China (Grants No. 4173072), and Foundation of Beijing University of Technology.

References

1. Maalej, W., Nayebi, M., Johann, T., Ruhe, G.: Toward data-driven requirements engineering. IEEE Softw. **33**(1), 48–54 (2016)
2. Guzman, E., Maalej, W.: How do users like this feature? a fine grained sentiment analysis of app reviews. In: 2014 IEEE 22nd International Requirements Engineering Conference (RE), pp. 153–162, August 2014
3. Chen, N., Lin, J., Hoi, S.C.H., Xiao, X., Zhang, B.: AR-miner: Mining informative reviews for developers from mobile app marketplace. In: Proceedings of the 36th International Conference on Software Engineering, ICSE 2014, pp. 767–778. ACM, New York (2014)
4. Carreo, L.V.G., Winbladh, K.: Analysis of user comments: an approach for software requirements evolution. In: 2013 35th International Conference on Software Engineering (ICSE), pp. 582–591, May 2013
5. Hariri, N., Castro-Herrera, C., Mirakhorli, M., Cleland-Huang, J., Mobasher, B.: Supporting domain analysis through mining and recommending features from online product listings. IEEE Trans. Softw. Eng. **39**(12), 1736–1752 (2013)
6. Zou, Y., Liu, C., Jin, Y., Xie, B.: Assessing software quality through web comment search and analysis. In: Favaro, J., Morisio, M. (eds.) ICSR 2013. LNCS, vol. 7925, pp. 208–223. Springer, Heidelberg (2013). https://doi.org/10.1007/978-3-642-38977-1_14
7. Blei, D.M., Ng, A.Y., Jordan, M.I.: Latent dirichlet allocation. J. Mach. Learn. Res. **3**, 993–1022 (2003)
8. Le, Q., Mikolov, T.: Distributed representations of sentences and documents. In: Proceedings of the 31st International Conference on Machine Learning (ICML 2014), pp. 1188–1196 (2014)
9. Lau, J.H., Baldwin, T.: An empirical evaluation of doc2vec with practical insights into document embedding generation arXiv preprint arXiv:1607.05368. (2016)
10. Rodriguez, A., Laio, A.: Clustering by fast search and find of density peaks. Science **344**(6191), 1492–1496 (2014)
11. Manning, C.D., Schütze, H., et al.: Foundations of Statistical Natural Language Processing, vol. 999. MIT Press, Cambridge (1999)
12. Mikolov, T., Chen, K., Corrado, G., Dean, J.: Efficient estimation of word representations in vector space arXiv preprint arXiv:1301.3781. (2013)

13. Panichella, S., Di Sorbo, A., Guzman, E., Visaggio, C.A., Canfora, G., Gall, H.C.: ARdoc: App reviews development oriented classifier. In: Proceedings of the 2016 24th ACM SIGSOFT International Symposium on Foundations of Software Engineering, pp. 1023–1027. ACM (2016)
14. Baeza-Yates, R., Ribeiro-Neto, B., et al.: Modern Information Retrieval, vol. 463. ACM Press, New York (1999)
15. Davis, F.D.: Perceived usefulness, perceived ease of use, and user acceptance of information technology. MIS Q. **13**(3), 319–340 (1989)

Mindmapping and Requirements Modeling

Streamlining Semantics from Requirements to Implementation Through Agile Mind Mapping Methods

Robert Andrei Buchmann[1](✉) , Ana-Maria Ghiran[1](✉) , Cristina-Claudia Osman[1] ,
and Dimitris Karagiannis[2]

[1] Business Informatics Research Center, Babeş-Bolyai University, Cluj-Napoca, Romania
{robert.buchmann,anamaria.ghiran,cristina.osman}@econ.ubbcluj.ro
[2] Knowledge Engineering Research Group, Faculty of Computer Science,
University of Vienna, Vienna, Austria
dk@dke.univie.ac.at

Abstract. **[Context and motivation]** Semantics are the essential asset that must be managed during requirements elicitation, and further made available to the implementation phase. Consequently, it makes sense to investigate how knowledge representation techniques can support both human-oriented and machine-readable requirements modelling to facilitate the transfer of semantics between the two phases. Semantic technology such as the Resource Description Framework (RDF) and methodologies such as Agile Modelling Method Engineering (AMME) may converge towards new methods of requirements elicitation. **[Question/problem]** How can requirements semantics be captured in a fashion that is diagrammatic, agile and streamlined to support the implementation phase? **[Principal ideas/results]** We introduce the notion of Agile Mind Mapping Method as an artefact that repurposes agile modelling methods for mind mapping practices and is enriched with an RDF-based semantic interoperability mechanism for transferring diagrammatic requirements descriptions to implemented software artefacts. **[Contribution]** Semantic technology, agile metamodeling and mind mapping best practices are combined in an elicitation method based on agile modelling artefacts that can streamline semantics from mind map-based requirements to semantics-aware implementations.

Keywords: Agile requirements modelling · Resource Description Framework
Agile Modelling Method Engineering · Mind mapping

1 Introduction

Mind maps are diagrammatic means of representing information about a topic that is hierarchically described through heterogeneous, visually radiating relations of heterogeneous semantics. Often, these relations are a mix of decompositions and specialisations, but may also be freely improvised relations, possibly linking to other topics having their own maps. Semantics and mnemonic cues are expressed not only through this

© Springer International Publishing AG, part of Springer Nature 2018
E. Kamsties et al. (Eds.): REFSQ 2018, LNCS 10753, pp. 335–351, 2018.
https://doi.org/10.1007/978-3-319-77243-1_22

radial-hierarchical structure, but also through distinctive visual attributes – icons, line styles and colours, data annotations.

While mind mapping techniques have primarily emerged from the field of psychology [1, 2], often recommending a pen-and-paper approach for quick results, nowadays they commonly employ software tools (a catalogue is maintained by [3]) and have been successfully adopted for requirements elicitation – e.g., [4, 5].

The evolution of mind mapping shows similarities with conceptual modelling, although having different origin and purpose. Conceptual modelling shares with mind maps the goal of supporting communication and understanding [6]; however, this is often shadowed by software engineering goals (e.g., code generation) or business process management goals (e.g., process simulation), giving a prominent role to standards that are aligned with such goals (e.g., UML, BPMN) and this in turn stimulated the shift from pen-and-paper diagramming towards modelling tools governed by metamodelling frameworks (e.g., the Meta-Object Facility [7]). The ambition of standardisation shadows the requirement of "agility" – a popular desideratum in software development, but less so with conceptual modelling languages, due to their typical ambition of global adoption and stability with respect to model-driven functionality. In conceptual modelling, "agility" should not be limited to content; it should also be extended to method and tool level – for the purposes of the work at hand, this type of agility is employed to tailor a conceptual modelling tool for mind mapping-based requirements elicitation practices.

Finally, a third paradigm and ingredient of this proposal is that of knowledge representation, aiming to ensure machine-readability and interpretability of semantics. An exemplary enabler in this context is W3C's Resource Description Framework standard (RDF) [8] which allows semantic representations, querying and reasoning over conceptual graphs that are amenable to Web-based distribution and processing, including reasoning through rules or Web ontologies.

The three ingredients – mind mapping, agile conceptual modelling and RDF are hereby intertwined in a proposed method, labelled as "Agile Mind Mapping Method". Requirements modelling is the motivational use case, due to the inherent need of transferring granular semantics from early to late stages of agile software development processes or to traceability tools.

The remainder of the paper is structured as follows: Sect. 2 provides background information on the ingredients of the proposed method. Section 3 introduces the problem in terms of addressed requirements and provides a solution summary. Section 4 highlights design decisions and usage patterns based on an expository implementation. Section 5 comments on related works. The paper ends with a concluding SWOT analysis that includes an outlook to future work.

2   Background

2.1   Mind Mapping

The practice of mind mapping was introduced as intuitive means for organising information – i.e., an alternative to note-taking, text-based understanding and memorisation of content. Radial diagramming (rather than unidirectional text), a reduction of text to keywords and iconic representations, semantic distinctions communicated through colours and shapes contribute to improved mnemonic effectiveness and the understanding of the "core topic" around which the map is built. However, at the time it was introduced its advocates were agnostic of potential software support and of the evolution of the conceptual modelling paradigm. Even in more recent times, practitioners [9] still stress the distinction between a mind map and concept maps/graphs (non-hierarchical and focusing on explicit relations rather than topics) or modelling graphs (typically perceived as being constrained by the syntax and semantics of some standard modelling language, e.g., UML).

The goal of this paper is to advocate a convergence of mind mapping and conceptual modelling practices using requirements modelling as an application ground. Conceptual modelling literature has already analysed cognitive shortcomings of established modelling languages – e.g., in [10], focusing on business process modelling languages, it is stressed that "[...] process models do not exploit colours, dimensions, sizes, etc. It is remarkable that process models typically have shapes (nodes and arcs) of a fixed size, and, even if the size is variable, it has no semantical interpretation..."; in a different context, the authors of [11] analyse shortcomings of a popular requirements modelling language. Modelling languages typically provide an invariant syntax and semantic space, being concerned more with ensuring visual distinctions among a limited set of concepts rather than enabling the flexible and free diagramming that is at the core of the mind mapping popularity. A notion of agility is therefore necessary in the world of conceptual modelling in order to bring it closer to mind mapping needs, as emphasised in the next section.

2.2   Agile Modelling Methods and AMME

Conceptual modelling languages and methods have evolved along two streams of thinking: (a) what the authors of [12] consider to be a blueprint-oriented thinking, benefitting from standardisation and unified metamodels that aim for reuse and stability; (b) the agility-oriented thinking that sacrifices reuse and global adoption for the benefits of situational productivity, domain-specificity or case responsiveness. While the first direction has led to the popularity of languages such as BPMN, UML in close coupling with reusable model-driven mechanisms (simulation, code generation etc.), the second perspective focused on methodologies (e.g., [13, 14]) and platforms (e.g., [15, 16]) allowing for a full customisation of modelling tools, languages and methods with respect to situational modelling use cases.

According to this second perspective, mind mapping may be considered an application area for which conceptual modelling methods can be tailored. However, when mind mapping is employed for requirements elicitation, new goals emerge, as highlighted in the work at hand: the transfer of semantics towards later development phases or for traceability purposes; and, tool support may include modelling tools that are repurposed and agilely customised for mind mapping.

One methodology enabling such agile customisation is provided by the Agile Modelling Method Engineering (AMME) framework [13]. A key technological enabler for this methodology is the ADOxx platform for fast prototyping of modelling tools, freely available at [16] (a formalisation of its meta-metamodel is available at [17]). The core artefact that is created with AMME is a "modelling method" (implemented as a tool), defined in [18] as comprising several building blocks:

- The *modelling language*, which includes semantics (modelling concepts and their machine-readable properties), notation (graphical symbols for each concept) and abstract syntax (well-formedness rules for connecting the graphical symbols – e.g., relation domains, ranges, cardinalities). For the purposes of the work at hand, the language has a core diagram type tailored for the common usage of mind maps, providing a balance between drawing freedom and prescription of concepts. The map's language is further enriched with prescribed conceptual models that can be linked to its branches/topics in order to provide structured detail about the map's topics – e.g., processes, actors etc.;
- The *mechanisms/algorithms* refer to model-based functionality. For the purposes of the work at hand, this includes a model export plug-in that serialises, in RDF graph form, the mind map's graph structure, including annotations and linked models;
- The *modelling procedure* prescribes modelling steps to guide the end-user. In this case, the procedure comes to replace the intuitive freedom of traditional pen-and-paper mind maps by imposing a minimal structure and annotation guidelines to help the user with idea structuring and the preparation of a diagrammatic structure that can be later interpreted by the semantics-driven implementations.

This notion of *modelling method* is characterised by agility if it is subjected to the iterative customisation process of AMME with the help of a prototyping environment (ADOxx). These were extensively applied and evaluated in the Open Models Laboratory collaborative environment (OMiLAB) [19], where a number of modelling tools have been deployed for domain-specific application areas (catalogued and presented in [20]). In the context of this paper's proposal, AMME is repurposed into an Agile Mind Mapping Method, to be overviewed in Sect. 3.

2.3   The Resource Description Framework

The Resource Description Framework [8] provides a graph-based data model that can be used to represent and manage conceptual graphs and their associated ontologies. RDF is supported by some graph database management systems (e.g., GraphDB [21]) and it comes with a standardised graph query language (SPARQL [22]), a variety of serialisation syntaxes (e.g., TriG [23]), means of embedding graphs directly in HTML-based user interfaces (e.g., RDFa [24]) and REST-based protocols for distribution and querying over HTTP (e.g., [25]).

The framework became popular as an enabler for the Linked Open Data paradigm [26] - itself a foundation for the Semantic Web vision. Sources of information that are coalesced in distributed RDF graphs vary from open knowledge derived from public sources like Wikidata or Wikipedia (e.g., the DBPedia service [27]) to enterprise data that can be semantically lifted from legacy data sources through various adapters (e.g., D2RQ for relational databases [28]).

In the context of this paper's proposal, RDF is employed to capture a complex semantic network having mind maps in the centre and semantic links to a variety of related models or arbitrary Web resources that are relevant at implementation time. The semantic network is obtained through a generic mechanism for serialising diagrammatic models regardless of the type of model (currently implemented for ADOxx) and can be further enriched by inference rules, considering the properties that need to be available for the implementation phase.

3   Problem Statement and Solution Summary

The ability to reuse the mind maps semantics requires effort that may be either computational (i.e., knowledge extraction) or supported by knowledge representation techniques. Our proposal advocates the second approach by introducing a conceptual modelling framework that combines the agile engineering of modelling methods (AMME) with RDF in order to ensure that the knowledge captured in mind maps becomes available to later development stages. In other words, the AMME principles are distilled in the hereby proposed Agile Mind Mapping Method, assuming several high-level requirements that form our problem statement:

- to support mind mapping with a balance of free diagramming and constrained conceptual modelling, driven by a prescribed metamodel;
- to empower requirements engineers to adjust the level of conceptual prescription (i.e., metamodel) – i.e., having a starting metamodel and the possibility to extend it and re-prototype their tool support via metamodelling;
- to support the interoperability and machine-interpretability of mind map semantics.

The proposed method is summarised in Fig. 1 through its key usage process, comprising the following stages and responsibilities:

1. *Mind mapping and modelling*: a conceptual modelling tool provides a model type for mind mapping, allowing both free diagramming and constrained modelling according to an initial multi-perspective modelling language. This is performed by a modeller (who may be a stakeholder or a requirements engineer) supported by modelling guidelines;
2. *Map linking and annotation*: the mind map is semantically linked to various models (e.g., process descriptions, organigrams) and arbitrary Web resources (e.g., documents, data) that are relevant at implementation time. Model-to-model links can be created by the same modeller as in the previous phase. Links to implementation-relevant data follow the declarative style of the Linked Data approach (the data does not need to already exist) and would require supervision from a data engineer involved in the implementation/design phases;
3. If the modelling language is not rich enough to capture necessary details, AMME is employed in order *to extend the language and to re-prototype the modelling tool*, thus returning to the initial step with a richer language/tool version. The modelling method engineer, guided by change requests, performs this step (ideally the roles of requirements engineer and modelling method engineer should merge);

4. *Knowledge externalisation as RDF graph*: the underlying graph structure of the mind map, its annotations and linked models are exported as machine-readable RDF graphs; the export is tailored to read the metamodel structure, therefore it automatically reflects any changes that are applied during Stage 3. Any modeller can perform this step, with only minimal guidance (e.g., declaring the namespace to be attached to all model elements in the RDF graphs);

5. *Rule-based graph enrichment*: rule-based inferences are applied to enrich the derived graphs for run-time semantic queries. This stages crosses to the design/implementation phases, requiring a data engineer with RDF expertise;

6. *Semantics-driven implementation*: the final graphs are published and become a knowledge base (technically, a "graph database"), to be used by software developers via semantic queries and REST-based access. This provides an alternative to code generation, which would be difficult to maintain under AMME, due to the non-standard and unstable nature of the modelling language.

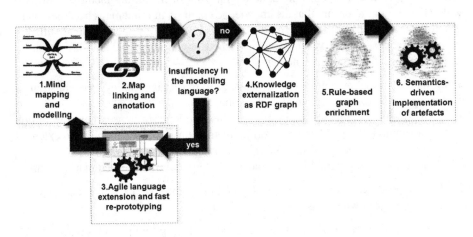

Fig. 1. The Agile Mind Mapping Method – a usage process overview

4   Design and Implementation Details

One of the advocated strengths of mind mapping is flexibility, understood as a quasi-absence of constraining rules. All the rules refer to visualisation (start in the centre, use a picture for the central idea etc.) and not to conceptualisation, since mind mapping was introduced as a domain-agnostic technique [29]. However, when applied to requirements elicitation at least a starting conceptualisation is needed to cover the key aspects that fall under the scrutiny of requirements analysis.

In order to balance the mapping freedom and conceptual prescription, a hybrid metamodel is employed in our proposal, to govern "the mind mapping language" and, consequently, the tool. This is suggested in Fig. 2 in a scenario built around an event planning and management company:

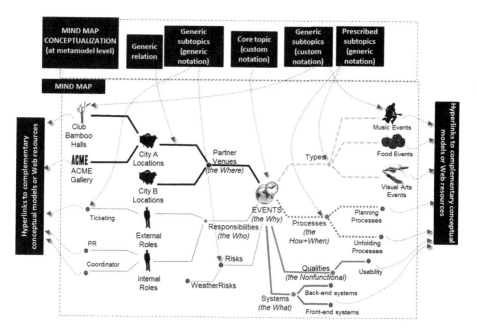

Fig. 2. The core mind map model type

On one hand, a minimal set of **generic constructs** is provided: a *core topic* (the map centre), the *generic subtopics* (on any level of the hierarchy except the centre) and the *generic relations* (visual connectors between topics). Both the core topic and the generic subtopics have (a) a minimal generic notation with convenient label positioning; and (b) the ability to replace this generic notation with arbitrary resizable graphics to allow full freedom in the choice of iconic notation for any element.

These generic constructs are complemented by more **specific concepts** (subtopic types) - the result of a conceptualisation tailored for requirements elicitation, derived from requirements modelling experience (see a project-based case reported in [30]). The frame of this conceptualisation is the Zachman Framework [31] – an informal ontology popular in Enterprise Modelling and Enterprise Architecture Management. The framework recommends several perspectives/aspects for describing enterprise information systems - these are adopted here as the dimensions along which requirements should be captured in a complex navigable semantic network: the *Why* (goals), the *How+When* (processes combined here with events), the *What* (developed systems), the *Who* (liable entities, roles), the *Where* (locations). The *Why* is the type of the map's "core topic", since requirements typically revolve around high level goals (goal modelling is commonly assimilated to requirements modelling, see also the case of the i* language [32]). The other perspectives correspond to prescribed subtopic types that may be included in the map, further (hyper)linked to dedicated types of models tailored for each perspective (e.g., process models for *How* subtopics, organigram elements for *Who* subtopics). The map together with these dedicated model types form the agile modelling language underlying this proposal, and are subjected to extensions during Stage 3 of the method overview (cf. Fig. 1).

In addition to the subtopics inspired by Zachman's perspectives, other dedicated subtopic types are prescribed – that of *Specialisation (Types)* to specialise the central goal (e.g., in Fig. 2 the event management company deals with three types of events under the assumption that processes and their requirements should be differentiated between these); and that of *Nonfunctional* requirements (*Qualities*). The user further has the possibility of freely adding subtopics beyond this prescription (e.g., the *Risks* subtopic visible in Fig. 2) - these can be annotated with resource identifiers in the sense of RDF (i.e., properties, entities from some existing database or ontology).

Figure 3 isolates a node of the mind map to show its core annotation schema (which is extensible through AMME with arbitrary hyperlinks to relevant documents).

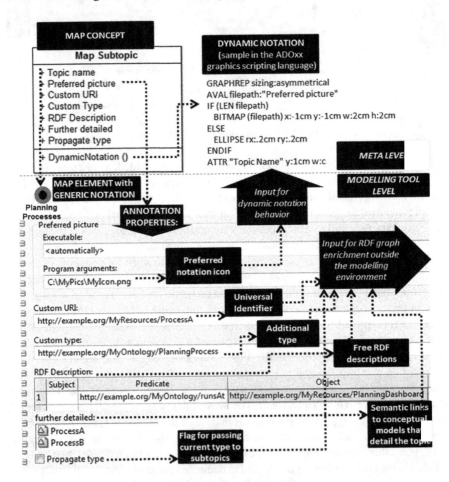

Fig. 3. Core description of a mind map concept

Each node in the map can be visualised according to a preferred icon loaded from external files (the *Preferred picture* slot). When keeping the generic notation, the map will be perceived as more relation centric, the visual focus being shifted to the chromatic and style variation of connectors; mind mapping practitioners recommend, however, the extensive use of icons and for this reason notational freedom is enabled (as opposed to the standard notations of popular modelling languages). Considering the goal of eventually exposing the map structure to implementation artefacts in the form of a machine-readable concept graphs, several annotations are dedicated to facilitate this: (a) the possibility of assigning reusable resource identifiers for the entities represented by map nodes (*Custom URI*); (b) the possibility of assigning types to those entities (*Custom type*), selected from some external classification/typing system (e.g., an ontology, the database to be developed); (c) the possibility of assigning arbitrary RDF triples to map nodes (*RDF description*). Similarly, each generic connector may receive identifiers to ensure explicit semantic distinction between occurrences (semantic distinction may also be achieved later, via rules).

Map nodes can be detailed into other types of models – i.e., goal subtypes are linked to other maps having them as a central topic (for more granular mapping) and other topics are linked to convenient conceptual models (e.g., business process models for processes, organisational structures for responsibilities, location maps with location descriptions) all conveniently enriched with properties that are deemed relevant at runtime (e.g., addresses for locations, contact data for responsibilities, endpoints supporting the process tasks). Such models are not detailed here as they may be modularly customised depending on the information that should be available to the implementation phase – they may even be standard model types (a reusable AMME-based implementation of UML, BPMN, Petri Nets, EPC and ER is presented in [33, 34]), but also customised or domain-specific model types (see the ComVantage modelling language described in [30, 35]).

All these models, regardless of their type (including the linked mind maps) are transformed into machine-readable graphs that *encapsulate the semantics exposed to the implementation phase* (amenable to reasoning), following the same generic transformation patterns - some are visible in Fig. 4 as they also apply to the mind map; a more extensive discussion on the mapping between diagrammatic patterns and RDF patterns was presented in [36]. Figure 4 shows some key SPARQL-based inference patterns that make use of the prescribed concepts (types) in order to derive semantics for the generic connectors (URI namespaces are avoided for readability). The bottom example also highlights: (i) the possibility to annotate generic connectors or topics with URIs, thus explicating the "meaning" of arbitrary connectors and topics; (ii) the possibility to infer transitively meaningful relations with the help of the dedicated flag attribute *propagate type* that can be switched by the modeller for both nodes and connectors (visible in Fig. 3); this inference extends the relation's meaning (e.g., haveRisks) over the inverse of subclass – the same mechanism also applies to the *further detailed* hyperlinks through which a map topic is linked to a conceptual model that describes it (as suggested in Fig. 5).

Figure 5 shows a graph fragment derived from a map having Music Events as the central topic. With the help of the inferences suggested in Fig. 4 the topic becomes

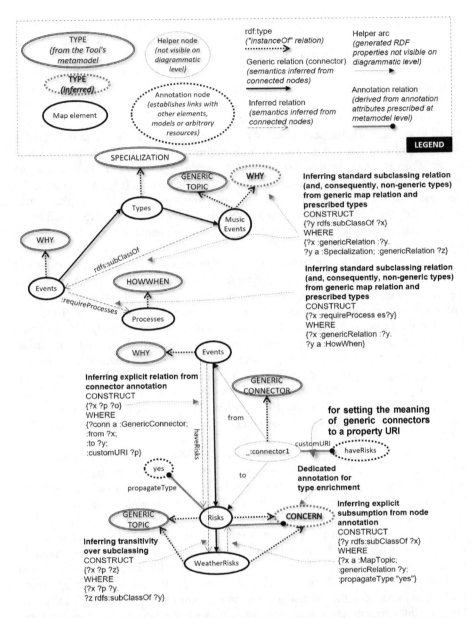

Fig. 4. SPARQL-based inference patterns for enriching the machine-readable map semantics

directly linked (via *requireProcesses*) to its required process models (filtered by a *Where* topic). Each task in these process models is further linked to performer descriptions (from an organisational chart providing more detail than the mind map's *Who* nodes) and to location descriptions (again, detailing the *Where* topics included in the mind map). Links may also be followed the other way around (from *Who/Where* nodes to tasks and

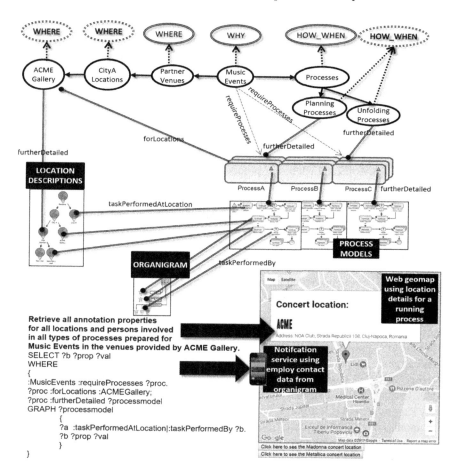

Fig. 5. Semantic query retrieving properties across the map links

processes). Implemented artefacts may then use this knowledge structure as a semantic database, via semantic queries that navigate across the structure comprising the map, linked models and inference-based enrichments (Fig. 5 suggests a Google map using model information for its location markers).

5 Related Works

This work was inspired by ideas proposed in [37] regarding the potential of mind map-aware application enhancements. There, the focus is on document management and none of their proposals involve a coupling between mind maps and semantic technology or conceptual modelling, as advocated in this paper. The feature of linking mind map nodes to external documents, which is commonly supported by mind mapping software (and emphasised by the contribution of [38]), is extrapolated in our work through the lens of the Linked Data paradigm, with links having not only a usability role, but also a semantic one - i.e., they are semantically distinguishable, query-able and an agile metamodelling approach allows their customisation. The link targets are not limited to documentation, they can be any Web resource (e.g., URLs of the artefacts to be implemented, ontology terms, elements of other models).

In other related works [39–41] mind maps are transformed into UML models and structured user stories. The authors also employ a metamodelling approach to facilitate the transformation but they make some simplifying assumptions about the semantics of the mind map's radial relations, in alignment with user story structures and UML models. Their final output is also UML models, employed for a validation feedback mechanism. By combining AMME and RDF, our proposal allows an agile customisation of model semantics; the output is not a model, but a machine-readable graph that acts as an RDF knowledge base that can be used at run-time. Authors of [42] propose a map-like structure which they characterise as being "aspect-oriented" (the Zachman framework dimensions of our proposal may be considered as "aspects"); their work is targeted towards developing an ontology editor.

Based on a recent survey on the interplay between ontologies and requirements engineering [43], we identified as prominent goals the checking of requirements consistency through reasoning (e.g., [44]) or ontology-driven guidance in requirements specification (e.g., [45]). In our work such functions are partly fulfilled by the Zachman-inspired metamodel governing the modelling tool – reasoning comes into play only after models are externalised as RDF, in order to enrich the knowledge exposed to the implemented artefacts. This doesn't necessarily involve ontologies in the traditional sense, but rather SPARQL-based rules over RDF knowledge graphs derived from interlinked models. Connectivity to external ontologies is possible – however, this opportunity was merely suggested and is left out of this paper's scope.

In another work that addresses the gap between formality and flexibility [46], users are empowered to contribute to a metamodel by assigning types to sketched elements. In our proposal, initial types are prescribed by the metamodel underlying the modelling tool, then additional types can be freely annotated as RDF resources (e.g., classes from some known ontology). The initial types may also be customised according to needs, with the help of the metamodelling features of the underlying platform (ADOxx) - however this assumes that the requirements engineer is supported with metamodelling guidelines/skills (an assumption also mentioned in Sect. 3).

6   Concluding Discussion

6.1   SWOT Analysis

The proposed method is a Design Science artefact and was first evaluated for its feasibility, by deployment in the form of a toolset comprising: (a) the modelling tool tailored for mind mapping (including complementary model types); (b) the interoperability mechanism for deriving the RDF graphs; (c) a proof-of-concept Web page incorporating properties retrieved from the mind map and inference results (see Fig. 5). The current state of the proposal has led to the following analysis:

Strengths: Compared with common mind mapping tools, the proposal advocates a hybridisation between a visualisation focus and a conceptual focus. Thus, users who do not care about conceptual modelling may use the prototype as a mind mapping tool; users who do not care about mind mapping may use it for conceptual modelling purposes (depending on the types of models linked to the mind map); and, finally, users working in requirements elicitation may benefit from both sides, including the possibility to derive a semantic database to further support the implementation phase.

Weaknesses: As examples show here, inferences are emulated through SPARQL queries for graph extensions – at least a partial delegation to OWL inference patterns is preferable, although that is limited by OWL expressivity.

Another weakness is a lack of full method evaluation in a project-based application. Partial evaluations have been applied for key ingredients of the method: the RDF export mechanisms (in terms of model retrieval performance [36] for project-based use cases); the understandability of several agile model types for app requirements elicitation (see [30]); and the effectiveness of visual diagramming for RDF graph creation compared with other RDF editing means (in [47]). Considering that the Agile Mind Mapping method as a whole is a Design Science artefact, the wide array of evaluation criteria summarised in [48] is applicable, and more holistic evaluation protocols must be designed (an outlook is discussed in Sect. 6.2).

Opportunities: The paper advocates a convergence of practices and technologies originating in different paradigms – i.e., mind mapping, metamodelling, Linked Data and requirements representation. Therefore it aims to inspire interdisciplinary work on how different representational options and flexibility can impact the understandability of hybrid mind maps and how the gap between requirements and implementation may be bridged with semantic technology. Other types of models used in requirements representation (e.g., goal models) could also be linked to the mind map's *Why* concept and subjected to the same knowledge streamlining.

Threats: The proposal depends on the uptake of the Agile Modelling Method Engineering methodology. The existing distance between mind mapping and conceptual modelling practices stems from a perception of modelling languages as being rigid languages that are too complex for mind mapping needs. This paper's proposal argues that an Agile Mind Mapping Method must provide both a flexible simple core aligned with the mind mapping tradition, as well as the possibility to agilely extend it with relevant conceptual models and inference enablers.

6.2   Evaluation Outlook

Due to complexity, the planned evaluation considers two foci:

A. Focus on the modelling tool. Usability and understandability are both supported and constrained by the underlying implementation platform (i.e., ADOxx). The choice of platform was not determined by its usability features, but by its ability to support AMME's agile conceptualisation, fast (re)prototyping of a modelling tool and the knowledge graph export. Still, the platform facilitates usability and understandability through some key features extensively employed in the work at hand – e.g., the scripting of dynamic and interactive modelling symbols, hyperlinks supporting meaning-driven navigation, a built-in modelling assistant driven by the metamodel constraints. However, since mind mapping tools are essentially visualisation-centred while modelling tools are conceptualisation-centred, comparisons must be quantified.

For *usability*, the planned experiment involves subjects of uniform skill and background (i.e., Information Systems students going through similar preliminary training and familiarisation, then selected based on a post-training assessment) and the typical usability metrics (e.g., completion rate and number of clicks/interactions when creating similar content in Freemind compared to the proposed tool). For *understandability* a generic evaluation protocol was devised and previously applied [30] for AMME-based tools, aiming to assess: (i) notation cognitive fit (measured by matches between concept labels and symbols, compensated by the modeller's ability to select preferred external graphics); (ii) the subject's ability to read models supported only by a symbol legend and tool tips (measured by the number of model elements correctly and explicitly mentioned); (iii) the ability to create models from narrative (measured by the number of model elements correctly created and linked).

B. Focus on the overall method productivity. Here we are interested in tracking project-based effort (i.e., person months) separated between the stages of the process depicted in Fig. 1 across comparable implementations. Currently the project EnterKnow [49] is under analysis across multiple incremental iterations, each iteration following the same process and involving the same human resources.

Acknowledgement. This work is supported by the Romanian National Research Authority through UEFISCDI, under grant agreement PN-III-P2-2.1-PED-2016-1140.

References

1. Buzan, T.: Use Your Head. British Broadcasting Corporation, London (1974)
2. Buzan, T., Buzan, B.: The Mind Map Book: How to Use Radiant Thinking to Maximize Your Brain's Untapped Potential. Plume, New York (1996)
3. Software for mindmapping and information organization – official webiste. https://www.mind-mapping.org/
4. Mahmud, I., Veneziano, V.: Mind-mapping: an effective technique to facilitate requirements engineering in agile software development. In: Proceedings of the 14th International Conference on Computer and Information Technology, pp. 157–162. IEEE (2011)
5. Jaafar, J., Atan, M., Hamid, N.: Collaborative mind map tool to facilitate requirement elicitation. In: Proceedings of the 3rd International Conference on Computing and Informatics 2011, pp. 214–219. Universiti Utara Malaysia Press (2011)
6. Mylopoulos, J.: Conceptual modelling and Telos. In: Loucopoulos, P., Zicari, R. (eds.) Conceptual Modelling, Databases, and CASE: An Integrated View of Information System Development, pp. 49–68. Wiley Press, New York (1992)
7. Object Management Group, The MetaObject Facility Specification. http://www.omg.org/mof/
8. The Resource Description Framework – official website. http://www.w3.org/RDF

9. The Mind Mapping Software Blog, Frey C.: Concept maps vs. mind maps – updated for 2016 (2016). http://mindmappingsoftwareblog.com/concept-maps-vs-mind-maps/
10. van der Aalst, W.M.P.: Process-aware information systems: lessons to be learned from process mining. In: Jensen, K., van der Aalst, W.M.P. (eds.) Transactions on Petri Nets and Other Models of Concurrency II. LNCS, vol. 5460, pp. 1–26. Springer, Heidelberg (2009). https://doi.org/10.1007/978-3-642-00899-3_1
11. Moody, D., Heymans, P., Matulevičius, R.: Visual syntax does matter: improving the cognitive effectiveness of the $i*$ visual notation. Requir. Eng. **15**(2), 141–175 (2010)
12. Loucopoulos, P., Kavakli, E.: Capability modeling with application on large-scale sports events. In: Proceedings of the 22nd Americas Conference on Information Systems 2016. Association for Information Systems (2016)
13. Karagiannis, D.: Agile modeling method engineering. In: Proceedings of the 19th Panhellenic Conference on Informatics 2015, pp. 5–10. ACM, New York (2015)
14. Frank, U.: Domain-specific modeling languages: requirements analysis and design guidelines. In: Reinhartz-Berger, I., Sturm, A., Clark, T., Cohen, S., Bettin, J. (eds.) Domain Engineering, pp. 133–157. Springer, Heidelberg (2013). https://doi.org/10.1007/978-3-642-36654-3_6
15. Kelly, S., Lyytinen, K., Rossi, M.: MetaEdit+ a fully configurable multi-user and multi-tool CASE and CAME environment. In: Bubenko, J., Krogstie, J., Pastor, O., Pernici, B., Rolland, C., Sølvberg, A. (eds.) Seminal Contributions to Information Systems Engineering, pp. 109–129. Springer, Heidelberg (2013). https://doi.org/10.1007/978-3-642-36926-1_9
16. BOC GmbH, ADOxx metamodeling platform – official website. http://www.adoxx.org/live/home
17. Fill, H.-G., Redmond, T., Karagiannis, D.: Formalizing meta models with FDMM: the ADOxx case. In: Cordeiro, J., Maciaszek, L.A., Filipe, J. (eds.) ICEIS 2012. LNBIP, vol. 141, pp. 429–451. Springer, Heidelberg (2013). https://doi.org/10.1007/978-3-642-40654-6_26
18. Karagiannis, D., Kühn, H.: Metamodelling platforms. In: Bauknecht, K., Tjoa, A.M., Quirchmayr, G. (eds.) EC-Web 2002. LNCS, vol. 2455, p. 182. Springer, Heidelberg (2002). https://doi.org/10.1007/3-540-45705-4_19
19. OMiLAB (Open Models Initiative Laboratory) – official website. http://omilab.org
20. Karagiannis, D., Mayr, H.C., Mylopoulos, J. (eds.): Domain-Specific Conceptual Modeling. Springer, Cham (2016). https://doi.org/10.1007/978-3-319-39417-6
21. Ontotext, GraphDB - official website. http://graphdb.ontotext.com/
22. W3C, SPARQL 1.1 Query Language. http://www.w3.org/TR/2013/REC-sparql11-query-20130321
23. W3C, RDF TriG – official specification. https://www.w3.org/TR/trig
24. W3C, Rich Structured Data Markup for Web Documents. https://www.w3.org/TR/rdfa-primer/
25. Eclipse RDF4j - official documentation. http://docs.rdf4j.org/rest-api/
26. Heath, T., Bizer, C.: Linked Data: Evolving the Web into a Global Data Space. Synthesis Lectures on the Semantic Web: Theory and Technology, vol. 1(1), Morgan & Claypool, San Francisco (2011)
27. DBPedia – official website. http://wiki.dbpedia.org/
28. Accessing Relational Databases as Virtual RDF Graphs (D2RQ) - official website. http://d2rq.org
29. Buzan, T.: Mind Mapping – official website. http://www.tonybuzan.com/about/mind-mapping/
30. Buchmann, R.A., Karagiannis, D.: Modelling mobile app requirements for semantic traceability. Requir. Eng. **22**(1), 41–75 (2017)

31. Zachman, J.A.: A framework for information systems architecture. IBM Syst. J. **26**(3), 276–292 (1987)
32. Yu, E.S.: Towards modelling and reasoning support for early-phase requirements engineering. In: Proceedings of the 3rd IEEE International Symposium on Requirements Engineering 1997, pp. 226–235. IEEE (1997)
33. OMiLAB Bee-Up – official website. http://austria.omilab.org/psm/content/bee-up/info. Accessed 20 Sept 2017
34. Karagiannis, D., Buchmann, R.A., Burzynski, P., Reimer, U., Walch, M.: Fundamental conceptual modeling languages in OMiLAB. Domain-Specific Conceptual Modeling, pp. 3–30. Springer, Cham (2016). https://doi.org/10.1007/978-3-319-39417-6_1
35. Buchmann, R.A., Karagiannis, D.: Domain-specific diagrammatic modelling: a source of machine-readable semantics for the Internet of Things. Cluster Comput. **20**(1), 895–908 (2017)
36. Karagiannis, D., Buchmann, R.A.: Linked Open Models: extending Linked Open Data with conceptual model information. Inf. Syst. **56**, 174–197 (2016)
37. Beel, J., Gipp, B., Stiller, J.O.: Information retrieval on mind maps-what could it be good for? In: Proceeding of the 5th International Conference on Collaborative Computing: Networking, Applications and Worksharing 2009, pp. 1–4. IEEE (2009)
38. Beel, J., Gipp, B., Müller, C.: "SciPlore MindMapping": a tool for creating mind maps combined with PDF and reference management. D-Lib Mag. **15**(11/12) (2009). https://doi.org/10.1045/november2009-inbrief
39. Wanderley, F., Silveira, D., Araujo, J., Moreira, A., Guerra, E.: Experimental evaluation of conceptual modelling through mind maps and model driven engineering. In: Murgante, B., Misra, S., Rocha, A.M.A.C., Torre, C., Rocha, J.G., Falcão, M.I., Taniar, D., Apduhan, B.O., Gervasi, O. (eds.) ICCSA 2014. LNCS, vol. 8583, pp. 200–214. Springer, Cham (2014). https://doi.org/10.1007/978-3-319-09156-3_15
40. Wanderley, F., da Silveria, D.S.: A framework to diminish the gap between the business specialist and the software designer. In: Proceedings of the 8th International Conference on Quality of Information and Communications Technology 2012, pp. 199–204. IEEE (2012)
41. Wanderley, F., Silva, A., Araujo, J.: Evaluation of BehaviorMap: a user-centered behavior language. In: Proceedings of the 9th International Conference on Research Challenges in Information Science, pp. 309–320. IEEE (2015)
42. Brinkschulte, L., Enders, A., Rebstadt, J., Mertens, R: Aspect-oriented mind mapping and its potential for ontology editing. In: Proceedings of the 10th International Conference on Semantic Computing 2016, pp. 194–201. IEEE (2016)
43. Dermeval, D., Vilela, J., Bittencourt, I., Castro, J., Isotani, S., Brito, P., Silva, A.: Applications of ontologies in requirements engineering: a systematic review of the literature. Requir. Eng. **21**(4), 405–437 (2016)
44. Siegemund, K., Thomas, E.J., Aßmann, U., Pan, J., Zhao, Y.: Towards ontology-driven requirements engineering. In: Proceedings of the 7th International Workshop on Semantics-Enabled Software Engineering (2011)
45. Farfeleder, S., Moser, T., Krall, A., Stålhane, T., Omoronyia, I., Zojer, H.: Ontology-driven guidance for requirements elicitation. In: Antoniou, G., Grobelnik, M., Simperl, E., Parsia, B., Plexousakis, D., De Leenheer, P., Pan, J. (eds.) ESWC 2011. LNCS, vol. 6644, pp. 212–226. Springer, Heidelberg (2011). https://doi.org/10.1007/978-3-642-21064-8_15
46. Wüest, D., Seyff, N., Glinz, M.: Sketching and notation creation with FlexiSketch Team: evaluating a new means for collaborative requirements elicitation. In: Proceedings of the 23rd IEEE International Requirements Engineering Conference, pp. 186–195. IEEE (2015)

47. Karagiannis D., Buchmann, R.A.: A proposal for deploying Hybrid Knowledge Bases: the ADOxx-to-GraphDB interoperability case. In: Proceedings of the 51st Hawaii Conference on System Sciences, University of Hawaii, pp. 4055–4064 (2018)
48. Prat, N., Comyn-Wattiau, I., Akoka, J.: Artifact evaluation in information systems design-science research – a holistic view. In: Proceedings of the 19th Pacific Asia Conference on Information Systems 2014, p. 23. Association for Information Systems (2014)
49. EnterKnow project – homepage. http://enterknow.granturi.ubbcluj.ro

A Persona-Based Modelling
for Contextual Requirements

Genaína Nunes Rodrigues[1]([⊠]) [iD], Carlos Joel Tavares[1], Naiara Watanabe[1],
Carina Alves[2], and Raian Ali[3]

[1] University of Brasília, Brasília, Brazil
genaina@unb.br, carlosjoel.tavares@gmail.com, naiara@gmail.com
[2] Center of Informatics, Federal University of Pernambuco, Recife, Brazil
cfa@cin.ufpe.br
[3] Bournemouth University, Poole, UK
rali@bournemouth.ac.uk

Abstract. **[Context&Motivation]** Personas are a technique used to guide developing products accommodating people diversity. They are archetypes reflecting common combinations of users' characteristics, needs and goals. Persons can add a human-centred facet to requirements engineering practice which is often revolving around the concept of business roles. **[Question/Problem]** Goal modelling is an example of mainstream requirements engineering approach driven by business roles and their responsibilities and needs represented as goals. Personnel in the system are expected to act according to this prescriptive specification. Personnel diversity is often seen as a customization and design issue. **[Principal idea/Results].** In this paper we propose to consider such diversity as a conditional context in requirements modelling and, as an approach, augment Contextual Goal Model (CGM) with personas as a new contextual dimension. Additionally, we propose an algorithm to analyse the achievability of CGM goals in the presence of the personas contexts variation. We evaluate our approach using a Mobile Personal Emergency Response System (MPERS) implemented as a prototype. **[Contribution]** Our persona-based modelling approach paves the way to augment requirements with a consideration of people diversity and enrich the business perspective with a more user-centred design facet.

Keywords: Contextual requirements · User-centred design
Goal-oriented requirements engineering

1 Introduction

A persona is a fictional character that represents a group of users of a given system. It is a design technique used in product development that complements other usability techniques, rendering the product development more effective and accommodative to diversity [1,2]. The use of personas puts a face on the user, making them as real as possible and helping in that sense making the design

© Springer International Publishing AG, part of Springer Nature 2018
E. Kamsties et al. (Eds.): REFSQ 2018, LNCS 10753, pp. 352–368, 2018.
https://doi.org/10.1007/978-3-319-77243-1_23

more human-centred. The personas are defined by their attributes, goals and any other information that might help the development process (e.g. age, skills, tasks, etc.). Such attributes and goals guide the development of a system solution and may provide a significant advantage during the research and conceptualisation stages of the design process [3].

Goal-oriented requirements engineering (GORE) uses goals for the elaboration, specification, negotiation, documentation and modification of requirements in system development [4]. Goal models (GM) provide the goals for which the system should be designed and a set of ways to reach those goals in prescriptive and pragmatic manners [5,6]. Personas, on the other hand, are synthesized into descriptions that include behavior patterns, goals, skills/capabilities, attitudes, and environment [1]. Therefore, goals and capabilities are core and also shared constituents for both goal modelling and personas making the integration of power between both techniques easier and natural.

GORE in general tends to take a business perspective where people are allocated to roles, responsibilities and permissions. However, we recognize that the individual levels cannot be normalized and would not be expected to play the same role in a similar and uniform way. On the other hand, the consideration of the personal differences case by case adds infeasible overhead to the engineers and introduce the need for personalizing the requirements [7]. We propose the use of personas as a feasible mechanism putting two perspectives together. First, as a way to handle the lack of consideration of users as people with personality and goals not necessarily completely aligned with their roles in the system. Second, as a normative way of operation to handle the complexity of taking into account a multitude of personal difference.

Persona information can be modelled as contextual conditions on the set of requirements and their alternative strategies of achievement following from their behavior patterns and capabilities. By context we mean *a partial state of the world that system operates* [8] specified as a formula or world predicate that must be fulfilled to enable the activation of a requirement and also its achievement through certain alternative pathways in the goal analysis. For example, consider a system that requires a person to specify their location and situation in case they require a prompt delivery of an ambulance. If the person is averse to technology, they might not be able to perform well such action in such emergency situation. However, such aversion is not exactly a personal goal or neither a system goal, but instead part of the person's characteristic that enables or hinders the need for certain goals and their alternative ways of achievements.

In this paper, we introduce the notion of personas as a source of context when modelling contextual requirements so that we empower requirements modelling practice with personalization and human-centred design facets. In addition, we propose a method for goal achievement sensitive to their actual set of personas. We formalize a structure where personas attributes and goals are then used to define the contextual operation the system. Therefore, the contributions of the paper are threefold. First, we propose a methodology that articulates the information of personas and map them to contextual goal models (CGM) [8] as contextual condition. Secondly, we propose an algorithm to analyse the achievability of CGM goals in the presence of the personas contexts variation. Lastly, we carry out an exploratory study performed on the Mobile Personal Emergency System (MPERS) [5] to assess the benefits and feasibility of the approach.

The remaining sections of the paper are structured as follows: Sect. 2 explores the background needed for understanding the paper. Section 3 we present our conceptual model and the methodology used in this paper. Section 4 presents the exploratory study we conducted on the Mobile Personal Emergency Systems (MPERS). Section 5 presents literature works most related to the focus of our work. In Sect. 6 we conclude our work and present future directions we envision.

2   Background

In this section we present a brief background needed for the understanding of our approach: Contextual Goal Models and Personas.

2.1   Contextual Goal Models

Contextual Goal Model (CGM), proposed in [8], extends classic Goal Models by the explicit presentation of the relationship between a goals and their achievement strategies and quality of those strategies on one hand, and the dynamic nature of the system surrounding, i.e. its context, on the other. Context is defined as *a partial state of the world in which the system operates and is relevant to its goals* [8]. It is a reification of that system surrounding in terms of concrete conditions [9]. Context and its different status operate as an adaptation driver when deciding the goals to activate and the alternatives to adopt and reach the activated goals. It also plays role in deciding the quality of those alternatives, i.e. their contributions to soft-goals. A context may be a patient's health status, a person's relationship status, a specific season of the year, etc.

The CGM presented in Fig. 1 depicts the goals to be achieved by a Mobile Personal Emergency Response System (MPERS) which is meant to respond to emergencies in an assisted living environment. The root goal is respond to emergency", which is performed by the actor Mobile Personal Emergency Response. The root goal is divided into four sub-goals: emergency is detected", [p] is notified about emergency", central receives [p] info" and medical care reaches [p] ([p] stands for patient). Such goals are then further decomposed, within the boundary of an actor, to finally reach executable tasks or delegations to other actors. A task is a process performed by the actor and a delegation is the act of passing a goal on to another actor that can perform it.

2.2   Persona Characterization

Persona is a fictional character, an archetype of a group of people of the real world [1,2]. It is a design technique widely used on product development. A persona is defined primarily by its objectives, determined in a process of successive

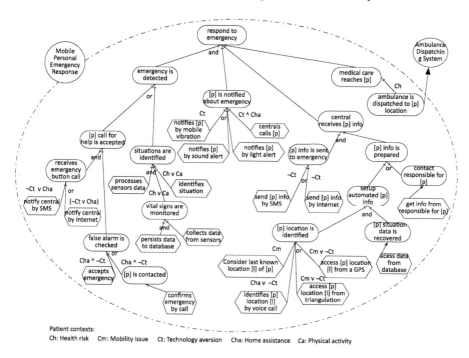

Fig. 1. A CGM for responding to emergencies in an assisted living environment, adapted from [5].

refinements during the initial investigation of the domain of an activity. The Persona structure is derived through a research process, which aims to collect information from various users of the system and, from this, create representative profiles for a group of users. Our persona, Mary Collins in Fig. 2, contains the characteristics: age, profession, attributes and goals, but that amount of attributes is not fixed, it depends on how detailed and fine-grained a persona description needs to be which is also dependent on the use and other design artefacts personas are intended to complement.

3 Persona-Based Modelling for GORE

In this section, we present our conceptual model and the methodology of using personas in conjunction with CGM to add human-centred contextual facets to the requirements model.

3.1 Persona for Contextual Goal Models

In this section we propose an extension to the CGM integrating it with personas. CGMs take into consideration contexts as conditions on (i) the options embedded in the system to be developed, i.e. functional requirements modelled as goals and

Mary Collins (Persona 1)

Age: 70 years
Profession: Retired

Attributes

- Live alone in a small house;
- Does not have a houserkeeper, only diarist every 15 days;
- Does other household chores;
- Fell at home once, but did not fracture any bone;
- Has osteoporosis type 2 at an early stage;
- Has diabetes, high blood pressure and heart problems;
- She is diurnal but wakes up twice at night to go to the bathroom;
- Has 2 childrens who lives in their homes;
- Don't have Wi-Fi at home.

Goals

- To avoid frustating experiences with technologies;
- To not to worry with her children;
- To feel safe by not falling down at home;
- To have quality of life.

Fig. 2. The characterisation of persona Mary Collins.

their strategies, and (ii) their quality modelled, i.e. non-functional requirements modelled as soft-goals. Attributes of the users that will actually interact with the system can be seen also as contextual conditions. By considering them at the goal level, usually used at the early stages of development, we add a human perspective early on in the development process. Our extension to the model is highlighted on Fig. 3. By including personas to our modeling, we can cater for the actual potential user groups of the software, allowing better specification of the user needs in the software, making the generic goals of the actors more assertive and more specific. In addition, the variability space presented through the space of personas representing users diversity allows identification of the impacts to the model to be used on properties like fitness to capabilities and usability. This means that the objectives of the persona can be checked against the objectives and options defined for the product to be developed, in this case the goal model of the system. Therefore, it is possible not only to define the system's functionalities but also to prioritize them from the point of view of the user, who is the one who interacts with the system. Our conceptual model depicted in Fig. 3 extends original definitions of the CGM, as our context definition is based on the persona's goals and attributes in its entirety. Major concepts of our model are: Goals, Persona, Context, Attributes, World Predicates, Facts *(a world predicate F is a fact for an actor A iff F can be verified by A. [8])*. The CGM contains a set of Contexts linked to its variation points. A Context can aggregate a set of World Predicates in a form of a logical formula and will be validated through a specific Persona. A Persona aggregates a set of Goals and Attributes. Attributes are associated with a set of contextual facts that are aggregated into the World Predicates which constitute the atomic propositions of a certain context.

3.2 Methodology

Our methodology comprises the following major steps: structuring personas attributes as contextual facts, characterizing personas contexts, mapping personas contexts into the CGM and checking the achievability of the CGM goals. We should note that our approach brings benefits to the process of goal-oriented requirements modelling independently from the technology used, i.e. KAOS, i*, Tropos. We explain such steps in the following sections.

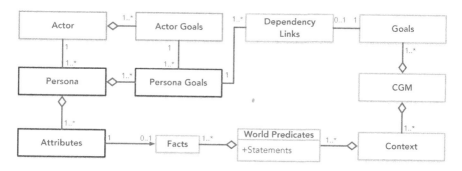

Fig. 3. Conceptual model of our CGM-based persona modelling approach.

Structuring Persona Attributes as Contextual Facts. The creation of personas relies on information gathered in the early requirements phase. Thus, the determination of the number, attributes, goals and types of personas depends on the potential stakeholders and the elicited requirements and purpose statement of the system. Prior to exploring how personas should be systematically analysed following our methodology, we first define how the informational content of a persona should be first mapped as contextual facts that can be integrated to the CGM [8]. In our work, we argue that persona attributes should be modelled as contextual conditions instead of functional requirements directly mapped as part of those sets of services a system should fulfill, in accordance with the argument in [7]. As such, we model each persona attribute as a contextual fact: *a world predicate for an actor A if the fact can be verified by A* [8]. We should note that the world predicate is a formula of logic predicates that specifies a context. In our work, the actor is archetyped as personas.

We formalize the description of the persona attributes into contextual facts as follows:

1. i is the id of the persona in the population of interest.

2. $A_i \in \{A_1, A_2,...,A_n\}$, where A is a set of attributes as nominal categorical variables of i.

3. Each attribute A_i may have a corresponding contextual fact F_j, where $i \leq j$.

4. $i = \bigcup\limits_{n=1}^{j} F_n$, the persona i is characterized as the union of F_j contextual facts.

Following the work of Chapman et al. [10], the persona attributes can be sorted as a key-value list, where each key is a nominal categorical variable instantiated by an attribute of the persona. For example, from the excerpt of the persona Mary Collins, we can have a list of attributes: A_1("Mary Collins") & B_1("high probability of fall incidents") & C_1("unfamiliar with technology") & etc., where 1 is the id that uniquely identifies the persona Mary Collins. Attributes A_1, B_1 and C_1 are categorical variables that could be accordingly mapped to contextual fact such as *name*, *healthProblem* and *techAversion*, respectively.

In the formalization of personas attributes above, note that F_j is an index function that characterizes the facts under study pertaining *all* personas. For a particular category variable, the purpose is to have the more variation as possible to significantly represent the target system. For example, in order to comprehensively represent a group of patients to be modelled for the MPERS, various types of illness and health risk may be represented in different persona representations.

Characterizing Persona Contexts. Once the persona's contextual facts are properly characterized, we then proceed to characterize all the contexts which will be further instantiated in the CGM to analyse if the system goals will be affected by the persona's characteristics as contexts of operation. To characterize the context that will be triggered by the persona we take in consideration the semantic information of the contextual facts. For example, in our persona Mary Collins the attribute B_1: "high probability of fall incidents" mapped into contextual fact *healthProblem* can take part of the context *healthRisk*. Other facts could compose such context if, for example, another persona is characterized with another *healthProblem* fact that could fit into *healthRisk* context.

Following the work in [8], we specify context as a predicate formula of and/or combinations of statements and facts. Note that the contextual facts in our work map only those relevant persona information that can be directly verified through data gathering, for example. In Fig. 4 we model context $Ch : healthRisk$. Such context is defined by the following predicate formula: $f1 \vee f2 \vee f3 \vee f4 \vee f5 \vee f6$ & $wp1$. Therefore, context Ch applies if at least one of such contextual facts is true (present) in the modelled personas *and* the health status of the patient is characterised either as low ($f7$), medium ($f8$) or critical ($f9$) status. In particular, for other fuzzy typed values, an analogous modelling can be carried out as characterised by $wp1$, which actual range values should be defined by the domain expert. We should note that it is out of scope of our current work to define an approach to elicit contexts. We assume that the contexts characterization into facts should rely on domain expert validation. However, one could also use other

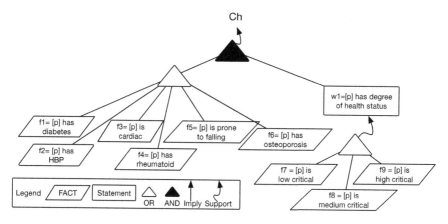

Fig. 4. Context modelling excerpt.

sources of information to extract relevant contexts from available information, if present, or conduct a data gathering of personas' relevant information via survey study following the work of Chapman et al. [10].

In Fig. 1 we illustrate five different patient contexts in the MPERS case study, where each context variant characterizes their own context formula. Namely, such contexts are the following ones: Ch: health risk, Cm: mobility issue, Ct: technology aversion, Cha: home assistance and Ca: physical activity. Once the contexts related to the persona are identified, the next step consists of the mapping of such contexts into the CGM. The contexts identified for the patients of the MPERS case study are presented in Fig. 1. Once the contexts (formula) of the CGM have been defined, it is then possible to define all the contexts that are triggered by a given persona. Given all those contextual facts of a persona, if a context formula evaluates to true for the facts of a persona, it means such context is part of the set of contexts triggered by a persona. We formalize such set definition as follows:

Definition 1 (Persona Context Set). *Let the mapping function $C\colon i \xrightarrow{C_j} \{T, F\}$ which returns true or false for the facts of persona i applied to context C_j. If $C_j(i) = T$, it means that $C_j \in \Omega$, where Ω is the set of contexts triggered by persona i.*

In case of our persona Mary Collins, she triggers the context set Ch, Cha and Ct. The trigger of Mary's Ch is due to the fact that at least one of the facts from $f1$ to $f6$ are part of Mary's context facts list. Actually, not only $f1$ but also $f2$, $f3$ and $f6$ are facts of the persona Mary Collins. While Ct is triggered by the fact she *is not technology friendly* ($f19$) and Cha is triggered by the fact she *has an assisted living device* ($f14$).

Structuring Persona Goals. Due to the fact that a persona represents user groups by using a rich and highly memorable description, they are easy to

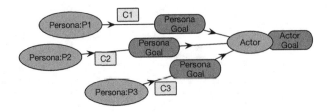

Fig. 5. The Relationship Between Actors and Persona Goals

understand during the whole development process. In our proposal, a persona has several goals to achieve by using the system. The goals of a persona can be described in a holistic manner using the persona's psychological characteristics, attitudes, motivations, and preferences. Therefore, persona goals encapsulate a comprehensive description of representative users' needs and expectations regarding the system under development. It also clarifies decision rationales to prioritize a particular goal. Initially, during the definition of a persona as described in Fig. 2, the requirements team should textually describe the persona attributes and goals. Following the proposal by [11], the persona attributes and goals previously defined in a textual format can be represented by means of goals, softgoals, or tasks. As such, an actor can be associated by different personas, in which each persona has his/her specific goals and contexts, as illustrated in Fig. 5. For instance, in our case study, actors can be patients and doctors. The group of patients as users is very heterogeneous and can be classified in specific personas such as: Mary who is averse to technology, Dorothy who has difficulty in walking, and Jennifer who does physical activity, has facility with technology but takes controlled medication. In our study, the actor doctor is represented by the persona Paul[1]. Then, we identify the extent to which each element contributes to the persona goal satisfaction. The persona goals have relationships with the CGM via dependency links. Therefore the satisfiability of the persona goals can be defined as follows:

Definition 2 (Persona Goal Satisfaction). *Let the context set Ω triggered by persona i, the actor goal Γ, which the persona goal is link dependent, and the target system CGM. The persona goal satisfaction property Φ_i is achieved when $(\Omega, \Gamma, CGM) \vDash \Phi_i$.*

For example, in the MPERS scenario, the patient actor they want to be assisted. While the actor representing the medical doctor they want to assist the patient. However, it not only suffices to know if their goal to either be assisted or to assist via the MPERS will be achieved. The context of the patient and the doctor also needs to be taken into consideration to make sure the persona instantiating the corresponding actors will have their goals satisfied. Therefore, the need to know the persona context is paramount to learn if the CGM goal will be reached.

---

[1] Such personas are available in the GitHub link for this paper: https://github.com/CJTS/REFSQ_2018.

So the satisfaction of the persona goal in the MPERS means that the root goal of the CGM was satisfied under the persona context set (e.g. Mary's context set) and its actor goal (e.g. be assisted via MPERS).

Goal Achievement Check. In our work, the persona goal satisfaction is carried out through the goal achievement check algorithm, where we leverage the achievability of goals in a CGM by adding the human perspective through the person context. Such expressiveness will enable richer adaptation decisions that not only consider the static achievability but also the achievability where the user context can be explicitly modelled and its effect on the fulfillment criteria of a goal. The achievability of a goal and the space of adoptable alternatives to achieve it are essential information to plan adaptation, seen as a selection and enactment of a suitable alternative to reach a goal under a certain persona context criteria.

In Algorithm 1 we evaluate the achievability of the system goals under the contexts triggered by the persona. The algorithm has as input information the Contextual Goal Model and the persona context facts. The algorithm is recursive, building on the fact that the CGM is a tree-structured model and that each refinement may be seen as a tree node. The Algorithm considers the root node of the CGM (line 1). Given the context facts that characterise the persona and a set of logical relations between the context variables, in line 2, the call to *getContextSet* method returns the context sets triggered by the persona to check if there exists a truth assignment for all variables that makes the conjunction of the persona context formula satisfiable. If such assignment exists, then the formula is satisfiable, otherwise it is unsatisfiable under the assumed logical relations.

After that, the contextual goal model is traversed considering the mapped persona context set and the tree structure of the CGM. The algorithm checks whether the goal node is itself applicable under the current persona context (line 3), returning NULL if it is not (line 4). In the particular case when the node type is a task (6) it can decide on the goal achievability and returns a plan consisting only of such task (line 9). If the node is not a task, the Algorithm starts defining an execution plan that fulfills the persona context set (line 11). For each of the applicable refinements (line 13), it will evaluate if it is achievable (line 14). If the refinement is achievable then, for OR-decompositions, the algorithm returns this plan immediately (line 17) and for AND-decompositions it is added to the complete plan (line 20). If the CGM node is not achieved the algorithm returns the root node of the failed subtree (lines 22–25). As such it means that in the fulfilment of that particular failing CGM node, better alternative strategies need to be addressed so that frustrations with the actual user do not happen under real life conditions. Finally, for AND-decompositions, should all refinements render achievable it will return the complete execution plan for the persona contextual information (line 28).

Algorithm 1. isAchievable(CGM cgm, ContextFacts personaFacts)

Require: CGM, PersonaFacts context facts
 1: Goal node ← cgm.getRoot()
 2: ContextSet persona ← getContextSet(personaFacts)
 3: **if** !node.isApplicable(persona) **then**
 4:     **return** NULL
 5: **end if**
 6: **if** (node.getType() == task) **then**
 7:     p ← new Plan(node)
 8:     p.achievable ← true
 9:     **return** p
10: **end if**
11: Plan complete ← NULL
12: deps ← node.getRefinements(cgm, persona)
13: **for all** Refinement d **in** deps **do**
14:     Plan p ← d.isAchievable(cgm, persona)
15:     **if** (p.achievable ∧ p!= NULL) **then**
16:         **if** (node.isOrDecomposition()) **then**
17:             **return** p
18:         **end if**
19:         **if** (node.isAndDecomposition()) **then**
20:             complete ← addPlanToPlan(p, complete)
21:         **end if**
22:     **else if** (node.isAndDecomposition()) **then**
23:         p ← new Plan(d)
24:         p.achievable ← false
25:         **return** p
26:     **end if**
27: **end for**
28: **return** complete

---

4   Feasibility Study

To evaluate our method, which mainly formalizes the information of personas and map them as contextual requirements, we implemented the Algorithm proposed in Sect. 3.2 and applied it in the MPERS CGM. The algorithm analyses the achievability of goals in a CGM when considering a certain persona and their attributes as contexts. The evaluation was designed according to the Goal-Question-Metric (GQM) framework [12] presented in Table 1. For this purpose, we evaluated the efficiency of the algorithm, run it to test the achievability of goals and the planning it yields for each modelled personas with the varying attributes and goals. The purpose was to provide a proof of concept and evidence for feasibility.

4.1 Experiment Setup

The study consisted in evaluating the methodology in the MPERS case study. We used the goal model provided in Fig. 1. We modelled four personas where three of them are patients (Mary, Jennifer and Dorothy) and one of them is a medical doctor (Paul). For the patients, we applied the five contexts modelled in Fig. 1. As for the medical doctor we applied three new contexts: *Cc: means of communication, Ci: means of information sharing, Che: means of assisting.* The evaluation was based on a prototype implemented in C#. The experiments were executed on an Intel(R) Core i5, 1.6 GHz and 4 GB of RAM. For the sake of space, we do not report all the detailed information of our feasibility study and the implementation details, but they can be accessed via our provided Github repository link.[2]

4.2 Results

Question 1: Is the algorithm efficient to come up with an execution plan? – We evaluated the time for the algorithm to come up with an execution plan considering the MPERS CGM in Fig. 1 for the four modelled personas. The results showed that the algorithm took at most 40.10^{-3} ms ($40\,\mu$s) to come up with an answer for each persona context. Therefore, the algorithm can be considered quite efficient for setup analysed.

Formally speaking, the algorithm can be proven as linear time complexity $O(n)$, where n is the number of nodes in the CGM. The major complexity of the algorithm is in the execution of each Refinement d in *deps* (lines 13–27). The algorithm recursively invokes itself for the CGM of the Refinement (sub goal, task or delegation). Since this invocation is performed on trees of height lower or equal to the CGM tree we can consider that the root node has n refinements and this is performed in $O(n_k)$ time, where n_k is the amount of nodes in the k sub tree of node n. Then, each node in the sub tree is visited exactly once. Therefore, the time to visit all n nodes is: $O(n) + O(n_k)$. That amounts to $O(n)$,

Table 1. GQM devised plan

Goal: Analysis of the achievability of the goals	
Question	Metric
Q1. Is the algorithm efficient to come up with an execution plan	Execution time
Q2. Does the algorithm allow testing and explaining persona-based goal achievability?	Yes/No
Q3. Are the plans provided by the algorithm correct?	% of correct plans

---

[2] Source code, goal model and evaluation of our approach are available at: https://github.com/CJTS/REFSQ_2018.

since summing across the number of children of each tree node is equivalent to summing over all nodes. We should note that, in the particular case that the root goal is not applicable the algorithm simply returns NULL in constant time, thus $O(1)$. Likewise, the call to the getType method returns in constant time (lines 3–9).

Question 2: Does the algorithm allow testing and explaining persona-based goal achievability? – We considered 19 distinctive facts for the considered personas. Such facts can be distributed in eight distinctive contexts: five for the patients and three for the medical doctor, as previously mentioned in the Study Setup and further explained in the Github link of this work. Having the root achieved for each persona means that the root goal of the MPERS' CGM is achieved and, therefore, considering the persona context, the system is able to meet its goals. Out of the four modelled personas, only Mary did not have the MPERS goals achieved. It happened due to the fact that Mary has technology aversion to some degree since she fears having frustrating experiences with technology (context fact $f19$). Such fact triggers context Ct and hinders the goal fulfilment that the *central receives [p] info* since its left subtree will be fulfilled if the patient does not have technology aversion. As a result, alternative solutions need to be devised (and included in the MPERS CGM) particularly related to the *[p] info is sent to emergency* goal, where people with technology aversion, like Mary Collins, may be able to guarantee their information is sent under an emergency situation without requiring them to be technology friendly.

Question 3: Are the plans provided by the algorithm correct? – Out of the four modelled personas, the algorithm provided two execution plans as presented in Fig. 6. We represent the two plans as one, where they differ on the highlights in red boxes. The activity in the red box labelled *Planning 1* corresponds to the available execution plan that is achieved in the context of Dorothy (patient) and Paul (medical doctor). While the activity in the red box labeled *Planning 2* corresponds to the available execution plan that is achieved in the context of Jennifer (patient). Note that the fact that Dorothy and Paul share the same

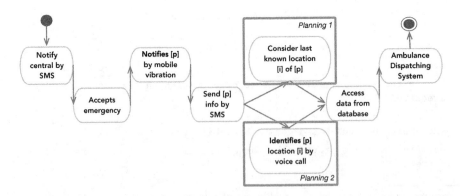

Fig. 6. Achievable plans for the provided personas contexts. (Color figure online)

planning does not mean they trigger the same contexts since their context sets are disjunctive. On the other hand, considering that Jennifer and Dorothy are both patients, they trigger different execution plans. While Dorothy has some difficulty in walking and therefore considered as having some problem on her ability to move *Cm*. In case she falls and her location identification is needed, the system will *Consider last known location of Dorothy*. The variability that the planning captured is exactly what has been conceived for those patients with mobility issue in the CGM devise. Therefore, the plans provided by our algorithm are correct.

5 Related Work

Several works studied Persona in Software Engineering context [13–16]. Haikara [15] tackles the subject in agile software development where the argument is that agile software development methods do not seem to address usability and interaction design issues enough and the author proposes an extension on the interaction design process by using personas. Castro et al. [16] use the personas technique and integrate it into the requirement analysis activity. They advocate the necessity to understand users who interact with the system. The work of Faily and Lyle [14] illustrates how personas can be integrated into software tools to support usability and software engineering. That works presents guidelines that software engineering tools should incorporate to support the design and evolution of personas. By using personas in the requirement analysis phase they can gain a better understanding of the user and can improve the usability of the system. Chapman et al. [10] propose a formal model to understand persona information in terms of factual attributes. They use such information to guide the extraction of a comprehensive variety of personas. In our work, we take personas a step further and embed them in the system requirements model so that we allow a more formal and automated support to the alignment between users diversity and the system at the early stage of goals and intentionality.

The works of [11,17] amongst the first to address personas in the context of a goal modelling process. They use the goals model to visualise and help validate personas. While in [17] the author is concerned with usability issues, in [11] the authors are concerned with trust issues. In our work, we use personas information as contextual facts and the impact personas-derived contexts will have in the goal model the personas might be embedded in. The work of Di Francescomarino et al. [18] tackles personas in the context of goal modelling and uses the User-Centered Design (a series of well-defined methods and techniques that comes from social sciences) towards that integration. Their work aims at defining a modeling framework that integrates the goal-oriented paradigm, process modeling and User-Cantered design techniques and methods to capture the intentional elements of the user (e.g. goals, preferences, assets, etc.).

The work in [8] proposes an explicit notion of context and its relation to requirements and applies that on goal model providing Contextual Goal Models (CGM). There are few works that adopt CGM as modelling baseline such as

Guimaraes et al. [5] and Mendonca et al. [19]. The work in [5] uses the concept of Pragmatic Goals to enhance the contexts of CGMs. Pragmatic Goals are the idea that a goal's interpretation varies according to context. While the work in [19] uses the CGM structure to provide quantitative dependability analysis by means of probabilistic model checking. Despite the benefits of their approach, they do not cater primarily for the human perspective which could hinder altogether their analysis processes in that aspect.

6   Discussion, Conclusion and Future Work

The use of persona as an enabling technique to personalize and add a human-centric aspect to business requirements was proposed. The premise is that this would make the system analysis closer to its personnel both in relation to their job role description and also unique personalities. While personas are usually used in the literature of HCI and usability, we argued that they can be equally useful at the early stages of requirements engineering including the intentionality and strategic interest modelling done via languages like goal modelling. Personas in this case are not only about how the users use the system typically but also about the alignment between their intentions and capabilities on one hand and the socio-technical solutions on the other.

Concerning the efficiency of our approach, we have shown the algorithm works in O(n) complexity. Therefore, the number of personas to be analysed would not be a computational issue. As for the optimal number of personas one should take into account, Chapman et al. [10] have already proposed an ideal number of personas previously. Nevertheless, the higher the number of the personas, the more complex to map their information into the goal model. On the hand, such complextity stems from the mapping of contexts into goals following the CGM background approach. As for the application domain benefit, all those that benefit from a goal-oriented modelling approach could benefit from our work, if the human perspective should be taken into account as any socio-technical system would require.

We recognize that a better management of our approach requires a more elaborated conceptualization of personas. This includes the distinction between different families of personas characterizers and relations amongst them and goals. Remarkable classes of these attributes include capabilities, personality traits, collaborative and competitive nature, intrinsic and extrinsic motivation and learning styles. This should also be mapped to goals for fitness and alignment. For example, a business goal which requires heavy dependency and interaction with other actors to achieve would not fit a persona who is introvert in personality and prefers well-defined tasks and less tolerant to deviation from the norm. In addition, personas goals could be of various families as well including social recognition, values, promotion goals, etc. which are aimed to be achieved in tandem with the business goals but not part of the contractual settings.

For future work, as a process of specification we may need to think of two parallel processes to allow a separation of concerns. The first strand would concern the business requirements modelling while the other looks at the personnel and their expectations and requirements in the first instance. This would enable independence before the triangulation stage would start. Such a mixed-method could be applied in an iterative and evolutionary style where argumentation and negotiation can be enabled. Participatory design principles and processes would be a potential fit. In summary, a human-centred approach to requirements modelling would also benefit from similar approaches adopted at the design stage but adapted to the level of abstraction and emphasis of requirements modelling. Additionally, a real-life case study will be addressed.

Acknowledgment. The authors would like to express their gratitude for the fruitful discussions with Shamal Faily, Felipe Pontes, Célia Ralha and Renato Pina during the development of this work. Genaína would like to thank CAPES-PROCAD for the partial financial support of this work.

References

1. Cooper, A.: The Inmates Are Running the Asylum: [Why High-tech Products Drive us Crazy and How to Restore the Sanity]. Sams Publishing, US (2004)
2. Pruitt, J., Grudin, J.: Personas: practice and theory. In: Proceedings of the 2003 Conference on Designing for User Experiences, DUX 2003, New York, NY, USA, pp. 1–15. ACM (2003)
3. Long, F.: Real or imaginary: the effectiveness of using personas in product design. In: Proceedings of the Irish Ergonomics Society Conference, pp. 1–10. Irish Ergonomics Society (2009)
4. Van Lamsweerde, A.: Goal-oriented requirements engineering: a guided tour. In: Proceedings of the Fifth IEEE International Symposium on Requirements Engineering 2001, pp. 249–262. IEEE (2001)
5. Pontes Guimaraes, F., Nunes Rodrigues, G., Macedo Batista, D., Ali, R.: Pragmatic requirements for adaptive systems: a goal-driven modeling and analysis approach. In: Johannesson, P., Lee, M.L., Liddle, S.W., Opdahl, A.L., López, Ó.P. (eds.) ER 2015. LNCS, vol. 9381, pp. 50–64. Springer, Cham (2015). https://doi.org/10.1007/978-3-319-25264-3_4
6. Yu, E., Mylopoulos, J.: Why goal-oriented requirements engineering. In: Proceedings of the 4th International Workshop on Requirements Engineering: Foundations of Software Quality, vol. 15, pp. 15–22 (1998)
7. Sutcliffe, A., Fickas, S., Sohlberg, M.M.: Personal and contextual requirements engineering. In: 13th IEEE International Conference on Requirements Engineering (RE 2005), pp. 19–28 (2005)
8. Ali, R., Dalpiaz, F., Giorgini, P.: A goal-based framework for contextual requirements modeling and analysis. Requir. Eng. **15**, 439–458 (2010)
9. Finkelstein Andrea, A., Savigni, A.: A framework for requirements engineering for context-aware services. In: Proceedings of the 1st International Workshop From Software Requirements to Architectures (STRAW 2001), pp. 200–201 (2001)
10. Chapman, C.N., Love, E., Milham, R.P., ElRif, P., Alford, J.L.: Quantitative evaluation of personas as information. In: Proceedings of the Human Factors and Ergonomics Society Annual Meeting, vol. 52, pp. 1107–1111. SAGE Publications, CA (2008)

11. Faily, S., Fléchais, I.: Eliciting and visualising trust expectations using persona trust characteristics and goal models. In: Proceedings of the 6th International Workshop on Social Software Engineering, pp. 17–24. ACM (2014)
12. Van Solingen, R., Basili, V., Caldiera, G., Rombach, H.D.: Goal question metric (GQM) approach. In: Encyclopedia of Software Engineering (2002)
13. Aoyama, M.: Persona-and-scenario based requirements engineering for software embedded in digital consumer products. In: 2005 Proceedings of the 13th IEEE International Conference on Requirements Engineering, pp. 85–94. IEEE (2005)
14. Faily, S., Lyle, J.: Guidelines for integrating personas into software engineering tools. In: Proceedings of the 5th ACM SIGCHI Symposium on Engineering Interactive Computing Systems, pp. 69–74. ACM (2013)
15. Haikara, J.: Usability in agile software development: extending the interaction design process with personas approach. In: Concas, G., Damiani, E., Scotto, M., Succi, G. (eds.) XP 2007. LNCS, vol. 4536, pp. 153–156. Springer, Heidelberg (2007). https://doi.org/10.1007/978-3-540-73101-6_22
16. Castro, J.W., Acuña, S.T., Juristo, N.: Integrating the personas technique into the requirements analysis activity. In: Mexican International Conference on Computer Science, ENC 2008, pp. 104–112. IEEE (2008)
17. Faily, S.: Bridging user-centered design and requirements engineering with GRL and persona cases. In: Proceedings of the 5th International i* Workshop, pp. 114–119. CEUR Workshop Proceedings (2011)
18. Di Francescomarino, C., Leonardi, C., Marchetto, A., Nguyen, C.D., Qureshi, N.A., Sabatucci, L., Perini, A., Susi, A., Tonella, P., Zancanaro, M.: A bit of persona, a bit of goal, a bit of process... a recipe for analyzing user intensive software systems. In: iStar 2010, Proceedings of the 4th International i* Workshop, p. 36. Citeseer (2010)
19. Mendonça, D.F., Rodrigues, G.N., Ali, R., Alves, V., Baresi, L.: GODA: a goal-oriented requirements engineering framework for runtime dependability analysis. Inf. Softw. Technol. 80, 245–264 (2016)

Author Index